D0396418

NEW DIMENSIONS
IN
AMERICAN RELIGIOUS HISTORY

Martin E. Marty

New Dimensions in American Religious History

ESSAYS IN HONOR OF MARTIN E. MARTY

Edited by

Jay P. Dolan *and* James P. Wind

William B. Eerdmans Publishing Company
Grand Rapids, Michigan

255 Jefferson Ave. S.E., Grand Rapids, Mich. 49503

Printed in the United States of America

Library of Congress Cataloging-in-Publication Data

New dimensions in American religious history:
a festschrift for Martin E. Marty /
edited by Jay P. Dolan and James P. Wind.
p. cm.
Includes bibliographical references.
ISBN 0-8028-3702-6 (hard)
1. United States — Religion. I. Marty, Martin E., 1928- .
II. Dolan, Jay P., 1936- . III. Wind, James P., 1948- .
BL2525.N485 1992
200′.973 — dc20 92-40425
CIP

Contents

NEW DIRECTIONS IN AMERICAN RELIGIOUS HISTORY

RELIGIOUS FUNDAMENTALISM

Introduction

> **festschrift** [G, fr. *fest* celebration + *schrift* writing] (1901): a volume of writings by different authors presented as a tribute or memorial esp. to a scholar *(Webster's Ninth New Collegiate Dictionary)*

IN AN AGE filled with thousands of qualifications, *New Dimensions in American Religious History* is, without qualification, a festschrift. It is a collection of essays written in tribute to Martin E. Marty, a scholar whose collection of accolades includes many like the one given by *Time* magazine when it named him "the most influential living interpreter of religion in the U.S." To be sure, this book is a tribute, not a memorial. Marty is by all accounts very much at full speed; some insist that he is accelerating. Author of more than forty books, recipient of dozens of honorary degrees, weekly circuit rider from campus to think tank to professional society to board of directors to denominational meeting, Marty keeps on interpreting America religiously. From posts at the University of Chicago, *The Christian Century,* and the Park Ridge Center, through his own newsletter *Context,* in countless articles, op-ed pieces, and interviews, Marty has provided perspective on American religion for more than thirty years. If one were searching for someone to honor, Marty is — in many senses of the word — a "natural."

This volume offers its tribute right at the borderline between "natural" and "unnatural" moments. Presented to him on the occasion of his sixty-fifth birthday, it is several years in advance of the time when Marty intends officially to "retire" (that date has been written into his 1998 calendar for years); it also comes midway in the course of the writing of his magnum opus, *Modern American Religion,* and long before all the discoveries of his massive fundamentalism project have been reported out. When one considers how prolific Marty has been while also engaged full-time in teaching and advising, the prospects of his eventual transition to "full-time" writing are humbling and daunting. So, in many ways, this volume is premature. On the other hand, Marty's impact is large enough, the accumulation of his insights and scholarly work is weighty enough, and he has been at his task long enough that it is "natural" for scholars to begin to call attention to his significance.

There is another reason, however, for the appearance of this volume at this particular moment. Historians, perhaps because their subject matter is so intrinsically messy, appreciate occasional neatnesses whenever they find them. Thus, they enjoy coincidences such as the fact that Abraham Lincoln and Charles Darwin, two individuals who shaped the thought worlds of Americans as much as any nineteenth-century figures, were born the same day, 12 February 1809. Those of us looking for other signs of tidiness might note the fact that two of the most important twentieth-century interpreters of religion, Andrew Greeley and Marty, also share natal dates, 5 February 1928. These kinds of convergences might tempt historians to dabble in astrological speculations; wisely, they often look for less exact patternings. Sometimes they even invent them. In this case, this festschrift appears exactly one century after the year (1893) that Marty selected to begin his four-volume recounting of modern American religion. As a way of honoring the audacity of Marty's attempt both to see the past century as a distinctive period in American religious history and to make sense of its turmoil, the contributors to this volume have written tributes that focus on the century in which so many new dimensions in American history — both secular and religious — became apparent.

Scholars leave their legacies through their publications and through their students. On the wall of Marty's Swift Hall office at the University of Chicago, above his desk, hangs a framed list, lettered in his own calligraphy, of more than fifty students who have completed dissertations under his supervision. A sign of his appeal as a teacher, his stamina as an advisor, and his endurance as a human being, the list has room for a few more names to be added. Those of us already on that list — including this volume's twelve authors — are aware that it took more of Marty's time to assist each of us through the many stages of doctoral studies than it did for him to write any of his books. Few of us can forget the carefully budgeted ten-minute appointments when

Marty would get immediately to our less-than-clear points, sharpen or restate the issue, spin off a list of books to read, suggest a seemingly impossible deadline, and still have time left to ask about some aspect of our personal life. His exam questions always forced us to learn what we knew and did not know and to reshape, connect, and synthesize our fragments of scholarly learning into webs of larger significance. In seminars he relentlessly pressed us to state the thesis of our thesis, always added another perspective to the mix we had assembled, and then, when we turned in our papers or chapters, he would edit our manuscripts with equal and ample measures of scholarly and literary scrutiny. At each encounter, we met a man with extraordinary energy, genuine responsiveness, incomparable erudition, and great love for learning and learners. Reflecting his heritage, Marty seemed to run like a fine Swiss watch, effortlessly, precisely, gracefully. Disciplined to the point of setting aside Thursday evening baths to read articles for *Context* and playful enough to foist the imaginary theologian Franz Bibfeldt upon us all, Marty provided entry to worlds of learning and opportunity that few of us had even glimpsed.

In *By Way of Response,* a deliberately unautobiographical story of his life, Marty invoked a favorite philosopher, Eugen Rosenstock-Huessy: "one book is about one thing; at least the good ones are." At one point or another in our graduate studies, most of his students heard that line — most likely when Marty was pruning away digressions from our projects. But Marty also applied that line to his own life. "The most rich and varied lives, I contend, are also 'about' one thing." In his case, that meant, "as an American religious historian in the face of the most jumbled and competitive melange of religiosities the world has ever known, my project almost naturally came to focus around the philosophical theme of 'the one and the many' and the political problem of 'pluralism.'"[1]

During a career that moved from Lutheran parish to editorial office to the Fairfax M. Cone Distinguished Professor of the History of Modern Christianity Chair at the Divinity School of the University of Chicago, Marty has probed pluralism across the broad range of American experience. In *Religion and Republic: The American Circumstance,* he admitted that "I am preoccupied with questions of land and landscape, city and city-scape, people and peoplescape. That is, the environment itself . . . has been seen to be somehow revelatory and redemptive in

1. Martin E. Marty, *By Way of Response* (Nashville: Abingdon Press, 1981), pp. 26, 28.

often overtly and consistently quiet ways."[2] Like his teacher Sidney E. Mead, Marty celebrated the Americanness of American religion. In this New World, the environment brought into being a "fragile" and "modest" type of pluralist polity that allowed the many religious and ethnic tribes to be a "one" — albeit a messy, rapidly changing, and factious one.

Those who have spent much time with Marty know that he is quintessentially peripatetic, always in motion, whether moving through the corridors of Swift Hall, flying from one side of the country to the other, or working at his stand-up desk in his study in Riverside, Illinois. It is little wonder, then, that the motion in American religion, rather than its fixed places and institutions, captured his imagination. In his one-volume history of five hundred years of American religious history, Marty made the energetic movers across the American landscape his central figures. The itinerants who crisscrossed oceans and frontiers, the dynamos responsible for new outbreakings of religious creativity, the entrepreneurs and seekers became his central interest. There was a oneness in all the diversity and chaos of their stories. Lines from French philosopher Jacques Maritain's *Reflections on America* seemed to capture it: "Americans seem to be in their own land as pilgrims, prodded by a dream. They are always on the move — available for new tasks, prepared for the possible loss of what they have. They are not *settled, installed.*"[3]

Through his many books and articles, and through the generation of students who pondered the multitudinous and pluriform directions of American religious history under his tutelage, Marty has attempted to respond to the many new dimensions in American religious history by finding one plot line that ran through it all — the distinctively American experiment with pluralism. The essays that follow show how some of his students are following some of his leads, moving beyond others, and struggling to find better ways to comprehend the richness of American religious history. Some of the essays — notably those by Sally M. Promey, William Sachs, Mark G. Toulouse, and Robert Choquette — celebrate the American search for oneness in spite of the efflorescent manyness of this nation's pluralism. They trace that search in works of art, on the pages of one of mainstream Protestantism's most

2. Martin E. Marty, *Religion and Republic: The American Circumstance* (Boston: Beacon Press, 1987), p. 2.

3. Maritain, quoted by Martin E. Marty in *Pilgrims in Their Own Land: Five Hundred Years of Religion in America* (Boston: Little, Brown, 1984), p. xiii.

public voices, *The Christian Century,* and beyond our borders as they follow our missionaries in Japan or seek to learn about our distinctiveness by examining the Canadian experience.

Other essays shift the focus toward particularity, as authors R. Scott Appleby, Timothy P. Weber, and Yaakov Ariel probe Catholic, Protestant, and Jewish forms of fundamentalism. These essays remind us that being American is seldom merely settling for oneness. Particularity, distinctiveness, schism, and conflict are the other side of our story.

A third group of essays, those by Catherine L. Albanese, Jay P. Dolan, Paul Westermeyer, L. DeAne Lagerquist, and James P. Wind, set off in new directions of historical inquiry — directions that push us into new and old forms of particularity at the same time that they uncover other signs of sameness. These essays take us into ranges of experience that the old types of church history — the kinds that were preoccupied with institutions and their elites — ignored. Here we come close to the lived religion of ethnic groups, women, questers after health, and people in the pews.

Not surprisingly, one will find evidence in Marty's writings that he has gone in all, or at least almost all of these directions, often leading his students, but also following them. His students' writings — here and elsewhere — are signs that another generation of American pilgrims, in this case a particular subspecies called historians, is still not settled, that they are prodded on, like their teacher, by the dream of better understanding. Their dream risks all of the inherited wisdom of the previous generations, and it keeps the American experiment in motion.

These essays form only an early stock-taking of the significance of Marty's teaching. After all, there are more of his students and colleagues to hear from. And if Marty is graced to live as long as the other great historians he never ceased to remind us about, then we can expect much more from him. More than once he told us that historians lived as long as Roland Bainton or Kenneth Scott Latourette did because they wanted to see how the stories they were writing turned out. The one that he is telling, which is also one that he shaped in many still-to-be-noted ways, should keep him writing and us reading and writing for a long time.

James P. Wind
Jay P. Dolan

PUBLIC RELIGION

"Triumphant Religion" in Public Places: John Singer Sargent and the Boston Public Library Murals

Sally M. Promey

John Singer Sargent's *Triumph of Religion* (1890-1919) is one of the more comprehensive cycles of religious art produced by a nineteenth-century American artist.[1] The *Triumph of Religion* does not adorn the walls of a religious institution, however. Rather, it occupies the entire third floor staircase hall of the Boston Public Library.[2] Although Sargent and many of his contemporaries considered the murals to be of major significance, they have received little scholarly attention either from art historians or from historians of American religion. In focusing my essay on Sargent's mural cycle, I propose to explore the *public* pictorial character of this expression of what might more accurately be called triumphant Christianity. Why would Sargent, an apparently nonreligious expatriate American painter, choose a religious subject for a project of this scale at the climax of his career? More specifically, why would he employ explicitly religious subject matter in a cycle commissioned for a public library? Finally, how would Sargent's public(s) respond to representations that failed to recognize the religious pluralism of turn-of-the-century Boston and, by extension, the United States? These are

1. This essay represents a preliminary stage of a larger project on art, religion, and the public sphere in the United States at the turn of the century.

2. See John Dillenberger, *The Visual Arts and Christianity in America: The Colonial Period through the Nineteenth Century* (Chico, Calif.: Scholars Press, 1984), p. 152.

The author gratefully acknowledges the support of the National Endowment for the Humanities in completing this essay.

questions to which I will direct my attention. But first, a brief sketch of historical background and a description of the murals themselves will aid the consideration of possible meanings and contexts for the mural programme.

On 17 September 1887, Sargent left his London home for the United States, where he spent the winter painting portraits of America's elite. Most of this American sojourn (and one that followed approximately a year and a half later) located Sargent in Boston (sometimes in New York), attending to the business of American commissions and exhibitions of his work.

In May 1890, Sargent and the trustees of the new Boston Public Library (1887-1895) reached a verbal agreement on the mural decoration for the gallery of the special collections floor at the top of the building's principal staircase. Architects Charles McKim and Stanford White had both campaigned for the selection of Sargent as muralist.[3] Sargent's friend, colleague, and studio-mate through much of this venture, expatriate American painter Edwin Austin Abbey, undertook the decoration of the distributing room on the second floor, and Pierre Puvis de Chavannes, a French painter, consented to provide the murals for the main staircase hall and corridor. The room allocated to Sargent's murals was a long vaulted hall with no windows on the library's uppermost floor. Skylights in the barrel vault illuminated the room, which measured 85 feet long, 23 feet wide, and 26 feet high to the top of the barrel vault. Along the east wall ran the balustraded stairwell; doors leading to special collections rooms punctuated the two end walls to the north and south and the west wall opposite the stairwell. Almost immediately, Sargent expressed his pleasure with the space assigned for his mural decoration. Because he would assume responsibility for decorating the entire third floor gallery, he could treat the space as a unified artistic whole; he could manipulate to his liking a relatively self-contained visual environment.[4]

The library's trustees left the subject matter of the murals to the

3. Charles F. McKim to Samuel A. B. Abbott, 9 May 1890 (Boston Public Library [hereafter BPL] Ms Bos Li B18b, Folder 2); McKim to Abbott, 3 November 1890 (BPL Ms Bos Li B18a, Folder 2); and McKim, Mead, and White to the Trustees of the Boston Public Library, 5 June 1893 (BPL Ms Bos Li B18a, Folder 2). See also Trevor J. Fairbrother, *John Singer Sargent and America* (New York: Garland Publishing, 1986), pp. 212-15; and Stanley Olson, *John Singer Sargent: His Portrait* (New York: St. Martin's Press, 1986), pp. 163-68.

4. See Charles Merrill Mount, *John Singer Sargent* (London: Cresset Press, 1957), p. 151.

discretion of the artist. Initially Sargent intended to depict selected themes from Spanish literature.[5] At some point early in his deliberation, however, he changed his mind and chose instead a subject he called the "Triumph of Religion — a mural decoration illustrating certain stages of Jewish and Christian religious history."[6] As the project developed, the completion of Sargent's mural cycle required installation in four chronologically sequential parts, over a period of twenty-four years from 1895 to 1919.

In 1895 Sargent installed the first mural panels at the north end of the gallery. The ceiling vault he covered with a panel representing (west to east) the "pagan" gods Moloch, Neith, and Astarte. The lunette directly below this ceiling vault depicted the Israelites afflicted and oppressed by Egyptian pharaoh and Assyrian king and by attendant Egyptian and Assyrian divinities and symbolic creatures. Elevated somewhat above the chaos of this scene, but still within the lunette, Sargent painted Yahweh, face covered by clouds and by the wings of cherubim, intervening on behalf of the children of Israel. The *Frieze of Prophets* completed this first installment of panels.

Not until 1903 did Sargent travel to Boston to hang the second installment in the mural cycle. He painted all of the murals in England, accompanying them, after completion, to the United States to supervise and participate in their placement. The 1903 installation, intended in its entirety for the south wall of the gallery, Sargent called the *Dogma*

5. As a painter, Sargent had a significant history with Spanish subject matter (e.g., *El Jaleo,* 1882, and *La Carmencita,* 1890) and demonstrated more than a passing interest in Spanish culture. He illustrated a book of Spanish and Italian folk songs; the subject of some of the images he made for the book's pages involved Spanish religion. Of particular relevance to Sargent's initial decision regarding subject matter, one of the special collections rooms adjacent to the hall to be occupied by his murals housed the impressive Ticknor Collection of Spanish literature. Further, Spain and things Spanish attracted a large number of Americans in these years surrounding the World's Columbian Exposition. The association of Spain with Columbus and Columbus with America magnified popular approbation of Spanish culture. See Nicolai Cikovsky, Jr., "*El Jaleo* in the Cult of Spain"; and Mary Crawford Volk, "Sargent, Spain and El Jaleo," in *John Singer Sargent's El Jaleo* (Washington: National Gallery of Art, 1992).

6. Sargent to Herbert Putnam [1895] (BPL Ms 1320.2). See also Herbert Small, *Handbook of the New Public Library in Boston* (Boston: Curtis, 1895), p. 52. Edwin Austin Abbey, whose ties to the Aesthetic Movement were much clearer than Sargent's, also changed from a more strictly "literary" to a "religious" topic for his murals in the distributing room at the Boston Public Library. He had first selected Shakespearean literature but instead painted *The Quest for the Holy Grail.* See Olson, *John Singer Sargent,* p. 216.

of the Redemption. In the lunette, the three persons of the Trinity appeared as three crowned men sharing one cope and one throne. Below the lunette, the *Frieze of Angels* contained eight figures holding instruments of the Passion of Christ. The two central figures (whose garments Sargent decorated with eucharistic symbols) supported the base of a very high relief *Crucifix* which compositionally united lunette and frieze. In this conception, Adam and Eve, bound by a single cloth to Christ's body, extend eucharistic chalices to catch the blood of Christ. The spike that pierces Christ's feet also nails the head of the serpent to the cross.

With the third installation in 1916, Sargent completed the ceiling vault and the corresponding niches on this south wall. In the niche to the east he represented the *Handmaid of the Lord,* balanced on the west by the *Madonna of Sorrows,* facing the *Handmaid* directly across the space of the gallery. Above, on the south ceiling vault, Sargent painted the *Fifteen Mysteries* or the *Meditation of the Rosary.* Thus, by 1916, the north and south ends of the hall, friezes, lunettes, and ceiling vaults, had been installed.

Also included in the 1916 installation was a series of lunettes for the three vaults along the east and west walls of the gallery, and accompanying ceiling decorations. Beginning with the lunette at the north corner of the east wall and moving south, the artist painted the *Fall of Gog and Magog,* the figure of Israel under the mantle of God's *Law,* and the *Messianic Era* as the fulfillment of Isaiah's prophecies. On the west wall, beginning at the northwest end, Sargent depicted *Hell* as a monstrous green beast in a fiery lair. In *Judgment,* the central lunette, an angel weighs souls in a balance and consigns them to *Hell* or to *Heaven,* the celestial subject of the third panel, located at the southwest end of the gallery.

Sargent contributed once more to his mural cycle in 1919, when he added personified representations of *Synagogue* and *Church* to the east wall above the stairwell. *Synagogue* he placed in closest proximity to the "Jewish" north wall; *Church* he located nearest the "Christian" south wall (Figs. 1 and 2, pp. 8-9). In 1919, then, Sargent Hall was finally completed. The public could view in its entirety this monumental work of a painter many considered to be America's greatest living artist.

A complex web of contexts (biographical, art historical, cultural) contributed to the significance of religious subject matter in the Boston Public Library. In terms of biography, the issue of nationality has long complicated discussion of Sargent's painting. While cultural influences from both sides of the Atlantic certainly figured in Sargent's attitudes and in his art, in this essay I minimize the European and accentuate the American, focusing on responses of an American public to works of art in an American institution.

Sargent's personal history provides no obvious reason for his decision to paint religion at the library rather than painting Spanish literature as he had first intended. In fact, his personal history would seem to distance Sargent from religion rather than involve him in its practice. Despite his father's membership in the American Church at Nice, his family's nomadic life-style precluded settled participation in the life of any one church or faith community.[7] John Sargent was raised by American parents who numbered Puritans and Moravian Brethren among their ancestors.[8] During the artist's childhood, however, his father made a point of allowing the children some latitude and flexibility in religious training.[9] There is no record that the mature John Sargent ever attended church regularly, and the testimony of acquaintances indicates that he did not. Of the painter's religious life as an adult, a friend expressed the opinion that he was "quite emancipated from all religious ideas."[10] His grandnephew believed that "Sargent was not in the least religious, and his objective and historical approach precluded any personal statement of faith."[11] In sum, when it came to religion, it seems that Sargent was more a spectator than a participant.[12] Though his experiences and attitudes were generally informed by Western Christianity and its symbols, religion was an idea to which the artist more or less subscribed, not a faith to which he committed himself.

7. Stanley Olson notes that Fitzwilliam Sargent was a sometime "staunch member of the American Church in Nice" ("On the Question of Sargent's Nationality," in *John Singer Sargent*, ed. Patricia Hills [New York: Harry N. Abrams, 1986], p. 17).

8. Olson, *John Singer Sargent*, pp. 274-7.

9. See Evan Charteris, *John Sargent* (New York: Scribner's, 1927), p. 5. For Vernon Lee's comments on Fitzwilliam Sargent's "puritanism," see pp. 245-46, 249; for her notes in this regard on the painter himself, see pp. 235-36.

10. Vernon Lee, in a 1937 assessment of the impression Sargent made on her in 1881, quoted by James Lomax and Richard Ormond in *John Singer Sargent and the Edwardian Age* (London: National Portrait Gallery, 1979), p. 9.

11. Richard Ormond, *John Singer Sargent: Paintings, Drawings, and Watercolors* (New York: Harper & Row, 1970), p. 89.

12. Olson claims that Sargent's great talent was observation, that in all of life, as in religion, Sargent was a "perpetual spectator" (Olson, *John Singer Sargent*, p. 155). Elsewhere, Olson describes Sargent's "Baedeker education" and comments on his "tourist" status, stating that the painter was "at home everywhere, and belonged nowhere" ("On the Question of Sargent's Nationality," pp. 23, 17).

Figure 1. John Singer Sargent, *Synagogue*
Courtesy of the Trustees of the Public Library of the City of Boston

Figure 2. John Singer Sargent, *Church*

Courtesy of the Trustees of the Public Library of the City of Boston

Personal religious conviction of the conventional sort did not lead Sargent to paint religion at the Boston Public Library.

What then did religion mean to Sargent (and to his publics) in the context of the library murals? Although the church-like quality of the special collections hall, with its barrel vault and its orientation with respect to the long axis, may have contributed to Sargent's decision regarding his murals' subject matter, the Boston Public Library, obviously, was not a church.[13] I will argue that Sargent borrowed the iconography of religion, filtered it through late nineteenth-century American aesthetic aspirations, and reframed that iconography within the civic sphere. In the Boston Public Library, the iconography of religion served the artist in several different ways. Religion in Sargent's murals incorporated, on the one hand, a general appeal derived from the association of religion with certain qualities highly desirable to the artist and his patrons. On the other hand, Sargent's depiction of religion also communicated a very specific particularized "religious" content. At the first and more generalized level, the subject of religion offered Sargent a twofold opportunity: it attracted adherents of late nineteenth-century exoticism, and it announced the ultimacy of the message.

Religion was for Sargent an exotic subject of the highest order. Other late nineteenth-century artists shared this assessment (especially those artists, like Sargent, who were attracted to one degree or another to the art and theory of the Symbolists, of the Aesthetic Movement, and even of the American Renaissance).[14] Within religion these artists found an "other" whose "otherness" both amplified and extended the two favored alternative expressions (gender and ethnicity) and carried the implications of "otherness" beyond the dimensions of space and time.

13. Fairbrother suggests that the quality of the space may have influenced Sargent's decision to paint religion (*John Singer Sargent and America,* pp. 217-18).

14. See Martha Kingsbury, "Sargent's Murals in the Boston Public Library," *Winterthur Portfolio* 11 (1976): 153-72; Doreen Bolger Burke, "*Astarte:* Sargent's Study for the *Pagan Gods* Mural in the Boston Public Library," *Fenway Court* (1976): 12-15; Charteris, *John Sargent,* pp. 62, 88; Carter Ratcliffe, *John Singer Sargent* (New York: Abbeville Press, 1982), pp. 9-13; and Mount, *John Singer Sargent,* p. 123. Symbolism and Aestheticism placed religious subject matter in an appealing historical, exotic, erotic framework that generally downplayed the religious subject's relationship to personal faith and amplified its identity with "primitive" and elemental feelings and with "elevated" thoughts and values. Sources contemporary with Sargent label his *Triumph of Religion* "symbolist" in contexts which imply that they intend the European usage. For recent scholarship recognizing this relationship, see Ratcliffe, *John Singer Sargent;* Kingsbury, "Sargent's Murals in the Boston Public Library"; and Burke, *"Astarte."*

The appeal of the transcendent and the elemental as well as the appeal of the "pagan" and the "primitive" was obvious to many who described the Boston Public Library murals.[15]

Sargent's longtime friend Vernon Lee (born Violet Paget) once remarked that the painter's favorite words included *strange, weird, fantastic,* and *curious.*[16] This comment summed up an important aspect of Sargent's life and of his approach to art. From childhood, much of his time had been spent seeing the sights of his world; this adventure continued into adulthood. While Sargent was and is perhaps best known as a portrait painter, from the beginning he produced other sorts of paintings too. He painted provincial oyster gatherers at Cancale, Spanish dancers and Spanish madonnas, dramatic Venetian interiors, Bedouins, a Moroccan woman perfuming herself and her garments in a ritualized manner. In portraiture as well, the artist often created exotic settings, stances, and costumes for his sitters. His paintings of Isabella Stewart Gardner, Ellen Terry, the Boit daughters, La Carmencita, and Elsie Palmer, for example, fit this exotic mode.

One of Sargent's earliest responses to the mural commission involved travel. Before the year was over he set out for Alexandria, Cairo, and other Egyptian sites, Athens, Olympia, Delphi, Constantinople, and a number of places in Spain. Later, in preparation for the south "Christian" wall, Sargent traveled to Ravenna and Sicily to view Christian and especially Byzantine monuments there. As a painter of the exotic, Sargent continued to do what his mobile childhood had best prepared him to do. He traveled. He saw the sights. He researched. He painted the "other" (divine and human) with the detachment of a perpetual tourist rather than the intimacy of a believer or a native citizen.

Sargent's exoticism was manifestly evident in the splendor of the visual setting he created. He attempted to capture the essence of the Pharaoh in ancient Egyptian conventions, of the Assyrian king and gods in an Assyrian vocabulary, of Byzantine Christian rites and medieval doctrine in Byzantine and medieval modes of visual expression,

15. See, for example, Ormond, *John Singer Sargent,* p. 28. Frederick W. Coburn noted the "evocation of the allied instincts of sex and religion, the sensory allure of pagan cults, the ecstatic throb of the Madonna worship" ("The Sargent Decorations in the Boston Public Library," *American Magazine of Art* 8 [February 1917]: 131; see also pp. 129ff.). In reference to the *Pagan Gods* vault, Ernest F. Fenollosa described the "ceiling's elemental world of cycles, brute powers, and lusts" (*Mural Painting in the Boston Public Library* [Boston: Curtis, 1896], p. 24).

16. Patricia Hills, "The Formation of a Style and Sensibility," in Hills (ed.), *John Singer Sargent,* p. 33.

suggesting that the ideas and values, the "spirit" of an era, might be transmitted through the manipulation of style.[17] At the south end of the room, Sargent depicted Christianity, the *assumed* common faith of the majority of the library's patrons, in a manner that reflected the devotion of very few, if any, of these patrons. Culling models from the forms and subjects of European, pre-Reformation, and often Byzantine Catholicism, Sargent represented Christianity as exotic mystery. Gold leaf, gilt haloes and moldings, bas relief, the artist's attention to the proper lighting of his work, and hieratic and ritualistic images combined to create the atmosphere of mystery and awe commented upon by his critics. That Sargent intended to evoke such feelings he made clear in a letter of November 1890 to friend Ralph Curtis: "The Boston thing will be (entre nous) Mediaeval Spanish and religious, and in my most belly achey mood — with gold, gore, and phosforescent Hellens. What a surprise to the community."[18]

In addition to the exotic appeal of the religious, and even more important in the context of the Boston library, Sargent meant his choice of subject matter to suggest the ultimacy of his mural cycle's message. Subject matter then underscored an associative content (regarding the permanence of the cycle's significance) already implied in the very form the project was to take. The public pictorial character of monumental decoration, of paintings cemented to the walls of a grand civic edifice, guaranteed the artist a large audience presumably over an extended period of time in a visual environment less conducive to rearrangement than a residence, gallery, or museum. Here the one many assumed to be the greatest artist of his time could inscribe his message for posterity.[19]

The sense of ultimacy Sargent claimed for his project certainly fit the aesthetic ideology of the architects and artists at work on the Boston library. Sargent painted his murals, after all, on the walls of one

17. "Unveil New Sargent Panels Today," *Boston Globe,* 21 December 1916 (Fine Arts Clipplings File, BPL); A. J. Philpott, "'Heaven' and 'Hell' as Pictured by John S. Sargent in his Decoration," *Boston Globe,* 24 December 1916 (Fine Arts Clippings File, BPL); Pauline King, *American Mural Painting* (Boston: Noyes, Platt, 1901), p. 127; and Small, *Handbook of the New Public Library,* pp. 53-55. See also Kingsbury, "Sargent's Murals in the Boston Public Library," p. 153.

18. Sargent to Ralph Curtis, 18 November 1890 (Boston Athenaeum, Sargent-Fox Papers, Box I, Folder 3). If not exactly a "surprise," the murals were certainly not what "the community" likely expected of Sargent.

19. Cf. Fairbrother, "Painting in Boston, 1870-1930," in *The Bostonians: Painters of an Elegant Age, 1870-1930* (Boston: Museum of Fine Arts, 1986), p. 46. Sargent considered these murals to be his grandest statement. See Olson, *John Singer Sargent,* p. 155.

of the premier monuments of the American Renaissance. And the *Triumph of Religion* met the requirements of this American awakening. Within the American Renaissance framework, the late nineteenth century was an age of public monuments dedicated to the enhancement and support of an American national story of mythic and religious proportions. Art and artists would play a formative role in the creation of a new America, a nation superior in culture and in morals to all its predecessors. Though practitioners of the American Renaissance adopted what now seems a conservative aesthetic, their agenda was nothing less than the transformation of civilization.[20] Looking to Europe and especially to the Italian Renaissance for cultural models, these artists and their patrons nonetheless understood themselves to be establishing a new American school of art. Sargent's American contemporaries viewed him as an eminently successful *American* artist, proof of a blossoming national tradition.[21] His murals for the public library represented perfectly what the American Renaissance meant by the inspiration of the art of ages past: Sargent borrowed from everyone and copied from no one. Sargent's critics and commentators pointed out affinities with Botticelli, Michelangelo, Tiepolo, Giotto, Masaccio. Ernest Fenollosa compared Sargent and these Boston murals to Michelangelo in the Sistine Chapel and declared that Sargent and the third floor gallery would become, like Masaccio's Brancacci Chapel, "a shrine for the pilgrimage of artists."[22] The Boston Public Library was, for its

20. On the American Renaissance in the visual arts, and particularly on this idea of the transformation of civilization, see Richard Guy Wilson, Dianne H. Pilgrim, and Richard N. Murray, *The American Renaissance: 1876-1917* (Brooklyn: Brooklyn Museum, 1979). While the American Renaissance was a movement promoted by a cultural elite, it reached multiple levels of society in one form or another (influencing, e.g., images on coinage, magazine covers, newspaper headings). Sargent's library murals were rapidly reproduced as prints available to the public. The *Frieze of Prophets* was most widely distributed. Above the figures, the photographic print form substituted English lettering for Sargent's Hebrew to ensure proper identification of each prophet by those unschooled in Hebrew. See, for example, the prints made by Cosmos Pictures Company, New York, and the large color print distributed by the Boston Public Library. And see R. H. Ives Gammell, "A Masterpiece Dishonored," *Classical America* 4 (1977): 47; David McKibbin, *Sargent's Boston* (Boston: Museum of Fine Arts, 1956), p. 45; and Walter Muir Whitehill, "The Making of an Architectural Masterpiece — The Boston Public Library," *The American Art Journal* no. 2 (Fall 1970): 29, 32-33.

21. Literature contemporary with Sargent's murals stressed the artist's Americanness. See Charteris, *John Sargent,* chap. 1; Small, *Handbook of the New Public Library in Boston,* p. 52; and *Vanity Fair* (November 1916): 76.

22. Fenollosa, *Mural Painting in the Boston Public Library,* p. 28.

creators and much of its public, an excellent example of the kind of collaboration of architecture, sculpture, and painting that typified the Italian Renaissance and that would typify the anticipated culmination and perfection of this Renaissance spirit in America. When John Sargent designed not only the murals but also the moldings, frames, electric fixtures, and lighting patterns for the gallery of the special collections floor, he was placing himself squarely within the expectations of the American Renaissance. Adopting the language of both church and state to suggest the ultimacy of cultural achievement represented in this enterprise, Frederick Coburn claimed that Sargent had created "an American Sistine Chapel, enshrined within a palace of democratic learning."[23]

Commentary and press employed explicitly religious language to communicate a content of ultimacy and sacrality. As repository of knowledge and culture, the public library was described as a "ritualistic center of civilization,"[24] and Sargent Hall in particular was called "a place of pilgrimage," a "Mecca of American scholarship."[25] Muralist and theorist Edwin Blashfield, a friend and promoter of Sargent, adopted just this sort of religious vocabulary in his plea for a public American art.[26]

> The temple and the cathedral spoke to the eye, but they spoke as loudly as did Iliad or Bible, and they told the same story. No one knew this better than did the priest, whether he were pagan or Christian. . . . All over the antique and medieval world . . . the priest set up the artist as schoolmaster, and his school became the public building.[27]

23. Coburn, "The Sargent Decorations in the Boston Public Library," p. 129. A poem by Oliver Wendell Holmes, read at the laying of the library's cornerstone on 28 November 1888, both reflected and reinforced this sanctification of American culture in the Boston Public Library. See Walter Muir Whitehill, *Boston Public Library: A Centennial History* (Cambridge: Harvard University Press, 1956), pp. 147-48.

24. Coburn, "The Sargent Decorations in the Boston Public Library," p. 136.

25. Edwin H. Blashfield, "John Singer Sargent," in *Commemorative Tributes to Cable, Sargent, Pennell* (American Academy of Arts and Letters, 1927), p. 32; and *Handbook of the New Public Library in Boston,* p. 51.

26. The American Mural Tradition was cultivated in the same civic soil as the American Renaissance. For an introduction to this material see Edwin H. Blashfield, *Mural Painting in America* (New York: Scribner's, 1928); and King, *American Mural Painting.*

27. Blashfield, *Mural Painting in America,* p. 5.

In the Boston Public Library, however, the public building was not the school of religion. It was, rather, the temple of civilization. This distinction is significant: a school of religion (a *religious* institution) teaches *religion;* a temple of civilization (a *civic* institution) sanctifies *civilization.* "The thoughts . . . summoned up [in the *Triumph of Religion*]," claimed Russell Sturgis, a critic for *Scribner's Magazine,* "are not the exclusive property of the devout, of believers, even of the religiously inclined."[28] The decoration of Sargent Hall was not intended to inspire belief in God; it was intended to inspire belief in America, belief in human progress, belief in knowledge, belief in freedom, and belief in art as an expression of such national greatness. The object of worship was culture and cultural knowledge. The space of the special collections gallery perhaps suggested the idea of the holy to Sargent, but, rather than teaching religion, the public building sanctified Western civilization and its progress. Fenollosa expanded upon this notion:

> The significance of the mural paintings in the Boston Public Library should now be plain. Here we have established the first great center of a future civic series. Here the principle is first openly, and on a large scale, acknowledged by the public authorities. By their act, and by this first blaze of achievement, we set Boston as the earliest of the seats of public pilgrimage, the veritable Assisi of American art. . . . That here already lie planted the seeds of the greatest school of painting the world shall have known, it is perhaps hardly extravagant to hope.[29]

Why religious art in the Boston Public Library? A certain religious content and vocabulary adhered to the institution itself and to its rhetorical context. Those who spoke and wrote this cultural agenda conflated the civic and the religious.[30] The idea of the public was itself

28. Sturgis, in "Sargent's New Wall Painting," *Scribner's* 34 (November 1903): 766.

29. Fenollosa, *Mural Painting in the Boston Public Library,* pp. 6-10.

30. Courthouse differed little, if at all, from cathedral. See Blashfield, *Mural Painting in America,* pp. 45-46, 179. While Blashfield wanted art to be more public, he also wanted the public to be more genteel. See Whitehill, "The Making of an Architectural Masterpiece"; and Whitehill, *Boston Public Library: A Centennial History,* for the debate on elitism and public art throughout the building and decoration of the Boston Public Library. See also T. R. Sullivan, *Passages from the Journal of Thomas Russell Sullivan, 1891-1903* (New York: Houghton Mifflin, 1917), pp. 133-35. An investigation of Sargent's public mural style in contrast to his more "private" portrait style might prove fruitful in this context.

sacred. The library's mission was to preach to the public the saving power of knowledge in a free society and to ground the public identity in this message. Critics late in the nineteenth and early in the twentieth centuries saw the Boston library as a sort of apotheosis of American culture and the tradition of free inquiry they understood to support American democracy.[31] All the more potent for this second associative meaning, religious subject matter made clear the bid for ultimacy, for sanctification. And a public setting suggested the contemporary object of worship.

But what of the particular narrative content of the mural cycle? Sargent's friends and friendly critics maintained that Sargent Hall represented the history of Jewish and Christian religious *thought* depicted in certain strategic moments or "stages" (Sargent's word) rather than as a recitation of events or lives.[32] The artistic evidence supports the reading of the mural cycle at the level of thought or idea. Despite the abundant use of visual *allusion,* Sargent Hall makes very few attempts at the kinds of visual *illusion* that connect the world of painting with the world of everyday life. While the large portions of the murals can be described as naturalistic, Sargent consistently moderated this appropriation of Renaissance aesthetic vocabulary, combining humanistic references with equally insistent medievalizing notations and containing the whole within a decorative framework. The molding and gilding serve to emphasize the decorative function of the murals, moving them from the beholder's space into the realm of abstraction. How appropriate that a temple of cultural knowledge should adorn itself with painted representations of the products of religious intellectual activity.

Though Sargent claimed to have painted the history of Christian and Jewish thought, he actually conceived of Judaism (and a number of Middle Eastern religions) as a prelude to Christianity. What Sargent had to say about religious thought was that it had evolved in an essentially qualitative fashion. For Sargent, the "triumph" of religion lay in the "evolution" of religion, in "progress" from more "primitive" to

31. The Boston library was founded in 1852 as the first state-supported free public library. The new McKim, Mead, and White building was financed by public funds, but much of Sargent's mural project was paid for with funds raised privately from among the cultural and economic elite of Boston. In spite of the relationship of the library's aesthetics to the desires and the pocketbooks of Boston's elite, contemporaries celebrated the library as a "people's palace."

32. Charteris, *John Sargent,* p. 107. For a specifically Symbolist interpretation of Sargent's murals, see Fenollosa, *Mural Painting in the Boston Public Library,* pp. 21-22.

more sophisticated forms.[33] The sequential installation of the Boston murals made the movement Sargent depicted even more evident to the public eye. Chronologically earlier (and evolutionarily "less developed") scenes the artist painted and hung first. From 1895 to 1903, when Boston citizens and critics had only the murals on the north wall to consider, the contrast between the "confusion" of the pagan cycle with its obscure symbolism and the clarity and humanity of the Hebrew representations occupied the public's attention. The calm grandeur of the prophets' monotheism succeeded the sensuality and violence of more "primitive" polytheistic religions. The critics saw the pagan gods and their attendants as "types of cunning and ferocity," their religion as "the unholy imagings of foolish and brutal men" — this in contrast to the nobility and "nude beauty of the kneeling Hebrew."[34]

But the prophets of hope (at the extreme east end of the *Frieze of Prophets,* on the northeast wall) literally pointed beyond themselves and their Jewish faith to the opposite end of the room with its representations of Christian faith and doctrine. Prior to 1903, Moses the lawgiver had occupied the focal point of the composition based both on his location as formal and compositional "keystone" to the door in the north wall and on the fact that his figure was modeled in the highest relief of any part of the murals. Moses was replaced in this distinction in 1903 by the *Crucifix,* in a similar location on the opposite wall but elevated and modeled in such high relief that it approached freestanding sculpture. The installation of murals on the south wall, and especially of the *Crucifix,* underscored the association between Sargent Hall and church. As one entered the hall, coming up the stairs, the *Dogma of the Redemption* confronted the spectator, suggesting at least visual similarity between the south wall of Sargent Hall and the altarpiece and crucifix at the front of a chapel or church. Not only was the *Crucifix* seen and intended as the compositional and artistic centerpiece, it also became the focal point for the interpretation of the *Triumph of Religion.* *Vanity Fair* reported that

> The Sargent contributions to the building form an organic whole. They express, taken all together, a philosophical idea. The aim of the painter has been to show the development of a religious idea,

33. In the *Handbook of the New Public Library* (1895), Small noted that "Mr. Sargent has described his complete scheme as representing 'the triumph of religion — a mural decoration illustrating certain stages of Jewish and Christian history' " (p. 52).

34. King, *American Mural Painting,* p. 136.

> which was also a social or legal idea. . . . Once the symbolism of the details of 'the crucifixion' is understood it will be seen at a glance that Isaiah and Jeremiah and the rest are hardly even links in a chain. They are rather explanatory spectators, like the chorus in a Greek play.[35]

The 1916 placement of the lunettes on the east and west walls underscored the "progression" already established in the 1895 and 1903 installations. At the northeast and northwest, closest to the north "Jewish" wall, Sargent located the lunettes of *Gog and Magog* and *Hell.* At southeast and southwest, in proximity to the south "Christian" wall, he located his *Messianic Era* and *Heaven.* Until the final installation in 1919, though, the Christian bias of the sequence was implicit principally in the *organization* of the cycle and not in the individual images themselves. In 1919, with the placement of the pendant images of *Synagogue* and *Church,* the bias underlying the cultural meaning of the entire sequence became explicit and unavoidable. Here Sargent portrayed the triumph of Christianity over Judaism in his personification of the blindfolded *Synagogue,* placed immediately below *Gog and Magog,* and the victorious *Church,* below the *Messianic Era.*[36] The artist lent formal credibility to the conceptual weighting of synagogue and church in their placement opposite the two large bookcases (constructed by Sargent on the west wall) that punctuated and balanced the two images and their framing devices. In his selective placement of these images in relationship to the staircase, Sargent structured his meaning around the spectator's own physical ascent and descent. The *Church* he located near the head of the stairs and the *Synagogue* over the foot of the stairs. The beholder ascended to the *Church* and descended beneath the *Synagogue.*[37]

35. *Vanity Fair,* November 1916, p. 76.

36. In support of arguments about the civic associations of the *Church* image, the passage from Isaiah quoted in the messianic lunette above the personified church (i.e., resting on "her" rather prominent shoulders) reminded the beholder that "the government" would be upon "the shoulder" of the messiah (Isa. 9:6).

While one may initially puzzle over the location of both images on the east wall, in the context of the entire room, the whole sequence is Christian. Jewish representations ultimately serve to point out "the foundation of the Christian faith upon Hebrew prophecy"; Sargent assigned them no integrity of their own apart from this function. According to the *Handbook of the Boston Public Library,* revised by Frank H. Chase (Boston: Association Publications, 1926), p. 58, Sargent intended the names of Jeremiah, Isaiah, Ezekiel, and Daniel on the arms of personified *Church*'s throne to communicate this content.

37. Actually, Sargent never completed the mural cycle he originally intended; the 1895 handbook of the Boston Public Library records his early plan to cover the

I have claimed that Sargent's murals cast religion as an analog for civilization. In the eyes of the artist and his public, the religious idea that the murals explicated hinged upon this association of Christianity with Western culture. As *Vanity Fair*'s critic put it, it was the impact of Christianity on civilization that produced astonishment and deserved attention.[38] Author and critic Pauline King asserted that "Mr. Sargent has gone straight to the result that he wished to obtain as Michelangelo did in the Sistine Chapel; and the subject, *The Triumph of Religion,* reflects the thought of our time as strongly as the *Last Judgment* does of that earlier period."[39] Certainly no one would have argued that Byzantine and medieval Catholicism represented the thought of increasingly less sectarian and increasingly more secularized Americans at the turn of the century. The post-Darwinian message had to be other than that. In a period much concerned with establishing a cultural identity and a cultural lineage for America, Sargent's excitement about this mural commission demonstrated his desire to make an enduring statement, in Boston, about his own nationality and about the American nation. Using a sacralizing vocabulary, Sargent created an aesthetic environment that his Boston public read as a vindication of American culture and that the artist meant to suggest both the integration of America into Western civilization and the future position of America with respect to that civilization.

The story Sargent told equated art as well as religion with civilization. The subject matter of his murals demonstrated a history of *religion;* the forms (with their referents and sources) suggested an ency-

---

east wall with a mural of Christ preaching to the nations (Small, *Handbook of the New Public Library,* p. 52). Preliminary sketches indicate that, by comparison with the completed images of synagogue and church, Sargent imagined his Christ preaching in a much less allegorical and hieratic presentation. Such a Christ, more stylistically accessible to its immediate public(s), would have suggested even more insistently the "superior" relevance of Christianity for contemporary civilization. In a letter to McKim dated 28 September 1893 (BPL Ms Am 562), Sargent referred to "my plans of doing three large panels along one wall of the hall, the subject being Christ preaching to the multitudes. . . . It will complete the room and be the keynote of my affair." As late as 1915, Sargent planned to paint this representation, which he now described as a Sermon on the Mount, between allegorical depictions of Synagogue and Church (Sargent to Josiah H. Benton, 8 October 1915 [BPL Ms Bos Li B18a, Folder 11]). It is, in fact, entirely possible that the painter abandoned this "keynote" subject in order to prevent further provocation of the considerable number of people opposed to his image of the *Synagogue.*

38. *Vanity Fair,* November 1916, p. 76.

39. King, *American Mural Painting,* p. 124.

clopedic history of *art.*[40] According to Sargent's images, the birthplace of Western religion was also the birthplace of Western art, and much of the history of Western art was clothed in forms suggested by the employment of art in the service of religion(s). In order to minimize negative associations between art and luxury, between art and corruption, American promoters of art had long found it necessary to link art with the highest moral and spiritual values.[41] Sargent was by no means the first American painter to suggest connections between the aesthetic sphere and the religious sphere.[42] In the Boston Public Library, the history of art could be told as a history of religion, and the history of religion could be told as a history of art. The art historical sources of Sargent's murals deserve closer scrutiny. It is, in fact, familiarity with one set of these sources that secures America's place at the pinnacle of civilization in Sargent's schema. In a gesture none too modest, the painter appropriated an image of his own making (*Fumée d'Ambre Gris,* 1880, Fig. 3) as a model for his *Church.* A painting (the *Church*) associated with a "historical" image *(Fumée d'Ambre Gris)* by a "modern" American

40. In their equation of art and civilization, Sargent's murals are similar to Samuel Morse's earlier, more literal *Gallery of the Louvre,* excepting the murals' evolutionary twist and more consistent (religious) subject matter.

Though the final results seldom resemble very closely any one "original," there is ample evidence of Sargent's concern with sources and precedents and of his extensive travels and sketching in the production of these paintings.

The special collections libraries on the third floor included the fine arts and music collections as well as a large number of books on religion and on American history and the Ticknor Collection of Spanish literature (see Small, *Handbook of the New Public Library in Boston,* pp. 63-65). Broadly speaking, Sargent may have understood the subjects of these books, taken together, to constitute a sketch of Western culture or civilization. The proximity of Sargent's murals to these adjacent collections suggests that Sargent may have been following in a time-honored tradition of library decoration, envisioning his project as a sort of freely interpreted visual catalogue (in style and form as well as subject matter) of the library's special collections. For a discussion of library decorations that fall more explicitly within this tradition, see Andre Masson, *The Pictorial Catalogue: Mural Decoration in Libraries* (Oxford: Oxford University Press, 1981).

41. For an intriguing discussion of this issue, see Neil Harris, *The Artist in American Society: The Formative Years, 1790-1860* (New York: George Braziller, 1966).

42. In the larger study that will follow the lines of this essay, I will devote considerable attention to Sargent's comments about the relationship of different styles in the murals to "the progress of belief towards a more spiritual [i.e., less 'material'] ideal" (Sargent to Herbert Putnam, 1895? [BPL MS 1320.2]) and to turn-of-the-century perceptions of the relationship between the aesthetic and the spiritual in the United States.

Figure 3. John Singer Sargent, *Fumée d'Ambre Gris*
Courtesy of the Sterling and Francine Clark Art Institute, Williamstown, Massachusetts

artist (Sargent) thus occupied a position of highest honor in the mural programme.[43]

But the progress of Western civilization was to be had only at a price: for Sargent, progress depended on hierarchical notions of religion, race, and culture. Sargent's carefully researched murals lent aesthetic and "scientific" credence to such notions.[44] The American people, in the decades after the introduction and popularization of Darwinian theory in the United States, were extremely familiar with this sort of cultural evolutionary schema. The great American expositions of the period presented similar images of progress allied with prejudice. This idea of progress (religious, cultural, moral, social) rested on assumptions of difference associated with assignments of value.[45] The murals, like the American fairs, presented a condescending view of the non-Christian world as at worst "barbaric" and at best "childlike."[46] Most subscribed to Sargent's cultural "religion of progress" (a civil form of millennialism) allied with the notion of the triumph of the modern over the primitive.[47]

But among Sargent's publics, Boston's Jewish community recognized the anti-Semitic bias inherent in the artist's murals of 1919. Those who did not fit the religious norm established by the murals objected to the display of that norm in a public institution that they had encouraged and supported. What is perhaps surprising is that they objected not to the entire cycle but only to its most blatantly prejudiced manifestation in the painting of the *Synagogue*. Not only did prominent Jewish leaders almost immediately confront the library's trustees and Sargent himself to request the removal of the painting of the *Synagogue* from the public library, but they took their case to the Massachusetts

43. Too much could easily be made of a connection between the *Fumée d'Ambre Gris* and the *Church*, however. In point of fact, Sargent himself appropriated the type for the *Fumée* from common Beaux-Arts usage. The "original" source, then, was likely French. Still, among late nineteenth-century *American* academic painters especially, the type proved extremely attractive. Sargent returned to this type on several occasions and even employed it in another painting for the Boston cycle, the figure of the *Law* in the lunette above and to the north of *Church*.

44. Cf. Robert W. Rydell, *All the World's a Fair: Visions of Empire at American International Expositions, 1876-1916* (Chicago: University of Chicago Press, 1984), p. 32.

45. Rydell, *All the World's a Fair,* p. 32.

46. Rydell, *All the World's a Fair,* p. 40; see also pp. 24-25.

47. Rydell, *All the World's a Fair,* p. 70. See also Richard Guy Wilson, "The Great Civilization," in Wilson, Pilgrim, and Murray, *The American Renaissance,* pp. 12-13.

state legislature.[48] In 1922 an act was passed authorizing seizure of this painting, but the act was repealed in 1924 for practical as well as constitutional reasons.[49] Feelings ran so high that a vandal spattered the *Synagogue* mural with ink. The physical damage was not permanent.[50]

Sargent produced his *Synagogue* and *Church* murals at precisely the time of growing ideological anti-Semitism in the United States in general and in Boston in particular.[51] Mass immigration of European Jews between 1880 and 1914 led to increasing agitation for quotas on immigration during the 1920s.[52] In fact, in 1894, the Immigration Restriction League was founded in Boston with the support of some members of the faculty of an institution no less distinguished than Harvard University.[53] In 1921 and 1924, the years most immediately surrounding Sargent's conflict with Boston Jews, immigration restric-

48. The objections were not unanimous. Among the less vehement reactions to the mural and even expressions of support by Jewish individuals was a letter from J. G. Moses (of the law offices of Davison, Moses, and Sicher) to the Librarian of the Boston Public Library dated 14 June 1922 (BPL Ms Bos Li B18b, Folder 2) in which Moses states that "the action of the promoters of this proposition [the act authorizing seizure] is calculated to foment rather than to lessen or remove race prejudice." See also a letter from Rabbi Otto Fleischner to Isabella Stewart Gardner dated 7 June 1922 (Archives of Isabella Stewart Gardner Museum). Fleischner had significant ties to the library as well as to the Jewish community: he had been appointed assistant librarian in 1900, a post he still occupied at least as late as 1917.

49. See the relevant correspondence collected in BPL MS Bos Li B18b, Folder 1, and copies of House Bills and the transcript of a public hearing in BPL MS Bos Li B18o. Charteris describes this episode in *John Sargent,* p. 209. See also Fairbrother, *John Singer Sargent and America,* pp. 233, 272n.36.

50. H. E. Thompson (of the Museum of Fine Art, Boston) to Charles Francis Dorr Belden, 25 February 1924 (BPL MS Bos Li B18o).

51. See David A. Gerber's introduction to *Anti-Semitism in American History,* ed. David A. Gerber (Urbana, Ill.: University of Illinois Press, 1986), p. 29. According to Gerber, the 1910s and 1920s in America constituted a period of "extra-ordinary" or "ideological" anti-Semitism. "Significant sectors of society . . . [were] willing to articulate publicly prejudicial views" in aesthetic, political, or economic terms (pp. 21, 29). These years saw the formation of the American Jewish Committee (1906) and the Anti-Defamation League of B'nai B'rith (1913) as well as the Leo Frank lynching in Georgia (1913) and the reestablishment of the Ku Klux Klan (1915) (pp. 22, 27).

52. Gerber, in *Anti-Semitism in American History,* p. 24.

53. At one point the League considered changing its name to the Eugenic Immigration League (*Anti-Semitism in American History,* p. 114). It was not Jews alone but "all cultural aliens" who were viewed as a threat to American unity and to the predominant culture (p. 119).

tions were imposed.[54] In the context of Protestant (and Catholic) patrician fears, Sargent's cultural evolutionary mural cycle, advocating a *relatively* "civilized" variety of anti-Semitism, must have been reassuring to many.[55] Sargent's murals depicted the Jews as a people of the past. The *Triumph of Religion* promoted a view of progress that relegated the Jews to a role as heroes of a bygone era, noble specimens, aged and broken in modern times.

Throughout the controversy, Sargent defended himself by insisting that his representation of *Synagogue* and *Church* was based on carefully researched medieval models. In a letter to Evan Charteris of October 1921, Sargent admitted,

> I am in hot water here with the Jews, who resent my 'Synagogue' and want to have it removed — and tomorrow a prominent member of the Jewish colony is coming to bully me about it and ask me to explain myself — I can only refer him to Reims, Notre Dame, Strasbourg, and other Cathedrals, and dwell at length on the good old times. Fortunately the Library Trustees do not object, and propose to allow this painful work to stay.[56]

Taking up the painter's defense, Sargent's friends and biographers accentuated the "accuracy" of his medievalist interpretations of Jewish and Christian religious institutions and the "impartiality" of his approach.[57] The 1926 edition of the Boston Public Library Handbook rallied to Sargent's cause (in the year after his death) and even labeled *Synagogue* and *Church* the "Mediaeval Contrast."[58]

To Sargent's mind, his sources were art historical, historical, and literary.[59] What he represented, he believed, was not the result of personal

54. *Anti-Semitism in American History,* p. 116.

55. See *Anti-Semitism in American History,* pp. 30-31.

56. Sargent, quoted by Charteris in *John Sargent,* p. 209.

57. *Handbook of the Boston Public Library,* rev. ed., pp. 55-58; Mariana Van Rensselaer, *Memorial Exhibition of the Works of John Singer Sargent* (New York: Metropolitan Museum of Art, 1926), p. xviii; Mount, *John Singer Sargent,* pp. 307-8; Charteris, *John Sargent,* p. 107.

58. *Handbook of the Boston Public Library,* rev. ed., p. 40.

59. Sargent likely consulted his copy of Emile Mâle's *Religious Art in France in the Thirteenth Century* as a source for the images of synagogue and church. Here he would have found support for his own cultural bias discussed in relationship to the same sculptural examples he mentioned to Fox in his letter of 1921. Mâle's text claimed that it was "only in relationship to the New Testament that the Old Testament has significance" (*Religious Art in France in the Thirteenth Century* [London: J. M. Dent & Sons, 1913], p. 133; see also pp. 186-93, 355, 377). Further, Mâle cited

religious choice but of careful translation of the monuments of art. According to Sargent, he consistently maintained a deliberate, considered, and spectatorial distance from his subject. He used a "medievalizing" style and referred his Jewish critics to the glass and sculpture of medieval cathedrals. Sargent's intention, as his biographer noted in 1927, was to "chronicle," not to "judge."[60] For Sargent, the "progress" of Christianity beyond Judaism was just as "objective" as were any of the "historical" details he sought to render with such archaeological accuracy.

While Sargent's mural cycle may have been objective in intent, it was, of course, subjective in content. Sargent discovered the models for his "Contrast" in historical sources, but the sources themselves reinforced the bias already inherent in Sargent's evolutionary schema. And Sargent did more than reiterate the religious biases of the past. He substantially modified medieval precedents to emphasize qualitative distinctions between the two institutions of synagogue and church. Rather than depicting two women of comparable age and beauty (as in his medieval models), Sargent gave Boston a synagogue that is aged and broken as well as blindfolded.[61]

Sargent delighted in dealing with multiplicity in exotic and foreign cultures, but, at least iconographically, he could not deal with multiplicity in his own time and place. Rather than acknowledging the increasing diversity of American civilization, he brought other places, other people, other worlds to Boston in order to depict the course of civilization from chaos to order, from confusion to clarity, from pluralism to unity. Sargent romanticized the "other," relegating it to foreign, distant, and "inferior" worlds. While he dealt rather more comfortably with the "Jew next door" (as, e.g., in painting the Asher Wertheimer family portraits), he could not deal conceptually with Jews and Judaism in the modern world. The hierarchical conception of religion in the murals mirrored a hierarchical conception of society.[62] The Christianity

---

a missionary impulse for the medieval representations of synagogue and church: to convince the Jews of the futility of their faith (p. 193).

Charteris does not indicate whether Sargent owned the English edition or the earlier French edition (1898). Since Sargent was fluent in French and, when it came to his own reading, preferred French to English literature, it is likely that he consulted this book in its original French relatively early in his preparation for the Boston library murals.

60. Charteris, *John Sargent*, p. 107.

61. Cf. Dillenberger, *The Visual Arts and Christianity in America*, pp. 154-55.

62. For a discussion of increasing cultural hierarchy in America in the late nineteenth century, see Lawrence W. Levine, *Highbrow/Lowbrow: The Emergence of Cultural Hierarchy in America* (Cambridge: Harvard University Press, 1988).

Sargent depicted was to religion in general as the cultural and aesthetic elite of the American Renaissance was to American democracy, or so the murals claimed. While it does not appear that Sargent was any more anti-Semitic than many of his contemporaries, in the Boston library paintings he accepted and even celebrated the fitness of the social order; he advanced an elitist notion of culture and the public sphere. Offering a worn perspective on the relationship of Christianity and Judaism (and, for that matter, on the relationship of West and East), Sargent's images presented the predominant Western cultural evolutionary view. Christians generally accepted this perspective as objective fact. Jews, with more at stake, recognized the affront.

Why would a presumably nonreligious expatriate American painter choose a religious subject for a project of this scale in a public edifice at the height of his career? I contend that these murals "belonged" in the Boston Public Library because of the aesthetic, religious, and cultural evolutionary conceptions of Sargent's turn-of-the-century patrons, especially of the American Renaissance, reinforced by some overtly similar European aesthetic ideas. In the end, what Sargent painted was not Spanish literature, not Greek myth, not even world religions (a title he deliberately rejected as "too comprehensive").[63] Through images recalling great cultures and great art of the past, in a location (Copley Square) whose other architectural monuments represented the intersection of culture, religion, and knowledge, Sargent depicted his summation of sanctified civilization.[64]

Within a few decades, the response to Sargent's murals moved from celebration to neglect, perhaps due in part to the uncomfortable disjunction between the cycle's particular "religious" content and its public context. In conservative aesthetic language, adapting styles and models from the past, Sargent promoted what had become a conservative social ideology. Boston Jews pointed out the inherent anti-Semitism of this ideology. In addition, others may have sensed that Sargent's view of the contrast between "savage" and "civilized" fit late Victorian assumptions better than it fit modernist primitivism (which was equally but differently biased). The murals have not aged gracefully. A too-vigorous cleaning in 1953 removed paint and gilding along with dirt.

63. In his descriptive letter to Putnam (1895?), Sargent explained, "I give the work a title in order to avoid such names as 'The Religion of the World' and others that are too comprehensive" (BPL Ms 1320.2).

64. Late in the nineteenth century, Copley Square was home to the Museum of Fine Arts (1876), Trinity Church (1872-77), and the new Old South Church (1875); see William L. Vance, "Redefining 'Bostonian,'" in *The Bostonians*, pp. 11 and 18.

Alterations in lighting patterns, changing both symbolic sense and degree of visual clarity, have further enshrouded the images in an artificially produced dusk.[65] Interestingly, the explanatory sheet on the Sargent Hall murals distributed by the library in the early 1990s is a reprint of a 1916 description of the first three installations (1895-1916).[66] While *Synagogue* and *Church* still adorn the Boston Public Library, in this library publication the controversial 1919 installation goes unmentioned. With the approach of the 1995 centennial of the "new" Boston Public Library, the murals' fortunes seem to be changing again, however. Provided that adequate funding can be secured, restoration of both the decorated surface and the lighting in Sargent Hall will soon expose these important images to closer scrutiny. In the contemporary pluralistic context, renewed visibility will almost certainly foster further discussion of past and present roles of religious images in public places.

65. See Gammell, "A Masterpiece Dishonored," pp. 49, 53.

66. "Judaism and Christianity: A Sequence of Mural Decoration Executed between 1895 and 1916. By John Singer Sargent, R.A." (Boston: Boston Public Library, n.d.).

Public Religion and the Crisis of American Protestantism in Japan, 1923-1940

W. L. SACHS

THE CONCEPT of a "public religion" has been a pivotal reference point in Martin Marty's analysis of American life. Marty has shown that since Benjamin Franklin, prominent Americans such as Jefferson, Lincoln, and Wilson have articulated national purpose in terms of a common faith that transcends ecclesiastical boundaries in order to secure national identity. Public religion has consisted in a consensus among mainstream Protestants about basic Christian beliefs that repudiates miracle and dogma in favor of a humane stress upon religion's role in earthly matters. Marty has delineated four phases of public religion, from the age of America's founders to the ideals of such literary figures as Melville and Thoreau, followed by the faith in democracy that John Dewey endorsed in the 1930s, and the revival of civic faith in the 1950s.[1] Public religion has embodied the aspiration of mainstream American Protestant churches to influence public policy.

Marty has shown that this American consensus about the churches' social role inspired a national sense of purpose. Historically, religious references have been important guideposts for policymakers and have encouraged denominational leaders to assume prominent roles in shaping national destiny. America's global task assumed religious significance, and Christian mission carried policy overtones. Public religion was a set of mainstream Protestant ideals about Christianity's social implications that legitimated an American sense of social establishment. But scant attention has been paid to the influence of

1. See Martin E. Marty, *Pilgrims in Their Own Land* (Boston: Little, Brown, 1984), pp. 154-64; and Marty, *Religion and Republic* (Boston: Beacon Press, 1987), pp. 60-61.

American public religion outside the United States. How has this fusion of faith and policy functioned as an American missionary strategy for inspiring public purpose in other cultures?

In a volume co-edited by Marty, William R. Hutchison has observed that American Protestant missionaries used their own cultural norms as means of assessing their task.[2] Mainstream Protestants from the late nineteenth century to World War II relied upon the ideal of a public religion as the missionary goal. They envisioned Christian mission not merely as individual conversion, nor as the creation of ecclesiastical structures, but as the dissemination of a model of social development in which a host culture would replicate the ideals of American public religion. They believed that technological advances and the emergence of democratic institutions should be grounded in a liberal Protestant form of Christianity, the only legitimate basis of a modern nation.

Japan offers a fascinating instance of the fate of American public religion in the mission field. This society never fell under actual rule by a Western power, but at times it hungered for Western cultural forms. By the 1920s; however, nationalism combined with xenophobia in a profound rejection of Western control. Under this strain, missionaries intensified their reliance on public religion as a means of buttressing their sense of control over Japanese social development.

I

In 1926 August Karl Reischauer, Professor of Comparative Religion at Meiji Gakuin (University), Tokyo, a missionary at a Presbyterian institution and father of a noted American Japanologist, argued that a new missionary era had begun. The modern world had broken through cultural and racial barriers, creating unity and interdependence. Missionaries could no longer presume an innate superiority over non-Western peoples nor presume to convert them simply by modernizing them. Neither conversion nor westernization, "our whole emphasis in modern Christianity is just this emphasis upon Christianizing all life's relationships; and that must, of course, include our relationships as

2. Hutchison, "Christianity, Culture, and Complications: Protestant Attitudes toward Missions," in *Pushing the Faith: Proselytism and Civility in a Pluralistic World,* ed. Martin E. Marty and Frederick E. Greenspahn (New York: Crossroad, 1988).

nations and races." The old form of mission overlooked cultural differences or dismissed them as unalterable social factors. Reischauer called for a new sense of cultural dynamism to guide mission and shift its focus from "saving souls" to "bringing new life to the ancient peoples of the world," establishing "the Kingdom of God on earth." In Japan, he wrote, "the normal activities of the people shall be Christian in spirit."[3] As a case in point, Reischauer argued that Shinto, Japan's cultural religion, must be transformed from a national loyalty into the Christian ideal of membership in God's kingdom. A public religion must ground nationalism in a higher loyalty.

The idea of cultural influence as the basis of Christian mission was not new. Dramatic growth in Protestant missionary activity in Japan occurred in the last third of the nineteenth century as the churches became a cultural force. As Japanese society embarked upon rapid modernization, the missionary role proved catalytic. Schools operated by the churches offered access to Western ideas, and their sudden popularity prompted missionaries to believe that Japan would be christianized as rapidly as it modernized. During the 1870s and 1880s American Protestants in Japan even adopted certain Japanese forms, such as the hiring of a Japanese army officer to drill students at St. Paul's Episcopal School in Tokyo in 1887.[4] In this way missionaries believed that they could express the gospel in a form that was both modern and recognizably Japanese. Christian belief, which they saw as the basis of successful modernization, could inspire the formation not merely of Japanese churches but of a Christian nation. By 1904, John McKim, Episcopal Bishop of Tokyo, believed that Japanese civilization was "essentially Occidental," a sign of Christianity's impending triumph.[5]

The initial phase of missionary influence in Japan encouraged the nation's rapid absorption of Western ways. In vague terms, missionaries hoped they could direct Japan's social development in such a way that the church would become the heart of a modern Japanese

3. Reischauer, *The Task in Japan* (New York: Fleming H. Revell, 1926), pp. 20, 39, 44, 47.

4. Report by John Gardiner, head of St. Paul's School, Tokyo, dated 30 July 1887, in Box 5 of the Japan Records, 1859-1953, of the Domestic and Foreign Missionary Society Records in the Archives of the Episcopal Church, Austin, Texas. I would like that express my gratitude to V. Nelle Bellamy, Ph.D., archivist, for permission to quote from these records, which are hereafter cited as JR.

5. McKim, "The Spread of Christianity in Japan," *The Spirit of Missions* 69 (September 1904): 653.

society.[6] Bishop Channing Moore Williams, the first Episcopal bishop and one of the first Protestant missionaries in Japan, recognized that the churches benefited from Japan's fascination with the West. He applauded the influence his church gained with leading Japanese citizens, and he acknowledged that all Protestants hoped to convert the influential social classes as means of access to the nation. However, Williams feared that popular Japanese interest in philosophers such as Thomas Huxley and John Stuart Mill portended a dangerously secular form of modernization. He insisted that Japan needed the church as an institution under missionary guidance so that, as it absorbed Western learning, it could "distinguish between what is true and what is false."[7]

As their influence in Japan grew in the late nineteenth century, Protestant missionaries envisioned cultural influence in Japan as the primary means of converting the nation to Christianity. They feared, however, that a generation of converts lured by a cultural rather than a religious message would sacrifice the church's distinctive identity and missionary control of church life would be lost. Unguided religious change might result in mere nationalism without a sense of membership in God's kingdom. In light of such concerns, Southern Presbyterians paid close attention to the textbooks chosen and the theology expressed in classes at Meiji Gakuin.[8] Similarly, Episcopalians gradually advanced Japanese men to the ordained ministry. It was not until 1883 that Channing Moore Williams ordained two Japanese deacons, twenty-four years after he began the Episcopal mission.

American missionaries felt that their caution had been justified as Japanese enthusiasm for Western culture faded during the 1890s and a period of nativistic reaction began. Emphasis on loyalty to Japanese ways intensified the civic role of Shinto and initiated a modern form of state religion. Protestant missionaries realized that their strategy for an indigenous Christianity had been ill-defined and had relied too heavily on the receptivity of Japanese society to Western cultural ways. They initiated new efforts to guide Japanese social development without identifying church and society. The first phase of a critical missionary strategy led to the erection of indigenous church structures

6. Irwin Scheiner, *Christian Converts and Social Protest in Meiji Japan* (Berkeley and Los Angeles: University of California Press, 1970), pp. 27-29.

7. Williams, Annual Report, 30 June 1880, JR, Box 23.

8. See Sandra Caruthers Thomson, "Meiji Japan through Missionary Eyes: The American Protestant Experience," *Journal of Religious History* 7 (June 1973): 255; and Augusta Moore Stoehr, "Mission Cooperation in Japan: The Meiji Gakuin Textbook Controversy," *Journal of Presbyterian History* 54 (Fall 1976): 339.

that American Protestants believed they could control. By the beginning of the twentieth century, American missionaries had embraced "self-support" as the goal of their work.

A concept generally used to indicate the goal of an indigenous church, "self-support" in Japan became the first Protestant response to nationalism.[9] Self-support involved the creation of Japanese leadership for self-sustaining churches, church schools, and hospitals. The underlying intention, which became clearer in missionary minds as they confronted nationalism, was the creation of a public religion. By the 1920s, the missionaries were hoping they could inspire a modern, Christian nation along American lines, and to meet that goal they felt it would be necessary to maintain a continuing presence in order to guard against secularism and nativism. In the 1920s American Protestant missionaries, as Reischauer stated, grasped a Japanese public religion as their goal.

II

"Indigenous churches in Japan have progressed more rapidly and to a further degree than those of any other section of the non-Christian world," James Cannon of Duke University claimed in 1925. "Japan has in a sense been the working laboratory, and experiments made here have been used as bases of work in other fields."[10] The goal of self-supporting churches had not been attained, but social issues weighed more heavily on the missionary mind. In 1923, one missionary feared that although Japan had modernized, democratic liberalism faced severe threats. "More energetic efforts should be made by the churches, Christian Associations, and other agencies of good-will to befriend and to Christianize the Japanese," wrote Galen M. Fisher. Missionaries must "do all in their power to promote the Christianization of the Japanese people." "Jesus Christ was the world's first great liberal and His in-

9. See my article " 'Self-Support': The Episcopal Mission and Nationalism in Japan," *Church History* 58 (December 1989): 489-501. There I show that "self-support," ostensibly a means of creating indigenous Christianity, actually allowed American missionaries in Japan to retain control of ecclesiastical structures. I now believe that "self-support" was the first phase of a missionary program that had as its goal a public religion.

10. Cannon, "Japanese Indigenous Christianity," *South Atlantic Quarterly* 24 (July 1925): 252.

creasing sway in Japan is the only sure guarantee of her becoming and remaining a liberal state."[11]

An apparent cause of increased missionary social concern was the massive earthquake that flattened much of Tokyo and Yokohama and caused considerable damage throughout Japan in early September 1923. Not only did church-supported facilities need to be rebuilt, but there was an awakening among missionaries to a pervasive social need. "A strong case could be made for the contention that industrialism has been more of a curse than a blessing to Japan," Fisher wrote in 1923. Conditions in mines and factories required amelioration, yet Japan's nascent labor movement seemed prone to Marxism. In the 1920s missionaries realized that modern life was fraught with dangerous possibilities and called for the Christianization of Japanese life. The "spirit and principles of Jesus Christ" must be injected "into the turgid thought currents that are sweeping the people."[12]

By the end of World War I, Japan "had become in the full sense an industrial state. As such she faced political problems of a kind new in her experience, arising both from the pressures of industrial wealth on political and social privilege and from the unrest that infused a growing urban proletariat."[13] Although the nature of this unrest was unclear to missionaries, they concluded that their influence was needed to complete Japan's national character. There was particular fear that political and religious extremism might infest students, the rising generation of Japanese leadership. Thus the churches during the 1920s created a series of groups for young men. Such groups proposed to teach Japanese students basic Christian principles, the ideals of democracy, and a Christian emphasis on social justice and the unity of all nations and races in Christ.

"The biggest and perhaps the most important work that has occupied my mind in the past six months is the organization of 'the Young Men's League of the Diocese of Tokyo,'" confided Episcopal priest Masatoshi Matsushita to his American superior in 1931. He feared that the "best minds have been taken away to Marxism."[14] In the same year, Paul Rusch, a notable Episcopal missionary, founded a Japanese

11. Fisher, *Creative Forces in Japan* (New York: Missionary Education Movement, 1923), pp. 64-65.

12. Fisher, *Creative Forces in Japan,* pp. 67, 202.

13. W. G. Beasley, *The Modern History of Japan,* 3d ed. (London: Weidenfeld & Nicolson, 1984), p. 214.

14. Masatoshi Matsushita, in the file of Charles Reifsnider, July 1931, JR, Box 124.

branch of the Brotherhood of St. Andrew, a church-run group for men and boys. By July 1933 he proudly reported that there were twenty-six Japanese chapters teaching Christian principles of social service and encouraging prayer for international harmony. Although Rusch hoped the Brotherhood would attract young Japanese men to the church, he laid greater emphasis on its potential for ameliorating secularism and social unrest.[15]

Other Protestant churches in Japan moved in a similar direction. They were concerned that previous generations of missionaries had taught a private form of Christianity that laid excessive stress on church growth. They hoped instead to forge a consensus among the churches about Japan's social needs.[16] In 1930 the Student Christian Movement originated under the auspices of the Japanese Y.M.C.A. The group's immediate leadership was Japanese, made up of young faculty at Christian colleges. But the movement received missionary impetus and embodied the public religion that American Protestants prized. The founders emphasized that God's power pervades all life and that Christianity is a faith that intends the redemption of history and harmonizes with scientific truth. The key plank was an emphasis on the kingdom of God as the tangible expression of salvation's advance within history.[17]

The kingdom of God became synonymous with public religion in the Japanese context. When they referred to the kingdom of God, leaders of the student movement such as Ju Nakajima and Enkichi Kan reflected the public ideals of their missionary mentors who had schooled them in liberal theology and American democracy. While the term "public religion" was rarely used, the "kingdom" embodied this social intention — namely, the idea of refashioning society into a cooperative community inspired by Jesus. It emphasized the search for the new relation between humanity and God that the American mainstream idealized.[18] It was assumed that the older missionary emphasis on education as the means of evangelizing had to be replaced by an assertive social criticism that affirmed the kingdom of God. This theme embodied the hope for a Christian social order like America's Protestant mainstream. Protestant "forces" had to apply "the gospel to the needs

15. Rusch, in a letter to John Wood dated 24 July 1933, JR, Box 126.

16. Kun Sam Lee, *The Christian Confrontation with Shinto Nationalism* (Philadelphia: Presbyterian & Reformed, 1966), p. 133.

17. Charles H. Germany, *Protestant Theologies in Modern Japan* (Tokyo: IISR, 1965), pp. 57, 72.

18. Germany, *Protestant Theologies in Modern Japan*, pp. 65, 73.

of daily life" and secure "the place of leadership" that they had achieved in the United States.[19]

Protestant emphasis on the kingdom expressed both an American hope and a critique of Japanese society. Church leaders decried the social forms of the past. They claimed that historically Buddhism had persecuted women and generally retarded social development and that such attitudes had been hardened by Confucianism. The advance of the kingdom entailed equal rights for men and women as well as freedom of the press and democratically elected officials. Yet the kingdom did not necessarily overturn all historic Japanese forms. Instead, the rise of God's kingdom could be seen in increasing respect for individual personality, the principle by which all social forms, ancient and modern, were judged. The customs of Japan's past "still represent spiritual forces which cannot be ignored" but which must be evaluated for their influence on individuals. The new factor "in the whole religious situation in Japan is the awakening sense of personality" — by which Protestants in Japan meant the individual's consciousness of being both a self and a social being whose unity lies in being part of God's kingdom. A key component of this public religion was the belief that the churches must guard the sanctity of individual personality against intrusive modern and national social pressures.[20]

The kingdom of God was thus the focus of missionary hopes that Christianity might provide the means to complete Japan's modernization. Christianity could engender forms of service that would eradicate evil social currents, guide national development, and secure the individual's sense of bond to the nation. Missionaries viewed public religion as the final stage in the creation of an indigenous Japanese Christianity, the amalgamation of Christian belief with modern Japanese form. Between 1929 and 1934, hope for a public religion reached its zenith in the "Kingdom of God" campaign and its leader, Toyohiko Kagawa.

By 1923, Protestant hopes fastened upon Kagawa, a young minister at work in the slums of Kobe. He returned to Japan in 1918 after three years of study at Princeton Seminary and wrote a book on the sources of poverty. He also organized mass meetings to demand better working and living conditions and universal suffrage and to call for an

19. Federation of Christian Missions in Japan, *Japan Mission Year Book* (Tokyo: Meiji, 1929), p. 119.

20. M. S. Murao and W. H. Murray Walton, *Japan and Christ* (London: Church Missionary Society, 1928), pp. 55, 57.

end to alcoholism and prostitution. He proclaimed himself a pacifist in the tradition of Tolstoy and upheld social service as the path to self-fulfillment. Following the patterns of leaders in the Christian Socialist and Social Gospel movements in Victorian Britain and America, Kagawa founded a labor federation and insisted that mobilization of workers had a Christian basis. He also founded a college at Osaka to train labor leaders. Well schooled in the ideals of public religion, and capable of attracting impressive public support, Kagawa epitomized the missionary hope for Japanese Christianity.[21]

In the 1920s and 1930s American Protestants spoke of Kagawa in hagiographic terms. One author called him a "miracle" of "purity" and "flaming idealism." Even as a child he was attracted to missionary teachings and appalled by poverty and ignorance. Fellow students shunned him when he aided beggars, yet he "fearlessly espoused unpopular causes and here on the threshold of his life showed an affinity for the prophets." He dared to advocate socialist principles, yet he "was a flaming evangel." In rural isolation for a year to recuperate from tuberculosis, he "poured brain and heart" into writing a novel while attempting to "evangelize the fishing-folk around him." Recovered, he headed for industrial slums, where he proclaimed Christ's love and taught a means of social organization.[22]

Kagawa seemed to be "a religious genius." Christ inspired in him the hope "for a Christian-social as well as a Christian-world order." He proclaimed a religion of "self-respect" that placed "before the people the model of a Christlike life." For him salvation meant "re-creation as living, hoping men and women."[23] He envisioned a day when the world would be renewed, its wealth equitably distributed, "the good cherished and the evil uprooted." A vision arose in him that the churches of Japan could "become a creative force mighty enough to fashion the nation's life according to the Christian pattern." Accordingly, in 1929 he called for a crusade to increase the number of Christians in Japan to one million, which he deemed essential to making the hope of a Christian nation plausible. He aimed his crusade at workers, social classes that Japan's missionaries had left untouched.[24]

The Kingdom of God campaign combined mass evangelism with

21. Fisher, *Creative Forces in Japan*, pp. 104ff.

22. William Axling, *Kagawa* (New York: Harper, 1932), pp. 3, 22-23.

23. Axling, *Kagawa*, pp. 115-16.

24. Margaret Baumann, *Kagawa: An Apostle of Japan* (New York: Macmillan, 1936), pp. 42, 89-90.

church-led social reform. Missionaries sensed that it expressed their hope for a public religion and applauded it as evidence that "the Christian forces are alive to the importance . . . of applying the gospel to the needs of daily life."[25] They hoped that Japan's churches were on the verge of the proper form of indigenous Christianity. After the campaign's inception in 1929, Protestant churches soon joined so that Kagawa was "still the religious genius and pivotal personality around which the Campaign moves but it is no longer a one-man movement." Focusing on preaching and evangelism, education and social reform, the movement's goal was "to establish the Kingdom of God ideals and spirit and the Kingdom of God way of life in every relationship and every sphere of the nation's life." As early as 1930, supporters claimed, large crowds attended mass meetings where Kagawa spoke and thousands in several cities signed cards indicating their faith in Christ.[26]

Though initially the response seemed impressive, by 1932 the campaign seemed to be stalling. In the first half of 1931 alone, thirty-one conferences were held to train workers from twelve denominations. Over 200 local campaigns enlisted two-thirds of Japan's Protestant churches and attracted over 8,000 new members. Yet there were still only 250,000 Christians in Japan — one out of every 400 persons — an increase of less than 50,000 converts. In 1932 Kagawa called for "a thousand times as much effort as at present." He blamed denominational differences, the churches' quibbling over intellectual abstractions of dogma and biblical interpretation, and the Western tendency toward individualism.[27] A missionary critic went farther, claiming that the movement had been imposed on the churches rather than emerging from them. The campaign did not embody indigenous Christianity but represented missionary infatuation with Kagawa.[28]

The appearance of recrimination signaled the decline of public religion in Japan. This decline is impossible to quantify, but a loss of heart among American missionaries became apparent in the early 1930s. Missionary enchantment with Kagawa faded, although he remained a respected spokesman. American Protestants acknowledged that the Kingdom of God campaign stirred tens of thousands of Jap-

25. *Japan Mission Year Book* (1929), p. 119.

26. William Axling, "The Kingdom of God Campaign," in *Japan Mission Year Book* (Tokyo: Meiji, 1930), pp. 141ff.

27. Toyohiko Kagawa, "A Real Kingdom of God Movement," in the *Japan Mission Year Book* (Tokyo: Meiji, 1932), pp. 91-92.

28. John K. Linn, "The Kingdom of God Movement: A Criticism," *Japan Mission Year Book* (1932), p. 102.

anese hearts, but they feared that it obscured denominational identity and sacrificed doctrinal precision.[29] Missionaries believed that the form of the church ensured the efficacy of its response to social problems and sensed syncretistic and nationalistic tendencies in the Kingdom of God campaign. Affirmation of Japan as a fatherland and of its glorious traditions rang throughout the campaign and left most missionaries troubled. American missionaries believed a public religion must preserve ecclesiastical identity and must offer a critique of modern society, not surrender to indigenous currents. Missionaries feared that in Japan there "is too much of a tendency to think of the church as a kind of club. The church has failed to influence social life and social relationships as much as it should."[30] One American missionary in Kyoto wrote in 1935 that the "largest part of our work is Social Service because I believe that to help people spiritually we must also help them mentally and physically."[31] The point of his letter was to request increased financial aid from American churches. American missionaries believed that the triumph of public religion required their oversight as well as Kagawa's appeals.

III

The Kingdom of God movement embodied the hope of American missionaries for a Japanese public religion. They viewed a public religion as the last phase in the creation of an indigenous Japanese Christianity. Missionaries envisioned a critique of modernity's flaws that stressed love of Japan and trust in the course of its social development. They also presumed that indigenous leadership and continuing missionary influence were not incompatible but would secure Christianity's social role. The missionaries were determined to show that Japan needed the church's social critique. However, the goal of a public religion was overwhelmed by a nationalism that Western ideals could not encompass. The collapse of public religion in Japan reveals the limitations of missionary policy in the face of social reality.

The basis of the Kingdom of God campaign, and of missionary hope for a public religion, began with the perception that moderniza-

29. Arthur Judson Brown, *One Hundred Years* (New York: Fleming H. Revell, 1936), p. 731.

30. *Japan Mission Year Book* (Tokyo: Meiji, 1933), p. 57.

31. J. Kenneth Morris, in a letter dated 23 January 1935, JR, Box 147.

tion had created a religious vacuum in Japan. "The present weakening of the old religious stimuli calls for serious consideration," the *Japan Mission Year Book* observed in 1929. "Like the rest of the modern world, Japan is passing through a religious revolution which demands a deeper and more fundamental analysis than has yet been given." Missionaries lamented the passing of rural and village life and the emergence of industrial society. Rapid rather than gradual development weakened historic social ties and gave rise to sectarian extremism. A variety of cults, ideologies, and theologies made up the "mingling currents of religious life in Japan."[32] These movements provided false sources of assurance for Japanese youth, who had no adequate vision of the nation. When they proposed a public religion, the missionaries believed that Christianity could supply the proper form of modern wholeness without which no nation could endure.

The missionary fear that Japan was susceptible to sectarian movements had a basis in fact. A variety of sects that had first emerged in the nineteenth century reappeared during the 1920s and 1930s, and a score of new ones joined them. Derivatives of Buddhism and Shinto, these "new religions" appealed to farmers and workers as means of personal healing and assurance that more formalized religious systems failed to deliver. Tenri-kyo, Hito no Michi Kyodan, and Reiyukai shared an emphasis on simple, personal piety with the promise of forgiveness of sin and individual salvation. Though each was suspect to the Japanese government as heterodox, all flourished by the early 1930s, and their appeal set the tone for the public religion that missionaries promoted.[33]

Kagawa's campaign was evangelistic because he sensed the power of personal appeal. But conversion in his framework led to public service, reflecting missionary hope that Christianity could serve to unify society. Public religion aspired to be a mass movement of national loyalty. Initially missionaries were eager to profess loyalty to Japan and often claimed that Christianity had produced modernity's greatest benefits. In the face of Japan's increasing militarism, many missionaries tried to reassure Japanese authorities of their benevolent intentions. In 1936, Episcopal bishop Shirley Nichols in Kyoto wrote, "I do not think or speak very much about militarism, nationalism, or any of the other isms. . . . Strange as it may sound, I think I may say

32. *Japan Mission Year Book* (1929), pp. 52, 49.

33. Shigeyoshi Murakami, *Japanese Religion in the Modern Century,* trans. H. Byron Earhart (Tokyo: University of Tokyo, 1980), pp. 83-90.

truly that to my mind not one of these movements . . . can be called unqualifiedly and essentially evil."[34] Nichols persisted in the conviction that a public Christianity could direct such movements toward a healthy sense of national identity.[35] The essence of public religion lay in the hope that Christianity could inspire Japan's masses. To this end, missionaries often were eager to show their loyalty to the nation and to endorse forces of national unity, until they threatened church life.

In December 1939, Nichols wrote reassuringly to Episcopal authorities in New York concerning a new government edict. All schools were required to display a tablet emblematic of the Imperial Shrine at Ise on a "kamidana" or "god-shelf" in a prominent location. The appearance of this regulation symbolized the assertiveness of State Shinto, the marriage of Shinto rites, an imperial cult, and frenetic nationalism that expressed Japan's militaristic ideology. Clinging to the hope of a public religion, Nichols reasoned that "there is no contradiction between the Christian faith and the showing of respect to the Imperial Family through this ritual." He cautioned, however, that ritual practices required by government decree risked placing Christians in an untenable position. Public religion could not be state religion.[36]

Nevertheless, motivated by their goal of a public role, many missionaries and Japanese Christians went to great lengths to convince government officials of their loyalty. When Japan invaded China, Christian groups generally endorsed the war and made loud protestations of patriotism. A few were less enthusiastic. "Christianity in Japan is losing its soul," an anonymous writer lamented in 1939.[37] For the sake of preserving an image of public influence, the argument ran, the churches supported the war and emperor worship. The ideal of a public religion had been a Christian "contribution to wholesome nationalism" through "the widespread relief of suffering, the promotion of positive social well-being, and the deepening of devotion. The Christian was the best patriot." But by the mid-1930s, the incompleteness of Kagawa's

34. Shirley Nichols in a letter to John Wood dated 15 May 1936, JR, Box 149.

35. S. H. Wainright, "Christian Influence upon Japanese Literature," *Japan Mission Year Book* (1930), p. 159.

36. Shirley Nichols in a letter to John Wood dated 5 December 1939, JR, Box 149.

37. "The Japanization of Christianity," *Christian Century,* 2 August 1939, p. 945. See also H. Henry Howard, "The Japanese Church Goes to War," *Christian Century,* 16 March 1938, pp. 332-34; and Stuart Lillico, "Christians and the Japanese Caesar," *Christian Century,* 24 May 1939, pp. 671-73.

work and pressure from State Shinto signaled the end of a public, missionary-led Christianity.[38]

The dilemma for missionaries lay in blurring the distinction between public religion's aspirations and modern Japanese social development. At first missionaries and their churches "began to absorb the nationalistic spirit" and even encouraged respect for Shinto shrines and state observances because they promoted national unity and were not, they believed, strictly religious. Shinto seemed a means for national purpose that missionaries cautiously endorsed, hoping to retain Christianity's social purpose and to convince Japanese Christians of missionary sympathy.[39] As early as 1929, missionaries expressed the concern that "maladjustment between the missions and the self-conscious, independent, struggling native churches" could prove disastrous for Christianity's social program.[40]

The emergence of State Shinto with expectations of ritual observance created a feeling of uncertainty among missionaries and eroded their role in indigenous church life. The same August K. Reischauer who in 1926 professed certainty about the task in Japan, by 1931 commented that "among present day Christian workers there are many who are less positive than men used to be in the matter of an essential Christian message and also less certain as to whether what is essential in Christianity may not also be had from other sources, perhaps from the best in non-Christian religions or from what is inherent in human nature as this is now expressing itself in various departments of the physical and social sciences." Rethinking the meaning of Christianity in a non-Western culture, missionaries sensed after Kagawa's campaign that their faith could not compel the masses and that they must rethink their message. They began to speak of Christianity as "a religion which has the good of society and the state at heart but which has its own standards for what the good life of the individual and the state should be, and which stands for values and purposes which transcend even patriotism and the state."[41]

There was bountiful confidence in Christianity's social potential

38. D. C. Holtom, *Modern Japan and Shinto Nationalism* (Chicago: University of Chicago Press, 1943), p. 82.

39. James Arthur Cogswell, "A History of the Work of the Japan Mission of the Presbyterian Church in the United States, 1885-1960," Th.D. diss. (Richmond: Union Theological Seminary, 1961), pp. 234-35.

40. *Japan Mission Year Book* (1929), p. 71.

41. Reischauer, "Towards a Philosophy of Religion in Japan," *Japan Mission Year Book* (Tokyo: Meiji, 1931), pp. 80, 85.

during the 1920s, but after Kagawa's campaign got under way, that confidence eroded precipitously. Missionaries turned increasingly away from a public religion toward a stress on the individual. One missionary who had founded schools and social service agencies in Kyoto concluded in 1937 that church-run education should no longer be practical or social in focus but "essentially spiritual." As church attendance fell rapidly, it was concluded that the Christian message should shift emphasis to the sanctity of the individual conscience. The question of whether Christians could participate in Shinto rites must not be ignored, for Christianity represented a countercurrent in Japanese society. Rather than absorption in nationalism, Christians must stand against the state or compromise the distinctive character of their witness. Increasingly missionary attention turned to the "Shrine Problem" and away from the idea of the kingdom of God.[42] Because the "influence of Christianity on public opinion is observable to a certain extent, but it is not measurable," Christians must play a critical role in Japan.[43]

The churches made little public protest against State Shinto because they lacked an effective public voice. Locally, however, instances of missionary disapproval began to appear. Kinjo College, a Presbyterian institution in Nagoya, agreed under government pressure in 1938 to send its teachers and students to attend ceremonies at the Atsuta State Shinto Shrine. In response, the denominational mission committee required all of its missionaries to sever connections with the school in 1939.[44] The "confusing and delicate problems arising for Christians in this country from the existence of Shinto as a state cult" by the late 1930s had been resolved by missionaries in favor of a new emphasis on individual conscience and the separation of church from state. This shift represented a new emphasis on ecclesiastical identity rather than public influence. But this change in focus was an admission that public religion as a missionary tactic had failed. Unable to direct their host culture, the missionaries were forced to distance themselves from Japanese society.[45]

In 1939 the last nail in the coffin of public religion was hammered in place. The Religious Organizations Law pressured Protestants to

42. *Japan Mission Year Book* (1933), p. 61.

43. J. Kenneth Morris in a letter to John Wood dated 25 May 1937, JR, Box 147.

44. Cogswell, "A History of the Work of the Japan Mission of the Presbyterian Church in the United States, 1885-1960," p. 272.

45. *Japan Mission Year Book* (1932), p. 45.

unite in a union church, the Nihon Kirisuto Kyodan, formed in 1941. Public religion ended on an ironic note. Nationalism's modern form emerged from Western influence of the sort that public religion envisioned.[46] In a context in which Christians remained a minority, however influential, public religion proved to be a vain transposition of Western ideals by missionaries who sought a device to perpetuate their influence. Truly indigenous Christianity came to Japan in 1940 and 1941 as missionaries were expelled and public religion proved to be a mirage. After 1945, Japan's churches shunned social influence and rebuilt their infrastructures with little sense that they wished to guide the reconstruction of society.

46. Cf. "Missions in the Lion's Den," *Christian Century,* 18 March 1936, pp. 424-25.

The Christian Century *and American Public Life: The Crucial Years, 1956-1968*

Mark G. Toulouse

One winter day in 1956, Martin E. Marty, still a graduate student at the University of Chicago, received a phone call from Harold E. Fey, newly named editor of *The Christian Century.* Fey, on the recommendation of the dean of the Divinity School, had read some samples of Marty's writing and decided to ask him to join the writing staff of the magazine. Marty accepted the offer with the understanding that he would finish his Ph.D. first and then, afterward, join the magazine part-time as he continued his parish ministry. In a book honoring Marty's achievements, it is no doubt appropriate to give some attention to *The Christian Century,* a journal with which he has been associated for over thirty years.

In November of 1956, as a "fresh-fresh Ph.D. and parish minister," Marty began "moonlighting" at the *Century*'s offices during his "off" times.[1] In the 23 January 1957 issue, his name appeared on *The Christian Century* masthead for the first time. For over three and a half decades, with journalistic wit and wisdom, he has chronicled the developments of American religious life. Several of his many books, particularly his earlier ones, emerged from this part-time journalistic vocation. After many useful years as secondary interpretations of American Protestantism, those books are now being re-read as impor-

1. Martin E. Marty, "How It Looks in the Moonlight," *Christian Century,* 3 November 1976, p. 947. In subsequent references, *Christian Century* will be abbreviated *CC.* Additional reminiscences about Marty's initial association with the *Century* can be found in "M.E.M.O: The Finishing Canter," *CC,* 28 January 1987, p. 95; and "M.E.M.O: 30," *CC,* 12 October 1988, p. 911.

tant primary source materials by historians wanting to address the story of Protestantism since the mid-fifties.[2]

The yellowing pages of *The Christian Century* represent an important resource as well. The journal's editors have consistently confronted the critical issues of American life during the last three to four decades — a time when, as Marty put it in 1961, American Protestantism had to learn to function as a "creative minority" within a new cultural context, that of "realized pluralism."[3] As the mainstream's major representative voice, the *Century* provides the modern historian with an excellent window into the very heart of the Protestant response to its changing modern environment.[4]

Part of the *Century's* self-identity has included its desire to be "an agent, a shaper, an initiator" for the mainstream of American Protestantism.[5] *The Christian Century* belongs to that class of religious journals one might designate as the "nudgers" of Christian leadership toward new understandings and new engagements with both the gospel and its application to society. As 1970 and 1989 surveys of *Century* readers revealed, that task has been aided over the years by the fact that subscribers to the journal generally identify themselves as more liberal than conservative — although the later survey revealed that newer subscribers reflect a general trend in the mainstream toward more moderate views.[6]

2. Examples of secondary sources turned primary sources include *The New Shape of American Religion* (New York: Harper & Brothers, 1958); *Second Chance for American Protestants* (New York: Harper & Row, 1963); and *The Search for a Usable Future* (New York: Harper & Row, 1969).

3. Marty, "Protestantism Enters Third Phase," *CC,* 18 January 1961, pp. 72-75.

4. Marty's defense of the "creative minority's" role reappears in his 1969 book *The Search for a Usable Future,* especially pp. 87-101. There are numerous indications of the *Century's* influence in mainline circles. Undeniably, it is among the most quoted of Christian periodicals. In the 1970s, a survey revealed that it was "the most widely read religious publication" among seminary students (see "Toot!" *CC,* 14 January 1970, p. 37), and year after year it has won "general excellence" awards from the Associated Church Press. Speaking of its earlier years, Donald Meyer pointed to its general representation of liberalism in American Protestantism: "Aside from the liberal seminaries, there was probably no agency more responsible for keeping the passion vital in the ranks of the ministry. Confident that it spoke for liberal Protestantism as a whole, in many ways its strengths were the strengths of the social gospel, its weaknesses the social gospel's weaknesses as well" (*The Protestant Search for Political Realism, 1919-1941,* 2d ed. [Middletown, Ct.: Wesleyan University Press, 1988], p. 54).

5. Marty, "How It Looks in the Moonlight," p. 948.

6. For statistics related to the surveys, see "Profile of You," *CC,* 27 May 1970,

When Marty first assumed his "moonlighting" perch on the fourteenth floor of 407 S. Dearborn Street, he and his colleagues sat prepared to witness and write about the dawning of a new day in American Protestantism. Religious, cultural, and political developments of the late 1950s caused an identity crisis of no small proportions for American Protestants. In the neighborhood of a year on either side of Marty's arrival at the *Century,* a great many symbolic events took place on both the international and domestic scenes, signaling dramatic change for the cultural context of American Protestantism. The mainstream would never be the same again.

Though it might be too early to offer an authoritative periodization of this newly modern mainstream Protestantism as it has stood in its relationship to American public life, perhaps a tentative offering would be helpful in stimulating further and hopefully more productive discussion of the topic. At least three general periods, each with its own particular characteristics, are discernible in the maze of events affecting both Protestants and American culture during these years. Though this essay addresses only the first one in any detail, the other two periods deserve at least a brief definition here.

The first of these three periods covers the years from approximately 1956/1957 to 1965, extending in some ways through 1968, from the end of the so-called cultural revival to the assassinations of Martin Luther King, Jr., and Robert Kennedy, the events signaling that the period had indeed come to an end. Protestantism's growing awareness of pluralism in American life and the associated awareness by the mainstream of its status as a minority group within the population constitute a portion of the identifying characteristics of the first period. The remaining portion of the period's identity was shaped when these twin realizations combined with the effects of external events to demand some kind of response. The mainstream, out of both its anxiety

---

p. 652; and "On Liberals, Moderates and Century Readers," *CC,* 17 January 1990, pp. 35-36. Currently, around 83 percent of *Century* subscribers are ordained, 98 percent are college educated, and 88 percent hold postgraduate degrees. Only 2.4 percent are minorities. Interestingly, the 1989 survey clearly showed that the subscription pool of *Century* readers is moving toward the more moderate end of the ideological spectrum. The subtle shift toward the right holds true generally for mainstream Protestantism as a whole over the last decade. In the *Century*'s case, it also reflects the influence of James M. Wall, the editor since 1972, who has toned down the ideological tenor of the magazine and conscientiously welcomed a much more diverse contributor list to the pages of the journal, including sophisticated and moderately conservative representatives of evangelicalism.

and its modern social piety, chose to place in motion an outward activism that altered its self-understanding and affected its sense of mission from that time forward.

In many ways, this first period was the period of unifying themes and optimism. Marty has described these years as "centripetal" in nature. Beginning with World War II, Americans began to rally together to address world problems. The onset of the Cold War, followed quickly by the American cultural revival of the mid to late fifties, each served in its own way as a catalyst toward achieving unity in the culture. Kennedy's "new frontier" and Johnson's "great society" offered promising domestic visions in the midst of an often anxiety-producing foreign policy. The Peace Corps, the war on poverty, the United Nations, the work of the World Council of Churches and the National Council of Churches, the promising merger of two fairly different congregational traditions in the United Church of Christ, the hopeful goals of the new Consultation on Church Union (COCU), the developments of Vatican II — all these events produced a centripetal force leading many of the more liberal church leaders toward expressing confidence that even so vast and powerful an enemy as segregation could be readily defeated. Even as late as the spring of 1965, the culture witnessed the march on Selma, civil rights legislation, and various other signs of progressive outlooks in bloom.

Then came the summer of 1965. Watts and escalation in Vietnam both appeared near the same time. Black power and the rise of Malcolm X proved to be profoundly disturbing to those who had hoped for easier solutions to racial difficulties. The tremendous diversity of Catholicism began to emerge. New religions, among them the Hare Krishna and the Jesus Cult, appeared. The drug culture surfaced from underground and went public. Beginning after midyear 1965, societal forces, using one of Marty's phrases, took a "centrifugal" turn.[7] The assassinations of Robert Kennedy and Martin Luther King, Jr., added the exclamation point. Protestant leaders turned inward and tribalism began to appear. These events ushered American Protestantism, and American culture in general, into a second period.

The second period overlaps, to some extent, the years of the first period. New beginnings are often rooted in the events that precede their

7. Marty and I discussed these "centripetal" and "centrifugal" forces in a phone conversation 21 August 1991. No doubt they will be major themes in the last two volumes of his projected four-volume analysis of twentieth-century American religion being published by the University of Chicago Press.

period of decisive influence. With due attention to the fluidity necessarily attached to arbitrary periodizations, I would say that the second period runs from 1965/1966 to 1979/1980 — from the appearance of secular theology to the emergence of reborn activists touting a Christian America. This is the period when the issues of public life forced their way *into* the theological and institutional centers of mainstream Protestantism.

Beginning with the "secular city," the mainstream's leaders were forced to deal in rapid succession with the positive implications and negative fallout associated not only with it but also with other particularistic and centrifugal movements, such as black power and theology and feminist interpretations accompanied by important linguistic and sexuality considerations. For this reason, this second period was generally characterized more by inward conflict than outward activism, though most certainly the period had its outward thrusts. The point worth noting, however, is that the inward conflict had its legitimate roots in the outward activism of the first period. It is hard to imagine anything resembling the second period without the formative activity of the first. Of course the period also witnessed a rising, much more sophisticated evangelical voice (*Sojourners* and *The Other Side,* for example) addressing matters in public life.[8]

The genesis and character of the third period are harder to nail down precisely. No doubt this is due to the fact that, as these words are written, the mainstream is probably still within the period's boundaries or, perhaps, just beginning to cross a line of some sort to enter into an as yet largely unassimilated fourth modern period.[9] One thing seems certain: the third period is largely defined by the dissatisfaction some Protestants had with the developments of the first and second periods.

If the second period constitutes the time when blacks, women,

8. The years of these first two periods are treated with considerable insight by Ronald B. Flowers in his *Religion in Strange Times: The 1960s and 1970s* (Macon: Mercer University Press, 1984).

9. Perhaps the work of David Tracy and some others is already moving in the direction of new possibilities for emphasizing both the "public" nature of theology and the practical activity demanded by all theological reflection. See, for example, Tracy's *Plurality and Ambiguity: Hermeneutics, Religion, Hope* (New York: Harper & Row, 1987); see also *Religion and Public Life,* ed. Robin Lovin (New York: Paulist Press, 1989). James Gustafson's two-volume *Ethics from a Theocentric Perspective* (Chicago: University of Chicago Press, 1981-1984) also points in new and exciting directions.

and some evangelicals came of age as particular movements through their self-understanding and their establishment of a power base, the third period is partially characterized by the actions of the "neo's": the redefining turn taken by old-time liberals newly styled as neoconservatives (e.g., Michael Novak and Richard Neuhaus); the significant neoconfessional return to an emphasis on the particularity of Christian tradition (e.g., George Lindbeck and Stanley Hauerwas), some of which has become so absorbed by the question of Christian identity that it has essentially denied a legitimate role for the church in the formation of public life; and the burgeoning political involvement of the neofundamentalists (e.g., Jerry Falwell and Pat Robertson).[10] Catholicism, during these years, gained its own authentic expression in relation to public life: authentically Catholic, authentically Christian, authentically public.[11] The Protestant mainstream has appeared, at least through the beginning of this last period, to become a side stream, no longer representative of the controlling current within American Protestantism as that current flows through public life.

In order to understand more about the nature of the events that started mainstream Protestantism into the new considerations and attitudes about itself and its relationship to culture during the last thirty-plus years, it makes sense to take a look at that first crucial period, 1956-1968. One can argue that those twelve years constitute one of the most important periods in American history for the formation of "modern" mainstream Protestantism. With unrelenting force, external events caused mainstream leaders to recognize and accept their minority status

10. On the neoconservative phenomena, it is instructive to read Richard John Neuhaus's contribution to the *Century*'s 1990 mind-change series, "Religion and Public Life: The Continuing Conversation," *CC,* 11-18 July 1990, pp. 669-73; it is also interesting to read James M. Wall's editorial, written at the beginning of this third period, "Neoconservatives Aim at Liberals," *CC,* 4 November 1981, pp. 1115-16. On neoconfessionals, witness the developments in narrative theology and its accompanying ethics of virtue, as set forth by Stanley Hauerwas, and the developments in the so-called "postliberal" theology of such people as George Lindbeck, as set forth more popularly by William H. Willimon. The crucial text, for the most part, is Lindbeck's *The Nature of Doctrine: Religion and Theology in a Postliberal Age* (Philadelphia: Westminster Press, 1984). Gabriel Fackre sets forth the tantalizing thesis that this neofundamentalism, as it has attempted to deal with what it views as increasing secularity in American public life, is itself best viewed as a secularization of faith. See his *Religious Right and Christian Faith* (Grand Rapids: William B. Eerdmans, 1982).

11. See, for example, the Catholic statement on living in a nuclear age, "The Challenge of Peace: God's Promise and Our Response," *Origins* 13 (May 1983).

in American culture and attempt to find a distinctive way of speaking to an environment they could no longer take for granted.[12]

Outward Activism: *The Christian Century* on Public Life, 1956-1968

The specific nature of events during these years definitely justifies setting them apart from those that follow. In a *Dædalus* article first published in the winter of 1982, Marty suggested that the end of the sixties brought a "generational shift."[13] Whereas the period under consideration exhibited the final effects of rising secularity and decreasing religious emphases (Marty dated the first generation from around the conclusion of World War II through the mid-sixties), the second generation (from the late sixties into the eighties) revealed more the pervasive "diffusion of religion." Interpretations of the "secularity" of culture had to give way to the meaning of a term like *modernity,* for at least the latter still enabled one to talk about the presence of religion. Marty's use of generations is helpful for defining cultural shifts but probably not definitive for understanding the nature of the mainstream's relationship to public life in America. By their very nature, generations last too long to account for the rapid changes in public Protestantism during these years.

A couple of years after Marty's essay appeared, Leonard Sweet also periodized modern Protestantism using the late sixties as a significant "shift" date.[14] Acknowledging Marty's generational paradigm but filling it with his own interpretation, Sweet developed a "two sixties" thesis. He described the character of the first sixties (1960-1967) as "bursting with belief, fresh hope, and high ambition" at the start. Yet, the events of these years, in his view, led to a crisis in authority and identity as liberal Protestants succumbed to a "culturalist Christianity" that finally brought discredit on the church and led to the general confusion, disarray, and demoralization that characterized the second sixties (1967-1971). Sweet

12. These are the defining characteristics of what I refer to as "modern" mainstream Protestantism: the recognition and acceptance by mainstream leaders of their minority status in American culture and their attempt to find a distinctive way of speaking to an environment they could no longer take for granted.

13. Marty, "Religion in America since Mid-Century," *Dædalus* 111 (Winter 1982): 149-63.

14. Sweet, "The 1960s: The Crises of Liberal Christianity and the Public Emergence of Evangelicalism," in *Evangelicalism and Modern America,* ed. George Marsden (Grand Rapids: William B. Eerdmans, 1984), pp. 29-45.

minced no words as he stated plainly and unequivocally that "theological dry rot worked its way through the edifice of old-line religion" during the first sixties. The forces of "relativism" and "pluralism," he wrote, left the liberals unable to speak a meaningful word either to their parishioners or to society at large. Evangelicalism, not without its own problems, emerged to fill the vacuum.

The *Century*'s pages verify the periodization in Marty's "generations" and Sweet's "two sixties," especially in designating the late sixties as a turning point. But why mark the late fifties as constituting another turning point, one that marks the beginning of a period when Protestantism began a new and different phase marked by "outward activism"? Part of the answer is found in the new and exciting leaders who emerged in both religious and political realms, including Martin Luther King, Jr., Pope John XXIII, and John F. Kennedy. Their respective roles symbolically mark the outlines of a new environment. But there is more to it than that. International events shook Protestantism's confidence in American superiority and, consequently, affected its own attachments to the culture.

In February of 1956, Nikita Khrushchev denounced Stalinism for its domestic crimes against the Soviet people and appeared willing to accept different forms of communism within the Soviet republic. The communist world began to take "polycentrism" seriously. Though few nations within the Soviet orbit resisted an ideological affinity, many of them sought some freedom from Moscow's domination. Khrushchev's attitude spawned new resistance movements in Poland and Hungary. Such national resistance to Moscow, however, never fit into Khrushchev's agenda. Soviet force halted both movements, the latter in an especially brutal fashion.

American concern over the willingness of Soviet leadership to brutalize its own people quickly turned into fear that such brutality might soon reach American shores. Late in the summer of 1957, the Soviets fired the first successful intercontinental ballistic missile (ICBM). On October 4, the Russians launched Sputnik, the first artificial satellite. A month later, another Sputnik orbited the globe, this time with a dog aboard. At the time, someone commented that the next one would have cows aboard — "hence, the herd shot 'round the world."[15]

15. Thomas G. Paterson, J. Garry Clifford, and Kenneth J. Hagan relate this anecdote in their *American Foreign Policy: A History,* vol. 2, 2d ed. (Lexington, Mass.: D. C. Heath, 1983), p. 494. More detail on all the foreign policy events of these years may be found on pp. 480-514.

Quips like these offered only a thin veneer covering a deep American anxiety.

In the wake of Hungary and Sputnik, American concern about Soviet power reached an all-time high in 1957. Several other events, however, seemed to weaken the Western moral condemnation of the brutal Soviet military action in Hungary. The nearly simultaneous invasion of Egypt by British, French, and Israeli troops did nothing to increase Western international credibility. Vice President Nixon's stormy "goodwill" visit to Latin American countries in the late spring of 1958 helped to instruct Americans about the strength of nationalist movements in the underdeveloped areas of the world, but Americans had a difficult time grasping the lesson, as events in Southeast Asia soon clearly demonstrated. Secretary of State John Foster Dulles's unwillingness to accept neutrality in the Cold War as anything other than communist sympathizing did not endear the United States to any of the developing nations.

The "Ugly American" image, as depicted in the 1958 novel of that name by William J. Lederer and Eugene Burdick, flourished. Since American Protestantism, particularly through its missions, had strong historic ties to the American image abroad, the movement had to deal with the dissatisfaction engendered by some of these international events.[16] The domestic scene, on the other hand, hardly helped to counteract any of these developments.

The 1950s "revival" of "religion in general" must be viewed as one of the dominating features of the domestic situation in America leading into these years. The number of Americans identifying themselves as church members rose steadily (five percentage points) during the early part of the decade ("the triumphant decade for the definition of church membership as going to church rather than being the church").[17] Congress added the words "under God" to the Pledge of Allegiance. Corporations and civic organizations decided that providing outlets for prayer made good business sense. Church building boomed. Religious book sales soared. Television, the propaganda potential of which people were only beginning to realize, spread religious images far and wide. Billy Graham's urban crusades were packed

16. See William R. Hutchison, *Errand to the World: American Protestant Thought and Foreign Missions* (Chicago: University of Chicago Press, 1987).

17. Leonard I. Sweet, "The Modernization of Protestant Religion in America," in *Altered Landscapes: Christianity in America, 1935-1985,* ed. David W. Lotz (Grand Rapids: William B. Eerdmans, 1989), p. 24.

with people, and he became America's best-known religious figure for the next several decades.

Given his propensity for the ironic, it should surprise nobody that Marty was the first American religious historian who suggested that the 1950s revival, rather than benefiting Protestantism, actually served as the agent to usher in the "post-Protestant" years of American life. The revival displaced more than revived Protestantism. It fostered "an attitude toward religion" that Marty claimed had "become a religion itself." Whereas the "old shape" of American religion had been "basically Protestant," the "new shape" was something else. Protestantism's power "as virtual monopolist in penetrating and molding the religious aspect of national culture" had "disappeared." For the most part, the cultural revival presented a God who was "understandable and manageable, . . . an American jolly good fellow."[18]

In an unsigned editorial at the end of year, Marty hailed 1958 as "the year the revival passed crest."[19] Graham seemed less able to generate massive support from all religious circles after his New York crusade. The gain in church membership fell off drastically compared to the general population growth. The voices of the "cultured despisers" of religion once again rose to rather vital expression. Mainstream Protestantism discovered the true meaning of religious pluralism. Even as early as 1955, Will Herberg pointed out that Catholicism and Judaism had joined the ranks of Protestantism as equal components of America's normative faith expressions.[20] Though Judaism exhibited little cultural power in those days, Catholicism's rise to prominence as a major player in the shaping of culture had a rather disquieting effect on all forms of Protestantism in the 1950s.

Another factor complicating Protestant complacency emerged with tenacious force during these years. Racial relations were ob-

18. Marty, *The New Shape of American Religion,* pp. 27-28, 32. Sidney E. Mead challenges the post-Protestant concept in an essay entitled "The Post-Protestant Concept and America's Two Religions," in his book *The Nation with the Soul of a Church* (New York: Harper & Row, 1975), pp. 11-28. Mead's point is that the "constitutional and legal structure" of the United States has never been Protestant. This is certainly true, but, prior to the 1950s, Protestants took that structure for granted, and most Americans interpreted it in ways fully consistent with Protestant values and beliefs. After the late fifties, such interpretations were challenged. See also chap. 4 of *The New Shape of American Religion* ("America's Real Religion: An Attitude"), pp. 67-89, especially pp. 73-74; see also pp. 37-39.

19. Marty, "The Year the Revival Passed Crest," *CC,* 31 December 1958, pp. 1499-1501.

20. Herberg, *Protestant-Catholic-Jew* (Garden City, N.Y.: Doubleday, 1955).

viously at the breaking point in 1956-1957. The yearlong bus boycott in Montgomery finally concluded with a favorable Supreme Court ruling regarding the desegregation of intrastate busing, but the battle for civil rights was clearly in its initial stages. In 1957, the Eisenhower administration suffered great embarrassment from the fact that the finance minister of the newly independent nation of Ghana was denied service at the Howard Johnson restaurant on Route 40 leading into Washington.[21] During the same year, Eisenhower had to send federal troops into Little Rock to ensure that black children would be admitted to public schools. Protestantism and emerging pluralism both had large stakes in the upcoming national debate concerning race and civil rights.

How did mainstream Protestantism attempt to deal with this new reality? Historically, the nature of Protestantism has exhibited not only a tendency to occupy ground but also an ability to critique those aspects of the culture it views as opposed to the transcendent will of God. These years confronted Christian leaders with the perplexing issues accompanying heightened racial tension and escalated involvement in the war in Southeast Asia. How did the mainstream respond to these issues? Might its response be interpreted as an aspect of the Protestant principle, the principle of prophetic protest in the name of higher authority? Or is Leonard Sweet right in condemning liberalism's response to these issues as evidence of cultural captivity and a lost sense of transcendent reference? The *Century*'s editorials and articles reveal that a simple Yes or No answer to either one of these questions is not really sufficient. Before filling in the lines of these answers, one must first understand the *Century*'s response to the rise of a sometimes hostile religious pluralism.

Living in an Age of "Displacement"

A term used by Marty helps to define the circumstances of the modern mainstream during this first period. In *Second Chance for American Protestants,* he argues that pluralism's "displacement" of Protestantdom as a "ground occupying" entity in America ended the "first chance for evangelical witness" to the culture. With this book, Marty defined the "second chance" as "a change to a different set of ground rules" that took seriously "the erosion and breakdown of one specific Christian

21. A brief account of this incident is given in "Insult in Delaware," *A.M.E. Zion Quarterly Review* 68 (1957): 51.

bond with culture."[22] Marty's naming of the context — the displacement of Protestantdom — stands unrefuted. The issue needing examination is what the mainstream did in response to it. How well did the mainstream respond to its "second chance"?

Like mainstream Protestantism in general, the *Century* did not accept pluralism easily. An editorial in June of 1951 carried the title "Pluralism — National Menace."[23] The author argued that the only "real hope that American society" would remain united rested in "straightforward, uncompromising resistance to any efforts by any group to subvert the traditional American way of life." The *Century,* occasionally speaking in rather conservative tones, feared the loss of Protestant hegemony as much as the next Protestant group.[24] But by 1961, the *Century*'s editors had no trouble affirming the more positive sides of "fully realized pluralism."[25]

Century *Support for Displacement*

Robert Wuthnow recently explained that "the very nature of our thinking and our social behavior takes place in terms of symbolic boundaries." These boundaries enable people to "make sense of [their] worlds" and hence are "fundamental to all of social life."[26] During the late fifties and early sixties, the *Century* staff grew more accepting of the changes in the "symbolic boundaries" of American life necessitated by recognizing the realities of radical pluralism; in fact, its members often endorsed more change than the government wanted.

Editorials opposed the placing of a crèche at Chicago's city hall in 1959. Editors sided with Jewish leaders against the 1961 decision of

22. *Second Chance for American Protestants,* pp. ix, 3, 8. Marty's original title for this book was *The Displaced Christian.* Editors at Harper & Row thought it would help sales to be "upbeat," so they changed the title. In discussing some matters related to this book, Marty, in a letter to me dated 19 June 1991, wrote that he still regretted Harper's insistence concerning this matter. "At any rate," Marty wrote, "I do think that it [the book] foresaw the changes that eight years later Dean Kelley began to chronicle and Roof-McKinney and all the rest did later."

23. "Pluralism — National Menace," *CC,* 13 June 1951, pp. 701-3.

24. For a discussion of the conservative nature of some of the magazine's viewpoints, see Martin E. Marty, "Peace and Pluralism: The *Century* 1946-1952," *CC,* 24 October 1984, pp. 979-83.

25. Marty affirms "fully realized pluralism" in "Protestantism Enters Third Phase," *CC,* 18 January 1961, pp. 72-75.

26. Wuthnow, *The Restructuring of American Religion* (Princeton: Princeton University Press, 1988), p. 10.

the Supreme Court upholding state "blue laws" mandating closing retail stores on Sundays. They argued very early (six years before cases went to court) that the military service academies needed to end the practice of mandatory chapel services. They questioned the legitimacy of congressional chaplains, and, although they supported the need for chaplains to the military, they wondered why the churches could not establish a religious civil service to take the place of military-paid chaplains.[27] The *Century,* with its sarcasm about prayer breakfasts and its unwillingness to publish one of President Johnson's annual "Thanksgiving Proclamations" because editors viewed it as a piece of "militaristic propaganda," demonstrated its rejection of old roles.[28] These Protestants knew they had to speak to the world on new terms. They spoke increasingly from outside locations as minorities rather than from the comfortable and secure confines of the inside elitist circles.

One of the clearest examples of the journal's openness to challenging America's symbolic boundaries is a 1967 editorial, probably written by editor Kyle Haselden, entitled "Who's Desecrating the Flag?" The editorial criticized groups that were pressuring Congress to pass a bill making it a federal offense to desecrate the flag. "The moment we make respect for the flag and love for the country mandatory," wrote the editor, "we make them impossible." Even though the editorial disclaimed any effort to defend flag burning, its author could not resist offering the observation that "an Amos or a Thomas Jefferson or a Tom Paine" might have burned a flag "for cause." The real desecration of the flag, insisted the editor, did not result from its being burned as much as from American toleration of ghettos, the delay of segregation, the disgraceful treatment of American Indians and Hispanic migrant work-

27. "No Creche at City Hall!" *CC,* 23 November 1959, p. 1365. "Blue Laws and the Court," *CC,* 19 July 1961, pp. 867-68. "Service Academies Require Chapel Attendance," *CC,* 4 March 1964, pp. 292-93. See also "Condemn Compulsory Chapel," *CC,* 11 November 1964, p. 1388. For a discussion of the first court case dealing with compulsory chapel attendance, see Dean Kelley, "The Case of the 'Wholly Secular' Chapel," *CC,* 30 September 1970, pp. 1166-69. On congressional chaplains, see "Erastianism on the Potomac," *CC,* 20 April 1966, p. 464; and "Pen-ultimate: Prayerful Sonorities for Senatorial Snorers," *CC,* 16 July 1969, p. 965. On military chaplains, see "Whither the Military Chaplaincy?" *CC,* 19 September 1962, pp. 1119-20. Debates about the chaplaincy continued throughout this whole period and beyond.

28. "Pen-ultimate: The Height of Humility," *CC,* 24 April 1968, p. 571. "Was God Listening When We Gave Thanks?" *CC,* 29 November 1967, p. 1516. The editors also viewed the presidential proclamation as a "chauvinistic justification of U.S. military intervention in southeast Asia."

ers, the "preoccupation of the country with power and pleasure," and, "more than anything else," the Vietnam War.[29]

It is interesting to note that the current *Century* editor, James M. Wall, has on several occasions taken a view of this question directly opposite to that of his predecessor in the editor's chair, defending a constitutional amendment or some other legislative action to protect the flag from flag burners. Is this a retreat from the *Century*'s willingness to defend challenges to the symbolic boundaries of American public life? Probably not. Though the head editor at the *Century* has had considerable influence in setting the journal's tone, at least as it is perceived by the reader, it would be oversimplifying too greatly to claim that staff members, even in the days of unsigned editorials, always agreed with all aspects of the lead editorials. In the days since the Eisenhower era of calm passed into the era of controversial issues, it became even more difficult to reach staff consensus on all the issues. The policy of signing editorials, fostered under Wall's leadership, has allowed for more personal responsibility on difficult questions. Wall's particular stance on the flag, however, no doubt surprised even some of his colleagues.

Wall has placed this conversation in the context of his more general belief that individual rights in our society too often supersede community claims. Wall's statement about the flag is, in some ways, a defense of what he would call "the ability of the community to guide its members away from irresponsibility." Though many liberals would agree that it is important to balance community claims over against individual rights, few would use the prohibition of flag burning to illustrate the principle. In what some have argued is a misuse of Tillich's distinction between signs and symbols, Wall has contended that the flag is a symbol that participates in the reality to which it points to the extent that the flag "is, in its fluttering presence on a flagpole, the nation itself."[30]

29. "Who's Desecrating the Flag?" *CC*, 14 June 1967, pp. 771-72.

30. See Wall, "Individual Rights, Community Claims," *CC*, 2-9 August 1989, pp. 707-8; and Wall, "The Dynamics of Flag-Burning," *CC*, 5-12 July 1989, pp. 643-44; see also Wall, "Protecting Speech, Protecting Symbols," *CC*, 27 June–4 July 1990, pp. 619-20. One critic said of Wall's use of Tillich, "I do not think it is a proper use of the Tillichian metaphor to leap from a symbol's 'participation' in an object to that symbol's *identification* with the object" (John W. Burkhart, "Reader's Response: Faith and Flag-Burning," *CC*, 16-23 August 1989, p. 757). Another critic warned that Wall's use of Tillich's distinction between sign and symbol ignored the equally important Tillichian distinction between symbol and idol (W. Paul Jones, "Reader's Response: Faith and Flag-Burning," *CC*, 16-23 August 1989, p. 758). See also "Readers' Response," *CC*, 16-23 August 1989, pp. 757-58; and "Letters," *CC*, 3 October 1990, pp. 884-85.

For many, the *Century*'s 1967 argument still makes more sense in questioning the wisdom of viewing "this piece of painted cloth" as having "some kind of inherent power to which men should supinely resign themselves or against which they are challenged to rebel."

Further evidence of the *Century*'s acceptance of the new pluralism of 1960s America lies in the editors' unflinching support for the Supreme Court in its gradual codification of Protestant displacement. This process took root, of course, with the Court's decisions related to prayer and Bible reading in the public schools during the 1960s. It is, perhaps, a testimony to the degree of displacement accomplished in public schools prior to 1960 that already in 1957 an article attempted to answer the conservative charge that educators had "taken God out of the classroom."[31]

Compared to neo-evangelical editors at *Christianity Today,* the *Century*'s staff seemed relatively uninterested in seriously advocating the Court's suggestion that the schools should teach objectively *about* religion.[32] Nor did the *Century*'s editors take up the more general question of how human values might be taught in public educational institutions. Since they regarded what passed for religion in the schools to be largely superficial anyway, they did not too much mourn its passing. In Martyesque style, for example, one editorial stated that the decision meant the government "*is* separated from any religious establishment, including establishment of religion-in-general."[33]

The concern about whether religion had a legitimate place in the curriculum of public schools did not surface seriously until a little later when even some liberals began to be concerned about the ethos settling

31. Birgil M. Rogers, "Are the Public Schools 'Godless'?" *CC,* 11 September 1957, pp. 1065-67. *Century* support for the Court can be found in the following: "Religion Cases Appealed to Supreme Court," *CC,* 20 June 1962, p. 767; "Court Bans Bible Reading in Public Schools," *CC,* 21 February 1962, pp. 220-21; "Politics of Prayer Stir the Nation," *CC,* 11 July 1962, p. 882; "Restating the Hard Lesson," *CC,* 18 July 1962, pp. 881-82; "Instructive Coincidence," *CC,* 25 July 1962, pp. 903-4; "Prayers, Bibles, and Schools," *CC,* 24 October 1962, pp. 1279-80; Edward O. Miller, "True Piety and the Regents' Prayer," *CC,* 1 August 1962, pp. 934-36. The *Century* has consistently fought various constitutional amendments designed to circumvent the court rulings on these issues.

32. See, for example, "Is the Supreme Court on Trial?" *Christianity Today,* 1 March 1963, p. 28. Though generally supportive of the decisions, the editors of *Christianity Today* expressed the hope that the school system would find a place for the Bible "as a sourcebook in the academic process" that might be used to inspire "a confidence in transcendent justice and objective morality."

33. "Prayer Still Legal in Public Schools," *CC,* 4 July 1962, pp. 832-33; see also "To Prevent Hysteria," *CC,* 17 April 1963, pp. 485-86.

into the schools.[34] The current editor, James M. Wall, spoke clearly to the issue late in 1990 when he expressed shock at the ethical insensitivity symbolized by the Michael Milken scandal on Wall Street and called for a proper discussion of "values in our public school system — a discussion that acknowledges the importance of our religious history."[35] It took liberals a while to feel their way back to a qualified support for the place of religious and moral values in public school settings. The secularizing tendencies of society helped to open their eyes.

A Slight Dragging of Mainstream Feet

Though the editors at the *Century* were willing, even anxious, to push for change in the symbolic boundaries of public life during these years, there were also certain areas of cultural life they simply took for granted. Affirmation of change in these areas occurred much more gradually. The sexual revolution, for example, greatly troubled the *Century* of the mid-sixties. The new availability of the birth control pill in 1964 caused mainstream writers to reevaluate their traditional arguments against premarital sex and found them learning how to stress the "full context of relationships" instead of the danger of pregnancy. The related arrivals of the "sexplosion" and the pill forced mainstream leadership to seek "a creative and relevant sex ethic."[36] Editors also pointed to a weakening of family life due to sexual freedom and began,

34. See, for example, DeMille L. Wallace, "Religion and the Public Schools," *CC*, 11 May 1966, pp. 612-15; Niels C. Nielsen, "Dialogue with Mrs. O'Hair," *CC*, 11 May 1966, pp. 615-18; Allan M. Parrent, "The Prayer Amendment Revisited," *CC*, 20 October 1971, pp. 1220-21; and Niels C. Nielsen, "Teaching about Religion: A Middle Way for Schools," *CC*, 4-11 January 1984, pp. 17-19.

35. Wall, "Scrambling for a Moral Vocabulary," *CC*, 5 December 1990, pp. 1123-24. For a presentation of the positive experiences of a high school teacher in teaching the Bible as literature, see Rose Sallberg Kam, "The Bible's Place in the Public School," *CC*, 20 November 1974, p. 1093.

36. Concerning the pill, see Peter A. Bertocci, "Extramarital Sex and the Pill," *CC*, 26 February 1964, pp. 267-70. In speaking of the changing sexual mores, *Century* editors and authors stressed the difference between standards of the world and those of the church, mostly without the accompaniment of a legalistic defense of old or rigid understandings of sex. See Robert E. Fitch, "The Sexplosion," *CC*, 29 January 1964, pp. 136-38; "Swedish Bishops Condemn Premarital Intercourse," *CC*, 24 June 1964, p. 821; "The Church and the Sexual Crisis," *CC*, 29 June 1966, pp. 823-24; Gordon Clanton, "Understanding Sex in the Age of the Pill," *CC*, 8 January 1969, pp. 43-47; and Joseph C. Hough, Jr., "Rules and the Ethics of Sex," *CC*, 29 January 1969, pp. 148-51.

for the first time, to deal with homosexuality as an issue. In 1963, the liberal religious view of homosexuality in America stressed its nature as "disease" rather than "sin." After 1967, the *Century* began to address issues related to homosexuality with increasing regularity.[37]

In general, editors opposed print and film censorship on "freedom of expression" grounds but deplored the spreading presence of pornography. But then even the slightest titillation could get their backs up. In 1960, the editors felt Elvis Presley's "revolting exhibitionism" on Ed Sullivan's television show, with his "two wiggles and . . . two songs," revealed clearly both "the depth of decadence" in society and the potential damage the new "media of communication" could wreak on family values.[38] The sixties, though increasingly liberal in social expressions related to sex, were clearly not the liberal decade in these areas for mainstream Protestantism.

Editorial positions on women's issues were few and far between until at least the mid to late sixties. Barely prior to the full blossom of the women's movement in America, Helmut Thielicke's view of the "vocation" of woman "to be lover, companion, and mother" probably

37. Winfred Overholser, "Homosexuality: Sin or Disease?" *CC*, 11 September 1963, pp. 1099-1101. The only previous mention of homosexuality in the *Century* during the modern period came in 1957, when an editorial noted its affirmation of the British government's decision to decriminalize homosexual acts between consenting adults; see "Treading Lightly in a Delicate Subject," *CC*, 18 September 1957, pp. 1092-93. After 1967, the topic was treated more frequently; see, for example, "Equality for Homosexuals?" *CC*, 13 December 1967, pp. 1587-88; "Religious Group Urges Recognition of Homosexuals' Rights," *CC*, 5 June 1968, pp. 744-45. Under Haselden's leadership (1964-1968), the *Century* endorsed equality for homosexuals but remained opposed to viewing homosexuality as a potentially normative condition. Shortly after Alan Geyer (1968-1972) assumed the editorship, the gay liberation movement began in earnest when, in 1969, police stormed a gay bar in New York's Greenwich Village. Within two years after that event, under Geyer's leadership, the *Century* became more open, though not committed, to understanding homosexuality as a state of being rather than as either a sin or a sickness. See "The Limits of Celebration," *CC*, 24 September 1969, p. 1213; "To Accept Homosexuals," *CC*, 3 March 1971, p. 276; and Elliott Wright, "The Church and Gay Liberation," *CC*, 3 March 1971, pp. 281-85. During Geyer's editorial stint, the *Century* published its first article advocating the ordination of homosexuals to ministry. It grew out of the first known ordination of a homosexual by the Golden Gate Association of the United Church of Christ. See W. Evan Golder, "Ordaining a Homosexual Minister," *CC*, 28 June 1972, pp. 713-16. For the most part, however, the 1970s was the decade when mainstream Protestants, in response to the homosexual rights battle in Dade County, grew more accepting of homosexual civil rights while at the same time refusing to accept for ordination those who practiced the life-style.

38. "What a Twisted Scale of Values!" *CC*, 25 May 1960, p. 630.

did not differ too radically from that of most mainstream Protestants in the country.[39] In a recent essay entitled "Women and the Churches," Barbara Brown Zikmund bemoaned the failure of churches, until the 1960s, to understand and help the women who were called out into the workplace during the Second World War.[40] The comparative lack of mention of women in *Century* indexes supports her complaint. When infrequent essays related to women did appear, they were usually written by Margaret Frakes, a member of the staff since 1949 who, as more perceptive readers might have realized, modeled a woman's career in religious journalism.

The *Century,* hardly a trailblazer in the women's movement, did nevertheless hitch up the wagons and follow once the movement started rolling. Even though editors completely overlooked the formation of the National Organization for Women in 1964, they increased their awareness of women's issues after 1963 largely due to the publication of Betty Friedan's *The Feminine Mystique.* Friedan's book exploded the popular myth that women find complete fulfillment as "wife and mother." The first mention of "women in business" is in the 1963 index, which also carries the first mention of "women theologians." This latter article, in direct response to the "feminine mystique" on college campuses, announced that "There *Are* Women Theologians" who might be called upon to counter such attitudes.[41] Outside of occasional and very general support for women in ministry, however, the *Century* did not say much about women's rights issues until 1970, when "women's rights" finally appeared as a separate index entry and the U.S. Senate considered the Equal Rights Amendment for the first time.[42]

Perhaps the most obvious dragging of Protestant feet with regard to acceptance of changing symbolic boundaries is illustrated by that area of the 1950s Protestant social posture known as anti-Catholicism. The *Century*'s position never equaled the more rabid varieties prominent in some conservative circles, and the editors of the journal were certainly more receptive to changes of attitude as time progressed than were most other WASP-oriented types. Nevertheless, a fear of Catholicism verging on anti-Catholicism was evident in the *Century.*

39. Thielicke, "Realization of the Sex Nature," *CC,* 15 January 1964, pp. 73-77.

40. Zikmund, "Women and the Churches," in *Altered Landscapes,* pp. 125-39.

41. "M.E.M.O: There *Are* Women Theologians!" *CC,* 28 August 1963, pp. 1053-54; see also Hannah Bonsey Suthers, "Religion and the Feminine Mystique," *CC,* 21 July 1963, pp. 911-12.

42. "I Didn't Raise My Girl to Be a Soldier: Sense and Nonsense about the ERA," *CC,* 25 October 1972, pp. 1056-58.

Today, it is not easy to remember a time when Catholicism seemed monolithic and rigidly intolerant of other Christian expressions. With some measure of legitimate rationale, pre–Vatican II mainstream Protestantism worried about what a politicized American Catholicism might try to accomplish in the name of the Vatican. Most Protestants feared the possibility of a powerful Roman Catholic politician. As early as 1956, the *Century* expressed concern when it looked as though John F. Kennedy might be chosen as a vice presidential candidate.[43]

Throughout Kennedy's presidential campaign four years later, the *Century* openly questioned Kennedy's fitness for high office based largely on his family's religious background, though it sought to avoid religious bigotry as it did so.[44] Harold Fey, probably a bit more disturbed by the Kennedy candidacy than most of the rest of his staff, was successful enough in avoiding the appearance of such bigotry that at least one reader wrote and accused the journal of being too "nonpartisan" in not pointing out clearly enough the problems a Roman Catholic president would present.[45] For most readers, however, Fey's vast editorial attention to this question must have been clear enough.[46]

In all its editorializing, however, the *Century* never said finally that Kennedy ought not be elected because of his Catholicism. Harold Fey was concerned; that much is clear. He was fearful of bloc voting on the part of Catholics, and seemed to discount the danger that Protestants might do the same.[47] Yet neither he nor any of the *Century* staff

43. "The Candidate's Religion," *CC*, 3 March 1959, pp. 251-53. "Drive on for Catholic Vice President," *CC*, 15 August 1956, p. 941.

44. "Moratorium on Bigotry," *CC*, 27 April 1960, p. 499; and "Religious Debate Must Continue," *CC*, 4 May 1960, p. 533.

45. Richard Yaussy, "A Catholic President?" *CC*, 7 July 1960, p. 829.

46. For examples of numerous editorials dealing with the question of JFK's religion and his candidacy, see "Candidate's Religion Remains a Proper Consideration," *CC*, 27 May 1959, p. 636; "Religion Plays Part in Wisconsin Vote," *CC*, 20 April 1960, p. 460; "Religious Affiliation," *CC*, 17 August 1960, pp. 939-40; "When Is a Catholic President Not Free?" *CC*, 24 August 1960, p. 966.

47. "Will Catholics Give Up Bloc Voting?" *CC*, 25 May 1960, p. 630; and "Religious Affiliation," *CC*, 17 August 1960, pp. 939-40. The *Century* went out of its way to show that Protestants could be more open than Catholics and vote outside of Protestant ranks. See "West Virginia Kills a Myth," *CC*, 25 May 1960, pp. 629-30; and "Democratic Delegates Were Two-Thirds Protestant," *CC*, 10 August 1960, p. 916 — though the author of this latter article admits that some Catholics voted for Stephenson and Johnson. A. Roy Eckardt wrote an article for the *Century* challenging those who refused to allow "that a Catholic may vote for a Catholic simply because he is honestly convinced that his candidate will do the country good" ("When Is Faith Not Faith?" *CC*, 14 September 1960, pp. 1050-52).

supported the statement of the National Conference of Citizens for Religious Freedom, signed by their own founder and longtime former editor C. C. Morrison, which stated that no Catholic should ever be elected president as long as Catholicism remained unchanged. The editorial staff dismissed that idea as "an indefensible thesis."[48] As the campaign wound down to its final days, and after the televised debates, editorials revealed less concern about religion as an issue, especially after Kennedy's famous speech to Houston ministers.[49] In October 1960, Winthrop S. Hudson pointed out what editors at the *Century* probably should have realized sooner when he wrote that "the religious faith" of both candidates had "been shaped more by the contemporary cultural climate than by the church."[50]

Concern about Catholicism's violation of society's symbolic boundaries also found expression in far too many editorials addressing questions of public aid to parochial schools and federal aid to public schools. Much of mainstream Protestantism, including the *Century*, opposed any federal aid for parochial schools. In their attempt to safeguard public funds from any Catholic encroachment, the editors tended to see Catholic conspiracies on these two issues almost everywhere.[51] Editorial preoccupation with these conspiracies led one reader to observe that "hatefulness seldom appears in your pages, but when it does, it is almost sure to be directed against Roman Catholics."[52]

48. "Religious Smoke Screen," *CC*, 21 September 1960, pp. 1075-77.

49. "Kennedy Clarifies Stand to Houston Ministers," *CC*, 28 September 1960, p. 1109. See also "Nixon Wins Round One," *CC*, 12 October 1960, p. 1171, where the editor confesses that he feels better about the "presidential caliber" of both men.

50. Hudson, "The Religious Issue in the Campaign," *CC*, 26 October 1960, pp. 1239-40.

51. See, for example, "No Federal Aid for Parochial Schools," *CC*, 26 October 1960, p. 1236; "Church Flexes Muscles," *CC*, 5 April 1961, p. 411; "Roman Catholic Church Goes for Broke," *CC*, 19 April 1961, pp. 476-77; "Long-Range Catholic Strategy," *CC*, 26 April 1961, p. 613; "Cardinal Spellman Tries Again," *CC*, 17 May 1961, pp. 508-9. When federal aid to public schools ran into difficulties, the Catholics were usually accused of being behind it (see, e.g., "The New Education Bill," *CC*, 8 March 1961, pp. 291-92; "Catholics Block Education Bill," *CC*, 5 July 1961, p. 822; and "Hierarchy Kills School Aid," *CC*, 2 August 1961, p. 924). When federal aid seemed to have a promise of success, it was usually believed to be due to compromise of some type in which Catholics could get something from the package (see "Federal Aid's Scylla and Charybdis," *CC*, 27 January 1965, pp. 99-100; and "H.R. 2362," *CC*, 17 February 1965, pp. 196-97). In 1959, the *Century* even expressed concern about the fact that 2,055 nuns and priests were teaching in public schools ("Not 'Captured' but 'Surrendered,'" *CC*, 15 July 1959, pp. 820-21).

52. Delbert Barley, "Reader's Response: The Beam in the Eye," *CC*, 27 June

Vatican II, the event, made clear what John F. Kennedy's election had suggested: smart gamblers should have hedged all bets when it came to predicting what Catholicism might do. But such sight was hindsight. When the *Century's* editors first received word of the possibility of a major ecumenical council, they viewed the announcement with grave pessimism. The Catholics might put on "an impressive denominational spectacle," but it was doubtful to these editors "that the meeting [would] be ecumenical in the true sense of the term." To contrast, the editors offered their version of a truly "ecumenical council," that of the Third General Assembly of the World Council of Churches scheduled to meet in Ceylon in 1961. The editorial suggested that Christians "need entertain no doubt as to the conclusion history will reach when it compares the two meetings."[53] Can anyone remember the Ceylon meeting?

By January 1963, the editors had come full circle to express their view that "the council may prove to be the most important religious event of our time," a view Marty repeated after it was all over.[54] After the promise of the Council became evident, the *Century's* pages demonstrated that mainstream Protestantism as a whole had broadened and deepened its own notions of ecumenism as a result. At the beginning of 1963, the *Century* dropped the "ungraceful and negative" word *undenominational* as a subtitle and substituted instead the more "graceful and positive" word *ecumenical.* A couple years later, an editorial reflected on that change by commenting that probably the "chief" pressure leading to the broadening of the *Century's* ecumenism in the early 1960s was the "great convocation of bishops, Vatican Council II."[55] Ten issues after Kyle Haselden replaced retiring editor Harold Fey in 1964, and a year before the completion of the Council's activities, the *Century* announced the addition of Michael Novak as its first Roman Catholic editor at large.[56]

Vatican II shattered any notions remaining among Protestants of

---

1962, pp. 814-15. Government's diplomatic ties to the Vatican were also closely watched by the *Century.* Editors spoke of Truman's "surrender to the pope" in 1951 (October 31), and continued the argument through the years.

53. "Catholic World Council Delayed Two Years," *CC,* 18 February 1959, p. 189; and "Pope John XXIII Plans a World Church Council," *CC,* 4 February 1959, p. 124.

54. See "Vatican without Walls," *CC,* 2 January 1963, pp. 3-4; and Marty, "Vatican II Was Just the Beginning," *CC,* 13 April 1966, pp. 455-57, where he states that Vatican II was "the greatest theological event of our times."

55. See "Typographically Your Century," *CC,* 2 January 1963, p. 4; and "Imperious Ecumenism," *CC,* 8 December 1965, pp. 1499-1500.

56. On the appointment of Novak, see "An Announcement," *CC,* 18 November 1964, pp. 1422-23. The journal also announced the addition of David Danzig, a Jew.

the Roman Catholic Church as monolithic. The dissent of the brothers Berrigan to the Vietnam War and the modernizing tendencies of women's religious orders served to clarify what many were beginning to see even before the midpoint of the Council. And yet, although Vatican II changed Protestant and Catholic relations forever, there still arose issues that complicated the relationship between the two Christian communities. The two big ones, especially in light of rising population figures, were birth control and abortion. The 1968 encyclical *Humanae Vitae* not only set the Catholic Church on "a collision course with the modern world" but also set back Protestant-Catholic relations as both groups sought to define their common public life.[57]

On still another "anti" front — anticommunism — the *Century* occasionally supported the status quo in American life. Prior to the Vietnam years, the *Century,* like almost everyone else in America in the midst of an uncertain cold war, tended to link democracy with God and communism with evil. Part of the fabric of public life in America during those years, perhaps the cross-stitch that held the symbolic boundaries in place, was the anticommunism every "American" shared. The editors at the *Century* shared it too.

Perhaps the worst of the journal's anticommunism in this period is displayed in a November 1961 editorial called "Confronting Communism." The author, probably Fey, described communism as a philosophy that must "obliterate religion." "Indeed, communism cannot remain communism and do otherwise." Though the editorial warned readers not to "commit the great blasphemy of confusing democracy with the kingdom of God," its author assumed absolute incompatibility between Christianity and communism. "Christianity and communism," it was argued, "cannot coexist in the same person any more than Christianity can share the same disciple with Buddhism or Islam."[58]

57. See Everett C. Parker, "Catholic Position on Birth Control Hardens," *CC,* 20 January 1965, pp. 71-72; Michael Novak, "The Ecclesiology of Birth Control," 14 April 1965, pp. 454-55; Michael F. Valente, "Contraception: Toward Decision," *CC,* 18 January 1967, pp. 77-79; and "Populorum Progressio," *CC,* 12 April 1967, pp. 460-61. On the abortion issue, see "Abortion Laws Should Be Revised," *CC,* 11 January 1961, p. 37; Lester Knsolving, "What About Therapeutic Abortion?" *CC,* 13 May 1964, pp. 632-35; and, from the Roman Catholic side, Michael Novak, "Abortion Is Not Enough," *CC,* 5 April 1967, pp. 430-31. Abortion became a much more heated issue after 1970. On *Humanae Vitae,* see "Human Life in Our Day," *CC,* 27 November 1968, pp. 1495-96; and James E. Allen, "How Catholics Are Making Up Their Minds on Birth Control," *CC,* 29 July 1970, pp. 915-18.

58. "Confronting Communism," *CC,* 15 November 1961, pp. 1355-56. Anticommunism in general is evident in "What Is behind the War Scare?" and "That

Under Fey's leadership, however, the *Century* also held positions that made it rather unpopular with average anticommunist groups and individuals. The journal strongly sought United Nations recognition of the People's Republic of China.[59] On the issue of space exploration, even given the threat of initial Soviet successes, Fey condemned American efforts as a "fantastic waste" of economic resources.[60] The *Century* welcomed the change in Cuba from Batista, who had been backed by the United States, to Castro, and it characterized the Bay of Pigs invasion as a "debacle."[61] Just after the Cuban missile crisis, editors insisted that Americans look to the "enemy within" for part of the cause of the crisis, especially "the shameful history of [American] exploitation of Cuba."[62] They also argued for de facto recognition of the East German communist regime in the Berlin crisis.[63] Clearly, the *Century's* anticommunism had some sophisticated and reflective edges to it.

By 1968, editorials addressed more frequently the shortcomings of American life. At approximately the time Alan Geyer became the new editor of the *Century,* replacing the ailing Kyle Haselden, the journal printed an editorial entitled "Universal Moral Myopia." The Soviet Union had just invaded Czechoslovakia, but the editor was in no mood to engage in simple anticommunist banter. Instead, he pointed to America's "two evils," racism and Vietnam, and stated that the Russian invasion should not serve as "a scapegoat for our own guilt." Geyer's editorial took seriously the situation in Czechoslovakia, but it compared the invasion to both the American intervention in Vietnam and the U.S.

Unthinkable War Could Break Loose" (*CC,* 30 October 1957, p. 1276); see also Reinhold Niebuhr, "Why Is Barth Silent on Hungary?" *CC,* 23 January 1957, pp. 108-10.

59. "No Change in China Policy," *CC,* 10 July 1957, p. 835.

60. "High Up Is Too Much," *CC,* 24 May 1961, p. 645; "Shall We Escape to the Moon?" *CC,* 14 June 1961, p. 732; "Claiming the Moon," *CC,* 19 August 1964, p. 1028.

61. "Defeat or Debacle?" *CC,* 3 May 1961, p. 547. The *Century* believed that the government should have been more accepting of Castro's victory over Batista in early 1959. Shortly after Castro took power, they published articles detailing the atrocities of the Batista regime. Though they were not Castro supporters, and became increasingly dismayed over his growing alignment with Moscow, they felt the United States had made several serious mistakes in its Cuban policy. See "Cuba Should Learn From Puerto Rico," *CC,* 14 January 1950, pp. 36-37; Carleton Beals, "Cuba in Revolution," *CC,* 4 February 1959, pp. 130-32; Beals, "Cost of Dictatorship in Cuba," *CC,* 11 February 1959, pp. 165-67; and "What Is Happening in Cuba?" *CC,* 7 March 1962, p. 286.

62. "The Enemy Within," *CC,* 7 November 1962, pp. 1343-44.

63. "Time to Turn," *CC,* 30 August 1961, pp. 1019-20.

invasion of the Dominican Republic. Communism, in other words, had no monopoly on immorality. Though Geyer was the least likely of all *Century* editors to utilize theological rationale (he was more given to critical discussions of foreign policy like those one might find in *The Nation* or *The New Republic*), in this particular editorial he pointed out that Americans "live as if the meaning of our lives was ours alone to create."[64] Other *Century* editors utilized a theological approach to the culture more regularly, one that often enabled the journal to assume a prophetic posture toward American society as a whole.

The Prophetic Principle at Work

Harold Fey and his staff believed the process of displacement afforded many new opportunities for the mainstream. Marty wrote a few books to detail his conviction that the new environment could enable Protestantism to recapture the prophetic voice so characteristic of early Christianity.[65] The prophetic voice had not been entirely absent in years prior to these, but, as John C. Bennett wrote in 1954, it had been largely "neglected" by the church in favor of the "healing ministry of the church."[66] The 1950s were the "peace of mind" decade, with an emphasis on "positive thinking." The prophetic voice did re-emerge during the later fifties and early sixties, particularly with regard to the two major social issues of the decade: race relations and the Vietnam War.

Race Relations

Fey wrote rather forcefully about minority issues for the *Century* in the years just before he became editor. Largely due to his influence in *Century* offices, the journal became a vocal advocate for Native American rights before many liberals had even begun to address the issue. His work in this area helped to halt the trend toward governmental termination of all contractual responsibilities regarding Indian welfare. Advocacy for Indian rights remained a strong feature of *Century* coverage throughout the years. In 1971, for example, an editorial called for

64. "Universal Moral Myopia," *CC*, 4 September 1968, pp. 1095-96.

65. In different ways, this topic is the dominant theme of three of Marty's early books: *The New Shape of American Religion, Second Chance for American Protestants,* and *The Search for a Usable Future.*

66. Bennett, "The Church as Prophetic Critic," *CC*, 6 January 1954, pp. 9-11.

protection of Indian bones and graves and respect for Indian rights over against archaeological intrusion, something Congress finally accomplished in 1990 with the passage of the Native American Grave Protection and Repatriation Act.[67]

The *Century's* editors during the early 1950s could hardly be classified as strategists in the war for civil rights, but they did try their hand at analysis and expressed sympathetic support for both the commanders and the ground troops. As Supreme Court decisions moved toward desegregation, editors wrote enthusiastic words and urged "Christian forces" to assume their responsibility to encourage a peaceful compliance. True to their liberal outlook, the editors were optimistic that Southern leaders would ensure a calm reception of the 1954 desegregation order.[68] Before long, they realized just how naive they were.

If there is a single turning point in the *Century* editors' posture regarding civil rights, it would have to be the period of nonviolent resistance in Montgomery during most of 1956. An editorial in January 1957 hypothesized that the Christian influence in the demonstrations involved in this action "may in the long run be seen to constitute the most important Christian achievement of 1956 in this country."[69] The next week, the editors issued a call to church leaders to become active in supporting the court's decisions.[70]

With the Montgomery bus boycott of 1956 occurring just as he stepped into the editor's chair, Fey began a much more intensive focus on black civil rights. Martin Luther King's contributions to the journal began in February 1957 and appeared regularly thereafter.[71] Fey proudly

67. During 1955, Fey began a series of articles about Native American for the *Century.* Later the series was published in a book entitled *Indian Rights and American Justice.* See also Fey, "America's Most Oppressed Minority," *CC,* 20 January 1971, pp. 65-68. On Indian gravesites, see "Let Sleeping Bones Lie," *CC,* 6 October 1971, p. 1157; and Dean Peerman, "Bare-Bones Imbroglio: Repatriating Indian Remains and Sacred Artifacts," *CC,* 6 October 1971, pp. 935-37. Fey also demonstrated his strong support for minorities through his consistent advocacy of more lenient immigration laws. See, for example, "Fling Wide the Gates," *CC,* 4 September 1957, p. 1028.

68. See, for example "No School Segregation, Says Supreme Court," *CC,* 26 May 1954, p. 627; and "The School Decision," *CC,* 2 June 1954, pp. 662-63.

69. "New Challenges Filed in Bus Segregation," *CC,* 9 January 1957, pp. 36-37.

70. "Battle Widens between Courts and Racists," *CC,* 16 January 1957, pp. 67-68.

71. King's contributions included the following: "Nonviolence and Racial Justice," *CC,* 6 February 1957, pp. 165-67; "The Most Durable Peace," *CC,* 5 June 1957, pp. 708-9; "The Church and the Race Crisis," *CC,* 8 October 1958, pp. 1140-41; "Pilgrimage to Nonviolence," *CC,* 13 April 1960, pp. 439-41.

announced King's appointment as an editor-at-large for the journal 8 October 1958.[72] Later, the *Century* had the distinction of offering the first national publication of King's "Letter from Birmingham Jail."[73] Mainstream Protestantism came to depend on the *Century* to report on and comment about every development in the area of civil rights. "Race Relations" as a category in the biannual indexes grew larger and larger. From 1963 to 1965, it contained more entries than any other subject, rivaled only in 1965 by "Catholicism," a close second.[74] Compare this coverage with that of the neo-evangelical journal *Christianity Today,* which did not even mention King by name until 17 January 1964, when he received two sentences noting the fact that he had been chosen *Time*'s "Man of the Year."[75] In 1966, the editors of *Christianity Today* were still using King to illustrate "lawlessness as a sign of our times."[76]

Early on, the *Century's* editors had sounded like the "white liberals" King's 1963 Birmingham letter criticized. For example, they asked for patience to enable time for education of whites before the government passed legislation granting greater enforcement in the Southern states. But by the early sixties such calls for patience had disappeared. March 1963 found them asking "How long, O Lord, how long?" Some of their increasing impatience obviously grew from fears that the Black Muslim extremists and other blacks who felt differently than King might gain the upper hand if solutions to the crisis were not forthcoming.[77] No matter whether the issue was civil rights, Vietnam, or urban renewal, the *Century* feared the activities of the radical element, and abhorred the use of violence to gain power in public life.[78] After the

72. Fey, "An Announcement," *CC,* 8 October 1958, p. 1135.

73. King, "Letter From Birmingham Jail," *CC,* 12 June 1963, pp. 767-73.

74. There were 129 entries in 1963, 155 in 1964, and 124 in 1965. "Race Relations" had 129 entries in 1966, but was surpassed by "Catholicism," with 178 entries. "Vietnam" surpassed both "Race Relations" and "Catholicism" in the number of entries in 1967.

75. "Personalia," *Christianity Today,* 17 January 1964, p. 46.

76. "Lawlessness: A Bad Sign," *Christianity Today,* 29 April 1966, pp. 29-30.

77. See "A Stitch in Time," *CC,* 26 February 1958, pp. 245-47; "Tokenism Frustrates Negro Hopes," *CC,* 20 March 1963, p. 357; "Violence Obscures Issue in Birmingham," *CC,* 15 April 1963, p. 636; "Racial Crisis Moves toward Showdown," *CC,* 22 May 1963, p. 667; "Can Negro Leaders Hold the Line?" *CC,* 3 July 1963, pp. 853-54; and "Demonstrations or Threats?" *CC,* 10 July 1963, pp. 877-88.

78. On Vietnam, for example, see "Rebels, Amnesty and Property," *CC,* 5 March 1969, p. 307; on urban renewal, see "Justice and Beyond Justice," *CC,* 24 February 1965, pp. 227-28; on civil rights, see "Racial Extremists Fill Vacuum" (in which Malcolm X is characterized as "deranged"), *CC,* 29 April 1963, pp. 539-40; and "The Pied Piper of Harlem," *CC,* 1 April 1964, pp. 422-23.

riots in Watts, they examined the root causes of violence and expressed the unsupported and characteristically liberal belief that proper legislation probably could have prevented it.[79] Such liberal sentiments were harder to justify after the summer of 1965.

By 1966, the editors were making distinctions between good black organizations and bad black organizations. Mainstream Protestants tended to meet the emerging diversity within black life on the basis of what they believed each group had to offer that was compatible with American life as they (mainstream Protestants) hoped it would be. In this way, at least, liberals were not much more understanding of the meaning of the black struggle than were conservatives. The editors of the *Century* supported the Southern Christian Leadership Conference, the NAACP, and the Urban League but warned against the "personal empire-building" of the Congress of Racial Equality (CORE), the Student Nonviolent Coordinating Committee (SNCC), and the National Committee of Negro Churchmen.[80] *Century* editorials never revealed any appreciation or understanding of the contribution of the black power movement to the ultimate success of the civil rights movement. It took outside authors to note that articulate "Negroes" such as James Baldwin, Dick Gregory, and James Foreman "do not share every value of white bourgeois culture" and that black power must be seen as "a reaction to inaction" rather than "reverse racism or some ugly form of nationalism."[81]

With perhaps too much "liberal" confidence in nonviolence, education, legislation, and litigation as the sole means to eliminate ongoing cultural conflict, these liberal editors never wavered in their support for civil rights in general. They spoke frankly on the issue and usually girded their comments with both theological concern and some measure of action. Harold Fey joined the march on Washington in 1963; Marty and Dean Peerman attempted to march from Selma to Montgomery in March 1965 when the whole marching group was turned back by state troopers and the sheriff's posse shortly after crossing the bridge over the Alabama River.[82]

79. "Does Anyone Really Care?" *CC*, 22 September 1965, pp. 1148-49.

80. "Black Power for Whom?" *CC*, 20 July 1966, pp. 903-4.

81. C. Lawson Crowe, "Rights and Differences: Some Notes for Liberals," *CC*, 4 November 1964, pp. 1359-60; Margaret Halsey, "Integration Has Failed," *CC*, 28 December 1966, pp. 1596-98.

82. See "Integrate the Integration March!" *CC*, 7 August 1963, p. 973; Fey, "Revolution without Hatred," *CC*, 11 September 1963, pp. 1094-95; and Peerman and Marty, "Selma: Sustaining the Momentum," *CC*, 24 March 1965, pp. 358-60.

The end of this period, however, found these mainstream leaders confused. "Negro" no longer served as an appropriate name for the African Americans. The name "black" became, as a *Century* editorial phrased it at the time, "a symbol of their new deepening negritude."[83] The editors were not quite sure what to do with that development. In 1968 both Martin Luther King, Jr., and Robert Kennedy were assassinated, and the movement's national cohesiveness died with King.[84] Demonstration tactics no longer seemed to work. The word *charisma*, so rightfully used to describe King, now "applied to men who exercise theirs negatively, and call for destruction and revenge." The editors recognized that new tactics were needed, but they had no idea what would serve the need. About all they could do was reach into their hearts and acknowledge the whole people's need for repentance, "even though only symbolic persons enact their crimes."[85]

Editorials anguished over Protestantism's defection from the cities and deplored the expansion of "racial ghettos." They urged Protestantism to develop "an inner city program consistent with its gospel."[86] The pro and con arguments related to urban renewal found regular expression in *Century* pages during these years, demonstrating that the mainstream had some difficulty determining what to think about these government-funded programs.[87] Editors at the *Century* supported urban renewal but lamented the presence of governmental "red tape" and criticized those who saw a way to make a quick dollar at the expense of the poor. Usually sounding paternalistic, even self-righteous, when arguing against other views, well-meaning liberals like Fey felt urban renewal represented the best hope for the "frightened, disadvantaged people" in the cities. They depicted such leaders as Saul Alinsky, whose Industrial Areas Foundation organized urban dwellers in order to give them a voice in their own affairs, as the enemy. Fey and others reasoned that uneducated urban people who were thus organized to

83. "A Fresh Look at Black America," *CC*, 25 October 1967, pp. 1340-41.

84. See Albert J. Raboteau, "The Black Church: Continuity within Change," in *Altered Landscapes*, pp. 77-91.

85. "Martyrdom Comes to America's Moral Leader," *CC*, 17 April 1968, pp. 475-76.

86. "How Do Churches Get Involved?" *CC*, 3 April 1963, pp. 420-21; "Are We Building New Ruins?" *CC*, 12 June 1957, p. 725; "The Rise of Suburban Power," *CC*, 11 October 1967, pp. 1275-76.

87. See "Open or Closed Cities?" *CC*, 10 May 1961, pp. 579-80; "Woodlawn — Open or Closed?" *CC*, 31 May 1961, pp. 685-88; and Fey, "Open or Closed Cities — A Reply to Replies," *CC*, 7 June 1961, p. 711.

seek power for themselves, most often through questionable means, were simply unable to see what was truly good for them.[88]

By 1968, *Century* editors represented a mainstream Protestantism attempting to ward off despair in any way it could.[89] In some ways these Protestants were harder on themselves than they had to be. Though the liberal program had not resolved the racial crisis, objective observers must surely admit that much had been accomplished since the late fifties. Major civil rights legislation had been passed and, to some degree at least, implemented. The failure of legislation to do the job entirely, from the perspective of many decades later, should not surprise anyone, especially those who recognize the sinfulness of human nature.

The earlier optimism among liberals gave way to a deeper appreciation of the depth of the sin, and of their own involvement in it. This realization helped them to focus attention on problems closer to home. Millions of blacks had moved into the cities, where Catholics met their needs better than Protestants, who had spent the latter portion of the decade leaving the cities for the suburbs. Black power soon turned into black theology and confronted Protestants with new challenges needing a response. Protestant energy over the next ten years had to be spent attempting to deal with problems related to racism in church life; mainstream white leaders, at least, seemed to consider that problem more immediately approachable than the problem of racism in society as a whole. The next decade witnessed the arrival of black Protestantism as a force within the mainstream complete with a distinctive and mature voice all its own.

Vietnam

Events in Vietnam occasioned the other major issue of the 1960s. The *Century* heralded the birth of the Republic of South Vietnam in November 1955 and said not another meaningful word about it until April 1962, when an editorial demanded that President Kennedy tell the truth about why "American soldiers [were] dying almost every day in South Vietnam."[90] The event that woke the *Century* from its slumber was the crash in the Pacific of a plane carrying ninety-three American soldiers

88. See "Exploiting Urban Decay," *CC,* 12 February 1964, pp. 195-96. For another view of Alinsky, see Sanford D. Horwitt, *Let Them Call Me Rebel: Saul Alinsky, His Life and Legacy* (New York: Knopf, 1989).

89. "The Incredibility of Integration," *CC,* 6 November 1968, pp. 1391-92.

90. "Give Us the Truth, Mr. President!" *CC,* 25 April 1962, p. 514.

to Vietnam. Why were there nearly five thousand American troops, accompanied by ships and planes, in a country over ten thousand miles away? If a communist takeover seemed imminent, why did the president not inform Congress to let it act accordingly in a proper debate concerning a declaration of war?

In 1962, these mainstream liberals feared the implications of a communist takeover in Southeast Asia as much as anyone else did. They did not question the fact that South Vietnam needed help. The domino theory made limited sense to them at the time. The editors objected primarily because Kennedy had acted alone when the United Nations should have been contacted to deal with the situation. While recognizing the legitimacy of the cause against communism throughout 1963 and 1964, editorials argued against expansion of the war and called for a peaceful, negotiated withdrawal.[91]

The prospect of a national presidential election at such a crucial time also frightened these editors. Just before the Republican National Convention in 1964, Harold Fey wrote an editorial entitled "Goldwater? No!" He feared that Goldwater might become the presidential nominee for the Republican party and that this candidate's ideological bent "would inflame the cold war" and probably escalate the war in Vietnam.[92] Just after Fey retired in September, Kyle Haselden, in one of his first tasks as editor, endorsed President Johnson for re-election ("Johnson? Yes!"). He was confident that a Johnson-Humphrey team would handle Vietnam with wisdom and could be trusted to avoid the "hair-trigger action" of a Goldwater. Johnson, he wrote, would work toward peace and prevent any move toward all-out nuclear confrontation.[93] Johnson's better history on civil rights also mattered to Haselden.

The *Century* endorsement not only cost the journal its tax-deductible status for a year but also led to an editorial shift toward a more realistic understanding of politics, including less willingness to wed Christian goals to the election of particular leaders. Johnson's policies

91. See the following editorials: "Vietnam Regime Ends in Blood," *CC*, 13 November 1963, p. 1392; "Southeast Asia Next," *CC*, 27 June 1963, pp. 799-800; "More War or Less in Vietnam?" *CC*, 11 March 1964, p. 326; "Getting out of Vietnam," *CC*, 23 December 1964, pp. 1582-83; "Urge Cease-Fire in South Vietnam," *CC*, 13 January 1965, p. 37.

92. Fey, "Goldwater? No!" *CC*, 1 July 1964, p. 851.

93. Haselden, "Johnson? Yes!" *CC*, 9 September 1964, pp. 1099-1100; see also "A Time for Cool Heads and Steady Hands," *CC*, 28 October 1964, pp. 1323-24. Self-righteousness about the necessity of support for Johnson over Goldwater is also evident in "The Churches' Mandate," *CC*, 18 November 1964, pp. 1419-20.

forced Haselden to eat his words, something few editors ever enjoy doing. Haselden's profound disappointment found expression as early as May 1965.[94] Later, *Century* editors Alan Geyer and James M. Wall, both prone toward Niebuhrian realism in general, pointed out the mistaken assumptions evident in the journal's endorsement of Johnson.[95]

The Pentagon papers revealed that Johnson, prior to the election, had already taken steps to escalate the war. By the end of 1965, troops in Vietnam numbered over 185,000; one year later they numbered 385,000, building eventually to over 540,000 troops. That these developments jarred the *Century* is clearly evident in its stronger opposition to the war after 1965. The 1964 Tonkin Gulf Resolution authorizing presidential authority to send American troops to Vietnam had originally brought barely a whimper.[96] By early 1966, editors had decided the resolution had blown "a hole in the Constitution of the United States big enough to drive an undeclared war through."[97]

In the interim, the editors became more openly critical of the domino theory and began to speak of the war as a "civil conflict" in which the aspirations of a proud Vietnamese people to conduct their own affairs were at work. They tired of cover-up words such as *democracy* and *freedom* and began arguing that the war's only purpose was the containment of the Chinese. They attacked the American use of "nonfatal" gas as a weapon, fearing an introduction of chemical warfare (a fear later realized). By 1965, Americans felt the domestic costs of the war more intensely, and editors took note of the war's effect on the "great society." They urged the involvement of the United Nations to work out a negotiated peace.[98]

By the end of 1965, editorials more frequently defended dissent. Stepped-up and indiscriminate bombing had its effect. The members of the staff became more active in expressing their own dissent.[99] Hasel-

94. Haselden, "Nothing Personal, Mr. President," *CC*, 26 May 1965, pp. 667-68.

95. Geyer, "Of Betrayal and Loyalty," *CC*, 30 June 1971, pp. 792-93. Writing in the context of the new religious right's involvement in the 1980 presidential election, Wall used the example of the 1964 election to point out that religious groups should refrain from the endorsement of particular candidates and, instead, trust the political process to work ("Don't Say 'Nuts' to the IRS," *CC*, 16-23 July 1980, pp. 723-24).

96. "An Echo, Not a Choice," *CC*, 19 August 1964, pp. 1028-29.

97. "Congress and the Undeclared War," *CC*, 16 February 1966, pp. 195-96.

98. See "Alternatives in Vietnam," *CC*, 10 March 1965, pp. 291-92; "The Issue Is China," *CC*, 23 March 1966, pp. 355-56; "Bad News from Vietnam," *CC*, 7 April 1965, pp. 419-20; "Paradise Deferred," *CC*, 28 July 1965, pp. 931-32; and "Christian Consensus on Vietnam," *CC*, 8 September 1965, pp. 1083-84.

99. See "Students' 'Sturm und Drang,'" *CC*, 3 November 1965, pp. 1339-40;

den and Marty were both members of the National Emergency Committee of Clergy Concerned about Vietnam, a group of religious leaders pressing the president to work toward negotiation and de-escalation.[100] Haselden joined the march on Washington in early 1967.[101] Alan Geyer wrote a defense of selective conscientious objection in early 1966, two years before he became editor of the *Century*.[102] Marty joined seventeen other religious leaders in signing a statement pledging "to risk fine or imprisonment to assist young men who resist the draft on grounds of conscience."[103]

Century opposition to the draft was clear throughout this period, well before Vietnam itself became an issue. At the pinnacle of the Vietnam War, editors argued that if America had to have a draft, it should be as equitable as possible. They were especially concerned about its tendency to include more blacks than whites, more poor than rich, more illiterate than educated.[104] Interestingly enough, in the late sixties, editors became rather vocal about the need to do away with the ministerial and seminary exemptions from the draft. These positions were consistent with support for conscientious objector status, it was argued, because removing the clergy exemption would force ministers to clearer expression of their convictions on the issue. They also felt it would free seminaries from the responsibility of "becoming hospices for disguised draft dodgers and cowards."[105] Strong editorial resistance to the war effort continued right down to the implementation of Nixon's "peace with honor," which the *Century*, under new editor James M. Wall, damned as the "final self-deception."[106]

The *Century*, throughout the conflict, attempted to speak in

---

"Defend Right of Dissent," *CC*, 10 November 1965, pp. 1372-73; "On the Antiwar Front," *CC*, 2 February 1966, pp. 132-33; "Is Dissent Traitorous?" *CC*, 1 June 1966, pp. 703-4; "The Foot in Mouth Syndrome," *CC*, 19 October 1966, pp. 1263-64; and "Dissenters Must Dissent," *CC*, 1 November 1967, pp. 1389-90.

100. See "Clergy Concerned about Vietnam," *CC*, 26 January 1966, pp. 99-100. This appears in a special issue of the journal dedicated to the Vietnam conflict.

101. See "Concerned and Committed," *CC*, 15 February 1967, p. 197.

102. See "Churches Default COs," *CC*, 30 March 1966, p. 389; and "In Good Conscience," *CC*, 22 June 1966, pp. 791-92.

103. See "Sidelights on the War," *CC*, 13 December 1967, p. 1589.

104. "Military Draft Is an Anachronism," *CC*, 11 December 1957, p. 1468; "The Draft Should End in June," *CC*, 16 January 1963, p. 71; "Time to Abolish the Draft," *CC*, 25 March 1964, p. 391; "What Kind of Draft?" *CC*, 15 March 1967, p. 333.

105. "Seminarians and the Draft," *CC*, 13 March 1968, pp. 316-17; "Draft the Clergy Too," *CC*, 1 February 1967, pp. 133-34.

106. "Honorable Peace: Final Self-Deception," *CC*, 7 February 1973, p. 139.

Christian terms about the war.[107] But editors did so piecemeal, here and there in editorials, without ever offering their own article-length theological arguments against the war. At several points they chastised the church for its silence and urged it to formulate a "Christian consensus" in order to address the issues involved. They wondered aloud if Christians were so "thoroughly dispersed in and absorbed by the general fabric of society" that any truly Christian opinion was impossible.[108] Though they were confident that their own understanding of the issues grew out of Christian commitments, they were never too deliberate in stating specific theological rationales.

Yet after rereading their editorials and weighing the evidence of what they chose to publish, including many articles utilizing theological and moral categories to analyze American involvement in Vietnam,[109] one cannot help but come away with the distinct impression that the editors' Christian faith served them well during these years. Though they failed to use sophisticated theological arguments to defend their positions, it is nonetheless clear that they spoke from faith in a transcendent God who meted out justice and cared deeply for the poor and outcast, whether in Vietnam or in America.

Conclusion

On Christmas Day 1968, the *Century* announced it was time for "reconstruction after renewal." The end of an era had come. "Humpty Dumpty [had] tumbled from the wall." With Pope John XXIII gone from the scene and no new or exciting Catholic leaders on the horizon, Catholicism faced what seemed to be "retrogression" as Pope Paul VI published his *Humanae Vitae.* The Protestant Consultation on Church

107. Two entire January issues of the *Century,* one in 1966 and the other in 1968, were devoted to exploring the Christian and moral dimensions of the war.

108. See, for example, "Christian Consensus on Vietnam," *CC,* 8 September 1965, pp. 1083-84; "Mindless and Mute," *CC,* 10 November 1965, pp. 1371-72; and "King Speaks for Peace," *CC,* 19 April 1967, pp. 492-93.

109. I would cite the following as examples: Alan Walker, "An Australian Looks at Vietnam," *CC,* 4 August 1969, pp. 958-62; William Henry Harris, "Morality, Moralism and Vietnam," *CC,* 22 September 1965, pp. 1155-57; Georgia Harkness, "The Churches and Vietnam," *CC,* 26 January 1966, pp. 111-13; Philip Wogaman, "A Moral Reassessment of Our War in Vietnam," *CC,* 4 January 1967, pp. 7-9; and Haig A. Bosmajian, "The 'Nonmorality' of Cruelty and Killing," *CC,* 23 August 1967, pp. 1065-67. Paul Ramsey used just-war categories for the other side in "Vietnam: Dissent from Dissent," *CC,* 20 July 1966, pp. 909-11.

Union faced tough days. Various radical theologies had come and gone. The editors lamented the current "theological adaptationism put on by cowed and fearful whitey theologians who bring no kind of judgment to the black religious and social movements" and announced, in Tillichian phraseology, that they were looking for "radicality that will call *all* human structures, establishments, patterns — including those of 'our side' — into question and put them under judgment." Finally, in view of both "Catholic disintegration and Protestant stasis," the editors said it was "time to start something."[110]

In the first issue of 1969, to underscore their point, the editors announced a change in the design of the title of their journal. The elaborate Gothic letters spelling out the words "**Christian**" and "**Century**" in equal type sizes gave way to a bold rendering of the word "**CENTURY**" in all caps, with the words "the christian," in plain and lower case type, resting above it. The accompanying editorial explained that the change recognized "the transition from a triumphalist model of Christendom to the witness of a servant church, given to serving humanity in its time. It is not really to haul down the flags; it is to raise up the possibilities of new Christian signs and signals."[111] But Protestantism seemed ill-prepared for the task.

In his introduction to American religion, Winthrop S. Hudson points to the "Protestant disarray" near the end of the sixties.[112] The fact that Protestants were in disarray can hardly be denied. Though astronauts walked on the moon in 1969, the superior technological and scientific developments of the age seemed impotent in the face of continued racism and prolonged war. Liberal hopes had clearly failed. Leonard Sweet has argued in a couple of locations that the events of this particular decade and the Protestant response to them caused a loss of transcendent vision and trapped the mainstream in a trendy embrace of cultural authorities.[113] This essay demonstrates that Sweet's generalization is a bit too sweeping.

By sometime around the middle of the decade, the outward conflict with public life had caused some mainstream Protestants to

110. "Reconstruction after Renewal," *CC,* 25 December 1968, pp. 1615-17. See Paul Tillich, *The Protestant Era,* abridged ed. (Chicago: University of Chicago Press, 1957), pp. 163, 230.

111. "Good-by to Gothic," *CC,* 1 January 1969, p. 4.

112. Hudson, *Religion in America,* 4th ed. (New York: Macmillan, 1987), p. 377.

113. See Sweet, "The 1960s," pp. 29-45; and "The Modernization of Protestant Religion in America," pp. 19-41.

look toward new forms of theological expression. The theology of hope found expression in America from the early sixties through the work of King. Shortly thereafter, hope led to the more activist theologies of Gibson Winter and Harvey Cox, whose desire it was to celebrate the God at work outside of the church.[114] As Cox put it in 1966, " 'following Jesus' will inevitably make us participants and not just onlookers in today's social revolution."[115] During the sixties, Cox and most mainstream Protestants became more aware of the "historically conditioned character" of the Christian faith. In response to the resulting crisis of faith, Cox first abandoned the religious symbols for the "secular city" and then, within a few years, returned to retrieve them in a more self-critical way, but always in a way that addressed the needs of the world.[116]

Other theologians dealt with the crisis of faith by embracing secularity to the point of proclaiming the "death of God."[117] This secular theology became the symbol for all the other developments that caused Leonard Sweet some twenty years later to condemn the late sixties mainstream as "a dispirited and ailing conventional Protestantism that had little to declare theologically and was seldom able to answer even the simplest questions about the faith, to say nothing of answering them with a distinctive or a strong voice."[118] Was this indeed the case? Or was Protestantism merely gearing up for an internal struggle that would force theologians and church leaders within it to take issues of race, sex, and class seriously? Perhaps it was only natural that the outward activism of the past decade would lead to the profound inward struggles of the next one.

Whether one speaks of Cox's "secular city" or the "death of God" theologians, the truth is that mainstream Protestantism did not spend much time endorsing these attempts to speak for a secularity charac-

114. See Winter, *The Suburban Captivity of the Churches* (Garden City, N.Y.: Doubleday, 1961); and *The New Creation as Metropolis* (New York: Macmillan, 1963). See Cox, *The Secular City: A Celebration of Its Liberties and an Invitation to Its Disciplines* (New York: Macmillan, 1965).

115. Cox, "The Place and Purpose of Theology: How I Am Making Up My Mind," *CC*, 5 January 1966, pp. 7-9.

116. Cox, "Tired Images Transcended: How My Mind Has Changed," *CC*, 1 April 1970, pp. 384-86.

117. Thomas J. Altizer and William Hamilton, *Radical Theology and the Death of God* (Indianapolis: Bobbs-Merrill, 1966); Paul van Buren, *The Secular Meaning of the Gospel* (New York: Macmillan, 1963).

118. Sweet, "The 1960s," p. 32.

terized by technology and optimistic industrial development. Most mainstream leaders of the next decade appropriated the criticism such theologies offered of a church too separate from the world's needs and too wrapped up in its parochial concerns to make a difference in the world but refused to endorse the more general and "secular" tendency to write the church or God off as inherently irrelevant in the modern world. As early as July 1966, for example, the Pen-ultimate column in the *Century,* spoofing religious bumper stickers, suggested a bumper sticker that would read "God is Dead is Dead."[119]

Secular theology never really stood much of a chance to achieve a sustained success among mainstream leaders, but it should be noted that in their own way secular theologies did help the mainstream take its first step toward recognizing that religion was actually diffused through all of culture. Shortly after the attempt to embrace secularity — and perhaps due to the failed attempt to capture its elusive character — many religionists and social scientists reached the conclusion that secularity was not all that secular. Religion was redefined in ways that must have seemed imperialistic to the pure secularist. Clifford Geertz, in fact, described "religion as a cultural system."[120] From yet another perspective, Robert Bellah, in his famous *Dædalus* essay, talked about the "civil religion" of American culture.[121] Many more examples from the period could be offered.[122]

On top of these confusing developments, mainstream Protestants had other struggles to contend with, struggles largely growing out of their earlier activism in public life. The 1960s had opened up an entire Pandora's box of issues that now vied for attention within the mainstream camp. Having accepted their minority status within the culture and found ways to act out of it, Protestants faced a new challenge in the next decade. The mainstream self-definition through the

119. "Pen-ultimate: Religious Bumper Stickers," *CC,* 13 July 1966, p. 899. An earlier spoof in the column encouraged people to apply to the "God is Dead Club" ("Pen-ultimate: Apply Now!" *CC,* 16 February 1966, p. 223).

120. Clifford Geertz, "Religion as a Cultural System," in *The Religious Situation: 1968,* ed. Donald Cutler (Boston: Beacon Press, 1968).

121. Bellah, "Civil Religion in America," reprinted in *Beyond Belief: Essays on Religion in a Post-Traditional World* (New York: Harper & Row, 1970), pp. 168-89.

122. See Marty's discussion of the 1970s recognition of the diffusion of religion in culture, "Religion in America since Mid-Century." For a discussion of some of the many religious aspects of American culture, see John F. Wilson's excellent study *Public Religion in American Culture* (Philadelphia: Temple University Press, 1979).

1960s remained largely male, white, and middle-class. By the end of the 1970s, the definition had been expanded to allow more significantly for female, black, Hispanic, and even homosexual expressions. Though largely still middle-class by the end of the decade, the mainstream had at least begun to incorporate some of the theological insights of the less empowered classes by way of liberation theology. Issues related to public life were no longer "those issues" outside the walls of the church (if they ever were); the late sixties through the seventies brought them crashing into the life of the church itself to the extent that the 1960s mainstream (read here "white, male, and middle-class") Protestants could no longer ignore them.

There can be little doubt that American Protestantism has been split asunder since 1957. Much of the division within it, as Robert Wuthnow recently suggested, has resulted from the issues facing the social and public life of the nation since World War II.[123] Social issues have certainly played a very important role in both theological and ecclesial constructions during these modern years. And, in many ways, these constructions have often been "over against" other Christian understandings. Yet Wuthnow's suggestion that the major lines of the division have been between religious conservatives and religious liberals probably needs some rethinking. The divisions of the last few decades have come more between liberals and liberals on the one hand, and conservatives and conservatives on the other. There seems to be as much a move toward the middle from among both groups as there is a move to the left or to the right among each of them. Divisions, however, remain.

What will accomplish the healing? What will bring the unity that "special issue" theology has lost for the church? This appears to be the major question of the 1990s. If Christians cannot address public life with any degree of unanimity, how can they expect to influence its development toward the Christian objectives of peace and justice? The church is almost powerless to address public life because there is no unified Christian voice and no powerfully expressed and accepted Christian ethic for non-Christians to take seriously. Yet, as always seems true for those who affirm the gospel, there are signs of hope in the midst of despair.

As hinted earlier, many Christians from among evangelicalism, post–Vatican II Catholicism, and mainstream Protestantism have found themselves growing closer together. Today, for example, the writings

123. Wuthnow, *The Restructuring of American Religion.*

of either of the first two groups are as likely to be found in the pages of the *Century* as those of the last group. Editorial positions of *Christianity Today* and *The Christian Century* on most social issues are more similar today than they were in the late fifties through the sixties and seventies. Both journals have moderated their understandings and redefined their identities in ways that have moved them more toward a common center than toward reinforcement of their previously polar isolation from one another.

Black theologians, feminist theologians, and theologians of Third World liberation have also discovered common ground, and many of their expressions have crept into the vocabulary of both evangelical and mainstream Christianity in the dialogues of the last decade. These past ten years have also witnessed a deep and ecumenical concern among many Christian groups to return to the importance of Christian tradition for ethical reflection. The "post-traditional" world advocated by Robert Bellah in 1970 has given way to one in which he has more recently expressed his belief that "only living traditions make it possible to have a world at all."[124] As diverse as those within the enterprise are, this common and self-critical search for the relevance of Christian tradition holds great promise for a more unified Christian witness in the modern world.

Finally, even the self-confessed intransigent and politically active neofundamentalists have changed in the last decade. The political arrogance and naive optimism so characteristic of their movement in the early eighties has given way to a new measure of wisdom and realism. They have had to learn to form coalitions with traditional enemies (e.g., Roman Catholics) and engage in the fine art of negotiation and compromise. As they have broadened their net, they have relaxed their rigidity. They have also learned that their political heroes are as likely to fail them as to please them. Perhaps they have learned, like the liberals of the 1960s, that it is less than wise to place Christian hopes in secular baskets woven by leaders with much different agendas.

Whatever the scene of things to come as American Christians approach the end of the second millennium since the time of Christ, one can rest assured that the times will be interesting, and Marty, along

124. Contrast Bellah's *Beyond Belief: Essays on Religion in a Post-Traditional World,* which celebrated the freedom of modern religion from traditional restraints, with his contribution to the *Century*'s How My Mind Has Changed series, "Finding the Church: Post-Traditional Discipleship" (*CC,* 14 November 1990, pp. 1060-64), from which this quotation was taken.

with his colleagues at the *Century,* will find plenty more to write about.[125] The radical pluralism of the past thirty-five years, and Christian recognition of it, seem almost to guarantee fascinating developments. If nothing else, the history of the 1950s and 1960s demonstrates that the reality of pluralism does not dictate either Christian isolationism or Christian paralysis. In its hope to put forth a meaningful Christian witness in the midst of the cacophony of contemporary public life, the multifaceted mainstream must pay particular attention to both its history and its theology. If its members do so, they might be able to renew their commitment to what Marty described in 1969 as "the search for a usable future."[126]

125. It is interesting to point out that by January 1996, Marty will have surpassed even C. C. Morrison's active writing tenure at the *Century* to claim the longest active tenure of any editor in the journal's history. Morrison, Marty, Dean Peerman, W. E. Garrison, and Paul Hutchison all have spent more than twenty-five years as active writers at the *Century.* Harold Fey spent twenty-four years writing for the journal. The longevity represented by these individuals has helped the *Century* maintain a consistent and conscious attempt to wrestle with the meaning of the Christian tradition for contemporary life.

126. Marty, *The Search for a Usable Future* (New York: Harper & Row, 1969).

Christ and Culture during "Canada's Century"

ROBERT CHOQUETTE

IN 1904, eight years after having first been elected prime minister of Canada, Sir Wilfrid Laurier declared to an Ottawa audience that he was putting forth every effort to make the twentieth century "Canada's century."[1] Like his predecessors and successors in the office of prime minister, his success or failure was largely determined by the skill with which he managed the relationship between the country's two founding peoples, the French and the English — one of the most significant aspects of which was the relationship between Canada's Catholic and Protestant churches.

It is my hope in this essay to contribute to a better understanding of both the social function and the nature of Canada's Catholic and Protestant Christian traditions, the churches that still represent 90 percent of the people of Canada. I will begin with a review of the state of Catholic-Protestant relations on the eve of "Canada's century" and then sketch the mutual development of these churches during the next hundred years, underscoring their isolation from one another until the 1960s and then their timid but real discovery of one another. It is my contention that a century of warfare, hostility, and ignorance was the result of the Canadian churches' having become dependents of the two separate Canadian cultures, the English-Canadian and French-Canadian. Christ's Canadian spokespersons had sold out to two different cultures.

The 1960s brought a new beginning for Canada's churches, however. Spurred on by world events such as Vatican Council II, the ecumenical movement in Protestant churches, and the sweeping sociocul-

1. Réal Bélanger, *Wilfrid Laurier* (Québec: Les Presses de l'Université Laval and Les Entreprises Radio-Canada, 1986), p. 253.

tural revolution, the two ecclesial communities slipped the cultural leash that had held them in check for a century and rediscovered the gospel. Several ironies emerge from the story, one being that to the degree that they have rediscovered the gospel, Canada's churches have lost the support of large numbers of their faithful. Another irony is that it is while celebrating cultural involvement or inculturation that Catholics and Protestants have recently reestablished the necessary critical distance between their Christian faith and the world around them. This record may give us some clues to a means of renewing the historiography of Canadian Christianity.

Twentieth-Century Canada: A Confessional and Cultural Road Map

Throughout the twentieth century, the people of Canada have overwhelmingly identified themselves as Christian. During the hundred years between 1881 and 1981, Canada's total population has multiplied by a factor of six, growing from 4 million to 24 million. During the same period of time, the percentage of Catholics in Canada has increased from 42 to 47 percent, with a corresponding decrease in the percentage of Protestants to the present 42 percent. Simultaneously the percentage of French-speaking Catholics has diminished from 72 percent (in 1881) to 55 percent (in 1981), with a corresponding increase in the percentage of English-speaking Catholics from 28 percent (in 1881) to 45 percent (in 1981).

In spite of secularist trends, the most recent census figures (1981) still report 90 percent of Canada's 24 million people as Christian, including more than 11 million Catholics and 10 million Protestants. Of the 42 percent of the population that is Protestant, more than 80 percent belong to five main churches; the largest are the United Church of Canada with 3.7 million adherents and the Anglican Church of Canada with 2.5 million, the balance being made up of Presbyterians (800,000), Lutherans (700,000), and Baptists (600,000). Pentecostals represent the sixth largest Protestant group, with 300,000 adherents.[2]

Although there have always been French-speaking Protestants in Canada, they have never been numerous. There is a significantly

2. John Webster Grant, "Protestantism and Society in Canada," in *Encyclopedia of the American Religious Experience,* vol. 1, ed. Charles H. Lippy and Peter W. Williams (New York: Scribner's, 1988), pp. 239-52.

greater balance among Canada's eleven million Roman Catholics, however: six million are French-speaking and five million are English-speaking. The long-standing identification of Roman Catholicism with French Canada on the one hand, and Protestantism with English Canada on the other hand, is probably related to their traditional geographic differentiation. Fully 80 percent of the French-speaking Catholics reside in the province of Quebec, and an even greater percentage of English-speaking Protestants reside in provinces other than Quebec. In any event, much to the chagrin of both linguistic and cultural minorities in all parts of the country, during most of the twentieth century, most Canadians have identified Quebec as Catholic and French and the rest of the country as Protestant and English. Many tend to forget that one in six French-speaking Canadians and two in five Catholic Canadians reside in provinces and territories other than Quebec.

Catholics and Protestants on the Eve of Canada's Century

Relations between Canada's Protestants and Catholics in the late nineteenth century were shaped by confessional, national, and international factors.[3]

The country's strong evangelical movement established a general tone of Protestant denunciation of both international and Canadian Catholicism. A centuries-old anti-Catholic rhetoric remained alive and well in many Canadian Protestant manses and newspapers.[4] One hundred years ago, the typical evangelical Protestant was convinced that a Catholic did not even merit the name of Christian. There were, of course, exceptions to the reigning bigotry. Many Protestant laypeople demonstrated unalloyed respect, friendliness, warmth, and generosity toward Catholic laity and clergy. Such was the case, for example, among most officers of the Hudson's Bay Company, the commercial monopoly that controlled not only the commerce but also

3. The following material is based in large part on work I have done in preparing a book entitled *Catholics Encounter Protestants in the Nineteenth-Century Northwest,* forthcoming from Western Canadian Publishers Ltd. and the University of Alberta Press.

4. See J. R. Miller, "Anti-Catholic Thought in Victorian Canada," *Canadian Historical Review,* 66 (December 1985): 474-94; and Miller, "Bigotry in the North-Atlantic Triangle: Irish, British and American Influences on Canadian Anti-Catholicism," *Studies in Religion/Sciences Religieuses* 16 (Summer 1987): 289-301.

the communications and government of Canada's vast Northwest (more than half of the present-day Canadian landmass) until 1870. Such was also the case among many Protestant clergy. Although official evangelical Protestantism regularly and vehemently denounced the "whore of Babylon," and "the poisoned pastures of Popery,"[5] a study of the actual experience of Protestant clergy reveals a number of instances in which they established genuine friendships with Roman Catholic priests. It was as if they felt compelled to preach a gospel of hatred and bigotry when they donned their official hats but then felt free to show a completely different face when they stepped out of their official roles.

The ecclesiastical Protestant mind-set was reinforced by ethnonational considerations. Until the formation of the Dominion of Canada in 1867, Protestants in the federating British colonies of Nova Scotia, New Brunswick, Quebec, and Ontario had been very much influenced — in fact, frequently controlled — by both British and American culture. The same was true of provinces and territories that later joined the Canadian federation.[6] Canadian Protestant churches manifested many of the same ideologies, trends, and divisions as their mother churches in Britain or the United States. However, after 1867 an English-Canadian national consciousness began to emerge, leading the Protestant churches away from foreign ties both British and American and pulling them into the orbit of a new Canadian Anglo-Protestant mind-set. Among other things, the new ideology translated into a growing trend toward the reunification of various Protestant churches, a corresponding softening of their attitudes toward one another, and a gradual but growing identification of Canadian Protestantism with English-Canadian nationalism.[7] Given that nationalism was destined to become "the dominant twentieth century form of

5. The phrase is from S. Tucker, *The Rainbow in the North: A Short Account of the Establishment of Christianity in Rupertsland by the Church Missionary Society* (London: James Nisbet, 1858).

6. For a recent general history of Canada see R. Douglas Francis, Richard Jones, and Donald B. Smith, *Origins: Canadian History to Confederation* and *Destinies: Canadian History since Confederation* (Toronto: Holt, Rinehart & Winston, 1988). For a general history of Christian churches in Canada since 1867, see John Webster Grant, *The Church in the Canadian Era* (Burlington, Ont.: Welch, 1988).

7. Canadian Presbyterians managed to unify their various branches in 1875. Methodists did likewise in 1874 and 1884. Anglicans organized the Canadian general synod in 1893. This unification movement among Protestant churches culminated in 1925 with the formation of the United Church of Canada, the result of the fusion of Canadian Methodist, Congregational, and Presbyterian churches.

religion,"[8] the Dominion of Canada was becoming the Dominion of the Lord.

At the turn of the twentieth century, some 40 percent of Canadians were Roman Catholic. Of these, 72 percent were French-speaking, and 28 percent either were in an English-speaking group or were in the process of assimilating into one. This Canadian Catholic Church was strongly ultramontane in its theology, polity, and discipline. Proud of three hundred years of history that went back to the earliest days of New France and included the epic saga of the Jesuit martyrs and the evangelization of the North American continent,[9] Canada's Catholic Church had not only survived the British conquest of Canada in 1760 but had since become (particularly since 1840) French Canada's only real powerful and credible voice in North America. Having revitalized itself after 1840, Canada's Catholic Church occupied a position of strength from 1900 to 1960 to which the country's other churches could only aspire. The province of Quebec began the twentieth century with one priest for every 500 faithful, but the number of men and women in religious orders grew by leaps and bounds, attaining a phenomenal ratio of one religious for every eighty Catholics in 1941, a total of sixty thousand men and women in orders. This legion of consecrated folk fanned out to evangelize every part of Canada as well as many parts of other countries; they also dominated every level of Catholic schools and social services. Indeed, in Canada, French and Catholic seemed interchangeable terms, although the number of English-speaking Catholics continued to grow.

Ethno-Cultural Protestantism in Canada

By the turn of the century, Protestantism was one of Canada's two primarily ethno-cultural fronts. Woven during the last third of the nineteenth century, and destined to last into the post–World War II era, the Protestant tapestry drew its principal strength from white Anglo-

8. Frank Underhill in a foreword to *Nationalism in Canada*, ed. Peter Russell (Toronto: McGraw Hill, 1966), p. xvi

9. For a summary of this history, see J. E. Robert Choquette, "French Catholicism in the New World," in *Encyclopedia of the American Religious Experience*, 1: 223-38. For a more detailed presentation of the religious history preceding 1776, see Robert Choquette, "French Christianity Comes to the Americas," in Charles Lippy, Robert Choquette, and Stafford Poole, *Christianity Comes to the Americas* (New York: Paragon Books, 1992).

Saxon Protestant people of Canadian, American, and British heritage. Patterns in the tapestry were produced by such threads as British imperialism, Protestant anti-Catholicism, English-Canadian nationalism, progressivism, xenophobia, and the dogma of progress. Protestant communions that had once competed with each other joined forces to repel invading hordes of Catholics, Eastern and Southern Europeans, and Asiatics, as well as to conquer and rule the vineyard of the Lord.[10] "His Dominion" was overwhelmingly envisioned as being white, English-speaking, Protestant, and superior. On the face of it, this meant that Catholics, French-speaking individuals, and foreigners were not welcome in Canada unless they were willing to assimilate as rapidly as possible into the English and Protestant majority.

Between Confederation and World War II, Canadian Protestant leaders denounced the threat to their "Canadian" identity posed by all who were different — Orientals, Slavs, Catholics, French Canadians, Mennonites, Mormons, and Jews. So it was that in 1910, S. D. Chown, a future General Superintendent of the Methodist Church, inquired, "Shall the hordes of Southern Europe overrun our country as the Huns and Vandals did the Roman Empire?"[11] In a popular novel published a year earlier, the Reverend C. W. Gordon of the Presbyterian Church drew a most unflattering comparison between the virtuous WASP folk of Winnipeg and the "steaming, swaying, roaring dancers . . . all reeking with sweat and garlic" at a Ukrainian wedding.[12] In a book published in 1913, the assistant superintendent of the Baptist Home Mission Board of Ontario and Quebec laid down his own rules for cultural assimilation: "We must endeavour to assimilate the foreigner. If the mixing process fails we must strictly prohibit from entering our country all elements that are non-assimilable. It is contrary to the Creator's law for white, black or yellow races to mix together."[13]

So it was that while Canadian English-speaking Protestant

10. On the nineteenth-century religious history of Ontario, see John Webster Grant, *A Profusion of Spires* (Toronto: University of Toronto Press, 1988), and William Westfall, *Two Worlds: The Protestant Culture of Nineteenth Century Ontario* (Montreal: McGill-Queen's University Press, 1989). On the ideological context of English Canada in the latter part of the nineteenth century, see Carl Berger, *Imperialism and Nationalism, 1884-1914: A Conflict in Canadian Thought* (Toronto: Copp Clark, 1969). On the ethno-cultural mind-set of English-speaking Canadian Protestants, see N. K. Clifford, "His Dominion: A Vision in Crisis," *Studies in Religion/Sciences Religieuses* 2 (1973): 315-26.

11. Chown, cited by Clifford in "His Dominion," p. 317.

12. Gordon, cited by Clifford in "His Dominion," p. 317.

13. Cited by Clifford in "His Dominion," p. 319.

leaders claimed that the spread of the gospel was their primary concern, they actually focused on Canadianization, which is to say assimilation of all into the Anglo-Saxon cultural block. With few exceptions, between Confederation and World War II, English-speaking Protestant churches in Canada were leading agencies of cultural assimilation into the WASP mainstream. This was also the prime purpose of Canada's public schools in all provinces except Quebec, where the public school system was confessional.[14]

Ethno-Cultural French-Canadian Catholicism

By 1911, Canada's powerful and well-staffed Roman Catholic Church had no rival in its effective leadership of the French-Canadian people, who numbered two million — 72 percent of all Canadian Catholics. Altogether, Catholics constituted 43 percent of Canada's population, but the Church was deeply divided along ethno-cultural lines.

After 1870, a painful series of clerical-political quarrels prevented Canadians from taking anything for granted in matters confessional, ethno-linguistic, or by extension political or constitutional. The Canadian domestic disputes began in 1869-1870, shortly after Confederation, with the *métis* insurrection in Red River led by Louis Riel. After this dispute was settled by the creation of the province of Manitoba in 1870, Riel continued to be hounded and persecuted for another five years by an Ontario-based nativist WASP lobby that refused to permit the granting of political amnesty to the leaders of the insurrection, Riel in particular. The protracted dispute eventually led to another insurrection — an armed rebellion this time — on the Saskatchewan River in 1885. The *métis* were crushed by the Canadian army, and Riel was hanged — retribution that simply served to transform a mentally unbalanced leader into a national folk hero of French Canadians.

Simultaneously, a series of school disputes in various parts of the country further embittered relations between Catholics and Protestants, French- and English-speaking citizens. The conflicts arose from a systematic attempt by Canada's WASP leaders to abolish the Catholic public schools that existed in most of Canada's provinces.[15] They man-

14. Newfoundland also had a confessional school system, but the province did not become part of Canada until 1949.

15. There were confessional public school systems in New Brunswick, Manitoba, Ontario, and the Northwest Territories as well as Quebec and Newfoundland.

aged to enact legislation abolishing confessional schools in New Brunswick in 1871; this was followed by similar legislation in Manitoba (1890), in the Northwest Territories (1892), and in Alberta and Saskatchewan (1905). In spite of clear and explicit constitutional guarantees, the Roman Catholics of Manitoba and the Territories, Alberta and Saskatchewan included, lost their right to Catholic public schools. In their place, the legislatures of these various provinces created public, "nondenominational" schools that were in fact Anglo-Protestant schools hiding behind a smokescreen of neutrality.[16] Indeed, the Canadian public schools, like public schools in the United States, became the new seminaries and temples in which all citizens were supposed to gather to worship the WASP idol that was paraded as the God of the Christians.

Catholics responded to this persecution by challenging some of the discriminatory laws in the courts and by reinforcing Catholic schools both private and public (where possible). For example, the majority of French-speaking Ontario citizens who had previously supported public schools shifted their allegiance to Catholic Separate schools. Given that an overwhelming majority of Canada's Roman Catholic clergy were French-speaking, the confessional fight over schools frequently appeared to be more ethno-cultural than confessional. During the late nineteenth and early twentieth centuries, while the crusade in favor of WASP hegemony waxed, French-speaking Catholic clergy identified ever more closely with the defense of French-Canadian rights. Indeed, between Confederation and World War II, a French-speaking clergyman in Canada was by definition a French-Canadian nationalist. Clerics (and nuns and brothers) in Quebec, where the French language and Catholic faith were secure, tended to view the battles that raged in Ontario and the Canadian West as the struggles of French-Canadian brothers in the faith heroically fending off the assaults of perfidious WASPs.

These confrontations culminated in the Regulation 17 fight in Ontario. Over a period of fifteen years (1912-1927), French-speaking citizens successfully resisted the government's attempts to ban French from Ontario schools. By the time the dust settled, the battle had in-

---

(Before the creation of the Yukon Territory in 1898 and that of the provinces of Alberta and Saskatchewan in 1905, the Northwest Territories included all their territory in addition to that of the present Northwest Territories.)

16. Alberta maintained the right to Separate schools, but they were merely public schools under a different name.

cluded litigation, strikes, confrontations between parents and police, public demonstrations, impassioned debates in provincial and federal legislatures, and two papal encyclicals. Given that by 1912 most Franco-Ontarian schools were in the Separate (Catholic) School system, were largely staffed by nuns and brothers, and were under the effective moral control of Catholic bishops, the Catholic Church was inevitably involved in the fight.[17]

So it was that by the early twentieth century, it seemed that everything conspired to weld together the destinies of the French-Canadian people and the Catholic Church of French Canada. In the minds of a growing number of French-Canadian nationalists (and most French Canadians *had* become nationalists), the school fights merely confirmed what they had suspected all along — namely, that the WASP block stood unified in wanting the annihilation of French Canada. French Canada was increasingly determined to resist.

Led by its clergy, French Canada gave itself a history of sacred origins in New France and interpreted its history in messianic and pastoral terms.[18] The great evil became the materialistic Anglo-Protestants with their immoral cities, exploitive industries, and filthy lucre. In contrast, French Canada was called to a spiritual vocation. Quebec's leading theologian, Louis-Adolphe Paquet, wrote in 1902,

> Not only do nations have a vocation, but some of them are called to a kind of priesthood. . . . My brothers . . . we have the privilege of being invested with this social priesthood that is reserved to elite nations. This religious and civilizing vocation is undoubtedly the

17. It should be noted that inasmuch as there were some English as well as French Separate schools, the language battle was necessarily joined *within* the Catholic Church as well. For more information on the overall cultural battle, see the following three volumes by Robert Choquette: *Language and Religion: A History of English-French Conflict in Ontario* (Ottawa: University of Ottawa Press, 1975), *La Foi Gardienne de la Langue en Ontario, 1900-1950* (Montréal: Bellarmin, 1987), and *L'Eglise catholique dans l'Ontario français du dix-neuvième siècle* (Ottawa: Editions de l'Université d'Ottawa, 1984). See also Chad Gaffield, *Language, Schooling, and Cultural Conflict: The Origins of the French-Language Controversy in Ontario* (Montreal: McGill-Queen's University Press, 1987).

18. During a half-century beginning in 1915, Father Lionel Groulx became French Canada's "national" historian. From his base in Montreal, Groulx wrote numerous historical works celebrating the glorious beginnings of French Canada, its more than three centuries of Christian witness, and its messianic vocation to evangelize the North American continent. Groulx is seen by some as the spiritual father of the Quebec independence movement.

> specific, special vocation of the French race in North America. Our mission is not so much to manipulate money, but to stir up ideas; it consists not so much in lighting the fires of industry but in maintaining and propagating afar the luminous effects of religion and thought. . . .
>
> The life of a tree is in its roots; the future of a nation is manifest in its origins. . . . When we count among our ancestors Clovis and Charlemagne, Louis IX and Joan of Arc, Vincent de Paul and Bossuet, are we not justified in claiming a distinctive role and a superior mission? . . .
>
> It is I, saith the Lord, who have formed this nation; I have established it for my glory, in the interest of religion and for the welfare of my church; I want it to persevere in its noble mission. . . . French Canada will only respond to God's designs . . . by keeping its individual character, its truly national traditions. . . .
>
> The language of a people is always a sacred trust. . . . Let us leave to other less-idealistic nations the feverish mercantilism, the gross naturalism that bind them to matter. Our ambition must aim higher.[19]

So it was that until the period after World War II — in fact, until 1960 — while typical Canadian WASPs considered it their foremost duty as Christians to "civilize" any and all who were different from themselves, typical French-Canadian Catholics considered it their foremost duty as Christians to stand on guard for the rights of French-Canadians. Of course, both groups were interested and active in other areas of concern (social, political, artistic, etc.), but only as long as the fundamental ethno-cultural social project was secure.

One fly in the neatly polarized ointment was the English-speaking Catholic group, bound to the French Canadians by religion but also bound to their WASP adversaries by language and culture.

Ethno-Cultural English-Canadian Catholicism

Canada's Catholic Church had been exclusively French-speaking until the end of the eighteenth century, when American, Scottish, and especially Irish immigrants began to arrive in growing numbers and to

19. Paquet, "La vocation de la race française en Amérique," sermon of 23 June 1902, reprinted in Emile Chartier, *Bréviaire du patriote canadien-français* (Montréal: Bibliothèque de l'Action Française, 1925), pp. 49-59; translation mine.

assimilate into the English-speaking population. Most of these English-speaking immigrants settled outside of Quebec, so that by the turn of the twentieth century, the majority of Canadian Catholics outside of Quebec were English-speaking.

These English-speaking Catholics found themselves in a double-minority situation, for they simultaneously constituted a linguistic minority within Canada's Catholic Church and a religious minority within English Canada as a whole.[20] As a linguistic minority, they came to resent the fact that they were constantly outnumbered at the decision-making level of the Catholic Church. They were also frustrated by the fact that they had to use French during their frequent dealings with French-speaking churchmen in Montreal and Quebec and clergy throughout the country. Beginning in the 1860s, many English-speaking clerics made an effort to find a better place in Canada's ecclesiastical sun by seeking to obtain the appointment of English-speaking bishops wherever they could and by endeavoring to sever the ties that bound them to the ecclesiastical centers of French Canada.

As a religious minority in Canada, these English-speaking Catholics found that they were required to bear the brunt of the anti-Catholic persecutions mounted by the WASP juggernaut, particularly in the matter of schools. In Canada's Northwest, for example, while the bishops and clergy that fought the discriminatory school legislation of the late nineteenth and early twentieth centuries were all French-speaking, the majority of the Catholic parents and children that were being denied their constitutional rights were English-speaking or in the process of assimilating into the English-speaking mainstream. Given the polarized public opinion of the time, the English-speaking Catholic community thus found itself damned by the WASPs if it sided with its French-speaking Catholic coreligionists and damned by the French Canadians if it sided with its English-speaking cultural brothers. Bishop Michael

20. Within the Catholic Church in Canada, the proportion of English-speaking faithful evolved as follows:

1881	28.3%
1911	27.7
1951	33.0
1981	45.2

There are no comprehensive scholarly studies of English-speaking Catholics in Canada; however, some information on this group is available in John Moir's "The Problem of a Double Minority: Some Reflections on the Development of the English-Speaking Catholic Church in the Nineteenth Century," *Histoire sociale/Social History*, April 1971, pp. 53-67.

Fallon, one of the English-speaking Catholics' foremost leaders, noted that they found themselves trapped between the upper millstone of French-Canadian nationalism and the lower millstone of Protestant bigotry.

Throughout most of the nineteenth century, the identity of Canada's English-speaking Catholics resided primarily in their Old World ethnic ties — more often than not, a Scots or Irish background. By the turn of the twentieth century, however, their group identity had changed to become primarily English-speaking Canadian. Scots and Irish ethnic solidarity was waning and being replaced by a growing sense of belonging to Canada's majority cultural group.[21] During the Ontario schools debate, and particularly during the Regulation 17 fight, when Ontario's English-speaking Catholic community was forced to choose between its French-speaking coreligionists and its English-speaking cultural brothers, it chose the latter overwhelmingly. During the subsequent half-century, most of the Irish- and Scots-Catholic institutions in Canada disappeared as English-speaking Catholics lost their ethnic identity.

Terminating Canadian Holy Bigotry

So it was that during the first half of the twentieth century, Canadian WASPs, English-speaking Catholics, and French Canadians each sought to convert Canadians to their particular Jesus. Given that the determining factor in the mind-set of each of the groups was cultural rather than religious,[22] the two English-speaking groups stood together fending off the claims of the French-Canadian Jesus, who had the gall to demand equality. The five mainline Canadian Protestant churches, representing the vast majority of Protestants, became in fact mere mouthpieces for the English-Canadian cultural majority, supported at every turn by Canada's English-speaking Catholic Church. Indeed, although officially

21. Mark McGowan presses this case regarding turn-of-the-century Torontonians in "'We Are All Canadians': A Social, Religious and Cultural Portrait of Toronto's English-Speaking Roman Catholics, 1890-1920" (Ph.D. diss., University of Toronto, 1988).

22. I first presented this thesis as it applied to early twentieth-century Ontario Catholics in *Language and Religion.* For an application of the thesis to the history of the archdiocese of Toronto, see *Catholics at the "Gathering Place": Historical Essays on the Archdiocese of Toronto, 1841-1991,* ed. Mark McGowan and Brian Clarke (Toronto: Archdiocese of Toronto, forthcoming).

united as one church, Canada's Roman Catholic Church was in fact two distinct churches, split along ethno-cultural lines. Canada's basic linguistic and cultural division had overwhelmed both Protestant and Catholic churches. Each was firmly held on a cultural leash, and in each the gospel of Jesus had become secondary, although few would have admitted it.

The Great Depression of the 1930s, the horrors of World War II, the onset of the atomic age, and the growing multicultural immigration to Canada provoked two decades of growing doubts about the adequacy of these exclusivistic ethno-cultural mind-sets. The upshot was that during the 1960s Canadian Protestants and Catholics began to rediscover the gospel — the gospel that taught that in Christ there is neither Jew nor Greek, neither slave nor free, neither man nor woman, for all are one in Christ (Gal. 3:28). And in the midst of the tidal wave of social and cultural change that was sweeping the Western world during the 1960s, there arose a special impetus for change from within the Roman Catholic Church itself.

Led by Pope John XXIII (1958-1963), the Second Vatican Council (1962-1965) had as its foremost concerns the reestablishment of contact and constructive dialogue between the Catholic Church and contemporary culture and society. Many Catholic bishops and theologians were convinced that they needed to build new bridges between the Roman Catholic Church on the one hand and contemporary arts, politics, and other religions and ecclesiastical bodies on the other — in short, with all of contemporary culture. The Council's most important statement in this regard is found in its pastoral constitution on the church in the modern world, but the same concerns are reflected in most other conciliar documents as well — in declarations bearing on the laity, Eastern churches, non-Christians, religious freedom, and other associated matters.[23]

Spurred on by the "quiet revolution" that was simultaneously transforming the province of Quebec,[24] Canada's bishops took a leading role in the Vatican II reform of the Catholic Church, while their own church was agonizing at home. As the Canadian clergy abandoned the ministry and the religious life in droves, more than half the faithful

23. For the whole range of documents, see *The Documents of Vatican II,* ed. Walter M. Abbott (New York: Guild Press, 1966).

24. The "quiet revolution" consisted of a thoroughgoing transformation of most areas of Quebec society and culture including education, moral values, political life, and religiosity.

ceased attending Sunday Mass, and the vast majority abandoned the sacrament of penance, while making their own decisions regarding the use of contraceptives despite clear Vatican directives on the matter.[25]

During the 1960s, Canada's mainline Protestant churches also showed a new willingness to reform and to improve their relations with any and all, including the Catholic Church. A sea change was occurring in relationships of Catholics and Protestants individually, as well as in relationships between Catholic and Protestant churches and Canada's cultural groups.

Cultures and Christian Churches: A New Relationship

It is ironic that out of a concern to arrest a perceived marginalization of the Catholic Church in the modern world, beginning in the 1960s Catholic bishops and theologians undertook to embrace contemporary cultures and in the process also managed to rediscover the God of the Christians.[26] Leading Catholic theologian Karl Rahner wrote that at Vatican II, the Catholic Church grew aware that it needed "to become at home in the diverse cultures of the world, [and] to become differentiated culturally."[27]

25. In 1991, many Quebec bishops estimated that a mere 15 percent of their flock were "practicing Catholics." Before 1960, more than 90 percent were members in good standing of the Catholic Church. Outside of Quebec, church attendance seems somewhat better, although public opinion surveys in 1991 reported that an average of only 23 percent of Canada's Christians (all churches) regularly attend worship on Sunday.

26. The basic official statements of the Catholic Church concerning its relationship to modern culture are Vatican II's Dogmatic Constitution on the Church *(Lumen Gentium)* and Pastoral Constitution on the Church in the Modern World *(Gaudium et Spes)* and Pope Paul VI's encyclical *Evangelii Nuntiandi* (1975), which was released following the 1974 meeting of the Synod of bishops studying evangelization. Recent theological literature on the theme of the Catholic Church and its relationship to culture is considerable; see, for example, Hervé Carrier, *Cultures notre avenir* (Rome: Presses de l'Université Grégorienne, 1985); Hervé Carrier, *Gospel Message and Human Cultures from Leo XIII to John Paul II,* trans. John Drury (Pittsburgh: Duquesne University Press, 1989); *Théologie et choc des cultures. Colloque de l'Institut catholique de Paris,* ed. C. Geffré (Paris: Editions du Cerf, 1984); J. Gritti, *L'expression de la foi dans les cultures humaines* (Paris: Le Centurion, 1975); Achiel Peelman, *L'inculturation. L'Eglise et les cultures* (Paris: Desclée, 1988); and P. Poupard, *Eglise et cultures. Jalons pour une pastorale de l'intelligence* (Paris: Editions SOS, 1980).

27. Rahner, "Towards a Fundamental Theological Interpretation of Vatican II," *Theological Studies* 40 (1979): 19.

Moving away from a humanistic understanding of culture as the ultimate refinement of human aspirations in the arts, Catholic leaders gradually came to acknowledge the primacy of the anthropological definition of culture as the total expression of human beings in society. Although hundreds of definitions of culture exist,[28] the one given by Jesuit sociologist Hervé Carrier accurately reflects the holistic meaning given the concept by contemporary Christian spokesmen:

> Culture is the humanized universe created wittingly or unwittingly by a human collectivity. It is the group's own representation of the past and its plan for the future, its typical institutions and creations, its habits and beliefs, its characteristic attitudes and behavior patterns, its original mode of communicating, working, celebrating, and creating the techniques and works that reveal its soul and its ultimate values. Culture is the typical mentality adopted by every individual who identifies with a collectivity; it is the human heritage transmitted from generation to generation.[29]

So it was that beginning in the 1960s, Christian leaders began to acknowledge the waning of ideologies and utopias and realized that it was the total human being that sought to define itself anew in its diversity of cultures. The Catholic Church decided that the dynamic concept of culture, the contemporary world's new paradigm, would become the Church's new privileged focus of activity. In the wake of Vatican II and Paul VI's *Evangelii Nuntiandi* (1975), in the 1980s Pope John Paul II began to describe the encounter between native cultures and the gospel as "inculturation," by which he meant "the incarnation of the Gospel in native cultures and, simultaneously, the introduction of these cultures in the life of the Church."[30]

In the eyes of the Catholic Church, a basic criterion of inculturation was the necessity of always distinguishing the gospel from a given culture, for Christian faith is not the product of any culture but of divine revelation, and hence it always remains radically different, transcending any and all cultures. At the same time, inculturation also entails an intimate transformation of cultural values by the gospel. Christians were called to evangelize not only individuals but also their

28. See A. L. Kroeber and C. Kluckhohn, *Culture: A Critical Review of Concepts and Definitions* (Cambridge: Harvard University Press, 1952).

29. Carrier, *Gospel Message and Human Cultures from Leo XIII to John Paul II*, pp. 4-5.

30. John Paul II, *Slavorum Apostoli* (1985).

milieu, their culture, never losing sight of the fact that in their capacity as evangelists they could not impose their own cultural values on other cultures.

These changes in Catholic Church policy were occurring at a time when Catholics were anticipating that by the year 2000, more than 70 percent of the world's Christians would live in the Third World and likely be disinclined to adopt the cultural values of Europe and North America that had for centuries accompanied Christian evangelization. The shift in the balance of power within the Christian church was necessitating a new understanding of the relationship between Christ and culture.

Christ and Culture in Canada: A New Relationship

Canada's three foremost ethno-cultural ecclesiastical bastions having begun to crumble in the 1940s, Christ began to reemerge from the rubble. Weak and tentative restructuring of Canada's leading churches began with the formation of the Canadian Council of Catholic Bishops in 1943[31] and the Canadian Council of Churches in 1944, which were meant to serve as coordinating bodies for all of Canada's bishops and for most mainstream Protestant and Orthodox churches, respectively. These new bodies did not really come into their own until the 1960s, however, when sweeping changes in Western society and in Canada's churches allowed them to take bold new steps.

Everything seemed to be possible in the 1960s. The Anglicans commissioned a leading Canadian popular historian to publish a critique of their church, and, by extension, of all Protestant churches in Canada. Pierre Berton's *The Comfortable Pew* (1965) soon became the best-selling book in Canadian history, despite (or because of) its frank criticism of Canadian Protestantism.[32] Meanwhile, Canada's Commission on Bilingualism and Biculturalism noted that Canada was experiencing the worst crisis of its history, citing calls by both the United Church of Canada (in 1964) and the Anglican Church of Canada (in 1965) for Canadian unity and equal rights for French-speaking Canadi-

31. For some years this body was known as the Canadian Catholic Conference.

32. Similar books were issued by the United Church of Canada *(Why the Sea Is Boiling Hot)* and by a group of Catholic laymen *(Brief to the Bishops)*.

ans. Canada's Catholic bishops made a similar plea in April 1967, on the occasion of the centennial of the confederation of Canada.[33]

In the same vein, during the next twenty-five years, Canada's Catholic bishops time and again professed their unalloyed support for linguistic and cultural equality for all in Canada. Statements to this effect were issued by the Canadian Conference of Catholic Bishops, the Quebec Assembly of Bishops, the Ontario Conference of Catholic Bishops, and other bodies. They issued pleas for more openness toward immigrants of all origins, for a greater measure of justice toward Indians, for the constitutional recognition of the rights of the French language in Ontario, for the recognition of the right of self-determination of the people of Quebec, and for the full equality of Quebec's minorities.

The bishops were endeavoring to apply to Canadian society the social teachings that came out of Vatican Council II and pontifical and episcopal social encyclicals of the 1960s, 1970s, and 1980s.[34] In 1983, these same churchmen shocked many to attention with their *Ethical Reflections* on the Canadian economy, an episcopal document that stirred up more controversy than any other Church document before or since. Therein, many Canadians witnessed for the first time the application to their own country of the Catholic Church's new social doctrine, which rested on the three pillars of the primacy of persons, of work, and of the common purpose of the world's goods.

In many respects, the contours of the Catholic Church's new social doctrine were similar to those of most mainstream Canadian Protestant churches during this period.[35] In fact, since the 1960s, Protestants and Catholics have cooperated as they never had before in a wide range of areas including social welfare, political activism, the rights of Canadian Indians, immigration policy, liturgical celebrations, theological education, shared evangelization, and the like. Ecumenists held protracted discussions intended to lead to the organic union of the Roman Catholic and Orthodox Churches and many mainstream Protestant churches.

33. Several of the social statements of Canada's bishops are reproduced in *Do Justice: The Social Teaching of the Canadian Catholic Bishops (1945-1986)*, ed. E. F. Sheridan (Toronto: Jesuit Centre for Social Faith and Justice, 1987).

34. The most noteworthy of these church documents were John XXIII's *Pacem in Terris* (1963); the report of the Medellin Conference of Latin American bishops (1968); Paul VI's *Populorum Progressio* (1967), *Octogesima Adveniens* (1971), and *Evangelii Nuntiandi* (1975); the report of the Puebla (Mexico) conference of Latin American bishops (1979); and John Paul II's *Laborem Exercens* (1981).

35. See Edward Pulker, *We Stand on Their Shoulders: The Growth of Social Concern in Canadian Anglicanism* (Toronto: Anglican Book Centre, 1986).

In fact, it could be argued that this period brought an end to ethno-linguistic bigotry among Canada's churches. One leading Canadian historian, Ramsay Cook, noted the significant fact that in 1965 the Royal Commission on Bilingualism and Biculturalism had managed to write 140 pages explaining Canada's linguistic crisis with very little reference to religion. "I would be prepared to state categorically that at no time before 1945 would it have been possible for a survey of French-English relations to have been written without devoting a very considerable amount of space to religious differences. . . . What has become of our old religious quarrels?"[36]

Indeed, Canada's churches seem to have slipped their cultural leashes in the 1960s. They no longer serve as the mouthpieces and the heavenly anchors for Canada's leading ethno-cultural tribes — namely, the WASP, the French-Canadian, and the English-speaking Catholic. They rediscovered the God of the Christians and simultaneously reestablished a more healthy critical distance between themselves and their respective cultures.

Many Canadian Christians of the 1960s and 1970s welcomed their new secular society and directed their churches to exchange their traditional cultic functions for a more prophetic and critical role in Canadian society. For example, whereas their predecessors had fought the good fight for the survival of French or the domination of English, after 1960 Canadian churchmen, both Protestant and Catholic, tended more and more to serve as moderators in disputes that were less and less frequently of their own making. They served to keep nationalisms in check by reminding people that there were other important aspects in civilization, fundamental things such as liberty and respect for others that should not be sacrificed on the altar of the nationalistic passion of a new tribalism.

We have noted that it is a fundamental dimension of the social doctrine of the Catholic Church that the Christian faith must not be identified with any culture. In other words, God remained wholly other while having become man — the doctrine of the Incarnation, which is central to Catholic thought. Although this was not new doctrine for the Catholics (it is in full accord with traditional Thomist and neo-Thomist theology), it had long been interpreted by both Roman Catholics and Protestants (e.g., Ernst Troeltsch) in a sense that led to the establishment

36. Ramsay Cook, "Protestant Lion, Catholic Lamb," in *One Church, Two Nations?* ed. Philip LeBlanc and Arnold Edinborough (Toronto: Longmans, 1968), p. 4.

of either a culture-Protestantism or a culture-Catholicism. Both models of society constituted acculturations of Christ — which is to say, they merged Christ with a given culture.[37]

Beginning in the 1930s, this theology was challenged by both the neo-Thomists among the Catholics (e.g., Etienne Gilson, Jacques Maritain) and by the influential neo-orthodoxy (European and American) of Karl Barth and H. Richard Niebuhr among the Protestants. One result was that in the 1960s and 1970s, Christians who were looking at their respective tribalisms with a new critical eye were supported by solid theological arguments from both Catholic and Protestant quarters. Christians were able to stand back from their respective tribes and find themselves together in Christ.

During the past twenty-five years, Canadian churches have thus reoriented their social teachings and their relationships with one another and society, but their new message has yet to penetrate very far into the minds of the people of Canada. On the basis of extensive opinion surveys conducted during the 1970s and 1980s, the sociologist Reginald Bibby concluded in 1987 that

> Religion, Canadian-style, is mirroring culture. . . . Culture leads, religion follows. . . . In this country, religion gives every indication of being something we create rather than something with a non-human dimension. . . . We are creating the gods. . . . Large numbers of Canadians are not going to return to the churches because they have little to which to return. . . . Culture calls most of the shots, and there is a fine line between translating the message and transforming it altogether. . . . If there are elements of religion that transcend culture . . . then religion on occasion at least should find itself . . . "contradicting the times." . . . If religion is to interact effectively with culture, then it has to be able to transcend culture.[38]

Postscript

The changing relationship between Christ and culture in twentieth-century Canada has produced a series of ironies. First, the churches flexed the most muscle when they were most bound to their respective tribes — that is, when each was furthest removed from an authentic Christian

37. For an excellent discussion of these issues, see H. Richard Niebuhr, *Christ and Culture* (New York: Harper & Row, 1951).

38. Bibby, *Fragmented Gods* (Toronto: Irwin Publishing, 1987), pp. 233ff.

catholicity and under the sway of powerful nationalisms. Second, this period of ecclesiastical muscle corresponded to that of the least sense of the majesty of God. Third, when this situation was in the process of being reversed, beginning in the 1960s, the new consciousness of both the majesty of God and the importance of one's neighbor developed in direct proportion to the loss of ecclesiastical adherents, revenues, political power, and the like. Indeed, as the cultic role of the Canadian Christian churches gave way to a prophetic role, clergy and laity left the churches in droves. Perhaps a fourth irony will be that in spite of all indices to the contrary, Canadians will nevertheless return to the Christian churches in droves. Professor Marty could well write of "the irony of it all."[39]

One lesson we can draw from this review of the relationship between Christ and culture in Canada is that it may be time for Canadian historians of religion to take serious stock of the specifically religious dimension of that history. It may well be time to put religion back into the history of religion. We have come a long way since the days of partisan confessional historiography that were with us not so long ago.[40] Now that the theories and findings of the social sciences (of cultural anthropology and social history in particular) have found their way into the landscape of the historiography of Canadian religion, perhaps it is time for historians of Canadian religion to become literate in theology. Former confessional church historians have frequently been accused of being "mere" theologians, and sometimes rightly so. Today's historian of Canadian religion should not forget, however, that it is not only useful but necessary to understand whereof he or she speaks. In the matter at hand, this includes becoming literate in theology without sacrificing any of the rest of one's expertise. Martin Marty would certainly agree, for he has always stood at the paradoxical junction of "this world" and the "wholly other," a stance that has allowed him to tell the truth, and that is typically Christian.

39. Marty, *Modern American Religion,* vol. 1: *The Irony of It All, 1893-1919* (Chicago: University of Chicago Press, 1986), p. xii.

40. For recent reviews of religious historiography in Canada, see John S. Moir, "Coming of Age, but Slowly: Aspects of Canadian Religious Historiography since Confederation," in the Canadian Catholic Historical Association's *Study Sessions* 50 (1983): 89-98; Mark G. McGowan, "Coming out of the Cloister: Some Reflections on Developments in the Study of Religion in Canada, 1980-1990," *International Journal of Canadian Studies/Revue Internationale d'Etudes Canadiennes* 1-2 (Spring-Fall 1990): 175-202; and Guy Laperrière, "L'Histoire religieuse du Québec: Principaux Courants, 1978-1988," *Revue d'Histoire de l'Amérique Française* 42 (Spring 1989): 563-78.

Religion and the Great American Argument about Health

JAMES P. WIND

IN 1983 Martin E. Marty wrote *Health and Medicine in the Lutheran Tradition,* a book that, even given Marty's wide-ranging interests, seemed a detour. The first in a multi-authored series now numbering ten published volumes and promising several more, Marty's book was much more than the momentary detour it initially seemed to be. The Health and Medicine in the Faith Traditions Series occasioned a much larger inquiry than its designers originally intended. Their probing of the complex relations among health, faith, and ethics in America has now taken on institutional form, with the creation in 1985 of the Park Ridge Center, which Marty shaped as founding president and which he still serves in a variety of ways. The Center in turn has produced a growing stream of publications that focus on the traditions, dimensions, and issues that interact and emerge when religion and health meet. Marty's early "detour" has widened to become a new avenue of inquiry into the larger story of American religion.

My purpose in this essay is not to tell the Park Ridge Center's story. Nor is it to reminisce about endeavors in which I was privileged to share with Marty as a colleague at the Center. Instead it is to grapple with a puzzle that Marty pondered in *Health and Medicine in the Lutheran Tradition.* There he made what for a historian can only be a "take-a-deep-breath" generalization. After surveying the extant scholarship on Luther and the Lutherans Marty stated, "In over 450 years, no book devoted exclusively to the subject [of well-being] in the Lutheran tradition has appeared or, at least, survived."[1] Six years later, in an address

1. Marty, *Health and Medicine in the Lutheran Tradition: Being Well* (New York: Crossroad, 1986), p. 10.

at the Carter Center in Atlanta, Georgia, Marty revisited this problem by commenting on conversations he had shared with authors who had probed "their" traditions in the Health and Medicine Series:

> In almost all cases, the authors reported that theirs turned out to be a lonely and often the very first act of gathering such resources of their traditions. Theological libraries contain tens of thousands of volumes, but in the age of skeptical reason, indifferentist toleration, and individualism, few authors or readers had been paying attention to the resources in the texts of faith traditions. That situation is changing suddenly, in theological schools, in history departments, in clinical settings and other places of healing. The challenge is to use what is there already and to find and produce more.[2]

Although historians tend to become increasingly cautious the closer their research gets to the present moment, Marty had risked another major generalization. He had spotted a significant change and was calling attention to it. The faith traditions of America had "suddenly" become sufficiently self-conscious about their relations to health and health care in modern (or postmodern) America to enter into a new period of scholarly reflection. In this essay I want to characterize this recent development as the latest stage in an argument about health that is as old as the religious traditions of America. Since the focus of this festschrift is on the most recent century of the American story, and since scholars have cleared only a few preliminary vistas for surveying this enormously large and complicated argument, this essay will have an exploratory and at times kaleidoscopic feel to it. But the result should be a sketch of the shape of an argument and a clearer sense of our own locations within it.

An Argument

The word *argument* carries with it many emotional and ominous overtones. We envision red faces, clenched fists, and inflexible or threatening stances. To be sure, the American pursuit of health has had these features, whether in battles over water rights on the American frontier or in boardrooms and executive suites of modern hospitals as decisions are made about allocation of scarce health-care resources.

2. Marty, "The Tradition of the Church in Health and Healing," *Second Opinion* 13 (March 1990): 61-62.

Here, however, *argument* means something more. In his now almost classic book *After Virtue,* Alasdair MacIntyre defines traditions as arguments. His important insight is that the various practices in which humans engage are actually fragments of great arguments. Our modern situation has resulted in the severing of connections between particular practices and the great traditions of which they were once an integral part. So moderns often do things without awareness of the larger background behind the particular behavior or practice chosen. (One of the reasons that Marty and his colleagues who pursued the relationship of health and medicine to the faith traditions found their task so novel and so difficult is that many of the connections between practices and their larger constitutive arguments had been broken or at least obscured.)

Yet, when scholars dig deeply enough, they find echoes and signals of an argument. Taken cumulatively, these signals suggest that there is still an argument going on, that there are living traditions that still fit MacIntyre's definition: "A living tradition . . . is an historically extended, socially embodied argument, and an argument precisely in part about the goods which constitute that tradition."[3]

For the most part in this essay I will focus on one great tradition, Christianity, and its debate within the American context about a cluster of health-related goods. However, it is important to acknowledge that the argument about the good called *health* that has developed in America is an argument involving many traditions — religious and otherwise. One could describe our American experience as an argument of arguments. (Even Christianity's argument is really a family of arguments, taking place among, within, and beyond the many denominations that complicate America's religious history.) Some of these arguments, such as those conducted by Native American traditions, predate the Christian arguments that have taken place here. Åke Hultkrantz, for example, has identified two "ideological complexes" among the pre-Columbian North Americans. Those who embraced the old hunting ideology concentrated on appeasing high gods or guardian spirits in order to maintain or restore health. Another major approach to health was embraced by Native Americans who manifested an ideology of cosmic balance. These earliest Americans concentrated on restoring cosmic harmony through their rituals rather than negotiating with

3. MacIntyre, *After Virtue: A Study in Moral Theory,* 2d ed. (Notre Dame, Ind.: University of Notre Dame Press, 1984), p. 222. I am indebted to my colleague Craig Dykstra for calling my attention to MacIntyre's definition.

guardian spirits.[4] Within each of these complexes, countless varieties of proposals and practices about how to retrieve lost souls from another world or how to restore cosmic harmony were offered as healers, shamans, and medicine women went about their tasks.

In the closing years of the century that is the focus of this volume, one can no longer walk the halls of a major metropolitan hospital without encountering bearers of many of the world's religious traditions, each embodying arguments about health and healing. Muslims invoke their *hadith* (prophetic traditions); Hindus draw upon traditions that derive from ancient Ayurvedic medicine; Africans bring Akan, Bantu, or *ngoma* practices and understandings; and so on. In each case, traditions are being represented and reinvigorated as new generations debate, ponder, and argue about what to do and believe.[5] Like most human arguments, the great American argument about health occurs at a variety of levels of consciousness and across many dimensions of human life. It is much more than a reflective debate or a dispassionate discussion. This argument is a collision of ways of life at the many intersections where human flourishing and survival is at stake.

What is the argument about? In a word, *health.* That word, of course, is so multivalent and so imprecise in modern discourse that it can mean everything and nothing. The meaning of *health* can range from "I'm feeling fine at the moment" to "the kidney in Room 311A is functioning well" to "the health of the global ecosystem is at risk." Such conventional usage suggests that our arguments about health can be narrowly focused or all-encompassing. In 1946, the World Health Organization (WHO) offered a definition that indicates how broad the argument can be. For the post–World War II architects of WHO, *health* equaled "complete physical, mental and social well-being."[6] Many, especially within the world of modern medicine, have opted for narrower, more focused definitions. For them, health has to do with the full and proper physical and mental functioning of the human person. As Christians and representatives of other American traditions built large urban hospitals, opened homeless shelters and food pantries, or

4. Hultkrantz, "Health, Religion, and Medicine in Native American Traditions," in *Healing and Restoring: Health and Medicine in the World's Religious Traditions,* ed. Lawrence E. Sullivan (New York: Macmillan, 1989), pp. 329-30.

5. For an excellent introduction to many of the world's religious traditions and their approaches to health, see Sullivan (ed.), *Healing and Restoring.*

6. The World Health Organization's definition is quoted and discussed in Daniel Callahan's, "The WHO Definition of 'Health,'" *Hastings Center Studies* 1 (1973), pp. 77-87.

created holistic health centers in their church basements, they were positioning themselves somewhere along the spectrum of meanings that hover around health.

In 1961 Paul Tillich offered one of the century's most complex and expansive definitions. For Tillich, a theologian, health was a "multidimensional unity" consisting of mechanical, chemical, biological, psychological, spiritual, and historical dimensions. Seeking to honor the precision of various narrow definitions, Tillich also sought to relate the various dimensions of health in an interactive model. An imbalance in one area — even too much of a good thing — could lead to dysfunction elsewhere.[7]

In this essay it will be necessary to work from Tillich's more complex and interactive understanding in order to grasp the full argument about health. As Americans came to terms with death, illness, madness, and suffering, as they sought to care, cure, and heal, to do justice and show compassion, as they interpreted the enduring mysteries of suffering, aging, birth, dying, and sexuality, as they wove all of those mysteries, problems, and experiences into individual biographies, ethnic, community, and national histories, they argued about one of the most elemental of all human goods: health. It was an argument about practices, institutions, and meanings.

About Practices

There are certain ways that humans care for each other. Some of them seem "natural." Like the animals, human parents care for offspring, build places to keep warm and safe, search for food, and defend against encroachers. But other ways that we care are unnatural, products of the cultures that we create. Over centuries these ways become practices, established patterns of behavior. They often take complex institutional form, and they participate in larger structures of meaning.

In the American argument about health, the religious communities contended over a wide range of practices. Most prominent among them were care for the suffering and dying, curing illness (something

7. See Tillich, "The Meaning of Health," in *On Moral Medicine: Theological Perspectives in Medical Ethics,* ed. Stephen E. Lammers and Allen Verhey (Grand Rapids: William B. Eerdmans, 1987), pp. 161-65. I discuss both Tillich's and the WHO definitions of health in "Health," in the *New Handbook of Christian Theology,* ed. Donald W. Musser and Joseph L. Price (Nashville: Abingdon Press, 1992), pp. 213-16.

quite different from care), and fostering well-being through health-producing disciplines. The debate went, inevitably, in every direction.

When the European settlers began to establish their colonies in North America, part of the baggage that they carried along consisted of established and distinctive patterns of pastoral care. In his *History of Pastoral Care in America: From Salvation to Self-Realization,* E. Brooks Holifield has traced the complex transitions that occurred in the practices of American clergy as they attempted to meet the spiritual needs of their congregation and community members. The magnitude of that change can be sensed by listening in on two pastoral conversations, one from the late nineteenth century and the other from the 1950s. In *Helps and Hints in Pastoral Theology* (1874), Presbyterian William Plumer described a visit he had made to a sick young woman. After the traditional pastoral prayer, she cried out in despair, "Oh, I am dying unprepared; do pray for me again. I am going to hell!" Plumer went to work on her salvation:

> There is something which God requires *you* to do. The Lord Jesus Christ has died on the cross of Calvary to atone for sin, that guilty sinners through faith in his name might be saved from destruction. God requires you now *to believe this truth,* and accept of the righteousness of his atoning blood as your covering from the guilt of sin.[8]

Seventy-seven years later, Carroll A. Wise, professor of pastoral psychology and counseling at Methodist Garrett Biblical Institute, shared a case from his experience. In *Pastoral Counseling: Its Theory and Practice* (1951) Wise held up as a model pastoral conversation one that helped a young woman clarify her feelings and experience the counselor's acceptance. The young woman went through a litany of modern struggles. She wanted to quit smoking but could not; she wanted to find a marriage partner, but her expectations were unfulfillable; her job was unpromising. In each case the counselor reflected her feelings back in an accepting manner. The "client" would present her feelings:

> I think that the trouble is that I have no goal in life. I just seem to live from day to day. I ought to have a goal. I do have one, in a way. But still I don't do much about it. I don't know if I am mixed up or what. Sometimes I feel it is a matter of security. I have never felt I

8. Plumer, quoted by Holifield in *A History of Pastoral Care in America: From Salvation to Self-Realization* (Nashville: Abingdon Press, 1983), pp. 161-62.

> had a home — that is, a real home. I had a place to live. But I never felt my parents cared for me.[9]

And the counselor would clarify: "It seems it has something to do with not having a goal and not feeling secure and loved at home?" As the subtitle of Holifield's history indicates, the caring task had become assisting self-realization rather than assuring salvation.

These two pastoral conversations are moments in a much larger and more complicated argument about the nature and purpose of pastoral care in America. As Holifield's book recounts, the argument crossed denominational lines and took place in numerous settings. It involved pastors, seminary professors, physicians, and psychiatrists. An important strand within that argument was the American encounter with psychotherapy. Some welcomed Sigmund Freud's insights and created pastoral psychology. Others shunned the therapy as counter to biblical and denominational doctrines. Another powerful strand of that argument began in 1925 as a reforming movement under the leadership of Anton Boisen and grew to take institutional form in clinical pastoral education, an approach to teaching pastoral care that is now firmly established in most seminary curricula and hospital chaplaincy programs. Voices of protest and concern about the drift of pastoral care have been raised as recently as 1976, in Don Browning's *The Moral Context of Pastoral Care,* and 1984, in Thomas Oden's *Care of Souls in the Classic Tradition.*[10]

There is no way that we can estimate the number of pastoral care interchanges that have occurred during the American experiment. But these interchanges were frontline situations in which the argument about care went on. In these small, often one-on-one interchanges, pastors and lay visitors brought traditions of caring into confrontation with new dilemmas and challenges. Behind the frontlines, as pastors attempted to improve their practice of ministry through books written for peers and students, the argument expanded to confront changing assumptions about care and human need. By itself, one situation of pastoral care seems like only a snippet of a great tradition's argument with its age. But when those snippets are put into relation with each

9. Wise, quoted by Holifield in *A History of Pastoral Care in America,* pp. 301-2.

10. Browning, *The Moral Context of Pastoral Care* (Philadelphia: Westminster Press, 1976); Oden, *Care of Souls in the Classic Tradition* (Philadelphia: Fortress Press, 1984).

other and with other facets of the argument, we begin to recognize just how extensive the argument was.

But the argument also was about healing and curing. In colonial America, the argument about healing involved encounters with medicine's limited repertoire and with a variety of folk remedies and wisdoms. For example, in the late seventeenth and early eighteenth centuries, the great Puritan preacher Cotton Mather advocated inoculation for smallpox at the same time that he affirmed that God was the Great Physician and sin the ultimate cause of sickness and disease. While the author of *The Angel of Bethesda* (which James H. Smylie has described as "the first book of medicine written on this side of the Atlantic") welcomed medicine's scientific gift, he drew an uncompromising line against witchcraft and the occult practices that were frequently employed in the colonial pursuit of health.[11] Alongside, in addition to, and occasionally in protest against these other strands of the argument about cure and healing, colonial and early national Christians prayed in church and at home for God's supernatural help, remembering Jesus' miracles of healing and his empowerment of the disciples to heal.

As the nineteenth century progressed, more voices were added to the argument. Medicine became a profession and joined forces with the modern research university to open up a wide variety of treatments and explanations that often challenged traditional assumptions about cure. Many members of America's religious communities welcomed the new medicine and, as we will see below, became partners in creating the new cathedrals of health care in which scientific medicine could be practiced. But others resisted. New religious voices, often coming from groups that placed a priority on health and healing, made the argument more complex and contradictory. Mary Baker Eddy, for example, rejected the Protestant type of accommodation that Mather had forged with science and invented her new Christian Science, with its alternative approach to healing and illness. Her type of science was really an idealism that asserted that there was "no Life, Substance, or Intelligence in matter. That all is mind and there is no matter." Eddy viewed illness and death as illusions that could be treated by Christian practitioners

11. For Cotton Mather's place in the Reformed tradition's argument about health and healing, see James H. Smylie, "The Reformed Tradition," in *Caring and Curing: Health and Medicine in the Western Religious Traditions,* ed. Darrell Amundsen and Ronald L. Numbers (New York: Macmillan, 1986), pp. 204-35. For a discussion of popular interest in witchcraft and the occult, see Jon Butler, *Awash in a Sea of Faith: Christianizing the American People* (Cambridge: Harvard University Press, 1990). For Mather's response, see pp. 72-73.

who *demonstrated* the healing that came when the truth about God and matter was proclaimed.[12] In his recent *Health and Medicine in the Christian Science Tradition,* the late Robert Peel, author of the definitive biography on Eddy and contemporary apologist for the tradition, provides ample evidence of how this small group within the American religious ecosystem continues to argue about cure. A cherished strategy is the testimonial of a healing. For example, Peel recounts a hazardous birth experience of a woman whose labor was impeded by a baby presenting a shoulder that was blocking normal delivery. After X-rays confirmed the problem, a physician advised an immediate Caesarean section delivery. The family joined with its practitioner and prayed. Fifteen minutes later, according to the published testimony, the woman requested re-examination. Normal delivery had become possible even though the medical authorities claimed that such a change was medically impossible.[13]

The Christian Scientists' argument with America about cure has extended into the courtrooms of the land, as the 1967 case of *Commonwealth of Massachusetts v. Sheridan* indicates. Ms. Sheridan was convicted of involuntary manslaughter for the death of her five year-old daughter, whom she had elected to treat with Christian Science.[14]

Eddy's teachings, although novel, were not the only claims made in the modern portion of the argument about cure. From within the more established mainline portion of the American religious community came a strong counterargument. Princeton theologian Benjamin B. Warfield delivered lectures under the title *Counterfeit Miracles* in 1918 that reasserted John Calvin's belief that medical cure is a gift from God. With Eddy firmly in his sights, but also taking aim at the newly emerging evangelical-fundamentalist strand of the argument represented by faith healers A. B. Simpson and A. J. Gordon, Warfield argued that

> Miracles do not appear on the pages of Scripture vagrantly, here, there, and elsewhere indifferently, without assignable reason. They belong to revelation periods, and appear only when God is speaking to His people through accredited messengers declaring His gracious purposes. Their abundant display in the Apostolic Church is the

12. For a presentation of Mary Baker Eddy's life and teaching, along with a historical overview of the Christian Science tradition, see Rennie B. Schoepflin, "The Christian Science Tradition," in *Caring and Curing,* pp. 421-46.

13. See Peel, *Health and Medicine in the Christian Science Tradition* (New York: Crossroad, 1988), p. 73.

14. See Peel, *Health and Medicine in the Christian Science Tradition,* p. 110.

> mark of the richness of the Apostolic age in revelation; and when this revelation period closed, the period of miracle-working had passed by also, as a mere matter of course.[15]

The argument about health was not confined to debates about how illness could be overcome, however. There were also numerous proposals for how one could prevent illness by following certain disciplines. Again, some of the made-in-America versions of Christianity led the way in shaping the argument. The Mormons, for example, maintained a life-style that was so successful in reducing incidences of cancer, heart disease, cirrhosis, and birth defects that by the 1970s leading medical journals were reporting studies that documented their distinctiveness. While the medical reporters frequently pointed to abstinence from tobacco and alcohol as the primary explanatory factors, other elements of the Mormon life-style also were acknowledged, such as low levels of promiscuity, early childbearing, abstinence from coffee and tea, and reduced stress.

This form of the argument was not conducted in seminar rooms or through literary salvos. Rather, the wards of the Mormon church and the homes of its members were places where Prophet Joseph Smith's *Word of Wisdom,* first announced in 1833, evoked a health-enhancing discipline.[16]

Other religious communities, such as the Adventists, made similar contributions to the argument by carefully nurturing healthy diets, rhythms of sleep, styles of dress, and proscriptions of "excessive" sex (especially masturbation). The Adventists are instructive for other reasons as well. The American argument about health did not simply occur between members of contending religious communities, or between their spokespersons and representatives of medicine, or in opposition to interpreters of the law. The argument was waged *within* these communities as well. In 1907 John Harvey Kellogg, the founder of the Battle Creek Sanitarium and one-time close ally of Ellen Gould White, the prophetess of Adventism, was disfellowshiped because he was not fully appreciative of "the gifts now manifest in the church" — that is to say, White. Kellogg, who had led the medical side of the Adventists' early health-care efforts, took the Sanitarium, the American Medical Mission-

15. Warfield, quoted by Gary B. Ferngren in "The Evangelical-Fundamentalist Tradition," in *Caring and Curing,* p. 493.

16. On the recent medical interest in the Mormon life-style and the significance of Smith's *Word of Wisdom,* see Lester E. Bush, Jr., "The Mormon Tradition," in *Caring and Curing,* pp. 414-15, 399-400.

ary College, and his flaked cereal with him, thus depriving the denomination of what would become a powerful source of income. White and her followers went on to create Loma Linda University as their new medical school, and eventually a new system of hospitals replaced the early Kellogg-run institutions.[17]

The mainstream religious communities were also struggling with discipline, with varying degrees of success. Most prominent among their efforts was the prohibition drive, which culminated in a constitutional amendment in 1919. The Methodists, drawing on a tradition of healthy-mindedness and discipline from the days when John Wesley wrote *Primitive Physick* in 1747, worked in both the North and the South in the period after the Civil War to prevent any consumption of alcohol. Even after the Twenty-first Amendment repealed the Volstead Act in 1933, the Methodist Board of Temperance cooperated with the Yale Center of Alcohol Studies, Alcoholics Anonymous, and others to combat what was coming to be called the "disease" of alcoholism. As late as 1959, a national survey indicated that 63 percent of Methodists endorsed voluntary abstinence and national prohibition. The United Methodist Church's *Book of Discipline* carried on the argument in 1972, announcing that abstinence from alcohol and marijuana was "a faithful witness to God's liberating and redeeming love."[18]

About Institutions

As the United States experienced the great modern processes of immigration, urbanization, industrialization, and bureaucratization, the traditional face-to-face patterns of care became increasingly inadequate. These modern pressures led many to attempt to reform existing institutions; they also became occasions for others to invent new ones.

The Social Gospel movement, for example, can be read, at least in part, as a profound questioning of the adequacy of nineteenth-century congregations, denominations, and other religious institutions to meet the life-and-death needs of people in the American cities. The argument took many forms and resulted in the creation of new cooperative institutions such as the Federal Council of Churches at the national

17. For a summary of the Adventist experience, see Ronald L. Numbers and David R. Larson, "The Adventist Tradition," in *Caring and Curing,* pp. 447-67.

18. See Harold Y. Vanderpool, "The Wesleyan-Methodist Tradition," in *Caring and Curing,* pp. 340-41.

level and many "institutional churches," hospitals, and other caring agencies in the greater metropolitan areas. It has continued throughout the century, going through various episodes of experiment and retrenchment as the national energies and resources waxed and waned.[19]

Congregations, the primary local religious institutions throughout the American religious story, experienced what Sidney E. Ahlstrom called "a tidal wave of questioning."[20] The questioning took many forms. Early in the twentieth century, the Reverend Dr. Elwood Worcester led Emmanuel Church, then the largest Episcopal congregation in Boston, into what Allison Stokes described as "the first American venture between clergy and doctors in the cure of souls." Through the congregation's program of lectures, classes, publications, and private counseling, clergy (Worcester and Samuel McComb) and physicians (Richard Cabot, James Jackson Putnam, and Isador Coriat) sought to infuse a "psychical movement" into the Social Gospel enterprise and a holistic perspective into health care. By 1909 the Emmanuel team of clergy and physicians had received over five thousand applications for a pre-Freudian type of psychotherapy and boasted as many as six hundred people in attendance for just one of its classes. When the Emmanuel Movement peaked in 1911, its leaders had addressed the nervous disorders of Americans in such popular magazines as *Good Housekeeping* and *Ladies' Home Journal*.[21]

Much later in the century, Granger Westberg made new attempts to change the character of congregations by developing Wholistic Health Centers in congregations. These attempts to make congregations into clinics staffed by doctors, nurses, and pastors, were attempts to bridge the steadily widening gap between the religious world of the local church and the medical world of the hospital. Westberg's original model, pioneered in the 1970s at Union Church in Hinsdale, Illinois, proved too costly and ambitious for most local congregations, so in the 1980s Westberg joined with Lutheran General Health Care System in Park Ridge, Illinois, to experiment with a "Parish Nurse" program. Here the idea was to add a nurse to the professional staff of a congregation

19. I have sketched the outlines of the debate about the relevance and value of American congregations in *Places of Worship* (Nashville: Association of State and Local History, 1990), pp. 106-9.

20. Ahlstrom, *A Religious History of the American People* (New Haven: Yale University Press, 1972), p. 604.

21. See Allison Stokes, *Ministry after Freud* (New York: Pilgrim Press, 1985), pp. 22-25.

so that the congregation's ministry could expand to include the primary health needs of its members and community.[22]

The argument about the role of the congregation was far more complex than either Worcester's or Westberg's experiments indicate. In 1988 Dr. Constance C. Conrad sampled a number of American congregations and identified twenty different "church models" for providing health-care services. Congregations were offering education, special advocacy, funding, and direct services in areas of nutrition, fitness, substance abuse, sexual behavior, environmental health, infectious diseases, chronic illness, and so on. Some congregations worked alone; more frequently they created coalitions of congregations, public health agencies, and denominational offices to carry out their ministries.[23] Taken as a whole, Conrad's catalogue of models indicates that the argument about congregational roles in the American pursuit of health is pervasive and increasingly variegated. In addition, others, such as theologian James M. Gustafson, urged congregations to play distinctive roles in the public debate about health by becoming "communities of moral discourse."[24] Advocates of this latter role seek to make congregations not merely frontline participants in the argument about health in America, but hosts and shapers of the very argument itself.

Not all of the institutional argument about health took place within and about congregations. Other arenas of conflict included the health-care professions, most notably medicine itself. The late nineteenth and early twentieth centuries were a period in which America powerfully reorganized its life around the idea of professions. The modern research university with its graduate schools, disciplines, and specialties joined with professional organizations to reorder American work and values. So determinative has this transition been in the formation of modern American life that Burton J. Bledstein has labeled the

22. See Granger E. Westberg and Jill Westberg McNamara, *The Parish Nurse* (Park Ridge, Ill..: Parish Nurse Resource Center, 1987).

23. Conrad, "A Vision of the Possible: A Sampling of Programs in Religious Communities," *Healthy People 2000: A Role for America's Religious Communities* (Atlanta and Chicago: The Carter Center and the Park Ridge Center, 1990), pp. 36-39.

24. Gustafson, "The Church: A Community of Moral Discourse," in *The Church as Moral Decision Maker* (Philadelphia: Pilgrim Press, 1970), pp. 83-95. I make explicit use of Gustafson's image in "Congregations and Medical Ethics," *Chicago Theological Seminary Register* 78 (Fall 1988): 5-13; and "The Congregation as a Place of Healing: One Congregation's Experience," *Second Opinion* 13 (March 1990): 76-88.

product of this change the "culture of professionalism."[25] The consequences of this change for American health have been enormous.

Physicians played pivotal roles in this transition. In *The Social Transformation of American Medicine,* Paul Starr summarized the magnitude of the change of the social place of the physician:

> In the nineteenth century, the medical profession was generally weak, divided, insecure in its status and its income, unable to control entry into practice or to raise the standards of medical education. In the twentieth century, not only did physicians become a powerful, prestigious, and wealthy profession, but they succeeded in shaping the basic organization and financial structure of American medicine.

The result, claims Starr, was the achievement of "professional sovereignty" that was paradigmatic and exceptional — "paradigmatic in the sense that other professions emulate its example; exceptional in that none have been able to achieve its singular degree of economic power and cultural authority."[26]

Members of various religious communities moved into this powerful professional context with distinctive religious commitments and perspectives. Their participation in the argument about health took several forms. David M. Feldman describes how Jewish physicians manifested their tradition's fundamental "mandate to heal." For Jews, "preservation of life and health is a mitzvah (commandment) of first rank; by permission and obligation they call for 'setting aside the rest of the Torah,' such as Sabbath and Yom Kippur." Building on a tradition with a rich legacy of medical practice, American Jews assumed preeminent places in the ranks of modern medicine. Names such as Jonas Salk and Albert Sabin, who overcame polio with their vaccines, represent the aggressive commitment to medical science that welcomed and discovered some of the great gifts of twentieth-century medicine.[27]

But while many members of religious communities became champions of scientific and high technology medicine, there were also religious voices from within the professions that expressed cautions

25. Bledstein, *The Culture of Professionalism: The Middle Class and the Development of Higher Education in America* (New York: W. W. Norton, 1976).

26. Starr, *The Social Transformation of American Medicine: The Rise of a Sovereign Profession and the Making of a Vast Industry* (New York: Basic Books, 1982), pp. 6-7, 28-29.

27. Feldman, *Health and Medicine in the Jewish Tradition* (New York: Crossroad, 1986), pp. 21, 47.

and, at times, grave concern. Dr. David Hilfiker, a family practitioner who began his career in Grand Marais, Minnesota, had a vocational crisis that led to a decision to become staff physician serving homeless men at Christ House in Washington, D.C. In the 12 January 1984 issue of *The New England Journal of Medicine,* Hilfiker went public about mistakes he had made in his practice, the most weighty being an unintentional abortion. After sharing his pain over his "mistakes," the physician protested the way his profession dealt with its failures:

> Doctors hide their mistakes from patients, from other doctors, even from themselves. Open discussion of mistakes is banished from the consultation room, from the operating room, from physicians' meetings. Mistakes become gossip, and are spoken of openly only in court. Unable to admit our mistakes, we physicians are cut off from healing. We cannot ask for forgiveness, and we get none. We are thwarted, stunted; we do not grow.[28]

Experiences of individual physicians, whether those of great discoverers like Salk or wounded healers like Hilfiker indicate that many of the key arguments about health are restricted to the private musings and personal deliberations of health-care professionals. But those arguments then take social form as the healers go about their business.

In *The Physician's Covenant,* William F. May, a Presbyterian ethicist, discloses how deep the professional arguments can be. May argues that a number of powerful metaphors are at work in modern medicine, that physicians often see themselves and are seen by others in one of a number of roles — as parents who make difficult decisions on behalf of others, as fighters who wage war against death, as technicians who master complex procedures and technology, as teachers who impart information and wisdom, or as covenant-makers who enter into privileged relationships with suffering human beings. May's book is a religiously informed argument in favor of covenantal and teacher images and in opposition to mere fighter or technician self-understandings. As physicians struggle with their own sense of their proper role vis-à-vis patients, they participate in an argument in which religious images and understandings have played a part and continue to do so.[29] William May's voice is just one of a growing cohort of medical ethicists, some

28. The article, "Facing Our Mistakes," is reprinted in Hilfiker's *Healing the Wounds: A Physician Looks at His Work* (New York: Pantheon Books, 1985), pp. 72-86.

29. See May, *The Physician's Covenant: Images of the Healer in Medical Ethics* (Philadelphia: Westminster Press, 1983).

clinicians and some academics, who are now lifting the argument about health to new levels.

America's religious communities also carried on the argument about health by creating their own new institutions, chief among them being the hospital, which in turn evolved into the medical center. In *The Care of Strangers: The Rise of America's Hospital System,* Charles E. Rosenberg recounts the history of the hospital in America. In 1800 there were only two institutions "dedicated exclusively to inpatient care of the sick," one in Philadelphia and one in New York City. Throughout the antebellum period hospitals were essentially almshouses that warehoused the dependent sick. "No gentleman of property or standing would have found himself in a hospital unless stricken with insanity or felled by epidemic or accident in a strange city." When the first survey of American hospitals was taken in 1873, 178 were counted (including mental institutions); they had less than fifty thousand beds among them. By 1909 there were 4,359 hospitals with 421,065 beds (not counting mental or chronic disease hospitals such as tuberculosis sanitariums).[30]

As dramatic as the surge in institutional creativity was during the late nineteenth and early twentieth centuries, the numerical boom of the hospital industry is only part of the story. The character of the institutions themselves had also dramatically changed: "Initiated in the late eighteenth and early nineteenth centuries as a welfare institution framed and motivated by the responsibilities of Christian stewardship, the twentieth-century American hospital has tended to see itself as a necessary response to scientific understanding and the hope of secular healing."[31]

Within the larger institutional history of the American hospital, religious communities made their own significant contributions. Sometimes, as when the Quakers invented the first American asylum (the Friends Asylum for the Insane outside Philadelphia) in 1817 or when Unitarians such as Dorothea Dix crusaded for new kinds of asylums that offered "moral treatment" later in the nineteenth century, religious leaders advanced the institutional argument to new levels.[32] At other times they offered denominational versions of existing institutions. The Methodists, for example, opened their first hospital, Seney Methodist Episcopal Hospital, in Brooklyn in 1882. By 1960 they were operating

30. Rosenberg, *The Care of Strangers: The Rise of America's Hospital System* (New York: Basic Books, 1987), pp. 4-5.

31. Rosenberg, *The Care of Strangers,* p. 8.

32. For the early history of asylums and "moral treatment," see Constance M. McGovern, *Masters of Madness: Social Origins of the American Psychiatric Profession* (Hanover, N.H.: University Press of New England, 1985).

seventy-six general hospitals in the United States. By the time of the Second Vatican Council, American Catholics were operating 950 hospitals, which served sixteen million patients a year. The Roman Catholic institutional presence also included 376 homes for the aged and 337 nursing schools.[33]

Many of these hospitals arose out of distinctive denominational identities and motives. They often served particular denominational and ethnic constituencies. As the twentieth century progressed, distinctive religious identities became increasingly problematic. Some, including Fredric Norstad, one of the founders of Lutheran General Hospital outside Chicago, entered the argument against particularity, arguing in the fifties, "I no longer believe in Church-owned hospitals. I don't see that they are any different from any other hospital." The choice facing religious hospitals was to adopt inclusive, ecumenical identities or to turn their energies away from high-technology medicine to other forms of health care. A few, such as Oral Roberts, attempted to create new, distinctive types of hospitals. Roberts's $150 million City of Faith Medical and Research Center in Tulsa, Oklahoma, was intended to be the "Mayo Clinic of the Southwest," but with a Pentecostal difference. Boasting accredited schools of medicine, dentistry, and nursing, a sixty-story clinic, a thirty-story hospital, and a twenty-story laboratory, the City of Faith set out to forge a new relationship between the worlds of faith healing and modern medicine. Each entering patient was assigned a physician, nurse, and prayer partner, a healing partnership that stretched both Pentecostal and secular approaches to cure.[34]

About Meanings

The arguments about practices and institutions participate in an enormous, convoluted, and sprawling argument about health-related meanings. As the religious communities of America have contended with one another and the challenges posed by the modern quest for health, they have found themselves in the midst of debates about almost all of their deepest beliefs.

The age-old question of the meaning of suffering continues to

33. Vanderpool, "The Wesleyan-Methodist Tradition," p. 339; Marvin R. O'Connell, "The Roman Catholic Tradition since 1545," in *Caring and Curing,* p. 136.

34. See Carter Lindberg, "The Lutheran Tradition," in *Caring and Curing,* p. 196; and Grant Wacker, "The Pentecostal Tradition," in *Caring and Curing,* p. 531.

demand answers. Throughout the history of the Christian tradition, a variety of understandings of suffering have existed in tension with each other. On the one hand, suffering is seen as the result of sin and the Fall. It is a tragedy, a powerfully heavy burden that humanity brought upon itself. Or it is punishment, God's chastising rod. On the other hand, suffering has at times been viewed as a means used by God to bring about spiritual growth.

All of these understandings vied and continue to vie with each other in the American argument. A few have gone as far as the great English preacher Charles Haddon Spurgeon, who late in the nineteenth century claimed that

> the greatest earthly blessing that God can give to any of us is health, *with the exception of sickness.* Sickness has frequently been of more use to the saint of God than health has. . . . A sick wife, a newly made grave, poverty, slander, sinking of spirit, might teach us lessons nowhere else to be learned so well. Trials drive us to the realities of religion.

In 1981, the American evangelist Billy Graham affirmed that the "fire of chastening purifies our lives and deepens our spirit." But he also made room for uncertainty: "When God allows these things to happen, there is a reason which will eventually be known to the individual — most likely not until we get to heaven."[35]

Others have found it more difficult to reconcile human suffering and divine causality. In the same year Graham found positive value in suffering, Rabbi Harold S. Kushner wrote the best-seller *When Bad Things Happen to Good People.* Writing out of his own experience of tragedy, Kushner sought to break the cause-and-effect linkage between God and human suffering.

> I believe in God. But I do not believe the same things about Him that I did years ago, when I was growing up or when I was a theological student. I recognize His limitations. He is limited in what He can do by laws of nature and by the evolution of human nature and human moral freedom. I no longer hold God responsible for illnesses, accidents, and natural disasters, because I realize that I gain little and I lose so much when I blame God for those things. I can worship a God who hates suffering but cannot eliminate it, more

35. Spurgeon and Graham are quoted by Timothy P. Weber in "The Baptist Tradition," in *Caring and Curing,* pp. 291-92.

> easily than I can worship a God who chooses to make children suffer and die, for whatever exalted reason.[36]

The argument about the meaning of suffering has taken place in the individual consciousness of numberless Americans, has been the subject of countless sermons, has lurked beneath many of the questions that Americans raised as they struggled with new quandaries posed by heroic treatments and prolonged processes of dying. Part of the question has had to do with the nature and existence of God. Another part has had to do with the origins of evil itself.

An example of how the question of suffering hides behind modern bioethical dilemmas was provided by ethicist Stanley Hauerwas in a discussion of the modern approach to care for the mentally retarded. Writing in response to the new "screening" diagnostic techniques that make it possible to identify retarded children long before they are born, Hauerwas asserted that "early abortion of handicapped children has become the medical 'therapy' of choice." Behind the issue was a secular approach to suffering: "Too often medicine becomes the means by which, in the name of humanity, we eliminate those who suffer." In his view, this modern understanding, which views suffering as a problem to be eliminated rather than as a mystery that can reveal, leads to an enormous deception about the nature of humanity. The quest for suffering-free existence masks the truth that "we are incomplete beings who depend on one another for our existence." At its root, his argument is with the Enlightenment tradition of autonomy, which, in his judgment, distorts our understanding of human nature itself.[37]

Another of the major topics in the argument about meanings has been human sexuality, especially in terms of its relationship to procreation. Perhaps no American religious community has been as torn over these questions as have the Roman Catholics. In *Health and Medicine in the Catholic Tradition,* Richard A. McCormick identifies "moments of development" in the Catholic argument from the time of Thomas Aquinas to the twentieth century:

> first, couples must *positively* pursue procreation; next, sexual relations are permissible if couples *do not positively exclude* procreation

36. Kushner, *When Bad Things Happen to Good People* (New York: Schocken Books, 1981), p. 134.

37. Hauerwas, *Suffering Presence: Theological Reflections on Medicine, the Mentally Handicapped, and the Church* (Notre Dame, Ind.: University of Notre Dame Press, 1986), pp. 160, 163, 10.

and other motives are acceptable so long as the act is not vitiated; finally, sexual relations are permissible even though there is the *intent to avoid* procreation (periodic continence).

The evolution from understandings of sexuality that were governed exclusively by procreation to understandings that allowed greater affirmation of human intimacy for its own sake was interrupted when Pius XI published the encyclical *Casti connubii* in 1930. Affirming that marriage and intimacy are secondary ends of of sexual expression and that procreation is primary, Pius condemned artificial contraception. Even the *aggiornamento* of Vatican II that sought to overcome the Augustinian dualism of natural law (procreation) in opposition to original sin (sexual desire) with an understanding of the integrity of the human person was unable to resolve the Catholic argument. In 1968 Pope Paul VI added his encyclical *Humanae Vitae,* which inflamed the argument further by, in the eyes of many, returning to the "procreative criterion." If the only appropriate purpose of sexual expression is procreation in the context of marriage, then extramarital sex, homosexuality, contraception, artificial insemination, and all other "unnatural" interventions into the procreative act are wrong.

The Catholic argument about healthy (moral) sexual expression quickly expanded to include other dimensions. Popes in Italy were creating pastoral and theological problems for bishops, theologians, and laypeople in the United States. A group of theologians meeting at Marquette University later in 1968 concluded that the encyclical had raised a host of questions about the teaching authority of the Magisterium. In 1980 American bishop John R. Quinn declared to a synod of bishops meeting to discuss the well-being of the family that many people of goodwill did not accept the "intrinsic evil of each and every use of contraception." He pointed to the Catholic Church's tradition of doctrinal development and insisted that "this problem is not going to be solved or reduced merely by a simple reiteration of past formulations or by ignoring the fact of dissent." And surveys of laypeople indicated that more than three-fourths of American Catholic women practiced some form of contraception and that more than 90 percent of those used methods condemned in official formulations.[38]

The argument about sexuality crossed all the denominations and manifested itself at many levels. At the same time that the Roman Cath-

38. For a summary and evaluation of the official argument about sexuality in the Roman Catholic Church, see McCormick, *Health and Medicine in the Catholic Tradition* (New York: Crossroad, 1984), pp. 86-104.

olic hierarchy was reiterating its traditional understanding, the Anglican Church was revising its prayer book in the opposite direction. The 1979 prayer book placed procreation last in its list of purposes for marriage; preceding it were "mutual joy" of the couple, and their "help and comfort." The Anglicans were also reconsidering homosexuality. In 1967 the General Convention of the Episcopal Church had urged its American members to study the question carefully. In 1976 the Convention affirmed that "homosexual persons are children of God who have a full and equal claim with all other persons upon the love, acceptance, and pastoral concern and care of the Church." In 1979 the Church's Commission of Human Affairs and Health concluded that homosexual behavior "constitutes a disqualification for ordination" but argued that if a priest, homosexual or heterosexual, could live "a life which is a wholesome example to Christ's flock," then that person could be ordained.[39]

As the twentieth century progressed, the constellation of arguments swirling around questions related to human sexuality and procreation steadily increased. The fierce abortion debate that emerged following the U.S. Supreme Court's *Roe v. Wade* decision on 22 January 1973 that made abortion a legal choice is but one example. Here religious groups played explicit public roles, as denominations adopted pro-choice or pro-life positions. Many of the mainline religious groups, with the notable exception of the Catholic Church, affirmed the right of women to have abortions, but they often disagreed over which circumstances were sufficient and which were not. Within the denominations, these statements occasioned further arguments, and many members of American religious communities joined the argument as they lobbied legislatures, picketed hospitals and clinics, or rallied in large public protests.

The burgeoning medical ethics industry that also emerged in the second half of the century is another sign of the proliferation of meaning questions that has occurred in the great American argument about health. Behind many of the field's often technical dilemmas — withdrawal of feeding tubes for dying patients, experimentation on human subjects, surrogate motherhood, organ transplantation, genetic engineering, and the host of issues related to human sexuality — are fundamental questions about the nature of the human being. The remarkable advances in our scientific knowledge and technological capacities during the twentieth century have rendered much of our

39. John E. Booty, "The Anglican Tradition," in *Caring and Curing,* pp. 258-59, 264-65.

conventional wisdom about human nature, whether that wisdom is religious or secular, problematic.

A third major meaning question has to do with death — what St. Paul called "the last enemy" (1 Cor. 15:26). Death is also the great enemy of modern medicine. Interestingly enough, much of the argument about American health, especially as medicine became more proficient at defeating or at least postponing death, has been about what kind of enemy it is. The arguments about euthanasia, the right to die, termination of treatment, and many of the risky experimental treatments, such as the artificial heart placed into the chest of Mormon Barney Clark by Mormon surgeon Dr. William DeVries in 1982, are topical evidences of a deeper argument about the meaning of death itself. That argument has been extensive and intricate. For the purposes of this essay, James M. Gustafson's argument about the penultimate value of human life distills the issue. "Physical life is the condition *sine qua non* for all other values of human life," says Gustafson; "thus there is always a presumption in favor of sustaining it, or in favor of research that will yield knowledge which will aid in its sustenance. But physical life is not of absolute value."[40]

In his writings about medical ethics, Gustafson regularly returns to classic Christian theological themes of the finitude and fallenness of human beings. He is concerned that modernity is turning human life into an absolute good, that humans are deceiving themselves about their own nature and the nature of the world, and, most importantly, that we are displacing God from the ultimate position in human concern. Because of its infinite pretensions, medicine is tempted to fight death as if preservation of life in whatever form is the greatest good, but in doing so it loses sight of the other goods of the creation. This argument about what earlier generations termed idolatry has been going on behind the scenes in the homes, universities, and hospitals of America for much of the second half of this century.

Gustafson's argument takes us to the nub of the American argument about health. In a recent interview he asserted that our culture needs to come to an acceptance of the fact of death, of human finitude. But then he raised a question about the value we place on health:

> Why aren't we asking what it is in our culture that exaggerates physical longevity as the desirable end of life? It can almost be said

40. Gustafson, *The Contributions of Theology to Medical Ethics* (Milwaukee: Marquette University Press, 1975), pp. 86-87.

> that health has replaced salvation as the chief end. What in our culture has given health the import that it has for us? The consequences of this are tremendous! I once read a sermon on the expulsive power of a great affection. Health has become the great affection, and it has the power to expel a great many things of value.[41]

Conclusion

This essay is an early and kaleidoscopic attempt to trace the contours and intricacy of an argument about health that has been a dominant concern of America's religious communities throughout their existence. It has also sought to render the argument more explicit, bringing many of its fragmented implicit dimensions into view. The great American argument about health has affected every dimension of American religious life, from the formal liturgies of worship to the institutions built by denominations to the courses taught at seminaries to the private lives of believers. The argument has taken place at many levels and in many forums — ranging from the local congregation to the denominational convention to the U.S. Supreme Court. It has challenged religious communities to answer some of the oldest questions of human existence in the context of ultramodern settings and practices.

The religious communities and traditions of America have responded to these challenges in a variety of ways. Some accepted modern medicine's gifts wholeheartedly and became, like the Jewish physicians Salk and Sabin, exemplars of modern scientific approaches of health. Others, such as Mary Baker Eddy's Christian Scientists and the early Pentecostalists, sought to oppose the materialistic and scientific approaches with radical alternatives. Still others, such as Samuel Worcester and his Emmanuel Movement or Granger Westberg and his parish nurses, sought to fashion new accommodations that stretched traditional understandings, practices, and institutions to include new ways of perceiving, acting, and ordering life that came from secular sources. At times these religious communities have seemed to act in clear opposition to the larger American culture that surrounded them. At other times they have seemed to follow the culture or even blaze the trail for new approaches to health. But each was a participant in an argument that reached across America at the same time that it was carried on within particular communities and traditions.

41. "All Things in Relation to God: An Interview with James M. Gustafson," *Second Opinion* 16 (March 1991): 95.

Where are we in the argument? None of the traditions seems immune to the effects of the controversy. Most are confused about their distinctive heritages; those who still remember their past practices and understandings find them difficult to retrieve and draw upon in our pluralistic context; many wonder about the viability of many of religion's institutions — denominations, congregations, church-related hospitals. A few — including the scholars mentioned by Marty — are beginning to move to a new stage in the argument.

In *Hospitality to Strangers,* Thomas W. Ogletree describes four distinctive moments of interpretation in normative traditions that may provide heuristic assistance to those trying to locate themselves within this great argument. The first of Ogletree's moments is "application" — the direct interpretation of a context in light of received (tradition-specific) common sense. This mode, still drawn upon by many who pray at the bedside of the ill, was the way that most members of American religious communities conducted the argument about health until the challenges of pluralism and new scientific approaches to health emerged in the American experiment. The second moment Ogletree calls "suspicion," and it occurs when axiomatic understandings fail or distort situations. The protests of the Social Gospel movement, the warnings of such ethicists as James Gustafson, and the experiments of those who pioneered in clinical pastoral education are examples of moments of suspicion about the ways in which conventional wisdom about health is being employed. Ogletree's third moment is the one that Marty pointed to in the quotations that occasioned this essay: "retrieval." Scholars such as Richard McCormick, William F. May, and the authors of the Health and Medicine in the Faith Tradition series are beginning "a new and deeper engagement with the longer traditions underlying the popular conventions which form present awareness." The fourth moment is what Ogletree calls "hospitality," a genuine encounter with "strange and unfamiliar meanings." It is a time when conversation with bearers of the genuinely new can lead to discovery and insight. The fourth moment in the interpretive process occurs after participants in the conversation have adequately prepared to encounter such differences and novelty.[42]

42. See Ogletree, *Hospitality to the Stranger* (Philadelphia: Fortress Press, 1985), pp. 112-21. I am grateful to Donald M. Braxton for pointing me to Ogletree's formulation. Ogletree is discussed at much greater length in Braxton's dissertation, "History and Responsibility: A Critical Comparison of Thomas Ogletree and Stanley Hauerwas" (Ph.D. diss., University of Chicago, 1992).

The great American argument about health seems to be situated about midway through Ogletree's hermeneutic process. Simple application of the wisdom of our various traditions seems increasingly problematic. Many voices of suspicion about our practices, institutions, and understandings have been raised throughout this century. But there are signs of retrieval occurring and some occasional attempts at hospitality. Whether these early efforts at retrieval will turn what has been a heated and fissiparous argument into a genuinely hospitable conversation about the health of the public (or better, the world) is the open question in the American experiment. For the argument to advance to that stage would require many more efforts at retrieval and equally strenuous efforts at carrying on a discourse in which each participant is prepared to offer a distinctive understanding or practice while being open to receiving those of the others. That rare combination of commitment and civility may be a difficult but necessary prescription for our cultural and religious ills.

NEW DIRECTIONS IN AMERICAN RELIGIOUS HISTORY

Body Politic and Body Perfect: Religion, Politics, and Thomsonian Medicine in Nineteenth-Century America

CATHERINE L. ALBANESE

Behold the great the sage M.D.
From College mill ground out;
A sheepskin his Diploma see,
A potent wand no doubt.

Arm'd with the title thus confer'd,
As with his lancet keen,
If so the public take his word,
No wiser head is seen.[1]

THE VERSE IS mid-nineteenth-century doggerel, spiced with a sarcasm that — if the word *scalpel* or similar were substituted for its *lancet* — might be attributed to a contemporary scorner of the medical profession. But this low estimate of American physicians, coming from the camp of unorthodox Thomsonian "herb doctors," expressed a common sentiment of its time. Regular physicians were often used grudgingly, with suspicion of their heroic procedures (the bleeding, blistering, and drugging of patients with mercuric compounds) and resentment at their bills. In its ordinary act of displeasure, the verse will serve as an introduction to a nineteenth-century discourse about power that, when scrutinized, can tell us much about social process. Moving from

1. "The M.D.," *The Thomsonian Scout,* 15 May 1842, p. 101.

concerns regarding social power to a rhetoric of the requirements for bodily perfection, this discourse illustrates how a public and political language can function to ease individuals into more privatized worlds. To add a second clause to my argument, this discourse suggests how a community can utilize a common — and covertly religious — rhetoric to preside over its own division and fragmentation.

In this context, two kinds of concerns frame my inquiry into the cultural world that produced the medical poem. First, I acknowledge a medical sociology and anthropology sensitive to issues of power. In a recent and lucid book addressing a contemporary set of issues, Peter Freund and Meredith McGuire alert us to the social construction of medical knowledge.[2] Such knowledge, they say, supports ideological agendas and legitimates the interests of already powerful individuals and groups. Summarizing a vast array of sociological and anthropological literature, the two authors point to a medical exercise of power orchestrated in a series of symbolic gestures through which professional dominance is achieved and maintained. Their work clears a path for understanding how a sick person, now as in an earlier era, might be inspired to acquire the trappings of a revolutionary.

Second, I acknowledge a recurring interpretive theme in American religious historiography and sociology. Contemporary American religion, we have been told, has become privatized, and American religious life is lived in a place apart from what Richard John Neuhaus has called the "naked public square." By the late twentieth century, according to Robert Bellah and his colleagues, the habits of American hearts could no longer be discovered in structures of community and tradition but instead in "autonomous individuals."[3]

The present, however, grew out of considerably older cultural events. Indeed, in his now-classic work *The Modern Schism,* Martin E. Marty located in the nineteenth century a profound shift in American culture — a shift by which "religious forces" learned to live with a "new social contract." According to the terms of this contract, religion addressed itself "to the personal, familial, and leisured sectors of life," while the public sphere became "autonomous" or came "under the

2. Freund and McGuire, *Health, Illness, and the Social Body: A Critical Sociology* (Englewood Cliffs, N.J.: Prentice-Hall, 1991); see especially pp. 203-58.

3. Neuhaus, *The Naked Public Square: Religion and Democracy in America* (Grand Rapids: William B. Eerdmans, 1984); Bellah et al., *Habits of the Heart: Individualism and Commitment in American Life* (Berkeley and Los Angeles: University of California Press, 1985); see especially pp. 275-96.

control of other kinds of tutelage." "An outer encompassing culture existed independently"; religion, on the other hand, was "inner" and "sequestered." Marty pointed to the 1840s as the key decade for a schismatic split between religion and the rest of culture, and he suggested that it was "possible to speak after these years of the privatizing of religion." Later, Marty more explicitly noted the role of Protestantism in American cultural transformation. If individual believers in the United States commuted between the two sides of a modern schism, that was because Protestantism provided an ideology for competition (and, thus, secularity and self-concern) in its "Christian individualism." So it was that Protestantism made the problem of community more acute.[4]

Such readings locate the significant transition in American culture — including religion — in the move from community to privacy. And they point to a historiographical set of questions that largely remain to be answered. How did the public culture — not just its religious infrastructure — become private? How, *in slow motion,* did the community come apart, and how did the autonomous individual emerge? Did the change that Marty saw in the 1840s occur all at once? Or could the tensions between what counted as public and what should be construed as private be seen at work earlier? And are there ways that we can begin to chart the process?

I

It is in an examination of Thomsonian herbal medicine, I believe, that we can bring together these concerns about an anthropology of power and about a historiography of politics and privatization. The world of the Thomsonians, although at first glance removed from my set of questions emphasizing religion, offers rich opportunities for a microstudy of power, politics, and perfectionism that casts light on religiocultural process. But first, who were Thomsonians, what was their movement, and where does it fit in a study of American healing?

Samuel Thomson (1769-1843), who led an army of healers already feuding internally as he lived, turned from New Hampshire farming to doctoring as a result of not uncommon experiences with

4. Marty, *The Modern Schism: Three Paths to the Secular* (New York: Harper & Row, 1969), pp. 98, 97-99; and *Protestantism,* History of Religion Series (1972; reprint, Garden City, N.Y.: Doubleday-Image Books, 1974), pp. 170-71.

illness and death among family members. Early, too, he was able to contrast the ministrations of "regular" physicians with a woman herbalist in the neighborhood and later with several "root doctors." He had a talent of his own, he discovered, with curing herbs, and soon his reputation spread.[5] Part of what distinguished Thomson from other rural root doctors, though, was his articulation of both a focused explanation of disease and a small, precisely ordered pharmacopoeia of herbal remedies. What distinguished him further was a combination of missionary zeal and entrepreneurial skill in publicizing and marketing his healing system.

According to Thomson — in his own version of ancient Greek four-element theory — earth, water, air, and fire composed the human form. But, in a departure from the Greeks, he maintained that the four were not equal. It was fire, Thomson argued, that "in a peculiar manner" gave "life and motion to the rest." Thus, when the body became "disordered," there was "always an actual diminution or absence of the element fire or heat" and the presence of the body's enemy, cold.[6] It followed that the successful healer needed to restore heat, and it followed for Thomson — with his early experiences with roots and herbs — that the way to do so was through these means.

By 1806, Thomson had begun to sell "Family Rights," which imparted the secrets of his herbarium along with instructions for the treatment of various disorders, and in 1813 he was awarded a patent. Members of his Friendly Botanic Society — composed of those who had purchased a Family Right — received an instructional pamphlet with blanks at key places that were filled in by agents only after the purchaser

5. See Thomson's autobiography, *A Narrative of the Life and Medical Discoveries of Samuel Thomson* (1822; reprint, New York: Arno Press, 1972), especially pp. 18-45. While Thomson is apologetic and self-aggrandizing in this volume, it remains the best source of biographical information about his early years and his prime. The best short secondary account of Thomson and his movement remains Alex Berman, "The Thomsonian Movement and Its Relation to American Pharmacy and Medicine," *Bulletin of the History of Medicine* 25 (September-October 1951): 405-28, 519-38. A recent and useful secondary account may also be found in William G. Rothstein, "The Botanical Movements and Orthodox Medicine," in *Other Healers: Unorthodox Medicine in America,* ed. Norman Gevitz (Baltimore: The Johns Hopkins University Press, 1988), pp. 29-51. For a more exhaustive treatment, see Alex Berman, "The Impact of the Nineteenth-Century Botanical-Medical Movement on American Pharmacy and Medicine" (Ph.D. diss., University of Wisconsin, 1954).

6. Thomson, *Family Botanic Medicine, with the Preparation and System of Practice, under the Nature and Operation of the Four Elements* (Boston: T. G. Bangs, 1819), pp. 4-5.

had pledged secrecy. Later, in 1822, Thomson published the most authoritative statement of his system in his *New Guide to Health,* a work that appeared in its tenth edition in 1835 and in its thirteenth and last in 1841.[7] With the publication, even, of a German-language edition in 1828 for Pennsylvania Germans, Thomson claimed in 1839 that more than 100,000 Family Rights had been sold and that about 3,000,000 people in the United States were using his medicine. And a follower, Aaron Douglas, boasted in 1842 that "three years ago Thomsonians were nearly as scarce as white crows, but now we can number one-third at least of our whole population converted to common sense."[8] More circumspectly, in our century Thomsonian scholar Alex Berman has concluded that it is "virtually impossible" to say how many adherents the Thomsonian system won, although he notes that in 1835, Mississippi's governor claimed that half of the state's population used Thomsonian medicine. In Ohio the same year, he observes, the Thomsonians declared they had half of the population, while even the regular doctors estimated one third. And a dozen years afterward in Virginia, possibly three percent of all physicians were Thomsonians.[9]

Thomson's movement came apart, however, after 1850, and before that its ranks were already filled with dissension and factionalism. Tensions arose mostly over the desire of many to obtain more (and more socially recognized) education and to professionalize — moves that the aging Thomson resisted strenuously. It is to the source of that resistance that I turn now, for Thomson's antiprofessionalism expressed an ideology that permeated his approach to healing and made of it a symbolic strategy in the pursuit of personal power

In brief, Thomson meant his medicine to be a revolutionary assault on the arsenals of professional privilege in order to restore power to the people. All of his writings underline this connection, and none with more nuance than his autobiography. First published in 1822, the *Narrative* never overtly spoke the language of national politics, but Thomson had been a child during the Revolutionary War years, and,

7. Thomson, *New Guide to Health; or, Botanic Family Physician* (Boston: E. G. House, 1822). Suggesting the geographical compass of the movement, the tenth edition was published in Columbus, Ohio, by Jarvis Pike and Company. Alex Berman cites the thirteenth edition in "The Thomsonian Movement," p. 418n.45.

8. Berman, "The Thomsonian Movement," p. 417n.44; Thomson, *Report of the Trial of Dr. Samuel Thomson* (1839), quoted by Berman in "The Thomsonian Movement," p. 407; Douglas, " 'Regular' Murder: Case of Mr. Douglass's Child, of Patterson" (letter to the editor), *Boston Thomsonian Manual,* 1 December 1842, p. 15.

9. Berman, "The Thomsonian Movement," p. 407.

in an echo of the Enlightenment ideology that supported the war, he declared that he published his autobiography to enable the public "to judge more correctly, whether I have taken that course in fulfilling my duty in this life, which the God of nature hath pointed out for me." He went so far as to concede that "learning may be a great advantage in acquiring a profession," but he emphasized that "that alone will never make a great man, where there is no natural gift."[10]

In fact, Thomson extensively appropriated the Enlightenment's language of nature and nature's law, which had been made familiar to Americans by the Revolution.[11] For example, he told how, in his childhood, a root doctor had successfully healed him of an ugly ankle wound because the "famous Dr. Kitteridge" was "governed in his practice by that great plan which is dictated by nature." On the other hand, Thomson's mother, who had died of "galloping consumption," had been "gallopped . . . out of the world in about nine weeks" by the regular doctors. They were "riders," Thomson wrote bitterly, and "their whip [was] mercury, opium and vitriol." Better, he thought, to "die a natural death" than to suffer their ministration. But best of all, at the time, to receive the help of someone like Dr. Kitteridge, whose "uncommon success" came from following nature, "evidence enough to satisfy any reasonable mind, of the superiority of it over what is the practice of those who become doctors by reading only, with their poisons and their instruments of torture."[12]

But as Thomson's discourse of nature already shows, nature's law did not reign in uninflected grandeur. From the first, for Thomson, it was law discovered in the midst of conflict, law pitted against alien and even demonic force. Thomson's ideological appropriation of the American Enlightenment served to introduce the rhetoric of the revolution and power to the people.

When Thomson's daughter was close to two years old, for example, the regular physician thought the child would die, covered as she was with canker sores. But Thomson believed she would live, and his concern was focused on keeping the sores from her eyes in order to prevent blindness. Distressed by the prospect of blindness and by the child's struggles to breathe, Thomson took matters into his own

10. Thomson, *Narrative*, pp. 13-14.

11. On the role of the concepts of "nature's God" and "nature's law" in the American Revolution, see Philip Davidson, *Propaganda and the American Revolution, 1763-1783* (1941; reprint, New York: W. W. Norton, 1978), pp. 111-16; and Catherine L. Albanese, *Sons of the Fathers: The Civil Religion of the American Revolution* (Philadelphia: Temple University Press, 1976), pp. 112-29.

12. Thomson, *Narrative*, pp. 22-24.

hands. He performed what was evidently the first Thomsonian "steaming" — a therapy later ridiculed in the standard diatribes of the day against the Thomsonian way. Thomson encircled his daughter and himself with a blanket and poured vinegar on a hot object between his feet. He maintained the heat for some twenty minutes, letting the steam envelop himself and the child, all the while keeping a cold-water cloth on the girl's eyes. The results, according to Thomson, astounded the doctor, for Thomson's daughter lived, and her father managed to save the sight in one of her eyes.[13]

Thomson became suspicious of "the practice of the doctors in prolonging a disease" and claimed that he could never reconcile himself to the belief that "a doctor could be any use if the fever must have its course, and nature had to perform the cure, at the same time the doctor gets his pay and the credit of it." Doctors, he found, "made much more sickness than they cured." But "if parents would . . . depend more upon themselves, and less upon the doctors, they would avoid much sickness in their families, as well as save the expense attending the employment of one of the regular physicians." There was "medicine enough in the country within the reach of every one, to cure all the disease incident to it."[14]

Repetitively — indeed, almost incessantly — Thomson inveighed against regular physicians and looked to the day when his own medical system would

> eventually be the cause of throwing off the vail [*sic*] of ignorance from the eyes of the good people of this country, and do[ing] away with the blind confidence they are so much in the habit of placing in those who call themselves physicians, who fare sumptuously every day; living in splendour and magnificence, supported by the impositions they practice upon a deluded and credulous people; for they have much more regard for their own interest than they do for the health and happiness of those who are so unfortunate as to have any thing to do with them.[15]

Born out of these convictions, the disease etiology of Thomson's system encoded a glorification of revolution and struggle for freedom. Indeed, there was a poetics of the flame and fire in his work. Reshaping the argument of Gaston Bachelard to my case, we might say that be-

13. Thomson, *Narrative,* p. 29.
14. Thomson, *Narrative,* pp. 30, 32.
15. Thomson, *Narrative,* p. 34.

cause Thomson chose fire as first cause, fire revealed more about him than Thomson himself told about it.[16] For the fire into which Samuel Thomson gazed was not unlike the fire of the Revolutionary War, and it burned a path, for him, to freedom.

Significantly, in Thomson's view cold was the "enemy" of the body and "its disease and death." In the disease situation, cold was engaged in a great battle with heat, and the body was the battleground. "If the heat gains the victory," Thomson wrote, "the cold will be disinherited, and health will be restored: but on the other hand, if cold gains the ascendancy, heat will be dispossessed of its empire, and death will follow."[17] Cold was lethal because it produced blockage or obstruction. "All disorders," Thomson proclaimed, "arise directly from obstructed perspiration." And while he recognized a variety of intermediate causes for the blockage — ranging from emotional to environmental and accidental — he insisted that the best medicines were those "most agreeable to nature, and efficacious in removing obstructions." Nor did the host of causes Thomson named threaten his unitary theory. "Whatever will increase the internal heat, remove all obstructions of the system, restore the digestive powers of the stomach, and produce a natural perspiration, is universally applicable in all cases of disease, and therefore may be considered as a general remedy."[18]

Behind the language of obstruction lay an implicit constitutional theory. There was a natural government of law for the body that the obstructive assault of cold would violate. The fire of the Revolution had removed the obstruction of the British army and foreign government, enabling the body politic to operate under its own government of "natural" law and constitution. Now the fire of Thomson's favorite remedies, lobelia and cayenne, routed obstruction and chased away the cold, restoring the body's constitutional system to its natural harmony.

16. See Bachelard, *The Psychoanalysis of Fire,* trans. Alan C. M. Ross (Boston: Beacon Press, 1968), p. 1.

17. Thomson, *New Guide to Health; or, Botanic Family Physician,* 1st Brockville (Canada) ed. from the 2d Boston ed. (Brockville: W. Wiles, 1831), as quoted by Jennifer J. Connor and J. T. H. Connor in "Thomsonian Medical Literature and Reformist Discourse in Upper Canada," *Canadian Literature* 131 (Winter 1991): 143.

18. Thomson, *Family Botanic Medicine,* pp. 5-6; and *Narrative,* p. 44. It is important to note that Thomson's disease etiology of blockage and obstruction appeared well before the public introduction of mesmerism, with its own disease etiology of blockage. The first mesmeric popularizer to arrive in America was Charles Poyen, in 1836. See Robert C. Fuller, *Mesmerism and the American Cure of Souls* (Philadelphia: University of Pennsylvania Press, 1982), especially pp. 16-47.

"The constitution of all mankind are [*sic*] essentially alike," Thomson taught; individuals differed "only in the different temper of the same materials of which they are composed."[19]

Always, though, the populist and patriotic rhetoric lurked behind the ordered facade of the body's constitution. Thomson had "suffered much" and endured "persecutions" to establish his system, he told readers, "that the people might become satisfied of its superiority over that which is practised by those styled regular physicians." He wanted to put it in the people's power to "become their own physicians, by . . . making use of those vegetable medicines" that were "the produce of our own country." These were "perfectly safe," "easily obtained," and "fully sufficient in all cases of [curable] disease . . . without any danger of the pernicious, and often fatal consequences attending the administering those poisons that the fashionable doctors are in the habit of giving to their patients."[20]

Meanwhile, even as Thomson juxtaposed the wholesome products of the American landscape with the artifices of "fashionable doctors," there were lingering traces of a contrast pervasively made at the time of the Revolution. Thomson spurned the mineral remedies of the regulars, imported as "foreign poisons" from England. The patriots, during the war, had self-consciously extolled the wholesomeness and strength of rural American life with its simplicity and homespun manufacture. And they had found its antithesis in the high style and inward "corruption" of old England, a place, for them, where the foppish and effete reigned supreme.[21] Samuel Thomson, apparently, had not forgotten.

19. Thomson, *Family Botanic Medicine,* p. 4. Thomson's remedies are first published, to my knowledge, in *The Constitution, Rules and Regulations to Be Adopted and Practiced by the Members of the Friendly Botanic Society* (Portsmouth, N.H., 1812), pp. 10-11. Even this document leaves blanks in places, presumably to be filled in later by the agent. For more on American medical constitutionalism among unconventional health theorists in the early nineteenth century, see Stephen Nissenbaum, *Sex, Diet, and Debility in Jacksonian America: Sylvester Graham and Health Reform* (Westport, Conn.: Greenwood Press, 1980), p. 19.

20. Thomson, *Narrative,* pp. 145-46.

21. Cf. the highly successful Revolutionary War–era farce *The Contrast,* by Royall Tyler (1787), which pitted the homespun patriot soldier Colonel Henry Manly against the effete Europeanized Dimple for the hand of Maria Van Rough (Tyler, *The Contrast: A Comedy in Five Acts* [1920; reprint, New York: AMS Press, 1970]). For a discussion of the political ideology of natural American wholesomeness during the period, see Catherine L. Albanese, *Nature Religion in America: From the Algonkian Indians to the New Age,* Chicago History of American Religion (Chicago: University of Chicago Press, 1990), pp. 47-53.

II

But Samuel Thomson was not alone. His views epitomized those of a movement that, however rent with internal division, was united in a similar series of affirmations. Like their founder, Thomsonians endorsed the Enlightenment principle of natural law, and as they did so, they spoke loudly in the dialect of natural right. As loudly, they proclaimed the power of the people to claim that right against chronic and life-threatening oppression by regular physicians. By the 1820s, members of one branch of the Friendly Botanic Society, with their own blend of resolve and doggerel, were singing their "new song" to announce the firmness of their "right" to use their country's medicines. They would hold to their "liberty"; "no monarchy is here," they proudly (and significantly) proclaimed.[22] And even in the early 1840s, one writer in a Thomsonian periodical could exclaim: "O America! Highly favored America! Boasted land of light and liberty! When will the day dawn that shall evince to our land and world, that we are a people capable of thinking and acting for ourselves, of knowing good from evil, of discriminating between medicine and poison!"[23] Another, in a different periodical, prayed for the day "that the *people* will assert their rights, exercise the grand prerogative of reason on this subject, and fortify themselves against the snares of crafty and evil doers."[24]

The memory of the Revolution, the sense of the battlefield, was still strong. The front-page editorial inaugurating the Burlington, Vermont, *Thomsonian Scout* plotted a distinctly military scenario for its readers. "One important object in our undertaking," explained the editors, "is, to reconnoitre the 'Regular' field, and watch the movements of the enemy."[25] Nor was the double entendre left to their readers' imaginations. Consider, for example, this exhortation from William S. Johnson, one of the editors:

> In the American Revolution the British red-coats were called *regulars,* because they were regular bred soldiers to the English war-services.

22. "A New Song," in Samuel Thomson, *Learned Quackery Exposed; or, Theory according to Art, as Exemplified in the Practice of the Fashionable Doctors of the Present Day* (1824; micropublished in "American Poetry, 1609-1900: Segment II" [New Haven: Research Publications, 1975]), p. 10.

23. L.S.K., "For the Thomsonian Scout," *Thomsonian Scout,* 15 June 1842, p. 118.

24. S., "Changes," *Boston True Thomsonian,* 15 August 1842, p. 370; italics in original.

25. "To Our Patrons," *Thomsonian Scout,* 15 November 1841, p. 1.

> Once the privileged class of ministers were called regulars, regular preachers. . . . At these enlightened times the college learned doctors, are called regulars, because they have had an act past [*sic*] granting to them the exclusive right and privilege over all who were not initiated into the *quack-salbar and latin* secrets. . . . But according to the progress of *things* at the present time, they soon will share the same fate of the other regulars, that we have above mentioned; that is, their regularism will be beaten off and will *go down to rise no more.*[26]

In more measured tones, the *Scout*'s second editor, P. Standish, mused on the transitions that accompanied all human institutions. The most republican of governments, he reminded readers, "in the lapse of time lose the purity of their principles, and become reversed." The same was true for religious sects, and — most to the point — for medical doctors. "Here," he lamented, "every thing is apparently lost sight of but that fine fangled name science." Standish was not always so philosophical, however. In the tradition of demonizing the British redcoats, he could point to the demonic work of the regular physician. The "fashionable doctor," he condemned shrilly, "upheld by popular influence, like a roaring lion . . . marches thro' our community, spreading devastation and slaughter, and debilitating and poisoning the constitutions of all whom he treats, who are fortunate enough to again get out of his clutches." "The result of doctor-craft" galvanized him for military action. " 'It nerves our arms and fires our souls for the battle' — that battle, which has already disrobed them of many of their exclusive privileges, that battle which still threatens an entire overthrow of their whole forces."[27]

Meanwhile, Thomsonians, including Samuel Thomson himself, invoked the Enlightenment ideology of nature to legitimate the governance of their healing protocols. James Osgood, for example, editorialized in the *Boston True Thomsonian* in words that recalled the Freemasonic Grand Architect presiding at the time of the Revolution. "No piece of mechanism ever came from the workshop of the great Architect unfinished or imperfect," he stated. Just as the sun had been "properly made, and then put in motion under the influence of certain fixed and unchangeable laws," so humanity was "made perfect, and was set in motion, subject to certain fixed and unchangeable laws." If human

26. J., "The Changing of Times," *Thomsonian Scout,* 1 October 1842, p. 175; italics in original. The masthead of the periodical lists its editors and proprietors as William S. Johnson and P. Standish.

27. S., [Untitled editorial], *Thomsonian Scout,* 15 July 1842, pp. 130-31; P. S., "Facts for the People," *Thomsonian Scout,* 1 December 1841, p. 12; italics in original.

beings had "lived in obedience to those laws," they would not have experienced "the necessity of this constant 'putting in' for repairs." But instead of heeding nature's warnings at small infractions of these laws, humans tried other alternatives. Perhaps, even, they stooped "to a regular, who advises another breach of the same law, to repair the injury sustained by a previous violation."[28] The implication was clear that the Thomsonian approach — following in the track ordained by nature and its architect — was superior.

Moreover, the Thomsonian approach was seen as superior *because* it was good government, in contradistinction to the approach of the medical faculty. It was perhaps with echoes of the failed parliamentary proceedings of the British that Osgood was ready to assign blame. The regulars had "virtually, as a body, if they have not done it in solemn conclave, *Resolved,* that the natural laws, established by God for the government of our being, shall be suspended while the body is diseased, for the purpose of testing the doctrine, whether one violation of law shall heal the wound caused by another violation."[29] Indeed, the Thomsonian William Crosby and others urged that "man-slayers" ought not to be licensed: "we think mankind had far better die natural deaths, than artificial ones."[30]

Most of all, however, nature would invigorate the masses of ordinary people as it had at the time of the American Revolution. Nature was the great democrat, and Thomsonians were the appointed press agents. The *Boston Thomsonian Manual* exhorted the New York State Medical Society to teach the people "to so prepare themselves, when in health, by study, reflection, and observation, that in time of sickness, they can administer to their own infirmities." Thomsonism was not meant to "displace one set of crafty and designing men to make room for another," warned the journal. Instead, without making a mystery of itself, Thomsonism should uphold its teaching that "men and women are as capable of being their own physician, as they are of doing any other business."[31] People should be their own physicians, reiterated William Johnson in *The Thomsonian Scout.* The editor was not advising

28. [James Osgood], "Editorial: Physic," *Boston True Thomsonian,* 15 September 1842, pp. 25-26.

29. [James Osgood], "Editorial: The Utility of Poisons," *Boston True Thomsonian,* 15 December 1842, p. 123; italics in original.

30. William Crosby et al., in an open letter to the medical faculty of Dartmouth College printed in *The Boston Thomsonian Medical and Physiological Journal,* 1 February 1846, p. 136. The printed letter bears a total of fourteen signatures.

31. *Boston Thomsonian Manual,* 1 June 1842, p. 219.

the reader "to exchange one doctor for another; but to become your own Physician and that of your family." "Were every man to study his own nature — and become his own Physician," he predicted, "diseases would rapidly diminish."[32] "It should be proclaimed from the house-top, that the people must be the guardians of Thomsonism," echoed still another writer in a different journal.[33]

Seemingly everywhere in the Thomsonian world, the message was the same. The distinguished (non-Thomsonian) pharmacist William Procter, Jr., writing of Thomson in the *American Journal of Pharmacy* in 1854, observed that "the idea that each individual head of a family should in medicine, *as in religion and politics,* think and act for himself, presented so inviting an aspect to the yeomen of the land, that his [Thomson's] medical system was adopted as a revelation."[34] Championing the revelation several decades earlier, Thomsonian Samuel Robinson extolled Thomson's *New Guide to Health* with a hymn to the masses couched in republican terms. "God has lodged the fund of common sense in the mass of the assembled multitudes," he exclaimed. "These assemblies were dear to every land of liberty; and it was on the appeal to that assembly, and its decisions, that the ancients established the maxim, so often in their mouth, *vox populi, vox Dei.*"[35]

What needs to be noticed about the voice of the people, however, is the domain in which it was exercised. Startlingly, the new American Revolution and the new "village Enlightenment" of the Thomsonians had translated the concerns of the commonweal into a more intimate dialect.[36] If, as Bryan S. Turner has asserted, "medicine is a political

32. J., "Study Your Own Nature, and Be Your Own Physician," *Thomsonian Scout,* 15 August 1842, p. 150.

33. A., "Necessity of Union among Thomsonians," *Boston Thomsonian Medical and Physiological Journal,* 1 March 1846, p. 162.

34. Procter, *American Journal of Pharmacy* 26 (1854): 570, quoted by Alex Berman in "Social Roots of the Nineteenth-Century Botanical-Medical Movement in the United States," in *Actes du VIIIe Congres International d'Histoire des Sciences,* Florence-Milan, 3-9 September 1956 (Florence: Gruppo Italiano di Storia delle Scienze, 1958), pp. 561-62; italics mine.

35. Samuel Robinson, *A Course of Fifteen Lectures on Medical Botany* (Columbus, 1829), pp. 18-19, quoted by Alex Berman in "A Striving for Scientific Respectability: Some American Botanics and the Nineteenth-Century Plant Materia Medica," *Bulletin of the History of Medicine* 30 (1956): 28. The Latin phrase means "the voice of the people is the voice of God."

36. I borrow the phrase "village Enlightenment" from David Jaffee, although I use the term without the literary focus that is Jaffee's (see Jaffee, "The Village Enlightenment in New England, 1760-1820," *William and Mary Quarterly,* 3d series,

practice," Thomsonian medicine was also *private* practice.[37] The landscape to be governed by the operations of a republicanism in accord with natural law was no longer the seductive — but public — "wildernesses" of the new United States. Rather, the Thomsonians invited Americans to survey a geography of personal pain and disease, to ease individual crisis and concern with an ideology formerly reserved for the collective. Wresting themselves from the corporate power of the regular doctors, Thomsonians were also removing themselves to their own private estates — outside the domain of the communal body politic.

III

On the other hand, William Procter had remarked that the head of a family should act for himself in medicine, as in *religion* and politics. There was a trinity here — medicine, *religion*, and politics, and religion occupied the middle ground. The placement was suggestive, as some of the Thomsonian rhetoric already cited hints. Like their observers, Thomsonians regularly linked politics to religion to medicine. The Enlightenment recourse to nature's God and the evangelical edge to the language with which Thomsonians spread their news suggest more questions — and the beginnings of answers — regarding the Thomsonian habit of mind. Can it be that, gazing into the fire of Thomsonian medicine, we can see a religious shadow reflected on the wall beyond? Can it be that what eased the transference of public rhetoric to private estate was the ready availability of a religious world?

In Thomson's autobiography, we see how close the religious world was. He wrote of his father's "severity" toward him in childhood, a trait the son suggested might be "the effect of his religion." His father was then "under the strongest influence of the baptist persuasion, and used to be very zealous in his religious duties," Thomson remembered, "praying night and morning and sometimes three times a day." Then, when the son was a teenager, the father "left the baptist persuasion and embraced that of universal salvation." "He was like another man in his house," Thomson recollected, and he added, too, that his mother re-

---

47 [July 1990]: 327-46). I am grateful to Professor Craig Hazen for bringing the Jaffee article to my attention.

37. Turner, *The Body and Society: Explorations in Social Theory* (Oxford: Basil Blackwell, 1984), p. 209.

mained a Universalist until her death.[38] Important here, in the father's move from Calvinism to the more freeing Universalist belief, we can trace a line from divine monarchy to human democracy in religious terms. And in the son's approval, we can read the beginnings of the refrain of "power to the people" and the perfectionism that came to characterize both his spiritual and somatic worlds.

For the son clearly understood his own healing work as a religious call. "I finally concluded to make use of that gift which I thought the God of nature had implanted in me," he reported. "And if I possessed such a gift, I had no need of learning, for no one can learn that gift. I thought of what St. Paul says in his epistle to the Corinthians, concerning the different gifts by the same spirit: some had the gift of prophecy, another the gift of healing, to another the working of miracles." To be sure his readers grasped what he was saying, Thomson underscored: "I am convinced myself that I possess a gift of healing the sick, because of the extraordinary success I have met with, and the protection and support Providence has afforded me against the attacks of all my enemies."[39]

Thomson's gift needed to be refined through education, he admitted — but not education of the ordinary professional sort. In one revealing testimonial outside his autobiography, Thomson claimed the God of nature was his "president and instructer [*sic*]; here I graduated; here I got my diploma." Out under nature's noonday sun mowing hay, Thomson said, he felt the most heat and life. And he confessed the divine creed and commandment that he had learned: "Open the obstructions caused by cold; promote perspiration; take off canker; and restore digestion, so that the food may keep up that heat on which life depends, and let all the people say, AMEN. Glory to the God of Nature, President of this college."[40]

In fact, though, there was more than glory to the healer's life. Indeed, Thomson's autobiographical *Narrative* was structurally a way of the cross, as he moved from persecution to persecution. Thomson presented himself as a prophet rejected in his own country, regularly accused by "fashionable doctors" of the death of patients whom they

38. Thomson, *Narrative,* pp. 18-19.

39. Thomson, *Narrative,* p. 40.

40. Thomson, *Learned Quakery Exposed; or, Theory according to Art. As Exemplified in the Practice of the Fashionable Doctors of the Present Day* (Boston: J. Q. Adams, 1836), pp. 45-46. So far as I can determine, this is the second edition of the work.

themselves had given up as hopeless, and finally indicted in 1809 for the murder of one patient, Ezra Lovett. Thomson endured the filth and bad conditions of the jailhouse and the contempt of the respectable. Finally acquitted by the Supreme Court of the state of Massachusetts, he nonetheless lost a civil suit against the doctor who had originally filed charges against him.[41] Later he was betrayed Judas-like by those most closely linked to him in his work. Thomson's humoral fire had, in his autobiography, been tried by another sort of fire. And this, as Thomsonians would agree, was "no more strange than that the glorious and benevolent system of the gospel should have met with opposition from its first introduction to the present day."[42] The implication was that, like the man of the cross, Thomson and his medicine had been made perfect.

As telling in symbolic terms, Thomson was obsessed by concerns for purity and perfection throughout his life. Alex Berman has written succinctly of Thomson's preoccupation with the purity of his medicines, his fears for their adulteration, and his concerns for the control of their distribution.[43] The seventy items that composed the Thomsonian *materia medica,* divided into six major groups of remedies, were often mixed by agents in ways not intended by Thomson and even combined by them with other substances to yield "improvements." Thomson himself warned against "spurious or adulterated articles," seemingly in vain, and as he aged grew more vitriolic in his efforts to preserve the purity of his pharmacopoeia.

Moreover, despite the inclination of some Thomsonians to pursue an increased income by exercising some creativity in blending Thomson's herbs in new ways, Thomsonians seemed as obsessed as Thomson himself with maintaining the pristine perfection of their sources. They refused to use regular drugstores, setting up their own stores, "depots," and infirmaries in competition. In fact, by 1834 the third National Thomsonian Convention, held in Baltimore, went so far as to resolve a formal boycott against established drugstores and apothecaries. Thomsonians continually worried about accidental introduction of poisonous drugs into their remedies, and they suspected the

41. For an account of both trials and the events leading up to them, see Thomson, *Learned Quakery Exposed,* 2d ed., pp. 94-111.

42. Members of the Friendly Botanic Society meeting in western New York state [November 1824?], quoted by Samuel Thomson in *Earnest Appeal to the Public* (Boston: E. G. Nouse, 1824), p. 27.

43. Berman, "Thomsonian Movement," pp. 519-29. Most of my account here is based on Berman's discussion.

integrity of pharmacists, who they believed might deliberately, for whatever reasons, substitute "poisons" for nature's purity.

IV

We need to notice, though, that nature's purity only reiterated evangelical purity. Robert C. Fuller has remarked that Thomsonians supplied "the physiological counterpart to the period's theological perfectionism."[44] And, significantly, Thomson's medicine flourished among religious come-outers. Indeed, American religious historian Nathan Hatch has noted that "the rise of Thomsonian medicine suggests the affinity in the early republic between sectarian medicine, republican politics and religious dissent." And he has pointed to the numbers of religious dissenters who turned to unorthodox medicine.

> Elias Smith and Lorenzo Dow became significant promoters of sectarian medicine. John Leland openly despised the pretensions of orthodox physicians. A prominent Methodist itinerant included both lawyers and doctors under the "wo" of prophecy. And the Mormon prophet Joseph Smith and his successor Brigham Young aligned the early Mormon movement closely with the Thomsonian botanic system.[45]

The case of Elias Smith is worth pursuing. Formally installed as pastor of the Baptist church in Woburn, Massachusetts, in 1798, Smith (1769-1846) later disdained the "new fangled ceremony" in which he and the others looked "like the cardinals coming out of the conclave after electing a pope." Converted to Jeffersonian republicanism in 1800 and pondering questions of monarchy and republicanism, he "became a republican from principle." The principle involved was "the interest of the people," and a year later he had left his pulpit, flirted briefly with Universalism, and then embraced the radical Christian movement. His mind, he said, was "delivered from *calvinism, universalism,* and *deism,* three doctrines of men." Now the impulse to purity and perfection could be translated into zeal to restore the church, to make it as it had been in New Testament times. And the republican freedom Smith found in the

44. Fuller, *Alternative Medicine and American Religious Life* (New York: Oxford University Press, 1989), p. 20.

45. Hatch, *The Democratization of American Christianity* (New Haven: Yale University Press, 1989), pp. 29-30.

politics of popular sovereignty could reach the domain of religion.[46] But politics and religion were not enough. Smith thought that there were "three important things in this life to attend to": *"Medicine, Government* and *Religion."*[47] By 1816, the year that his autobiography first appeared, Smith had purchased a Family Right from Samuel Thomson.

The following June, Smith became Thomson's general agent, selling Family Rights and herbal medicines to others. The two collaborated more and more closely, as Smith began to assist Thomson in preparing his own autobiographical *Narrative* for publication. But they had a falling out or a series of them. Smith formed a rival botanic society in 1820, and two years later he published his own medical guide to compete with Thomson's. The embittered Thomson was not reluctant, in his autobiography, to accuse Smith of failing to repay debts, of siphoning off members of the Friendly Botanic Society to form his own, and of attempting to claim proprietorship of Thomson's autobiography at copyright-filing time. What most enraged Thomson was evidently the book that Smith had published. Thomson charged that Smith, in his *Medical Pocket-Book, Family Physician and Sick Man's Guide to Health,* had taken credit for another man's ideas and work. "It is true that he has made alterations in the names of some of the preparations of medicine; but the articles used and the manner of using them is the same as mine. It is also a well known fact, that he had no knowledge of medicine, or of curing disease, until I instructed him."[48]

But plagiarism or not, Elias Smith's commitment to irregular medicine was genuine, and by 1826 he had published a second work, *The American Physician and Family Assistant.* Moreover, despite his antipathy toward Smith, Thomson himself corroborated the major linkages in his former agent's career. He nowhere summarized the motivating force behind his own and Elias Smith's life better than in his ostentatious *Address to the People of the United States:*

> There are *three* things which have in a greater or less degree, called the attention of men, viz. *Religion, Government,* and *Medicine.* In ages past, these things by millions were thought to belong to three classes

46. Elias Smith, *The Life, Conversion, Preaching, Travels, and Sufferings of Elias Smith,* 1 (1816; reprint, New York: Arno Press, 1980), pp. 278-79, 284, 293; italics in original. See the treatment of Smith in Hatch's *Democratization of American Christianity,* pp. 69-70.

47. Elias, quoted by Berman in "Social Roots of the Nineteenth-Century Botanical-Medical Movement in the United States," p. 562; italics in source.

48. Thomson, *Narrative,* p. 161; the entire account appears on pp. 146-61.

> of men; *Priests, Lawyers* and *Physicians.* The *Priests,* held the things of *religion* in their own hands, and brought the people to their terms; kept the Scriptures in the dead languages, so that the common people could not read them. These days of darkness are done away; the Scriptures are translated into our own language, and each one is taught to read for himself. *Government* was once considered as belonging to a few, who thought themselves, *'born only to rule.'* The common people have now become acquainted with the great secret of government: and know that *'all men are born free and equal'.* . . .
>
> While these, and many other things are brought where *'common people,'* can understand them; the knowledge and use of *Medicine,* is in a great measure concealed in a dead language, and a sick man, is often obliged to risk his *life,* where he would not risk a shilling.[49]

Meanwhile, as Thomson and Smith struggled to free themselves from the shackles they felt to be binding them, their fractured relationship signaled the fractures that were part of the Thomsonian movement as a whole. Eclectics and Physio-Medicals, Improved Botanics and True Thomsonians, Independent Thomsonians, Reformed Botanics, and others all laid claim, at least in part, to a Thomsonian heritage. The doctrine of power to the people spawned a do-it-yourself mentality in medicine, as in politics and religion, and do-it-yourselfism can be isolating. To return to the case of Elias Smith, though, it was political change and — as important — religious change that had preceded medical change; and the sequence of the three was instructive. If the political order, even in its democratic manifestation, prescribed for society as a collective, it was religion that turned attention to the soul and self. So religious and political change cross-fertilized each other, as it were — and spread to other aspects of culture.

In the volatile atmosphere of evangelical revival and come-outer sect formation, some nineteenth-century Americans were drawn by the Thomsonian heat even as they learned to attend to an intimate geography in religion. They appropriated a public and political language for use in reference to the physical territory of their bodies through the funneling device of evangelicalism. Still more, evangelicalism's missionary model and its Arminianized message of human ability joined in a rhetoric of perfection to be sought and found.

49. Thomson, *Address to the People of the United States* (Boston, 1817), p. 1; italics in original. Internal evidence suggests that the *Address* was first published in the Boston *Herald.* Thomson's "poetry" in *Learned Quackery Exposed* also tellingly links "Law, Physic, and Divinity"; see "Ingratitude" and "Three Crafts," in *Learned Quackery Exposed* (1836), pp. 16-17, 17-20.

At the same time, from another quarter the village Enlightenment supported evangelical religion with a religion of its own. With the deism of the Enlightenment overlooked as innocuous, its popular hymns to nature and to nature's God provided a different kind of religious support for the transition from body politic to body ailing. Since individual consent was the basis of the Enlightenment political message, it was not surprising that the focus could shift from what the individual consented to — natural law as expressed in the public governmental order — to the individual doing the consenting. The atomism that was the unexamined secret of Enlightenment doctrine could spin out a revised scenario under the impress of revival Arminianism and the new evangelical order.

What I am suggesting, then, is that the privatization that a twentieth-century generation of scholars has found dogging American religion and its surrounding culture came about through precisely the kinds of transitions that are evident in the Thomsonian episode. And the privatization came as an act of resistance and subversion, a refusal to play the power game as the collective ideologists prescribed. As one Thomsonian author argued, Thomson succeeded in his campaign of medical reform *"by subverting the theory and practice of the medical profession and establishing his own in the hands of the people."* There was, the writer tellingly put it, "no work except the subversion and establishment of a new religion of equal magnitude."[50]

And in the end, it was the same Enlightenment that had given birth to the new order of the ages that, through Thomsonianism and similar movements, muted it and dispersed its force. As Robert Fuller has noticed, there was irony in the way that the Enlightenment search for a universal first principle or set of principles gave the plausibility of science to the Thomsonian and other healing systems. But there was further irony in the way the rhetorical basis of the communal order was used to undercut it. The "irony of it all," though — to borrow a phrase from Martin Marty — is that the processing agent that hardened rhetoric into act was the collective passage through the evangelical fire.[51]

In sum, the Thomsonian story points to the utility of studying

50. "Dr. Thomson's Grand Object [from *Learned Quackery Exposed*]," *Boston Thomsonian Manual,* 1 October 1844, p. 291; italics in original.

51. Fuller, *Alternative Medicine and American Religious Life,* p. 13. I am of course using the phrase "the irony of it all" in a different context and time frame from those explored in Marty's *The Irony of It All, 1893-1919,* vol. 1 of *Modern American Religion* (Chicago: University of Chicago Press, 1986).

nineteenth-century irregular medicine as a cultural domain in which important social transitions were being played out. That some Americans elaborated complex cultural messages in terms of their own bodies was a function of the multiple worlds in which they lived. That these messages so strongly concerned nature, natural law, and libertarian revolution suggests the power of the political even as people (who were perhaps collectively powerless amid increasing social change) emptied the discourse of public content. And finally, that the messages upheld the significance of a quest for perfection suggests the equal power of religion. Hence, Samuel Thomson and his people may tell us as much (and perhaps more) about religious and general cultural changes and about how these processes worked as they tell us about getting well. Medical acts, they tell us, may be exercises and strategies of personal power. Perfect bodies may be sought as appropriate counterparts for perfect — and privatized — spirits.

To say this in another way, in the anthropology of power that was being negotiated, control of one's body or the loss of it signaled a series of other social contests and processes, all of them intricate and entangled with one another. Because of symbolic continuity — the persistence of a public language — as Martin Marty has argued, the "modern schism" was disguised. In one long cultural moment, the Thomsonians suggest *how* in the context of a struggle for power major aspects of culture moved toward privatization, *how* people slipped into position for what Marty has called "epochal shifts," and *how* religion got to be relocated. If, to quote Marty again, by the twentieth century religion had "become escapable," and if modernity came to be defined "in the chopping up of life and the impelling of choice upon private citizens," the Thomsonian episode can illustrate the ways that these things happened.[52] To understand American individualism and the cult of empowerment through privacy in contemporary religion and culture, there may be no better strategy than to call the Thomsonian doctor.

52. Marty, *Modern Schism,* pp. 100-101; *A Nation of Behavers* (Chicago: University of Chicago Press, 1976), p. 23; and *The Public Church: Mainline — Evangelical — Catholic* (New York: Crossroad, 1981), pp. 99-100.

New Directions in American Catholic History

Jay P. Dolan

In 1964 Henry F. May wrote an important article entitled "The Recovery of Religious History." In this article, May pointed out that the writing of American religious history was undergoing a renaissance. According to him, one group that contributed the least to this revival was Roman Catholics.[1] This is no longer true. In the years since May wrote that essay, the historical study of American Catholicism has enjoyed a revival. It has become more integrated into the mainstream of American religious history, and in the process it has broken away from the traditions of the past and has begun to chart new directions for the future. In order to appreciate the significance of this change, it is necessary to understand the historiographical tradition that dominated the first half of the twentieth century.

Peter Guilday (1884-1947) was the most significant historian of American Catholicism in the first half of the twentieth century. The author of several books, he is best remembered for his two major biographical studies, *The Life and Times of John Carroll, Archbishop of Baltimore, 1735-1815* (1922) and *The Life and Times of John England, First Bishop of Charleston, 1786-1842* (1927). Trained as a historian at Louvain University in Belgium, Guilday wanted to professionalize the study of American Catholic history. For this reason he became the driving force behind the founding of the *Catholic Historical Review* in 1915, and four years later he founded the American Catholic Historical Association. In addition, he taught at Catholic University, where in 1914 he inaugurated a seminar in church history to train students in the study of American Catholicism. More than anyone else, Peter Guilday was responsible for

1. May, "The Recovery of American Religious History," *American Historical Review* 70 (1964): 90-91.

the revival of American Catholic history in the twentieth century, a field of study that had become moribund after the death of John Gilmary Shea in 1892. Through his teaching and writing he influenced a generation of historians, most notably John Tracy Ellis, who eventually succeeded Guilday as the premier historian of American Catholicism. Because of his influence and prominence, Guilday's understanding of history and his ideas on how denominational history can best be written are essential for an understanding of the writing of American Catholic history in the twentieth century.

In the appendix to his biography of Bishop John England of Charleston, South Carolina, Guilday wrote, "for many years to come, historians of the Catholic Church in the United States must content themselves with a biographical presentation of its past." The reason he gave for this was "that, owing to the scattered and unorganized condition of our archival sources, the more prudent method is to center around the great figures in our Church the story of their times; with the hope that, as the years pass, our documentary knowledge will be increased and the institutional factors of our Catholic life become more salient and tangible." Having said this, Guilday then went on to state that the life and times of John England "may well be taken as the history of the Church in the United States during the twenty-two years he presided over the See of Charleston."[2] In this statement Guilday made two important points. First, historical biography was the key to unlocking the past, and second, the goal of this opening to the past was to understand more fully the history of the institution or, as he put it, "the institutional factors of our Catholic life."

Guilday also followed two other key principles in his writing. He viewed his historical work as a form of apologetics. In other words, history rightly written would prove that Roman Catholicism was the true church, and this would provide an important defense against the critics of Catholicism. In endorsing this principle, Guilday showed himself to be a true representative of the Counter-Reformation mentality that had been developing among Catholics since the sixteenth century. The other principle that guided Guilday was to seek episcopal approval for what he wrote; for this reason he was very cautious about what he wrote and would, as he put it, "quietly overlook" anything that was detrimental to the church and its leaders.[3] Such caution was

2. Guilday, *The Life and Times of John England, First Bishop of Charleston (1786-1842)*, 2 vols. (New York: America Press, 1927), 2: 555.

3. Guilday, quoted by David O'Brien in "Peter Guilday: The Catholic Intel-

indicative of the atmosphere that was prevalent in the years following the condemnation of modernism, when church leaders looked upon scholars with a great deal of suspicion.

Thus Guilday and his generation of historians were guided by four principles in their work: (1) they concentrated on biographical studies, (2) these studies formed the foundation for an institutional history of Catholicism, (3) the goal of their work was to defend the truth of Catholicism, and (4) they were selective in writing church history, producing what could be called "history without the warts." Institutional, biographical, apologetical, and promotional — these were the four characteristics of American Catholic history in the first half of the twentieth century. That this was so should not be surprising. Guilday and his contemporaries were writing in the age of the Counter-Reformation, an age that exalted the episcopacy, emphasized the institutional nature of the Church, and sought to defend the Church against Protestant attacks. Their historical writing carried the imprint of this era.

John Tracy Ellis, whom Guilday described as his "providential successor,"[4] became the personification of American Catholic history for the post–World War II generation of scholars. Ellis completed his doctoral studies in medieval history at Catholic University in 1930 and subsequently published his dissertation, *Anti-Papal Legislation in Medieval England (1066-1377).* Shortly afterward, he entered the seminary to prepare for the priesthood. After ordination to the priesthood in 1938, he joined the faculty at Catholic University. In 1942 he published his second book, *Cardinal Consalvi and Anglo-Papal Relations, 1814-1824.* Trained as a medievalist and exhibiting a keen interest in modern European history, Ellis did not appear to be a likely heir to Guilday. But when Guilday's health failed, the rector of Catholic University asked Ellis to take over Guilday's courses in American Catholic history. Ellis's reply was typically straightforward: "I do not know anything about the field." The rector's reply was equally blunt: "You can learn, can't you?" That brief exchange in 1941 launched the career of John Tracy Ellis as a historian of American Catholicism.[5]

Ellis's writings were of two types. The first type, which re-

---

lectual in the Post-Modernist Church," in *Studies in Catholic History in Honor of John Tracy Ellis,* ed. Nelson H. Minnich, Robert B. Eno, and Robert F. Trisco (Wilmington, Del.: Michael Glazier, 1985), p. 270. This is an excellent essay on Guilday.

4. O'Brien, "Peter Guilday," p. 261.

5. John Tracy Ellis, *Faith and Learning: A Church Historian's Story* (Lanham, Md.: University Press of America, 1989), p. 31.

sembled the work of Guilday, appeared most noticeably during the 1940s and early 1950s. It emphasized a biographical approach to religious history as well as a focus on the institution. The best example of this phase of his work is Ellis's two-volume study of Cardinal Gibbons, *The Life of James Cardinal Gibbons, Archbishop of Baltimore, 1834-1921.* Published in 1952, it followed in the tradition of Guilday: more than a biography, it was a history of the life and times of Gibbons. The second type of writing reflected Ellis's interest in social and cultural history, an interest most likely kindled when he studied with Arthur Schlesinger, Sr., at Harvard University in the spring of 1942. The one book that best exemplifies this style of history is *American Catholicism,* which appeared in the the Chicago History of American Civilization series, edited by Daniel J. Boorstin. The book originated as a series of four lectures given at the University of Chicago in 1955. In this study, social movements, issues, and organizations occupy center stage.

By the 1950s the essay had become Ellis's chief form of publication, and in numerous essays, many of which originated as lectures, he charted a new direction in American Catholic historical studies. The most memorable of these essays was a paper he read at the 1955 meeting of the Catholic Commission on Intellectual and Cultural Affairs entitled "American Catholics and the Intellectual Life." Later that year it appeared in *Thought,* a Catholic journal, and was subsequently published as a pamphlet. In this phase of his career, Ellis wrote about such issues as the intellectual life, higher education, religious freedom, and the education of priests.

Unlike Guilday, Ellis did not view church history as a branch of apologetics. He did not believe that church history "was meant to edify . . . and unpleasant episodes . . . were simply to be kept out of sight." Moreover, he continually urged truthfulness in the writing of history and was himself very critical of the Church and its leaders if he thought it necessary.[6] Nonetheless, he was writing in the 1940s and 1950s, and he manifested a defensive attitude that was still common among Catholics at that time. In his best-seller *American Catholicism,* he frequently pointed out the contributions that Catholics had made to the United States and made statements that were gratuitous and misleading. One such statement pertained to the issue of race in the twentieth century.

6. For a good example of Ellis's endorsement of truth in historical writing, see Ellis, "The Ecclesiastical Historian in the Service of Clio," *Church History* 38 (March 1969): 110.

After mentioning a few examples in which the Church had advocated integration, Ellis concluded that the "Church often has anticipated the most enlightened public sentiment on matters of this kind."[7] What he failed to mention were the many actions of church leaders that defended the status quo of segregation. In speaking about bishops and politics, he claimed that the hierarchy left "complete freedom of political action" to the people. That was not entirely accurate either, since there have been times when bishops have tried to influence the politics of the people.[8] In making these and other such unwarranted statements, it seems clear that Ellis was trying to paint the best possible picture of American Catholic history. Even though he did not hesitate to criticize the Church and its leaders, he often slipped into an apologetic style of writing. This becomes very clear when his 1956 history of American Catholicism is compared with the 1958 study written by Robert Cross, a Protestant layman, *The Emergence of Liberal Catholicism in America.* Cross's book manifests none of the defensive and apologetic tone of Ellis's study.

Unlike many historians of Catholicism in the Counterreform era, Ellis did not evidence prejudice and suspicion toward other religions; rather, he urged toleration and understanding. In many other respects, however, Ellis's way of writing history was similar to that of Guilday.

Like Guilday, Ellis endorsed the idea of "scientific history"; in other words, history must be based on documentary evidence. As he put it, "no documents, no history." In his study of Gibbons, he stated that he wanted "to allow the documents to speak for themselves so that the reader might have all the evidence before him."[9] The historical biography was also central to Ellis's writing, and the subjects of his biographies, like those of Guilday, were distinguished bishops. His other writings were also very institutionally oriented. Ellis was clearly a historian of the institutional Church, and the dissertations he directed at Catholic University provide rather conclusive evidence of this. The vast majority of them were either episcopal biographies or institutional

7. Ellis, *American Catholicism* (Chicago: University of Chicago Press, 1956), p. 146. For another view of the hierarchy's attitudes on race in the twentieth century, see Stephen J. Ochs, *The Desegregated Altar: The Josephites and the Struggle for Black Priests, 1871-1960* (Baton Rouge: Louisiana State University Press, 1990).

8. See Ochs, *The Desegregated Altar,* p. 92. The best example of this would be the 1886 mayoral election in New York City.

9. Ellis, quoted by Jack Douglas Thomas, Jr., in "Interpretations of American Catholic Church History: A Comparative Analysis of Representative Catholic Historians, 1875-1975" (Ph.D. diss., Baylor University, 1976), pp. 169-70.

histories.[10] In *American Catholicism,* Ellis makes a telling statement in this regard: "The question of nationalist feeling among the American Catholics, often so closely related to lay trusteeism, can be studied within the Church's hierarchy of these years more closely than they can be studied within the numerous and widespread clergy and laity." In other words, the best way to understand the people was to study the bishops. This was a very clerical view of church history, and subsequent historical studies have demonstrated how narrow a point of view it was.[11]

Despite the parallels between the work of Ellis and Guilday, Ellis did offer something new and unique to American Catholic history. He became a publicist for reform in the American Catholic Church and "used history as an instrument to promote changes he believed necessary to American Catholicism." Like the progressive historians of an earlier generation, "he possessed a present-mindedness that related events and developments of the past to questions of contemporary interest, and he used his addresses and publications to initiate change as well as to describe and explain it."[12] Some of the issues that he addressed included the use of the vernacular in worship, selection of bishops, religious liberty, higher education, and the intellectual life. No other historian of American Catholicism matched Ellis in this regard. It was this aspect of his writing that has gained him the most fame.

Timothy T. McAvoy, C.S.C. (1903-1969), was another historian of American Catholicism in this era who achieved a measure of distinction. Born and raised in Indiana, he entered the Congregation of Holy Cross after high school and studied at the University of Notre Dame. After graduating from Notre Dame in 1925, he studied theology in Washington, D.C., and was ordained a priest in 1929. Immediately after his ordination, he was appointed archivist at the University of Notre Dame; in 1933 he joined the university's history department. A major development in his career as a historian took place in 1935, when he entered the graduate history program at Columbia University; five years later he received his doctoral degree. When McAvoy returned to Notre Dame, he resumed his work as archivist and remained in this

10. See Ellis, *Faith and Learning,* pp. 45-51, where he writes about his students and their work.

11. Ellis, *American Catholicism,* p. 46; on lay trusteeism, see Patrick W. Carey, *People, Priests, and Prelates: Ecclesiastical Democracy and the Tensions of Trusteeism* (Notre Dame, Ind.: University of Notre Dame Press, 1987).

12. J. Douglas Thomas, "A Century of American Catholic History," *U.S. Catholic Historian* 6 (Winter 1987): 41, 44.

position until his death in 1969. He also taught in the history department and was appointed chair of the department in 1939, a year before he received his Ph.D.; his tenure as chairman lasted until 1960.

Despite his heavy administrative responsibilities as archivist and chair of the history department, McAvoy found time to do research and to write. He published many articles, both scholarly and popular, and he also wrote several books. His major work was a study of the Americanist episode, *The Great Crisis in American Catholic History, 1895-1900*, published in 1957. He also wrote a general history of American Catholicism entitled *A History of the Catholic Church in the United States*, which was published shortly after his death in 1969.

At Columbia University McAvoy was trained as a professional historian in one of the nation's premier history departments. Two key ideas that he undoubtedly learned at Columbia shaped his thinking as a historian for the remainder of his life. The first was the importance of the frontier thesis (the assertion that the process of Americanization and democratization took place most emphatically along the frontier); the second idea was that American Catholic history must be integrated into the social, political, and economic history of the nation. Both of these ideas were manifested in his doctoral dissertation, "The Catholic Church in Indiana, 1789-1834." A study of frontier Catholicism, it was an attempt to combine religious history with the social, economic, and political history of the Indiana frontier. In incorporating the frontier thesis into his writing, McAvoy acknowledged that "he used the term frontier to cover those changes in European civilization which had been effected in the new and rich land this side of the Atlantic, and attempted to find in that term or those forces an explanation for the changes in Roman Catholicism once it had become established in the new world."[13]

McAvoy differed from Guilday in that he did not view history as a branch of apologetics and he did not rely on biography as much as Guilday did in his efforts to interpret the past. His dissertation was a social history of Indiana frontier Catholicism, and this suggested that this style of history might shape his work in the future. In fact, late in life he stated that the history he had written was "a history of Catholic people, not the traditional list of clergymen, buildings, and occasional politicians."[14] Despite this claim, McAvoy never pursued the style of

13. McAvoy, *The Americanist Heresy in Roman Catholicism, 1895-1900* (Notre Dame, Ind.: University of Notre Dame Press, 1963), p. 305.

14. McAvoy, quoted by Walter Romig in *The Book of Catholic Authors*, 6th series (Grosse Pointe, Mich.: N.p., 1966?), p. 260.

history evident in his dissertation. McAvoy's view of the way prelates defined American Catholicism was much the same as that of Ellis and Guilday. As he put it, "one could characterize to a great extent the Catholicism of New England, of the Middle Atlantic dioceses, of the Middle West, and the like by the character and interest of the bishops and archbishops who led the church in that region."[15] Moreover, when McAvoy wrote his general history of American Catholicism, the episcopal perspective shaped the way the book was written. Where McAvoy differed from Guilday and Ellis was in his efforts to interpret the Catholic past.

The key to McAvoy's interpretation was his thesis about the formation of the American Catholic minority. He first presented this in 1948, and it remained a constant theme in his writing for the remainder of his life. The thesis was most clearly presented in a 1948 essay published in the *Review of Politics* in which McAvoy argued that "what there is of a distinctive Catholic culture is the result of the interaction between the doctrinal unity and this political, social, and economic divergence. It took its dominant form during the stormy years immediately before the Civil War."[16] According to McAvoy, the Catholic minority was formed as a result of the interaction between Anglo-American Catholics who traced their roots back to colonial Maryland and the immigrants who arrived in the United States prior to the Civil War. The "cultural leaven" in this process was the Anglo-American group, which pointed the way to Americanization for foreign-born Catholics. The union of the Anglo-American group with the immigrant groups created, in McAvoy's judgment, "a distinctive American Catholic cultural group." The place where this could be "most clearly observed was the Middle Western frontier. There the immigrant groups living away from the cities yielded more quickly to the general cultural trends." As he put it, Catholics "were quickly Americanized" in these regions. The Anglo-Americans provided the cultural leadership for the Catholic minority, and the immigrants offered a new style of aggressiveness through "their staunch defense of their religion" during the nativist crusades of the antebellum period. McAvoy also noted that the nativism of "the eighteen-forties and fifties furnished the hammer and anvil by which this distinctive Catholic cultural unity was created." The last sentence of

15. McAvoy, "The American Catholic Minority in the Later Nineteenth Century," *Review of Politics* 15 (July 1953): 280.

16. McAvoy, essay reprinted as *The Formation of the American Catholic Minority, 1820-1860* (Philadelphia: Fortress Press, 1967), p. 2.

the essay summarizes McAvoy's thesis very well: "But the gradual Americanization of the masses of non-English Catholic immigrants with the old Anglo-American Catholic group as a nucleus, is an understandable process and one as American as all the other combinations of immigration and the frontier which constitute our American civilization." Briefly put, McAvoy's minority thesis was his explanation of how Catholics became Americans.[17]

In emphasizing the difference between the early colonial and national period of Catholic history and the antebellum era of immigration, McAvoy had pointed out a very important aspect of that history. The history of American Catholicism is more than just the history of nineteenth-century immigrant Catholics. In fact, in order to understand this immigrant era, it is necessary to have a thorough understanding of the early national period. McAvoy understood this and attempted to explain the interrelationship between the two periods. By stressing the antebellum period and the nativist crusade as the "hammer and anvil" on which American Catholicism was shaped, McAvoy underscored the importance of this era in shaping the minority mentality of Catholics in the United States. McAvoy's insistence on the importance of midwestern Catholicism was an important corrective to the exclusive focus on Atlantic-coast Catholicism that characterized much of the historical writing at this time. In seeking to point out the differences between American and European Catholicism, evident not only in this essay but in much of his writing, McAvoy was attempting to show how American Roman Catholicism really was. He was offering an interpretive historical analysis of how Catholics became American, and he was the first historian of American Catholicism to attempt this. Nevertheless, his interpretive thesis never attracted much support.

There are several reasons for this. First of all, the argument was not presented clearly and convincingly. McAvoy's writing style sometimes made it difficult for the reader to follow his argument. Lacking clarity, the interpretation never marshaled many supporters. In addition, McAvoy did not present much evidence to support his thesis about the importance of the Anglo-American group of Catholics. In his dissertation he demonstrated his command of the midwestern phase of Catholicism in the early national period, but he never did the research needed to document his thesis about the Anglo-Americans being the cultural leaven of the American Catholic minority. He was not correct

17. McAvoy, *The Formation of the American Catholic Minority, 1820-1860*, pp. 12, 26, 22, 4, 31.

when he asserted that the French clergy in the United States "were actually defenders of the Anglo-American group against an Irish invasion" and that they promoted the interests of the Anglo-American Catholics. Here, as was often the case in this and other of his essays, McAvoy simply did not offer the necessary evidence to support the generalization. He did not explain who the Anglo-Americans were; indeed, throughout this and other essays their identity for the most part remains a mystery.[18] Finally, his appropriation of the frontier thesis of Frederick Jackson Turner, though not total and uncritical, led him to exaggerate the ease with which Americanization took place on the frontier as opposed to the city. Moreover, support for Turner's thesis was quickly fading in these years, and McAvoy's incorporation of it in his work weakened the credibility of his argument. Even in his 1969 general history of American Catholicism, McAvoy's Catholic minority thesis did not emerge any more clearly or more convincingly. It was a bold attempt to offer an interpretation of American Catholic history, but it failed.

McAvoy's best work was his history of the Americanist crisis. Though this too suffers from his obscurantist style of writing, it is a thoroughly documented study of a very complex period of history. In recognition of its importance, the book received the John Gilmary Shea award of the American Catholic Historical Association in 1957 as the best book published in Catholic history for that year.

In spite of the differences that set them apart from each other, Guilday, Ellis, and McAvoy did share a common quality. The major focus in their writing of American Catholic history was on the clergy (specifically the hierarchy), and their influence was such that all of American Catholic history at this time took on this quality. Henry J. Browne, a student of Ellis at Catholic University, commented on this in a survey of the writing of American Catholic history from 1947 to 1957. After noting the emphasis on episcopal biography and the influence that Ellis in particular had in this regard, Browne concluded that "this zeal for episcopal biography has been an outstanding characteristic of the period coming to a close."[19] Other works that Browne noted as having been

18. For a different interpretation of this early period of Catholicism, see Patrick W. Carey, *People, Priests, and Prelates;* and Jay P. Dolan, *The American Catholic Experience: A History from Colonial Times to the Present* (Garden City, N.Y.: Doubleday, 1985), pp. 101-26.

19. Browne, "American Catholic History: A Progress Report on Research and Study," *Church History* 26 (Dec. 1957): 372.

produced during the decade were histories of religious communities, histories of dioceses, and studies of a few lay organizations.

A decade later, David J. O'Brien wrote a similar essay and concluded that "the dominant characteristics" of American Catholic historiography were "the same today as noted by Henry J. Browne a decade ago: heavy emphasis upon episcopal biography, intense concern with the internal controversies of the late nineteenth century; lack of interest in non-Irish Catholic groups and in the supposedly conservative nineteenth century bishops; and an almost total neglect of Catholic thought and of the period since World War I. Of equal significance, many works are unoriginal, avoiding all but the most cautious and judicious interpretations."[20] The reason for this, according to O'Brien, was that the historians had a very institutional understanding of the church, and hence tended to tell "the history of the Church . . . in terms of the hierarchy with episcopal biography the typical mode of study."[21] But O'Brien noted that the winds of change were blowing across the landscape of American Catholic historiography, and a new understanding of the Church was emerging in the aftermath of the Second Vatican Council. In addition, social changes in the 1960s had radically altered the historical environment in the United States. A new day had dawned for both the Church and the nation. Awareness of this on the part of historians "might," said O'Brien, "suggest alternative modes of analysis of the history of the Catholic Church in this country."[22] That is just what has happened since O'Brien made that prediction. A new understanding of the Church has emerged "at a time when American Catholics themselves" have been "experiencing rapid social and intellectual transformation," and this twofold revolution has transformed the writing of American Catholic history.[23]

In the quarter century that has passed since the closing of the Second Vatican Council, the scholarly study of Catholicism has undergone substantial change. A new code of canon law has appeared, scholars have transformed the study of the Bible and of worship, and a new perspective has changed the Catholic understanding of ethics. Together with these changes has emerged a new type of church history. This is evident in both Europe and America, and though the roots of

20. O'Brien, "American Catholic Historiography: A Post-Conciliar Evaluation," *Church History* 37 (March 1968): 82.

21. O'Brien, "American Catholic Historiography," p. 87.

22. O'Brien, "American Catholic Historiography," p. 88.

23. O'Brien, "American Catholic Historiography," p. 80.

this shift can be traced back to the 1940s and 1950s and the emergence of a new social history, for Catholics the influence of Vatican II cannot be underestimated. It created an atmosphere that encouraged such intellectual exploration and creativity. Within American Catholicism, this new religious history (the phrase "church history" is no longer in vogue) has taken on a variety of styles or methods.

In 1968, two historians who have since become major interpreters of the American Catholic past — David J. O'Brien and Philip Gleason — published their first books, each of which was based on the author's doctoral dissertation research. O'Brien wrote *American Catholics and Social Reform: The New Deal Years,* and Gleason wrote *The Conservative Reformers: German-American Catholics and the Social Order.* Gleason's interests lay in the area of intellectual history, and by 1968 he had already published several articles that clearly indicated the themes he would investigate in the years ahead. O'Brien had also published some articles by this time, and these too suggested the concerns that would occupy him in the future. The contributions of these two scholars offered the first indications that American Catholic history was moving in a different direction. O'Brien and Gleason were laymen, and both of them were trained as American historians, not church historians; neither of them was interested in doing the traditional episcopal, institutional history that had set the standard for such a long time.

Gleason studied with Thomas T. McAvoy at the University of Notre Dame, but his interests were quite different from McAvoy's. Gleason would describe himself as an intellectual historian who studies the history of immigration and most specifically the theme of Americanization. He first examined these issues in his doctoral dissertation, and he has continued to examine them throughout his career. One of his overriding concerns has been the role of religion in the process of Americanization, and he has argued that an understanding of the historical development of the American identity cannot be achieved without a consideration of the role of religion. This is where Catholicism enters into his work — as a force that has helped to shape the American identity both in the nineteenth and twentieth centuries. Because of his interest in both intellectual history and the history of American Catholicism, Gleason has devoted much of his career to studying Catholic higher education. He has published several articles in this area; most notable are his essays on Catholic thought and culture in the 1920-1960 era. Rather than concentrate on the institutional history of Catholic higher education, Gleason has directed his energies toward understanding the cultural and intellectual forces that shaped this educational enterprise.[24]

Over the course of thirty years and in more than forty articles, Gleason has carved a niche for himself as one of the premier historians of American Catholicism in the twentieth century. Moreover, his writings clearly represent a turn away from the episcopal, institutional focus of the pre–Vatican II era. In focusing on new issues, Gleason has sought to integrate the historical study of Catholicism with the study of American thought and culture. This was a constant theme in the writing of Thomas McAvoy, and even though he himself never accomplished this goal, his student has achieved it in an impressive and creative manner. Gleason has demonstrated that the writing of Catholic history, when done well, can have important implications for understanding American history.

David O'Brien was cut from a different cloth than Gleason. A 1960 graduate of the University of Notre Dame, he acknowledged that he was a "relatively unreflective Catholic" who was secure in his faith at the time of his graduation. But the decade of the 1960s changed that for him. "Vatican II," he wrote, "the racial crisis in America, the assassination of our heroes, the Vietnamese conflict, these provided the context of my young adulthood and shattered my certainty."[25]

As a graduate student in history at the University of Rochester, O'Brien began to explore new intellectual horizons. His four years there were, in his words, "my real introduction to the intellectual life." His new understanding of history, specifically the concept of historical consciousness, allowed him to cope with the changes that were shaking the foundations of Catholicism and "to see the erosion of certainty as a quite natural fruit of honesty and commitment to truth, and to regard the new situation, however ambiguous, as a ground for the renewal of faith and hope."[26] After he completed his doctoral work in 1964, he

24. Some of Gleason's essays have been published in two collections, *Keeping the Faith: American Catholicism Past and Present* (Notre Dame, Ind.: University of Notre Dame Press, 1987) and *Speaking of Diversity: Language and Ethnicity in Twentieth-Century America* (Baltimore: The Johns Hopkins University Press, 1992); he also wrote a major essay entitled "American Identity and Americanization" for the *Harvard Encyclopedia of American Ethnic Groups* (Cambridge: Harvard University Press, 1980), pp. 31-58.

25. O'Brien, "The Historian as Believer," in *Journeys: The Impact of Personal Experience on Religious Thought*, ed. Gregory Baum (New York: Paulist Press, 1975), p. 66.

26. O'Brien, "The Historian as Believer," p. 67.

took a teaching position at Loyola College in Montreal. Canada was alive with political ferment in those years, and at Loyola O'Brien met academics "whose whole lives blended scholarly work with political responsibility and action." This impressed him immensely, and he clearly began to see his career as a historian intimately bound up with the larger question of the renewal of the church and the world. In an autobiographical essay written in 1975 he put it in the following manner: "the Catholic intellectual must assist his religious community in the arduous and difficult process of reform and renewal . . . in order to allow the light of the Gospel to be a more effective force in the liberation of men and women from bondage to ignorance, oppression, and death."[27]

The issue that decisively pushed O'Brien in this direction was the Vietnam War. Like many young intellectuals in these years, he "became almost totally preoccupied with the war." The personal crisis sparked by the war became a "profoundly religious crisis" as well — "a people's loss of faith and confidence in themselves and their brothers and sisters," as he put it.[28] So it was that by the late 1960s, O'Brien had become an activist scholar, a historian who wanted to integrate his scholarly work with activities aimed at political and social reform. Like many of his generation, he had become politicized, and this influenced his historical writing. His commitment to Catholicism persuaded him to channel his historical skills into the study of American Catholics. In a 1990 essay he recalled that "someplace along the way I made a more or less conscious decision to locate my work in the context of the Roman Catholic community in the United States. In particular, I chose to look at my work within that segment of the community which was working for renewal in the context of a commitment to peace, social justice, and human liberation."[29]

His first book, *American Catholics and Social Reform,* reflected his interest in social and political thought. It was a study of how Catholics "in the 1930s interpreted and applied the social teachings of the Church to American problems."[30] His interests clearly were centered on the relation of Catholicism to the larger society and how it tried to influence the welfare of that society. His next book appeared in 1972. Entitled *The*

27. O'Brien, "The Historian as Believer," pp. 62, 75.

28. O'Brien, "The Historian as Believer," p. 75.

29. O'Brien, "Faith, Work and Experience in Religion and Intellectual Life," *Cross Currents* 40 (Summer 1990): 200.

30. O'Brien, *American Catholics and Social Reform: The New Deal Years* (New York: Oxford University Press, 1968), p. vii.

Renewal of American Catholicism, it was a tract for the times in which O'Brien urged Catholics to renew the Church and the world. Their time had come socially and politically, said O'Brien, and now they must become involved in the building of a better world. During the rest of the seventies O'Brien wrote numerous essays in which he advocated the renewal of American society by the application of Catholic social teachings on justice and peace. He also became very involved with the Catholic Committee on Urban Ministry, a "network of social-action people around the country who offer one another personal support and share resources in the overall effort to move the Church toward the implementation of recent social teachings."[31] In 1974 he began to work for the National Conference of Catholic Bishops in planning a national conference to celebrate the nation's bicentennial in 1976. Known as the Call to Action conference, it brought together clergy and laity to discuss issues of justice in American society. Both a scholar and a reformer, O'Brien was following the tradition of the Progressive historians who sought to apply their scholarly talents to the reform of society. As a Catholic, O'Brien sought to do this through the Church, even to the point of working full-time for the National Conference of Catholic Bishops in planning the Call to Action conference.

In the 1980s O'Brien continued to write numerous essays related to his concern for justice in the world. He also wrote a history of the diocese of Syracuse, New York, entitled *Faith and Friendship: Catholicism in the Diocese of Syracuse, 1886-1986*. Published in 1987, it was an effort to write a people's history of the Church. Then in 1989 he published *Public Catholicism.* This book reflects O'Brien's life-long concern with the relationship of Catholicism and American society. It is an interpretive history of Catholicism from the eighteenth century to the present woven around three expressions of this relationship — what he calls republican, immigrant, and evangelical Catholicism.

Philip Gleason sought to interpret the American Catholic past from the perspective of the intellectual historian. He did not feel comfortable taking up the cause of the renewal of American Catholicism. In this regard he was very much like his mentor, Thomas T. McAvoy. David O'Brien followed more in the tradition of John Tracy Ellis, who "used history as an instrument to promote changes he believed necessary to American Catholicism."[32] O'Brien was never satisfied with being just a historian. He wanted to do more than interpret the past. He

31. O'Brien, "The Historian as Believer," p. 200.
32. Thomas, "A Century of American Catholic History," p. 41.

wanted to change the world by reforming the Church in the spirit of the Second Vatican Council.

What was new and different about Gleason and O'Brien was that they broke away from the type of history that was dominant among previous historians of American Catholicism. Gleason offered new ideas and categories to interpret the past; O'Brien brought a new perspective to the past — what he came to call the perspective of a "public Catholicism" — and he consciously used history in his attempt to reform the Church and the world. Neither of these scholars evidenced the apologetical concern of earlier historians. They were writing in the post–Vatican II era, when Catholics felt more at home in the United States than ever before and were no longer so self-conscious and defensive about their religion. Nor were they writing for the approval of the hierarchy. Gleason and O'Brien represented the first wave of the new breed of American Catholic historians. Nonetheless, they were both very traditional in the sources they used and the methods they followed in their historical writing. The issues they have examined are also traditional themes in American Catholic historical writing. Gleason's major writings examine the process of Americanization, a theme that McAvoy and others had wrestled with for some time. O'Brien's focus on social movements follows in the tradition of Aaron Abell, one of his teachers at Notre Dame, and his desire to reform the Church follows the path blazed by Ellis.

But even though Gleason and O'Brien have both offered new insights into American Catholic history, they nevertheless represent just the first stage of a new age in the writing of American Catholic history. A new generation of historians, educated at a time when social history was coming into vogue, has gone beyond them. This next generation of scholars is asking different questions of the past and seeking new sources and new methodologies in its attempts to answer these questions. Their new style of history has transformed the study of American Catholicism.

The new social history that developed in the 1960s and '70s favored the intensive study of individual communities. Stephan Thernstrom's book *Poverty and Progress: Social Mobility in a Nineteenth Century City,* published in 1964, became a classic example of this type of history. A study of a single community, Newburyport, Massachusetts, it focuses on a group of people, the inarticulate working class, rather than just individuals, and it searches for patterns and structures in the community that influenced the social mobility of the people. Thernstrom's study combines all the traits of the new social history that was to dominate the historical landscape for the next twenty years. It was virtually impossible for any young historian writing in the 1970s to escape the influence of this new school of thought. This was as true for historians of American Catholicism as it was for historians of American labor.

Among the first community studies of American Catholicism was my own dissertation, done at the University of Chicago under the direction of Martin E. Marty. Published in 1975 under the title of *The Immigrant Church: New York's Irish and German Catholics, 1815-1865*, it touched on several themes that were prominent in historical writing in the 1970s. These included the immigrants, the parish, and the religion of the people — all studied in the context of a single community. Marty's major influence in the writing of this book was his insistence that I try to recapture the religion of the people; each time I failed to do so sufficiently, he would urge me to find new sources and new ways to accomplish this. Another community study of this type was the work of Charles Shanabruch, *Chicago's Catholics: The Evolution of an American Identity*. Published in 1981, it examined the ethnic diversity of Chicago Catholicism during the era of immigration. June Granatir Alexander's book *The Immigrant Church and Community: Pittsburgh's Slovak Catholics and Lutherans, 1880-1915* (1987) is an excellent study of an immigrant community using the parish as the focal point.

This focus on the parish was something new in American Catholic history. Parish histories have traditionally been documents of solely parochial interest, volumes assembled in celebration of some special anniversary. They tend to celebrate the glories of the parish and its clerical leaders in a very uncritical manner. But with the new emphasis on community studies, the parish became a more viable institution to study. It was seen to provide a unique window to the history of a neighborhood and its people. Theologically the study of the parish also made sense. The new theology of the Vatican II era stressed the local church, the people of God, and the parish community best represents the incarnation of this idea. Historians of American Judaism and Protestantism also began to study the local congregation, and before long congregational studies became a buzzword among historians. As regards the history of American Catholicism, the most ambitious parish history study was published in 1987, a two-volume collection of six lengthy essays entitled *The American Catholic Parish: A History from 1850 to the Present*. Its uniqueness was its attempt to offer a history of American Catholicism using the parish, rather than the bishop, as a key organizing principle. The essays are organized on a regional basis to facilitate comparisons about the development of the Church in various regions of the country.[33]

The new social history stressed the study of groups, not just individuals, and it sought to recover the history of the inarticulate lower classes. Known as "bottom up" history, it fired the imagination of many historians and persuaded them to study such groups as slaves, laborers, and immigrants. Immigration history was also undergoing substantial development in these years, and this blended nicely with the emphasis on "bottom up" history. Also part of the equation was the civil rights movement and the stress on black history and the history of other minority groups. Then came the emergence of the new ethnicity, and attention was directed toward such white ethnic groups as Italians and Polish. All of these developments in the late 1960s and early 1970s resulted in an explosion in the study of immigrant communities. Many of these gave some peripheral attention to religion, most often Catholicism, given the large numbers of Catholic immigrants during the nineteenth century. Others were more explicitly centered on the theme of religion, such as Silvano Tomasi's *Piety and Power: The Role of Italian Parishes in the New York Metropolitan Area* (1975) and Joseph John Parot's *Polish Catholics in Chicago, 1850-1920* (1981). Both of these studies use the parish as the key organizing principle in their research. A study of black Catholics also was published during this period, the first such study in many years — Cyprian Davis's *History of Black Catholics in the United States* (1990).

An important development in the post-sixties era was the emergence of women's history. This has transformed the study of American history, and its impact on religious history has been significant as well. One of the essays in Mary Jo Weaver's study of the emergence of the women's movement within contemporary American Catholicism, *New Catholic Women* (1985), is a treatment of the exclusion of women from American Catholic history, a problem that has eased somewhat in the years since. The area that first attracted the attention of historians was the history of women religious. Mary Ewens's book *The Role of the Nun in Nineteenth Century America* (1979) was a pioneer study of this topic. Since then many studies of women religious orders have appeared. In recent years, historians of American women religious, most of them members

33. The authors of these essays are Joseph J. Casino for the parish in the Northeast, Michael J. McNally for the Southeast, Charles E. Nolan for the South Central region, Jeffrey M. Burns for the Pacific States, Carol L. Jensen for the Intermountain West, and Stephen J. Shaw for the Midwest.

of religious orders themselves, have formed their own organization and regularly publish a newsletter and convene conferences. Margaret S. Thompson, a laywoman and historian at Syracuse University, has written numerous essays on the history of women religious from the perspective of a women's historian.[34] Debra Campbell has also written an important essay that emphasizes the role of women in twentieth-century American Catholicism.[35] Karen Kennelly edited *American Catholic Women: A Historical Exploration* (1989), a collection of essays that clearly suggest that the history of American Catholic women is still in its early stages of development. James J. Kenneally recently published *The History of American Catholic Women* (1990), a single-volume work chronicling the contributions women have made to American Catholic history.

Another area of inquiry virtually unmined by historians of American Catholicism until the 1970s was the religion of the people. The use of new types of sources, such as prayer books and sermons, and the methodological influence of such anthropologists as Clifford Geertz and Victor Turner have influenced this genre of history. In one of my own studies, *Catholic Revivalism: The American Experience, 1830-1900* (1977), I sought to uncover the religion of the people by examining the parish mission — its sermons, rituals, and structure. Joseph Chinnici has written extensively on the theme of piety and recently published a book on this topic entitled *Living Stones: The History and Structure of Catholic Spiritual Life in the United States* (1989). This comprehensive synthesis is most original in its interpretation and offers an entirely new perspective on the history of American Catholicism from the late eighteenth century to the present. Ann Taves's study *The Household of Faith: Roman Catholic Devotions in Mid-Nineteenth Century America* (1986) was another important study of Catholic piety. By focusing on the devotional literature of Catholicism, Taves was able to explore the rise of devotionalism in the nineteenth century and its role in shaping the Catholic mind of this era. In his study of Italian devotional practices *The Madonna of 115th Street: Faith and Community in Italian Harlem, 1880-*

34. E.g., Thompson, "Women, Feminism, and the New Religious History: Catholic Sisters as a Case Study," in *Belief and Behavior: Essays in the New Religious History*, ed. Philip VanderMeer and Robert Swierenga (New Brunswick, N.J.: Rutgers University Press, 1991), pp. 136-63; and "Sisterhood and Power: Class, Culture, and Ethnicity in the American Convent," *Colby Library Quarterly* 25 (Sept. 1989): 149-75.

35. See Campbell, "The Struggle to Serve: From the Lay Apostolate to the Ministry Explosion," in *Transforming Parish Ministry: The Changing Roles of Catholic Clergy, Laity, and Women Religious*, ed. Jay P. Dolan, R. Scott Appleby, Patricia Byrne, and Debra Campbell (New York: Crossroad, 1989).

1950 (1985) and in his more recent work on devotion to St. Jude,[36] Robert Orsi has demonstrated how a historian with imagination and new methodological tools can mine the riches of popular devotions.

Another area of inquiry is the historical development of theology. Gerald P. Fogarty's study *American Catholic Biblical Scholarship: A History from the Early Republic to Vatican II (1989)* is a fine example of the insights a historian can bring to the intellectual heritage of Catholics. In *The Diocesan Seminary in the United States: A History from the 1780s to the Present* (1989), Joseph M. White examines the education of priests and the place of theology in that education. Theological modernism did establish a foothold among American Catholics, and R. Scott Appleby's study *Church and Age Unite: The Modernist Impulse in American Catholicism* (1992) provides an examination of the rise and fall of this school of thought.

In addition to these new areas of inquiries, historians have also turned their attention to more traditional themes. Diocesan histories have been a staple of American Catholic historiography for many years, but historians are now writing these histories with a new perspective, giving a fresh look to a traditional topic. Leslie Woodcock Tentler's history of the archdiocese of Detroit, *Seasons of Grace* (1990), is a fine example of this new style of diocesan history. Another example is Thomas W. Spalding's *The Premier See: A History of the Archdiocese of Baltimore, 1789-1989* (1989). Histories of religious orders have seldom appealed to those outside the orders, but some new studies seem to be turning this around. In *Desegregating the Altar: The Josephites and the Struggle for Black Priests, 1871-1960* (1990), Stephen J. Ochs studies the Josephite order and their struggle to ordain black priests. More than a history of the Josephites, the book offers a compelling explanation of why there are so few black Catholic priests in the United States. Christopher Kaufmann wrote a history of the Sulpicians that was much more than an institutional study — *Tradition and Transformation in Catholic Culture: The Priests of Saint Sulpice in the United States from 1791 to the Present* (1988). Bishops have always counted historians among their admirers, and this does not appear to be changing. A volume edited by Gerald P. Fogarty, *Patterns of Episcopal Leadership* (1989), includes essays on prominent bishops by some of the best traditional church historians. Fogarty himself is certainly one of the best of the new

36. Orsi, "'He Keeps Me Going': Women's Devotion to Saint Jude and the Dialectics of Gender in American Catholicism, 1929-1965," in *Belief in History: Innovative Approaches to European and American Religion*, ed. Thomas Kselman (Notre Dame, Ind.: University of Notre Dame Press, 1991), pp. 137-72.

generation of church historians, and his study *The Vatican and the American Hierarchy from 1870 to 1965* (1982) is an excellent reminder that traditional church history, when done well, can be as revealing and engaging as the new religious history that has developed since the 1970s. Another example from this genre would be James Hennesey's general history *American Catholics: A History of the Roman Catholic Community in the United States* (1981).

This brief survey of the new directions that American Catholic historiography has taken since the 1970s indicates that the scholars writing American Catholic history have made a radical departure from their counterparts in the 1950s, who were characterized chiefly by their "zeal for episcopal biography." Even more telling than the new themes, sources, and methodologies that have been introduced are differences in the background of the new breed of historian compared with the background of those who wrote in the Guilday era. In 1920 the membership of the American Catholic Historical Association was 90 percent male, and of the 172 individuals who belonged to the association, 64 percent were priests. It was an overwhelmingly male, clerical preserve. At a conference in 1990 at the University of Notre Dame on the history of twentieth-century American Catholicism, fifty papers were presented. About half the people who presented papers were female (46%), and 84 percent of the presenters were lay men or women; only 16 percent were clerics. Also significant is the educational background of the new historians. In the Guilday-Ellis era, those who wanted to become historians of American Catholicism almost without exception studied at Catholic University. That is no longer true. The new generation of historians has studied at a considerable variety of universities, both private and public, Catholic and secular. Having left the Catholic ghetto, they not only came under the influence of a more diverse scholarly community but were also exposed more directly to the winds of change that influenced American universities more generally in the 1960s and 1970s. Before long, the "consensus" view that dominated historical writing disintegrated, and the new generation of historians remade American history. Along the way, they also remade American Catholic history.

The new Catholic history that has emerged since the 1970s differs in a number of ways from the writing of the Guilday-Ellis era, but one feature that is especially noteworthy is its lack of coherence. In the 1940s and 1950s, American Catholic history was distinguishable by its institutional focus and its endorsement of the concept of the progressive Americanization of the Church and its people. There was a consensus about the history of the American Catholic experience. That is no longer true. The variety of topics that historians now study, the differences in their methodologies, and the variety of perspectives and beliefs that they bring to their work have shattered that consensus. This is not peculiar to American Catholic history; it is symptomatic of American history in general. Many historians have lamented this lack of synthesis, and yet the new social history of the United States in general and of Catholics in particular has demonstrated that history is never as simple as the historians would like it to be. History is complex and never yields to the simple interpretation. The consensus view of the past has given way to a rich diversity in historical studies generated by the use of new types of sources and new methodologies as well as the asking of new questions about the past. In the case of American Catholic history, such diversity has revealed the richness of the American Catholic past, nurturing a vision of that past that is much broader than was possible in the Guilday-Ellis era. Because it is so diverse and multifaceted, American Catholic history can now be integrated much more easily into the general history of the United States. This is especially noticeable in the area of immigration history, intellectual and cultural history, and women's history, as well as the study of popular religion. The diversity of the new American Catholic history does not mean that coherence and synthesis are something of the past. There is sufficient coherence in the new history that a new and fresh interpretation of the past can be attempted. This is what I tried to do in *The American Catholic Experience: A History from Colonial Times to the Present* (1985).

Compounding the problem for historians of American Catholicism is the ingredient of ideology, or how scholars interpret the changes that the Catholic Church has undergone since the Second Vatican Council. One school of thought interprets recent developments in American Catholicism in a very negative manner. According to this perspective, the unity of the 1940s and 1950s has been shattered and the culture of Catholicism has disintegrated. Philip Gleason has best articulated this point of view in his recent collection of essays *Keeping the Faith* (1987). Another school of thought endorses the changes that have occurred, and, while acknowledging the obvious disintegration of the culture of Catholicism prevalent in the pre–Vatican II era, it supports the idea of historical development and is more hopeful about the future of Catholicism. David O'Brien would be representative of this point of view.

Such difference of opinion is not unusual among historians. What is unusual is that many American Catholic intellectuals no longer feel comfortable with their Church. In the past, Catholics grappled with their relationship with American society — Should they be insiders or outsiders? Should they assimilate more readily or cling to their traditions more tenaciously? Now the key issue is the Church. Having finally achieved acceptance in American society and no longer having to fight against discrimination, Catholics now find themselves trying to come to grips with a Church and an ecclesiastical culture that in the past seemed never to change. Is it now changing too fast? What has happened to such traditional practices as confession and fasting? Are there any moral standards left? Do the clergy respect the opinion of the laity? Where does the authority of the pope begin and end? Of course, such questioning and discontent is not confined to the United States. It is visible throughout the world. In the United States it has been influenced by the broader cultural and political divisions between liberals and conservatives. The ideological fault line that has divided American society since the 1960s did not stop at the door of the Church. It has entered the sanctuary and reshaped the American religious landscape. It has also entered the academy and the writing of American Catholic history. Scholars of both points of view are engaged in the writing of this history, and in recent years some individuals have politicized this diversity of opinion to the point of claiming that some of the new generation of historians are seeking to "rewrite the American Catholic story line in order to prop up the sagging cause of 'progressive' Catholicism today." The new breed of historians, in the opinion of their most persistent critic, George Weigel, want to use history for "various partisan purposes in today's struggles over the meaning of orthodoxy, authority, and ministry."[37] Indeed, it is true that the division of opinion and belief that now permeates the Catholic community has influenced the writing of American Catholic history. Whether or not this has resulted in a distortion of the past for partisan purposes is an entirely different question. How this issue is resolved should make the future of American Catholic historical studies interesting, perhaps even exciting. No doubt it will also lead the study of American Catholic history in a new direction.

37. Weigel, "Telling the American Catholic Story," *First Things,* November 1990, pp. 48, 43. In this essay Weigel asserts that I am the chief culprit in this reinterpretation of American Catholic history, and he cites as evidence my book *The American Catholic Experience: A History from Colonial Times to the Present* (Garden City, N.Y.: Doubleday, 1985). Though I am flattered by the attention he gives to my work, I find his argument very unconvincing. The main problem with it is that it is based on opinion rather than historical data. Nonetheless, Weigel's essay is an example of how ideology and a person's understanding of the Church can politicize the study of American Catholic history.

Twentieth-Century American Hymnody and Church Music

PAUL WESTERMEYER

I. Lacuna

In an Editor's Column for *The Hymn* in July 1988, I wrote the following:

> Earlier this year, Martin E. Marty, church historian at the University of Chicago, sent a letter to a number of us, asking us to nominate articles for a fifteen volume reprint series dealing with Modern American Religion. He indicated that he was sending the letter to people "with many different fields of expertise and approaches, to allow for a wide range and a good deal of representativeness." I assumed he expected me to suggest an article dealing with church music or hymnody. Other themes would be amply covered by the rest of his nominators.
>
> The requirements for the articles were these: 1) the best 2) journal articles 3) dealing historically 4) with modern American religion, meaning basically twentieth century, though we could reach back to the 1880s, to which I added 5) concerning hymnody and church music.
>
> I could not think of anything immediately, but assumed that was just a deficiency in my memory. So I looked up bibliographies I had prepared, searched likely journals and my own notes, had the Elmhurst College Library run a computer check, and sought advice from friends and colleagues. All the searching yielded nothing. There are historical articles which deal with earlier periods and other countries or include twentieth century America as part of a larger sweep, there are articles with historical allusions and discussions of opinion which often relate to narrow or specialized topics, there are matters of theory and practice, and there are some books perhaps slightly

> more helpful than journals; but, unless I have missed something (which is entirely possible), there are no hard-nosed historical treatments in journals about twentieth century religious music or hymnody. There certainly is no body of literature on this topic![1]

More recently, Victor E. Gebauer addressed this same lacuna:

> Church musicians who search for their professional roots are puzzled by the virtual silence regarding 20th-century church music in "secular" histories of American music even though church music is covered extensively in reference to previous centuries. One finds, moreover, no comprehensive history of church music which even acknowledges present conditions, though some limited studies have appeared within recent years.[2]

There probably are some superficial reasons for the lack of historical analyses of twentieth-century church music. One might be that we write histories about things only after we have attained some distance from them, and our century is too close to us. There is some truth to that, but it is also true that we already have histories about all sorts of other topics in the twentieth century. Why not church music as well?

Another superficial reason might be the usual American religious historiographical dilemma. How do you make sense of things, or allow the overall shape of the story to find expression, when you are presented with a multiplicity of denominations and the temptation to

1. Paul Westermeyer, "Editor's Column: A Call for Twentieth Century Hymnic Histories," *The Hymn* 39 (July 1988): 5.

Since I wrote this, *The Hymnal 1982 Companion,* vol. 1, ed. Raymond F. Glover (New York: Church Hymnal Corporation, 1990) has been published. It contains three articles about twentieth-century hymnic history: Paul Westermeyer, "Hymnody in the United States from the Civil War to World War I [1860-1916]," pp. 447-73; David Farr, "Protestant Hymn-Singing in the United States, 1916-1943: Affirming a Heritage," pp. 505-54; and Russell Schulz-Widmar, "Hymnody in the United States since 1950," pp. 600-636.

2. Gebauer, "Problems in the History of American Church Music," *The Hymn* 41 (October 1990): 45. Gebauer's footnote at this point (p. 48) reads as follows: "The last major work devoted to American church music in any comprehensive fashion was Leonard Ellinwood, *The History of Church Music,* rev. ed. (New York: DaCapo Press, 1970), originally published in 1953. An example of a recent study, limited in scope, is Talmage W. Dean, *A Survey of Twentieth Century Protestant Church Music in America* (Nashville: Broadman Press, 1988). The first full-length American church music history was Nathaniel Gould's *Church Music in America* (Boston: A. N. Johnson, 1853)."

write a series of separate histories? That is a problem, of course. But historians have faced it in other areas. Why not in church music?

Philipp Harnoncourt, a European liturgical scholar, might have found a way to view the problem in a less superficial way by locating its origins in the nineteenth century. He has explained that composers then began to compose works for no particular purpose except people's amusement. That removed music from its earlier relation to the whole of life, to festivals, celebrations, praise of God, events of state, and play. Further, as composers felt they had to express their religious feelings, the congregation became an audience. Simultaneously church music was isolated: concert music was considered too worldly, so contemporary pieces were seldom performed in church, and a new thing called a "sacred style" developed.[3] Harnoncourt might argue that by the twentieth century, church music in the Western world was a cut-flower arrangement with no life left in it. And nobody is much interested in chronicling what is dead.

Handt Hanson, the musician at Prince of Peace Lutheran Church in Burnsville, Minnesota, who has used a popular idiom in the worship services he plans, gives a similar picture from a different perspective. Taking the best figures he could find, correlated to the widest age group possible, he compiled the following statistics for what people listened to on the radio in 1987 in the Twin Cities:

Type of Music	Percent of Listeners
Classical	2.8%
Country Western	17.0%
Jazz	0.0%
Folk	0.0%
News/talk	17.0% plus
All religious	3.1%
Top 40 and rock	66.0%

Hanson points out that the music most often used in churches fits nowhere in this tabulation. He doesn't use the term, but he too is pointing to what might be called a "sacred cut-flower style."

3. See Harnoncourt, "So sie's nicht singen, so gleuben sie's nicht," *Liturgie und Dichtung,* vol. 2 (St. Ottilien: EOS Verlag, 1983), pp. 165-67. For an English translation, see "If They Don't Sing It, They Don't Believe It," in *The Hymnology Annual,* vol. 1, ed. and trans. Vernon Wicker (Benton Harbor, Mich.: Patterson, 1991), pp. 4-35.

Daniel Kingman, one of the few American music historians who has addressed twentieth-century church music at all, makes a similar point. He has said that the "liturgically and aesthetically oriented middle- and upper-class churches will continue to attract the services of enough talented and highly competent composers to keep things alive there artistically," since the market is not large enough to be degraded by commercialism. "But in the case of popular religious music, it would appear that its life as we have known it for three hundred years — a period of exuberance, of vitality, and of spontaneous self-renewal — may be over." In 1979 Kingman saw no new life and argued that, apart from survival in isolated rural areas and specific efforts toward preservation and revival — as of shape-note hymnody — "a tradition of indigenous religious music genuinely 'of the people' is dormant, if not dead."[4]

The distinction Kingman makes between "liturgically and aesthetically oriented music" and "music genuinely 'of the people' " is part of the puzzle here. As Victor Gebauer has pointed out, until Gilbert Chase wrote *America's Music from the Pilgrims to the Present*, music historians presupposed that the subject of American church music history was the sort of music that was refining itself in imitation of European models.[5] Chase called that presupposition into question and argued that American music is not simply a European offshoot but has its own separate identity and integrity. So what is an American history of church music about — high art that is presumed not to be of the people, "popular religious music" that is presumed to be "of the people," or both? Are the assumptions accurate? And how does this come out in the twentieth century?

It may be that the failure to report about twentieth-century American church music has nothing to do with music at all but is related to the way the culture generally and historians specifically regard the

4. Kingman, *American Music: A Panorama* (New York: Schirmer Books, 1979), pp. 170-71. In the second edition of this book (1990), Kingman deleted these comments about the disappearance of popular religious music and spoke instead about gospel music as "a significant segment of the American popular music industry" and an American export (p. 162).

5. Gebauer, " 'Look Again!' Writing about American Church Music," *Currents in Theology and Mission* 16 (June 1989): 182. For evidence in support of his thesis, see Nathaniel Gould, *Church Music in America* (Boston: A. N. Johnson, 1853); and John Tasker Howard, *Our American Music — Three Hundred Years of It* (New York: Thomas Y. Crowell, 1954). Chase's *America's Music from the Pilgrims to the Present* was first published in 1955; a third revised edition was published by the University of Illinois Press in 1987.

church. Ann Douglas says that modern mass culture has picked up "the sentimental peddling of religious belief for its nostalgic value."[6] Patrick Keifert summarizes Douglas's argument for our period and says, "In short, religion becomes women's business and the women's place is securely in the private and domestic domain."[7] That is to say that in the United States in the twentieth century, the church is privatized and no longer regarded as having any public relevance. And that would mean that the church's music is irrelevant and not worth discussing.

Whether the church's activity in connection with such social issues as the fight to enact Prohibition, the civil rights struggle, the Poor People's Campaign, the Vietnam War, the abortion debate, and the like can be characterized as irrelevant is for others to determine, though there is surely much that is true in Douglas's and Keifert's analyses. The problem, however, lies in the fact that about 47 million people attend religious services each weekend across the United States, and most of them sing. And even for those who sing half-heartedly or not at all, the issue of what is sung and what is not sung at worship has traditionally been a matter of significant interest. On the whole, the music used in worship has a profound impact on the memories and feelings and lives of believers — a strange sort of irrelevance.[8]

What is even more to the point for our purposes, however, is another of Victor Gebauer's comments. He notes that "more people know of Randall Thompson through church and school experiences than have even heard of the West coast experimental composer Harry Partsch. Yet Partsch's work is treated as a vital element in American culture [by historians of American music], while Thompson is ignored completely by Hamm and Chase and given only passing mention by Hitchcock and Kingman."[9]

6. Douglas, *The Feminization of American Culture* (New York: Avon Books, 1977), p. 3.

7. Keifert, "A Challenge to Public Worship," undated manuscript, p. 9.

8. I have no hard data to substantiate the assertion that the music of worship is important in the lives of believers, but in discussions with congregations I have served or visited with my worship classes and choirs, as well as in surveys that churches have taken concerning their worship, music and hymnody always play a critical role. My hunch is that the public life of people is more profoundly influenced than we think by a religious group and its music, even if this is very difficult (or impossible) to measure.

9. Gebauer, "Look Again!" p. 183. The references to Hamm and Hitchcock are to Charles Hamm's *Music in the New World* (New York: W. W. Norton, 1983) and H. Wiley Hitchcock's *Music in the United States: A Historical Introduction,* 3d ed. (Englewood Cliffs, N.J.: Prentice-Hall, 1988).

No matter how irrelevant some analysts may consider twentieth-century church music to be, I would argue that no picture of our period would be complete without a consideration of it. It may or may not be on the cutting edge of musical developments, it may or may not have been isolated, it may or may not be high art, it may or may not be folk art, and it may be some or all of these in some curious combination. Whatever it is, it generates tremendous passions and exerts strong influences. The following is an attempt to propose some possible organizing schemes for understanding the roles it plays.

II. Twentieth-Century Church Music and Hymnody

One way to cut through the confusion concerning contemporary church music is to listen to a twentieth-century composer who carefully researched folk music. Bela Bartok wrote, "let us consider how is it possible to reconcile music based on folk-music with the modern movement into atonality, or music based on twelve tones. Let us say frankly that it is not possible. Why not? Because folk tunes are always tonal. Folk music of atonality is completely inconceivable."[10]

The point Bartok makes here gets at the heart of the absence of church music from twentieth-century historical discussions. Though Arnold Schoenberg is not the twentieth century's greatest composer, the atonal or twelve-tone music with which he is associated and its serial progeny have in large measure set the terms for serious Western twentieth-century musical culture and discussions about it.[11]

At its heart, church music is a folk idiom, because its center is what the people sing. The people, the folk, as Bartok says, have always sung melodies around a tonal — or modal (Bartok's meaning includes modal) — center, and much of the music their musicians have used has, not unexpectedly, employed such a center as well. This is not to say that atonality or any harmonic pallet is by definition ruled out of church music or that the meaning of "folk" is narrow; indeed, twentieth-century American church music has included everything from gospel and protest songs with only I, IV, and V chords to black and white spirituals to colorful uses of common-practice harmony to the most

10. Bartok, in *Contemporary Composers on Contemporary Music,* ed. Elliot Schwartz and Barne Childs (New York: Holt, Rinehart & Winston, 1967), p. 77.

11. Cf. William W. Austin, *Music in the Twentieth Century* (New York: W. W. Norton, 1966), p. 194.

complex atonal, polytonal, and aleatory music, in addition to past styles from every period along with neoforms and imitations. It is simply to say that the center of gravity has not been atonal, and in that sense the church has been out of step with the terms of serious twentieth-century Western musical culture. It is not surprising, therefore, that those who chronicle this culture would omit church music.

The fundamental problem is much deeper than church music. Church music is simply one of the most obvious illustrations of the twentieth century's division between the arts and the public at large. Whether church music represents a prophetic witness on behalf of the human race's deepest musical longings against a derailed and esoteric twentieth-century musical culture,[12] or whether our serious musical culture represents a prophetic witness against a public and a church stuck in a dead end of nostalgia, or whether there is some truth to both of those assertions, only future historians will tell. The point here is that, because of the nature of church music, in the twentieth century one has to assess it from grounds other than those of twentieth-century musical composition. Four organizational schemes suggest themselves: teachers and scholars, hymns and hymn books, music and musicians, and societies and schools. To these I will add a post-Puritan conclusion.

1. Teachers and Scholars

The starting point for the studies in this volume is 1893, the year Philip Schaff died. Perhaps that is significant in our search for an organizing principle here, for among his many other pursuits, Schaff was a hymnological scholar whose article on German hymnody in Julian's *Dictionary of Hymnology* can still be profitably used today.[13] Is there a thread of teachers and scholars, intellectual successors to Schaff, that weaves its way throughout the century and suggests some vitality to hymnology and church music as disciplines? The answer is Yes. The thread is made up of individuals who have offered us insights into both the discipline and its practice.

The thread begins with Louis Benson (1855-1930). A lawyer who studied at Princeton Seminary, Benson was ordained in 1886, served for six years at the Church of the Redeemer in Germantown, Penn-

12. See Henry Pleasants, *The Agony of Modern Music* (New York: Simon & Schuster, 1955).

13. Schaff, "German Hymnology," in *A Dictionary of Hymnology,* ed. John Julian, 2d rev. ed. (1907; reprint, New York: Dover Publications, 1957), pp. 412-18.

sylvania, and then became hymnal editor for the General Assembly of the Presbyterian Church, USA. He spent the rest of his life doing research, writing, editing, and teaching about hymnody at Auburn Seminary and Princeton Seminary. His book *The English Hymn* (1915) grew out of a series of lectures he delivered at Princeton Seminary in 1907 and 1910. Benson edited the Presbyterian hymnal in 1895, revised it in 1911, assisted the Southern Presbyterians in their hymnal editing, and edited *Christian Song* in 1926 and *The Smaller Hymnal* in 1928 for the Presbyterian Board of Christian Education.[14]

Contemporaneously with Benson, Luther D. Reed (1873-1972) was beginning his work. Reed lived much farther into the twentieth century than Benson, and his interests ranged beyond hymnody to worship and music more generally. A teacher at Philadelphia Seminary in Mt. Airy, Pennsylvania, Reed was one of the primary editors of texts and music in 1917 for the *Common Service Book* of the United Lutheran Church in America and forty-one years later for *The Service Book and Hymnal* of the Lutheran Church in America. His books *The Lutheran Liturgy* (1947) and *Worship* (1959) summarize his work and its Anglicanizing tendencies. With the Pittsburgh organist Harry G. Archer, he edited two books of Gregorian chant for the offices.[15]

Winfred Douglas (1867-1944), an Episcopalian, also had interests that extended beyond hymnody to church music, musicology, and worship. Douglas was a native of New York who graduated from Syracuse University with a bachelor's degree in music and then worked as a voice instructor and organist/choirmaster before he was ordained in 1893. He served briefly as a curate and musician at the Church of the Redeemer in New York City, but, because of poor health, he moved to Evergreen, Colorado, from which he traveled and to which he returned for the rest of his life. During one recuperative period, he lived among the Hopi and Navajo Indians and became an expert in Indian culture. Shortly thereafter he studied abroad, including a time at the Benedictine Abbey of Solesmes. On his return to the United States, he put his newfound knowledge to use as Director of Music at the Community of St. Mary in Peekskill, New York, and he became known as an authority on Gregorian chant. He spoke at

14. For bibliographic information on the 1895 Presbyterian hymnal and selected other twentieth-century hymnals, see the chronological listing at the end of this essay.

15. *The Psalter and Canticles Pointed for Chanting to the Gregorian Psalm Tones with a Plain Song Setting for the Order of Matins and Vespers* (New York: Christian Literature, 1897) and *The Choral Service Book* (Philadelphia: General Council Publication Board, 1901).

many seminaries, including Seabury-Western in Evanston, Illinois, where in 1935 he delivered the Hale Memorial Lectures (published in 1937 as *Church Music in History and Practice*). Though Douglas had a hand in the Episcopal *Hymnal* of 1916, two and a half decades later he packed all his knowledge and experience into editing the *Episcopal Hymnal 1940,* a landmark for which he is justly well known.

Benson, Reed, and Douglas represent English and European orientations. They all were influenced by the nineteenth-century Oxford Movement, which, along with parallel denominational movements, has had a considerable impact on twentieth-century American church music. One could add people to that cluster who were less influenced by the Oxford Movement but who still had an English or European orientation. Erik Routley (1917-1983), the twentieth century's foremost hymnologist, who wrote voluminously and came from England to Westminster Choir College in 1975, is a good example.[16]

As the century progressed, there came others who were oriented more specifically to American matters, among them George Pullen Jackson, Donald Hustad, and Jon Michael Spencer.

George Pullen Jackson (1874-1953) complained that the singing of American urban congregations and the hymnals from which they sang omitted American folk hymns.[17] Jackson studied at the Royal Conservatory of Music in Dresden and at Vanderbilt, Munich, Bonn, and Chicago universities. After completing his dissertation at the University of Chicago on Romantic literature, he joined the German department at Vanderbilt in 1918. He then developed an interest in the Sacred Harp Singers and similar Southern groups. In a book entitled *White Spirituals in the Southern Uplands,* he introduced this haunting, gapped, pentatonic music to a wider public, which contributed to its increasing use in American hymnals.[18]

Donald Hustad (b. 1918) represents the evangelical wing of

16. For a chronology of Routley's life and a list of his works, see *Duty and Delight: Routley Remembered,* ed. Robin A. Leaver et al. (Carol Stream, Ill.: Hope Publishing, 1985).

17. See Jackson, *Spiritual Folk-Songs of Early America* (New York: J. J. Augustine, 1937), p. 223.

18. Jackson, *White Spirituals in the Southern Uplands: The Story of the Fasola Folk, Their Songs, Singings, and "Buckwheat Notes"* (1933; reprint, New York: Dover Publications, 1965). Jackson also wrote *White and Negro Spirituals* (1944; reprint, New York: Da Capo Press, 1975) and *The Story of the Sacred Harp* (Nashville: FIX, 1944). For a chart of the increase in the interest in this music, see Harry Eskew, "Southern Harmony and Its Era," *The Hymn* 41 (October 1990): 34.

American Christianity. A graduate of Fletcher College, he earned his doctorate in music from Northwestern University in 1963. After holding a number of posts in and around Chicago — among them staff musician at WMBI, associate professor of music at Olivet College, organist-director at First Methodist Church in Park Ridge, and director of the Sacred Music Department at Moody Bible Institute in Chicago — he joined the Billy Graham Evangelistic Association as team organist and director of the "Crusader Men" on the Hour of Decision. He left the Billy Graham organization to teach at New Orleans Baptist Theological Seminary and then moved on to take the position of Professor of Church Music at Southern Baptist Theological Seminary in Louisville, Kentucky. Hustad has edited numerous hymnals, the last of which was *The Worshiping Church* in 1990. His book *Jubilate! Church Music in the Evangelical Tradition* (1981) grew out of his own pilgrimage: it is a broad description of church music in which gospel hymnody is cogently described and supported, along with its allied forms and theological presuppositions.

The last of this group is a more recent teacher and scholar. Just beginning his career, Jon Michael Spencer (b. 1957) has in the space of a few years written numerous studies about themes related to black sacred music in America. He has studied at Hampton University in Virginia and Washington University in St. Louis, where he earned his Ph.D. in music composition. After teaching at Duke University Divinity School, he went to Bowling Green State University in Bowling Green, Ohio, where he now teaches. In addition to numerous articles, his books include *As the Black School Sings: Black Music Collections at Black Universities and Colleges, with a Union List of Book Holdings* (1987), *Sacred Symphony: The Chanted Sermon of the Black Preacher* (1987), and *Protest & Praise: Sacred Music of Black Religion* (1990). Spencer is also founder and editor of *The Journal of Black Sacred Music*.

One could add many names to this list in and beyond the traditions already mentioned. The latter category, for example, might include a string of Roman Catholic scholars beginning in the nineteenth century at St. John's Abbey in Collegeville, Minnesota, or with John Baptist Singenberger (1848-1924), who founded the Caecilian Society and edited the magazine *Caecilia;* the church's elder Jewish cousins and their work, such as A. Z. Idelsohn's *Jewish Music in Its Historical Development* (1929) and Eric Werner's monumental two-volume work *The Sacred Bridge: The Interdependence of Liturgy and Music in Synagogue and Church during the First Millennium* (1959, 1984); Daniel W. Patterson and his equally monumental work, *The Shaker Spiritual* (1979); or, outside any specific tradition, Orpha Ochse and her *The History of the Organ in the United States* (1975).

There has been no dearth of twentieth-century teachers and scholars working on hymnody and church music. As in all disciplines, some have produced better work than others, but on the whole it has immeasurably increased our understanding. The work itself has been richly diverse, and it has come from a rich diversity of sources and individuals, many of whom have themselves been practitioners.

2. *Hymns and Hymnals*

Hymnals have been edited and published throughout the twentieth century in the United States, as a look at the list of titles at the end of this essay will show. There have been so many publications and so much activity that, at first glance, it seems unwieldy. But it does have a shape.

At the beginning of our period, hymnody was driven by three forces: an ecumenical and historic breadth, gospel hymnody, and social concerns. The first two of these forces are symbolically linked to 1895; a call for the third came a little later. In expanded versions, these forces continued throughout the century, with the second two gradually encompassed in the net of the first.

The denominational hymnals, though they are widely dispersed, can be broadly organized into three clusters, around the early, middle, and latter parts of the century. The books with which Benson, Douglas, and Reed were associated — the Presbyterian Hymnal of 1895 (revised in 1911 and supplemented in 1917), the Episcopal *Hymnal* of 1916, and the Lutheran *Common Service Book* of 1917 — represent the first cluster; the Episcopal *Hymnal 1940* and many other hymnals on either side of it represent the second; and the *Lutheran Book of Worship* of 1978 represents the third, a cluster that is still growing.

The major denominational hymnals of the twentieth century have been influenced by an increasingly inclusive ecumenical and historical breadth. The hymnals that Benson, Reed, and Douglas were associated with at the beginning of the century were tinged with Victorian sentiments, as one might expect, but essentially they were controlled by the ecumenical hymnic activity that had begun in the nineteenth century. *Hymns Ancient and Modern* (1861) — which brought together a broad ecumenical cross section of hymns from the entire history of the Christian church — was their model. This influence was felt even where one might not expect it, by the Baptists in *Sursum Corda* (1898), which E. H. Johnson edited.

Gospel hymnody challenged the church's broader historic hymnic consciousness. The Dwight Moody–Ira Sankey campaigns in the last quarter of the nineteenth century produced a body of hymnody that was collected in 1895 in *Gospel Hymns Nos. 1 to 6 Complete.* That collection contained cheery triplicate and dotted rhythms, enticing mild chromaticism, almost all major keys, and a lack of dissonance or musical argument to create tension. It developed into the even lighter, semi-sacred, and more commercial music of the Billy Sunday era after the turn of the century, such as "His Eye Is on the Sparrow" and "Ivory Palaces" from Charles Alexander's collections, Ina Ogden's "Brighten the Corner Where You Are," and George Bernard's "The Old Rugged Cross." It often took over Sunday schools altogether and made inroads into mainstream Protestant services as well. Sometimes songs in this style virtually replaced an entire hymnic heritage, at least in the Sunday school, if not beyond, as in the case of the German Evangelical Synod of North America (the denomination the Niebuhrs came from), which in its *Elmhurst Hymnal* (1921) gave up its German chorales. Independent publishers ground out pamphlets of gospel hymnody in great numbers.

The third force can be identified with a call by Walter Rauschenbusch for a hymnody associated with the Social Gospel. In his *Evangeliums-Lieder* of 1891, Rauschenbusch himself had translated Ira Sankey's gospel hymns into German, but after the turn of the century, he attacked Christian hymnody generally and gospel hymnody specifically on the grounds that it avoided service to humanity and postponed corrections of social ills to a future life. He argued for a Social Gospel hymnody that would "voice the new social enthusiasms."[19] His cry found expression in a couple of publications — Henry Sloane Coffin's *Hymns of the Kingdom of God* and Mabel Mussey's *Social Hymns of Brotherhood and Aspiration.* The challenge of its message, the task of creating new hymns, and the lack of gospel hymnody's enticements combined to keep Social Gospel hymnody from being a strong force or exerting a large popular appeal. Hymns with societal themes were not absent from the period,[20] but they did not have the proportions or attractions of gospel hymnody.

Denominational hymnals, however, were influenced by hymns with societal concerns and gospel hymnody. For example, the Presbyterian hymnal of 1895 which Benson edited was "virtually free of gospel

19. See Jon Michael Spencer, "Hymns of the Social Awakening: Walter Rauschenbusch and Social Gospel Hymnody," *The Hymn* 40 (April 1989): 19.

20. See Paul Westermeyer, "Hymnody in the United States from the Civil War to World War I (1860-1916)," in *The Hymnal 1982 Companion,* vol. 1, ed. Raymond F. Glover (New York: Church Hymnal Corp., 1990), pp. 447-51.

hymnody, tipping its hat in that direction with the inclusion of 'He Leadeth Me' and 'I Love To Tell the Story.' "[21] Benson's revision in 1911, however, included more hymns with a social emphasis, and, just before the Anglican chants at the back of the book, a section of twenty-nine hymns gathered under the heading "Evangelistic Services" was added. The Southern Presbyterians were even more influenced by gospel hymnody.[22]

All of this is not to say that denominations jettisoned their own hymnic lores. Though there were exceptions, such as the Presbyterians largely giving up their metrical psalms and the German Evangelical Synod of North America giving up its chorales, as a general rule American denominations in the twentieth century did not deny their individual traditions. Instead, they continued to combine them with a cross section of other hymnic materials, adapted to their own idioms and confessional postures. *The Hymnal 1940* of the Episcopal Church, a classic production, best illustrates this pattern, but a spate of publications by other denominations up through the *Pilgrim Hymnal* and *Service Book and Hymnal* of 1958 point to the same general flow.

The stretch of time from the publication of the Presbyterian hymnal in 1895 to the publication of the books just mentioned in 1958 could be described positively as a period when successive hymnal revisions developed steadily in ecumenical and historic breadth. On the other hand, it could also be characterized as a period during which "a frozen repertory [was] reshaped according to denominational needs."[23] The 1960s changed that. The 1960s fostered what has come to be known as a hymn explosion. It began in Scotland, in response to a perennial cry of the period that "nobody's getting down to writing the hymns for our time."[24] With Erik Routley as the catalyst, meetings were held between 1961 and 1969 at the Scottish Churches House in Dunblane. The participants included clergy, poets, musicians, teachers, and scholars who discussed hymnody seriously in relation to the present and then produced texts and music that were published as *Dunblane Praises* and *New Songs for the Church.*[25]

There was no comparable meeting in the 1960s on this side of

21. Morgan F. Simmons, "Hymnody: Its Place in Twentieth Century Presbyterianism" (unpublished typescript), p. 5.

22. Simmons, "Hymnody," pp. 8-9.

23. Russell Schultz-Widmar, "Hymnody," in *The Hymnal 1982 Companion,* 1: 600.

24. Ian M. Fraser, "Beginnings at Dunblane," in *Duty and Delight,* p. 171.

25. For a chronicle of these meetings and sketches of the personalities who attended, see Fraser, "Beginnings at Dunblane."

the Atlantic, but such publications as *Songs for Today, Hymns for Now,* and the *Hymnal for Young Christians* gave voice to the same need for new paths.

This ferment created a whole body of new hymns. The hymns from England by Fred Pratt Green, Timothy Dudley-Smith, Fred Kaan, and Brian Wren very quickly came into use in the United States, but the United States also provided its own hymn writers in Thomas H. Troeger, Jaroslav Vajda, Jane Parker Huber, Carl Daw, Gracia Grindal, and others. Canada provided Margaret Clarkson. The hymns of these writers run a wide gamut, from the traditional evangelical writing of Margaret Clarkson to the social passion of Brian Wren to the rich imagery of Thomas Troeger to the brief, evocative phrases of Jaroslav Vajda.

The ferment did not create only texts. It and the new texts themselves stimulated new tunes and harmonizations. Calvin Hampton took old hymn texts and wrote new tunes for them, often with complex accompaniments. Carol Doran and Thomas Troeger collaborated on their creations; Doran wrote and continues to write tunes and harmonizations in song-like contemporary idioms that are consciously wedded to specific texts. Carl Schalk has written remarkably singable tunes, even for unrhymed texts of Jaroslav Vajda that would seem to resist such settings.

There has indeed been an explosion of new material, but new texts and tunes tell only part of the story. In addition to the new, the century's high-level historical momentum toward increasing ecumenical breadth led to the inclusion of the old as well as the new in hymnals, including the white Southern spirituals that Jackson researched, black spirituals, "folk" and "popular" idioms, and a variety of Hispanic, Asian, and African hymns. There has also been a revival of psalm singing — not only of metrical psalms but all sorts of chant versions as well.

All of this has made elements of gospel hymnody more accessible to some who had earlier rejected it and elements of the more historic repertoire more accessible to some who had earlier rejected it. The cleavages have not been resolved, but gospel songs have gradually been folded into the broader context of the church's hymnody.

That does not exhaust the story, however. Hymn explosions signal reformations or revolutions, and this one was no exception. Hymnody prior to 1960 was not immune to the world around it. The temperance movement had its temperance hymnody.[26] The Episcopal hymnal of 1916 and the 1917 supplement to the 1895 Presbyterian

26. See Paul Westermeyer, "Chicago and Hymnody: A Tourist's Guide," *The Hymn* 28 (April 1977): 73.

hymnal "reflected the fact that the nation was at war."[27] Both of these hymnals included Rudyard Kipling's "God of Our Fathers, Known of Old," Francis Scott Key's "O Say Can You See," and Julia Ward Howe's "Mine Eyes Have Seen the Glory of the Coming of the Lord." The editors of the Episcopal hymnal in 1916 "included several of the best chorales, [but] because of war-time animosity against Germany, felt it necessary to camouflage them with English names. . . . HERZLICH TUT MICH VERLANGEN became PASSION CHORALE. . . . *The Hymnal 1940* . . . continued this practice."[28] The rejection of German chorales by the Evangelical Synod of North America was due, at least in part, to the same wartime fervor.

Hymnals published before 1960 were not without their hymns or even sections on brotherhood, obedience, service, and love, but, like the products of every culture, they reflected the period's blind spots. Jon Michael Spencer has pointed out that the "liberative lag" in black Protestant hymnody and in white Protestant hymnody is a counterpart of white supremacy.[29] The two were mirror images of one another: neither group saw, for example, the degradation of Africa in "From Greenland's Icy Mountains" or the degradation of the African or African-American in "Wash Me and I Shall Be Whiter Than Snow" — or, if they saw, they did not perceive what such texts did to them or to their brothers and sisters in the other race; or, if they perceived, they made no effort to change the situation.

The period since the beginning of the 1960s is no doubt afflicted with its own blind spots that future historians will see better than we. But the ruptures of the 1960s — the Second Vatican Council; the assassinations of Jack Kennedy, Robert Kennedy, and Martin Luther King, Jr.; the racial conflicts and riots that followed; the Vietnam War and its aftermath — created a new world in which past blind spots suddenly became eyesores. A new and conscious response to the culture took shape. While not the optimistic Social Gospel that Rauschenbusch might have had in mind, it was a social consciousness nonetheless, though postponed to the end of the century and chastened by its horrors.

Sometimes the new hymn writing addressed social issues head on, as Rauschenbusch presumably had called for. But a new consciousness also raised questions about language itself. At least three broad

27. Simmons, "Hymnody," p. 10.

28. William J. Reynolds, "The Hymnal 1940 and Its Era," *The Hymn* 41 (October 1990): 38.

29. See Spencer, "Black Denominational Hymnody and Growth toward Religious and Racial Maturity," *The Hymn* 41 (October 1990): 41-45, especially p. 44.

issues emerged. First, such King James English as "thee," "thy," and "vouchsafe" seemed outdated, and new earthen vessels in twentieth-century English seemed required. Second, the nature of language in relation to justice and peace was examined. How did the words of a hymn program the singers to perceive justice? Did the generic use of the male pronoun discriminate against women? Did language about the deaf and dumb match the injustice of washing blacks white? Did militaristic hymns program the singers to violence or idolatrous tribal persuasions? Third, the nature of poetry and especially hymnic poetry was considered, at a time when there was little or no consensus about what "good" poetry or art or music or architecture might be.[30]

These issues forced hymnal editors not only to make new choices from among an overwhelming variety and number of texts and tunes, in and out of their own traditions, but also to confront and answer some complex questions: How much updating and changing of historic texts is advisable? Can a generic male pronoun ever be used? What about male pronouns used in reference to God? What happens to the poetry or the "rights" of a dead poet when changes are made? To what extent do the texts belong to the community once they leave the hands of the poet? What business do editors have changing texts that are ingrained in people's memories?

The momentum of hymnody should be noted here. Though hymnody does respond to the culture — and, at points of shift as in the 1960s and beyond, the influence is especially great — it also goes on as if it is independent of the culture. Most hymnal committees consciously or unconsciously realized this and tried to stay in touch with their constituencies. The popularity of "Onward, Christian Soldiers," for example, got it into the Methodist hymnal of 1989 against the better judgment of many Methodists on and off the committee.

The Lutheran Book of Worship of 1978 was the first major response to the new situation. Committees now working on hymnals are still dealing with these issues.

3. *Music and Musicians*

Musicians have already been mentioned in the above two categories, and they will appear in the fourth, so this heading overlaps the others

30. A good illustration of the dilemma can be found in John Cage's *Silence* (Cambridge: MIT Press, 1961).

and may seem artificial. But that point itself suggests the character of the twentieth century.

During some periods in the West when the church served as a patron of the arts and supported composers and performers, this category would have been packed with many significant compositions for the church by the major composers of the period. That would not have been the case for the story of the pre-Constantinian era, however, and it is not the case in our post-Constantinian period. American churches have by and large not supported the arts. There have been some full-time musical posts in churches, but even large churches that could support full-time musicians have often had part-time employees or volunteers with varying degrees of competence. Some churches have even driven away their best musicians by resisting the contemporary musical syntax those musicians were of necessity driven to employ.

But that should not be taken to mean there has been no musical activity. The activity best organizes itself into two categories which might be divided into what the people sing and what the people hear.

What the people sing assumes a community — in the case of the church, a congregation or choir. I have in mind here the music that is in the ear of a given community. It has included a wide variety of styles and performance practices: Old Regular Baptists in Blackey, Kentucky, with lined-out hymns in an old New England style; Mennonites without instrumental accompaniment; Sacred Harp singers; Dutch Reformed metrical psalm singers; Norwegian Lutherans with a klokker, German Lutherans with rhythmic chorales; black congregations utilizing blue notes; rural congregations singing with a fervor that included their own rhythmic and melodic twists; urban and suburban congregations singing with a fervor of their own, but in a more conventional twentieth-century style; jazz masses at congregations in New York, Washington, Chicago, and other cities; Hispanic congregations with guitar and rhythm instruments; Southern Baptists with a song leader; Russian Orthodox choirs singing, virtually from memory, nineteenth-century versions of Byzantine chant. Some of this could not be notated very easily, and some of it, when notated, did not sound in performance like the notation. Sometimes it was lackluster and downright awful (and so, it should be noted, was some music made by professionals!), but sometimes it has also been remarkable in both spirit and music.

As ethnic groups were amalgamated into the broader societal net and the nomadic culture of the century increased, in many cases these communities either diminished or disappeared altogether. These changes gave rise to new communities of people with different backgrounds and memories who were forced to fashion new songs. This painful struggle characterizes many groups at the end of the twentieth century.

The musical leaders of these groups — organists or other instrumentalists, choir directors or song leaders — have included professional musicians, such as Mary Oyer of the Mennonites and Paul Manz of the Lutherans. But they have also included countless amateurs who were anonymous beyond local communities. Whether professional or amateur, those who were successful leaders sensed the musical and spiritual idiom of their people and were able to release, energize, and nourish it.

If the styles of the music that people sang were broad, the religious music that people heard in the twentieth century was broader, if not amorphous. At its broadest, it included everything from large works with religious themes, such as Leonard Bernstein's *Mass* or Duke Ellington's *Sacred Concert,* to small pieces that fit into church services, such as hymn settings and psalm settings and anthems and voluntaries in every style from monophonic chant to aleatory to atonal. I have no room here to begin to catalogue any of this. The number of anthems written in the twentieth century alone probably exceeds the sum of all such pieces written before the twentieth century. (Many of them are not worth reporting about, to be sure, but some of them are quite well crafted.) A brief glimpse at some individuals involved will have to suffice.

The first is one of the most innovative of America's native-born and trained composers, Charles Ives (1874-1954). Ives used the hymnic musical materials of American Protestantism and wove their themes together with techniques that were to be typical of twentieth-century music. David Ewen points out that Ives worked with polyrhythms before Stravinsky, dischords before Bartok, polytonality before Stravinsky and Milhaud, atonality before Schoenberg, quarter tones before Haba, tone clusters before Cowell, and chance music before Boulez.[31] Until 1902 Ives served as a church organist in New England and New York City, but he gave it up because he realized that people had rights that his stacks of thirds and consecutive dissonances tended to negate. He became an insurance agent so he would be free to write

31. Ewen, *The World of Twentieth Century Music* (Englewood Cliffs, N.J.: Prentice-Hall, 1969), p. 394.

the kind of music he heard. It was a uniquely American civil religious product.[32]

Other American-born twentieth-century composers were less innovative but important nonetheless. Horatio Parker (1863-1919), an organist-choirmaster and professor of music at Yale University who was one of Ives's teachers, wrote the oratorio *Hora Novissima* in 1893 based on a text of Bernard of Cluny. T. Tertius Noble (1867-1953), an Englishman by birth, came to St. Thomas's Church in New York, developed a boy choir, and came to be known for his free harmonizations of hymn tunes. Leo Sowerby (1895-1968) was born in Grand Rapids, Michigan, but made his home in Chicago, where he taught at the American Conservatory and served St. James Episcopal Church beginning in 1927. He stood in the Romantic tradition like Parker and Noble but utilized more dissonance and less traditional progressions. Randall Thompson (b. 1899) was a teacher, not a church musician, but he wrote well-crafted and sensitive sacred choral music that has been used by many choirs in church services and sacred concerts. His "Alleluia," *The Last Words of David,* and *The Peaceable Kingdom* are good examples.

Other musical personalities of the twentieth century left their marks on American church music by means other than just their compositions. W. Lynwood Farnum (1885-1930), born in Sutton, Quebec, worked in Montreal, Boston, and New York as an organist. An unusually gifted recitalist and teacher, Farnum moved the organ to a dignified role in worship and made it an important recital instrument. F. Melius Christiansen (1871-1955), a native of Norway, founded and developed the famous St. Olaf Choir with his settings of pieces from the Lutheran Germanic and Scandinavian hymnic and folk song heritage. St. Olaf has carried on the high musical quality of Christiansen's legacy right up to the present with such musicians as John Ferguson and Anton Armstrong. Paul Manz (b. 1919), an organist who studied with Flor Peeters in Belgium, brought organ improvisation to remarkable heights in the service of the people's singing. Many of his organ pieces have been published, as have some of his choral works.

32. The first paper I wrote for Martin Marty was "Charles Ives: A Musical Manifestation of Protestant and American Civil Religious Motifs" (17 December 1970). His willingness to deal with a topic like this and to help me with it, his continuing help through my dissertation and beyond, his ability to let the data reveal the plot, and his uncanny capacity to help me, like others, to see clearly what I was perceiving dimly — all this made it possible for me to begin sorting out the story and the issues that are related to this article. I am deeply grateful to my mentor for many things, these among them.

Each of these personalities, along with others such as John Finley Williamson and Clarence Dickinson, who will be mentioned later, have influenced and trained numerous men and women who have gone on to serve churches and schools across the American continent and beyond. They represent an ecumenical array of theory and practice in which many traditions have amicably lived side by side, often nourishing one another.

Twentieth-century American church music has also been immeasurably enriched by European influences. One of the most obvious of these is the person of Igor Stravinsky (1882-1971) — probably the greatest twentieth-century composer, comparable to Pablo Picasso for pictorial art — who came to the United States at the outbreak of World War II. His return to the Orthodox faith stimulated his *Mass,* which he wrote in the tradition of Western masses in such a way that it could be used at an actual mass. It stands as a monument of twentieth-century church music along with his *Symphony of Psalms*.

A less obvious but very important influence came from European teachers. One example is Flor Peeters, who has already been mentioned as Paul Manz's teacher. His organ method was used by numerous American organ teachers. Nadia Boulanger (1887-1979) is another example. Even before she came to the United States to teach during the Second World War, she had already taught many American musicians in France. Composers and organists who worked in churches were deeply influenced by her. They in turn influenced their students with her incisive insights from a Faure-Stravinsky center.

European music from the past and the present, widely published both here and abroad, was another influence. American organists have regularly studied and played the music of J. S. Bach, César Franck, Ralph Vaughan Williams, Olivier Messiaen, and many other European organ composers, known and unknown. Choirs have sung the music of Bach, Brahms, Mozart, Verdi, Distler, and many other European choral composers.

American church musicians have not been untouched by European organ building either; indeed, in 1991 there are small and very able organ builders throughout the country. Nor have they been untouched by European performance practice studies; they have assiduously followed them. That is not to say that Europe controls them anymore, if it ever did. They have generated their own research and can be quite independent about it.

Finally, back in this country, the influence of Robert Shaw (b. 1916), the retired conductor of the Robert Shaw Chorale and the

Atlanta Symphony Orchestra and Chorus, must be noted. Shaw served as a church musician at First Unitarian Church in Cleveland and said some interesting things there, but his remarkable influence as a choral conductor is far more significant.[33]

4. Societies and Schools

Societies and schools give further evidence of the ecumenicity of the twentieth century. Some societies had relatively narrow interests — for example, the Methodist Church Music Society founded in 1935, the American Guild of English Handbell Ringers in 1954, the Moravian Music Foundation in 1956, or any of the denominational societies that were formed or became active in the latter half of the century. But the most broadly influential societies were founded earlier and were ecumenical.

The American Guild of Organists (AGO) was organized just before the turn of the century, in 1896, "to advance the cause of organ and choral music" and "to improve the proficiency of organists and conductors." It organized itself by chapters, each with regular meetings. Regional and national meetings occur at larger intervals with an ecumenical array of topics, concerts, recitals, and services. The AGO has conducted examinations, offered certificates, and consistently pressed for high quality in American church music.

The Hymn Society in the United States and Canada (formerly the Hymn Society of America) was organized in 1922 with a more precise concern for congregational song. Both a scholarly and a practical society, it has published hymnological studies and promoted indexing and has sponsored hymn festivals and new hymn projects. Both the AGO and the Hymn Society have journals, *The American Organist* and *The Hymn,* respectively.

Schools represent another instance of ecumenicity. Peter Christian Lutkin (1858-1931) became dean of the School of Music at Northwestern University in Evanston, Illinois, in 1896. Shortly thereafter he started a department of Church Music that reached beyond the Methodist roots of Northwestern and the geography of the Midwest.

33. For some of Shaw's comments in the context of his work as a church musician, see Joseph A. Musselman, *"Dear People" . . . Robert Shaw* (Bloomington, Ind.: Indiana University Press, 1979), pp. 179-85. For a very perceptive and helpful study of American approaches to choral singing, see Howard Swan, "The Development of a Choral Instrument," in *Choral Conductings,* ed. Harold A. Decker and Julius Herford (Englewood Cliffs, N.J.: Prentice-Hall, 1973), pp. 4-55.

Clarence Dickinson (1873-1969), a founder of the AGO, became Professor of Music at Union Seminary in New York in 1912. In 1928 he established the School of Sacred Music at Union, which reflected a wide denominational breadth in both its practice and scholarship. It served church musicians from all over the country and utilized the ecumenical opportunities that New York City provided.

Westminster Choir College was founded by John Finley Williamson (1887-1964) in 1926. It grew out of his work at Westminster Presbyterian Church in Dayton, Ohio, and represented his approach to revitalizing choral music. It involved choirs for all age groups and a big, dark, choral sound. Westminster was not nearly as eclectic as Union, but it was not limited to one denomination either. It first appealed largely, however, to the "nonliturgical" portion of the Protestant mainstream, though that has changed more recently.

Several liturgical counterparts to Westminster emerged with more limited denominational ties. One was Trinity School of Church Music for the Episcopal Church. It operated in New York City from 1912 to 1918. Another was the Pius X School of Liturgical Music, founded in 1918 at the Manhattanville College of the Sacred Heart. It and the Gregorian Institute of America, founded in 1941 with correspondence courses, primarily served Roman Catholics. None of these schools had the impact of the more ecumenical institutions, however, or even of other schools that included church music and organ in their purviews — Oberlin College, Indiana University, the University of Nebraska, and Eastman School of Music, for example. The Southern Baptists developed the largest church music programs at their seminaries in New Orleans, Louisville, and Fort Worth. While their students have not been widely ecumenical, their professors have been deeply involved in ecumenical activities. Harry Eskew and David Music, for example, have served as editors of *The Hymn*.

5. Post-Puritan

Sydney Ahlstrom called the 1960s post-Puritan.[34] He meant that Reformed and Puritan impulses no longer functioned as the dominant forces to which everyone in the culture had to relate. A dream died. In a sense, as Don McLean put it in his popular song "American Pie," the music died.

34. Ahlstrom, *A Religious History of the American People* (New Haven: Yale University Press, 1972), p. 1079.

Neither hymnody nor church music in general went unscathed. Coalitions and financing came apart. The School of Sacred Music at Union Seminary in New York, the leader during much of the century for training church musicians of all denominations, closed its doors in 1973. That closing symbolized a new period in which Protestants lost a sense of coherence in their music and its leadership. After the Second Vatican Council finished its deliberations in 1965, Roman Catholics also entered a new world. Latin masses were replaced by vernacular masses, and there was a scramble to set the new, hastily devised vernacular texts to music. Guitar masses were prepared quickly and reflected the haste in their substandard quality and lack of durability. Protestants were influenced by guitars as well. Protest songs, guitar chords, choruses, and melodic lines without much substance all entered much of America's worship. Organs were used less or simply retired.

Geoffrey Beaumont's *Twentieth Century Folk Mass,* "gospel rock," and "gospel folk" began to appear in England in the 1960s and were soon picked up in the United States. At first some dismissed them as too secular, but gradually they found some acceptance. Congregations quickly discovered, however, that they had to sort out what was entertainment from what worked for continued, participatory, congregational use in worship. For instance, it did not take churches very long to figure out that *Jesus Christ Superstar,* a modern Passion setting in a popular style, functioned basically as entertainment.

The turbulence of the 1960s was short-lived. By the mid to late 1970s and early 1980s, organs were back in full use and guitarists hard to find. Congregations simply expanded their horizons to include a multiplicity of styles.

It appeared that a new consensus had been achieved. But by the early 1990s it seems clear that whatever consensus there might have been has fallen apart. More and more hymnal supplements are being published, and there are increasingly strong demands for "alternative" worship services on the one hand and "traditional" worship services on the other. In most large urban centers on any given weekend, one can find Latin Roman Catholic Tridentine rites sometimes with classic mass settings of the Ordinary by Mozart or other comparable composers, high Episcopal services with incense and processions and English anthems, Protestant services with less historic liturgical practices but with first-rate organists and choirs whose congregations pride themselves on the highest standards, churches and fellowships in which currents of renewal have taken various shapes, churches that follow their hymnals and books of worship relatively scrupulously, churches that deviate from them slightly, churches that deviate from them greatly, churches where "folk" materials are used, churches that are folksy, churches in which planning for worship is regarded as irrelevant, "entertainment evangelism" considerably amplified by electronic equipment, and all sorts of mixes and worshiping activities between and among these extremes.

Church music and hymnody in the early 1990s represents an incredible array and diversity. It extends from the twentieth-century compositional techniques of Daniel Pinkham (b. 1923) to the neogospel style hymns and hymn tunes of Gloria (b. 1942) and William (b. 1936) Gaither, from the finest organs to the most sophisticated electronic equipment — with the widest possible range of styles and theological points of view to support these styles.

If any consensus is to be reached, I have no sense at this writing of what it will be. Most of the battles are as much within denominational groupings as they are between denominations. That could presage new configurations, or it could indicate a continual broadening of the spectrum. Old coalitions may not hold, but the same issues that H. Richard Niebuhr identified in *Christ and Culture* are still present for music as well as for other matters. At this point I can do no more than briefly sketch the outlines of the changing landscape.

Evangelicals and fundamentalists — for our purposes here, a group including Southern Baptists, the Assemblies of God, television evangelists and their followers, megachurches, and those who choose these as their models — are living at both extremes of Niebuhr's Christ-in-culture and Christ-against-culture paradigms. They manage to hold these extremes together not in paradox or schizophrenic confusion but by maintaining them in different areas of their experience. In order to relate to the culture, to appeal to a popular mind-set and "bring people to Christ," they use popular musical styles without hesitation or embarrassment, no matter how superficial they may be — a Christ-of-culture position. On points of moral teaching, however, they oppose the culture's "liberal" drift and argue against anything that would appear to accommodate moral ambiguity or a pluralism that might give rise to questions about such matters as prayer in schools — a Christ-against-culture position.

This group manages to hold onto the two extremes not by means of sleight of hand or trickery. (Granted, there is hypocrisy in this camp, as the recent debacle of television evangelists has indicated, but there is hypocrisy everywhere, and its presence or absence does not make or break any position.) It manages to hold onto both positions because it locates sin at only certain points in the culture, and musical syntax and associations are not among them so long as the music is put to "saving" purposes. That is why this group feels free to use radio and television and all the modern electronic technical wizardry that is available, while at the same time attacking the media and even popular music for its godless slant. That is why this group feels free to use the sounds of popular culture while attacking the immorality of the culture. Their principal concern is not an assembled body of Christ that sings but rather individual decisions for Christ and moral activity with the emotive power to propel evangelistic activity — whether it be huge throngs that get carried along in a wash of electronic sound or individuals watching such events in living rooms on television screens.

The three mediating paradigms — traditionally identified with Roman Catholics as Christ above culture, Reformed bodies as Christ transformer of culture, and Lutherans as Christ and culture in paradox — are more complex and ambiguous. All of them require people gathered in one place so they can be nourished by word and sacraments, and all of them — though in different ways — require a gathered body that sings. They cannot therefore embrace the electronic media with the same abandon as the more fundamentalist groups, and they are nervous about sound that submerges or overpowers the people. (Similar concerns have long been expressed about musical accompaniment by organs or other instruments, so this is not a new issue; it is simply the case that audio technology has made it much easier to drown out the natural human voice.)

The Christ-above-culture folk may use sounds from the popular culture, but never as ends in themselves. The sounds always lead beyond themselves to something like the purity of Gregorian chant and its polyphonic progeny. Even sound in general is not considered an end in itself; it must always point beyond itself to the silence of pure love. The congregation may not sing vigorously (there is a theological reason why Catholics don't sing), or they may participate by listening to a choir. But they need to assemble to do this, and sounds that submerge or substitute for the congregation are only passing cultural accommodation to achieve something of greater value.

Those who take the Christ-transformer-of-culture position identify at one level with the popular: Calvin viewed music as a tool that could be used to make the word go down easier. But Calvin also spoke of the necessity for weight and majesty in church music. Here the point is not that music leads beyond itself but that the music transforms (actually the word through the music transforms). As Francis Williamson recently suggested to me, psalm singing for Calvin was a transforming, sanctifying activity. This makes the singing of the people extremely important, and the absence of instruments in Geneva and Reformed practice more generally was no accident. Although representatives of this group today have accepted instruments, they continue to believe that the purpose of church music is to transform lives, and they find anything that substitutes for the people's song to be misguided.

Those who take the Christ-and-culture-in-paradox position reject both the wholesale embrace of the culture and the wholesale rejection of it, on the grounds that it is fully sin-soaked and yet the object of God's grace. Like Luther, they know about the possibility of perverting the gift of music with "erotic rantings" and, also like Luther, they regard music as one of God's greatest gifts, which is to be used with gratitude regardless of its source, as long as well-crafted and durable creations result. Of course, today this group does not have the luxury that Luther enjoyed of being able to draw easily from a body of genuine folk music as a basis for new church music. Luther could carve out a setting of Psalm 46 or Psalm 130 from the hardy quarry of German folksong, but to attempt the same thing in our commercial culture from the idiom of a Coca Cola or Honda jingle would be quite a different thing.

At the end of the twentieth century, the distinctions among the practices of these groups are blurring. Any group may initially sound like any other group. Despite the seeming similarities, however, the basic issues remain the same.[35]

III. Reflection

What then have church music and hymnody been about in twentieth-century American life? The answer is the highest art of the past and present and the most banal materials one can imagine, the most difficult music played and sung by highly trained musicians and the most familiar texts and music sung by anonymous congregations. Church music and hymnody have been about all sorts of things, and the ferment at century's end points to the complexity. How it will turn out is for the next century's historians to ponder.

35. I have expanded these last seven paragraphs into "The Present State of Church Music: Historical and Theological Reflections," *Word and World* 12 (Summer 1992): 214-20.

Appendix: Representative Chronological List of Some Twentieth-Century Hymnals and Hymn Collections in the United States of America*

Gospel Hymns Nos. 1 to 6 Complete. New York: Da Capo Press, 1972. Republication of "Excelsior Edition" of 1895.

The Hymnal Published by Authority of The General Assembly of the Presbyterian Church in the United States of America. Edited by Louis F. Benson. Philadelphia: Presbyterian Board of Publication and Sabbath-School Work, 1895.

Sursum Corda: A Book of Praise. Edited by E. H. Johnson. Philadelphia: American Baptist Publication Society, 1898.

Hymnal of the Evangelical Church. St. Louis: Eden Publishing House, 1899.

The Choral Service Book. Edited by Harry G. Archer and Luther D. Reed. Philadelphia: United Lutheran Publication House, 1901.

The New Psalms and Hymns: Published by Authority of the Presbyterian Church in the United States. Richmond: Presbyterian Committee of Publication, 1901.

Church and Sunday School Hymnal. Scottdale, Pa.: Mennonite Publishing House, 1902.

Revival Songs No. 2. Chicago: E. O. Excell, 1902.

The Pilgrim Hymnal with Responsive Readings. Boston: Pilgrim Press, 1904.

The Methodist Hymnal: Official Hymnal of the Methodist Episcopal Church and the Methodist Episcopal Church, South. New York: Methodist Book Concern, 1905.

The New Praise Hymnal: A Collection of Scripture Readings, Church Hymns, Gospel Songs, and Anthems, Being the "Praise Hymnal" Revised and Enlarged. Edited by Gilbert J. Ellis and J. H. Fillmore. Cincinnati: Fillmore Brothers, 1906.

Songs of the King. Chicago: Scoville & Smith, 1906.

Hymns for the Kingdom of God. Edited by Henry Sloane Coffin and Ambrose White Vernon. New York: A. S. Barnes, 1931 (first edition 1909 or 1910).

The Lutheran Hymnary: Published by Authority of the Norwegian Evangelical Lutheran Synod, the Hauge's Evangelical Lutheran Synod and the United Norwegian Lutheran Church in America. Decorah: Lutheran Publishing House, 1913.

*For a list of hymnals in use in American and Canadian churches in 1986, see Harry Eskew, "Bibliography of Hymnals in Use in American and Canadian Churches," *The Hymn* 37 (April 1986): 25-30.

Social Hymns of Brotherhood and Aspiration. Edited by Mabel Hay Barrows Mussey. Boston: Universalist Publishing House, 1914.

Joy to the World: For the Church and Sunday School. Edited by E. O. Excell. Chicago: Hope Publishing, 1915.

The Hymnal: As Authorized and Approved for Use by the General Convention of The Protestant Episcopal Church in the United States of America in the Year of Our Lord MCMXVI. New York: Church Pension Fund, 1916 (1st edition 1918).

Common Service Book of the Lutheran Church: Authorized by The United Lutheran Church in America. Philadelphia: Board of Publication of the United Lutheran Church in America, 1917.

Wartburg Hymnal for Church, School and Home. Edited by O. Hartwig. Chicago: Wartburg Publishing House, 1918.

Elmhurst Hymnal and Orders of Worship for the Sunday School, Young People's Meetings and Church Services. St. Louis: Eden Publishing House, 1921.

Hymns of the United Church. Edited by Charles Clayton Morrison and Herbert L. Willett. Chicago: Christian Century Press, 1922.

Baptist Standard Hymnal. Edited by A. M. Townsend. Nashville: Sunday School Publishing House, 1924.

The Hymnal and Order of Service Authorized by The Evangelical Lutheran Augustana Synod. Rock Island, Ill.: Augustana Book Concern, 1925.

The Parish School Hymnal. Philadelphia: Board of Publication of The United Lutheran Church in America, 1926.

Church Hymnal. Scottdale, Pa.: Mennonite Publishing House, 1927.

The Psalter. Grand Rapids: William B. Eerdmans, 1927.

University Hymns with Tunes Arranged for Men's Voices. New Haven: Yale University Press, 1931.

The Concordia Hymnal: A Hymnal for Church, School and Home. Minneapolis: Augsburg Publishing House, 1932.

The Methodist Hymnal: Official Hymnal of the Methodist Church. Nashville: Methodist Publishing House, 1932.

Union Hymnal: Songs and Pravers for Jewish Worship. 3d edition revised and enlarged. N.p.: Central Conference of American Rabbis, 1932.

Christian Science Hymnal. Boston: Christian Science Publishing, 1932.

The Hymnal: Published by Authority of the General Assembly of the Presbyterian Church in the United States of America. Philadelphia: Presbyterian Board of Christian Education, 1933.

The Colored Sacred Harp. Edited by J. Jackson. Ozark, Ala.: J. Jackson, 1934.

The Pilgrim Hymnal. Boston: Pilgrim Press, 1935.

Original Sacred Harp (Denson Revision). Haleyville, Ala.: Sacred Harp Publishing, 1936.

The New Church Hymnal. Edited by H. Augustine Smith. New York: D. Appleton-Century, 1937.

The Mount Mary Hymnal. Compiled and arranged by Sister Mary Gisela. Boston: McLaughlin & Reilly, 1937.

Hymnal for Church and Home. Blair, Neb.: Lutheran Publishing House, 1938.

Christian Worship and Praise. Edited by Henry Hallam Tweedy. New York: A. S. Barnes, 1939.

Broadman Hymnal. Edited by B. B. McKinney. Nashville: Broadman, 1940.

Allen African Methodist Episcopal Hymnal. Nashville: African Methodist Episcopal Church, 1941.

The Church Hymnal. Washington: Review & Herald Publishing Association, 1941.

The Hymnal: Containing Complete Orders of Worship Authorized by the General Synod of the Evangelical and Reformed Church. St. Louis: Eden Publishing House, 1941.

The Lutheran Hymnal: Authorized by the Synods Constituting the Evangelical Lutheran Synodical Conference of North America. St. Louis: Concordia Publishing House, 1941.

Order of Worship (Partial Edition) for the Reformed Church in the United States [from 1866], Published with the Hymnal of the Reformed Church [from 1920]. Philadelphia: Board of Christian Education of the Evangelical and Reformed Church, 1942.

The Hymnal of the Protestant Episcopal Church in the United States of America 1940. New York: Church Pension Fund, 1940 (published 1943).

Enekeskonyo: Hungarian Psalter-hymnal. St. Louis: Eden Publishing House, 1947.

Christian Youth Hymnal. Philadelphia: Muhlenberg Press, 1948.

Hymns: The Church of Jesus Christ of Latter-Day. Salt Lake City: Deseret Book, 1948.

Office Hymns of the Church together with the Official and Some Additional Sequences in Their Plainsong Settings with Latin and English Texts. Edited by Carl F. Pfatteicher and Dudley Fitts. Boston: McLaughlin & Reilly, 1951.

The Brethren Hymnal Authorized by Annual Conference, Church of the Brethren. Elgin, Ill.: House of the Church of the Brethren, 1951.

Christian Worship: A Hymnal. Philadelphia: Judson Press, 1953.

AMEC Hymnal. Nashville: AMEC Publishing, 1954.

A Hymnal for Friends. Philadelphia: Friends General Conference, 1955.

The Hymnbook. Edited by David Hugh Jones. Richmond: John Ribble, 1955.

Baptist Hymnal. Edited by W. H. Sims. Nashville: Convention Press, 1956.

The Hymnal. Independence, Mo.: Herald Publishing House, 1956.

The Hymnal of the Evangelical United Brethren Church. Dayton: Board of Publication of the Evangelical United Brethren Church, 1957.

Pilgrim Hymnal. Boston: Pilgrim Press, 1958.

Service Book and Hymnal Authorized by the Lutheran Churches Cooperating in the Commission on the Liturgy and Hymnal. Minneapolis: Augsburg Publishing House, 1958.

Christian Hymnal. Hesston, Kans.: Church of God in Christ, Mennonite, 1959.

The Baptist Standard Hymnal with Responsive Readings. Nashville: Sunday School Publishing Board, National Baptist Convention, 1961.

Hymnal of Christian Unity. Edited by Clifford A. Bennett and Paul Hume. Toledo: Gregorian Institute of America, 1964.

The Book of Hymns: Official Hymnal of the United Methodist Church. Nashville: United Methodist Publishing House, 1964.

Church School Hymnal for Children. Edited by R. Harold Terry. Philadelphia: Lutheran Church Press, 1964.

Hymns for the Celebration of Life. Boston: Beacon Press, 1964.

Songs for Today. Edited by Ewald Bash and John Ylvisaker. Minneapolis: American Lutheran Church, 1964.

The English Liturgy Hymnal. Chicago: Friends of the English Liturgy, 1965.

Hymns and Songs of the Spirit. St. Louis: CPB Press, 1965.

Hymnbook for Christian Worship. St. Louis: CPB Press, 1965.

The Methodist Hymnal. Edited by Carlton R. Young. Nashville: Methodist Publishing House, 1966.

Hymns for Now: A Portfolio for Good, Bad, or Rotten Times. Chicago: Walther League, 1967.

Allelu! Booklet with the Second Mass for Young Americans. Music and texts by Ray Repp. Chicago: Friends of the English Liturgy, 1967.

Hymnal for Young Christians. Chicago: Friends of the English Liturgy Church Publications, 1967.

Songs of Salvation. Music and texts by Sister Germaine. Chicago: Friends of the English Liturgy Church Publications, 1967.

Hymnal and Liturgies of the Moravian Church. Elk Grove, Ill.: Walter M. Carqueville, 1969.

Hymns for Now II. St. Louis: Lutheran Church–Missouri Synod, 1969.

Hymns of Glorious Praise. Springfield, Mo.: Gospel Publishing House, 1969.

The Mennonite Hymnal. Edited by Kester Hoestetler, Walter Yoder, and Mary Oder. Scottdale, Pa.: Herald Press, 1969.

A New Song. N.p.: United Church Press, 1969.

Worship Supplement: Authorized by the Commission on Worship, Lutheran Church–Missouri Synod and Synod of Evangelical Lutheran Churches. St. Louis: Concordia Publishing House, 1969.

Hymns of Glorious Praise. Springfield, Mo.: Gospel Publishing House, 1969.

Hymnbook for Christian Worship. St. Louis: Bethany Press, 1970.

The Worshipbook: Services and Hymns Prepared by the Joint Committee on Worship for Cumberland Presbyterian Church, Presbyterian Church in the United States, The United Presbyterian Church in the United States of America. Philadelphia: Westminster Press, 1970.

Worship. Edited by Robert J. Batastini. Chicago: G.I.A. Publications, 1971.

Worship Hymnal. Edited by Paul Wohlgemuth. Hillsboro, Kans.: Mennonite Brethren Publishing House, 1971.

Christian Hymnary. Uniontown, Pa.: Christian Hymnary Publishers, 1972.

The Covenant Hymnal. Chicago: Covenant Press, 1973.

Morning Praise and Evensong: A Liturgy of the Hours in Musical Setting. Notre Dame, Ind.: Fides Publishers, 1973.

Psalm Praise. Chicago: G.I.A. Publications, 1973.

The Hymnal of the United Church of Christ. Philadelphia: United Church Press, 1974.

Hymns for the Living Church. Carol Stream, Ill.: Hope Publishing, 1974.

Baptist Hymnal. Nashville: Convention Press, 1975.

Break Not the Circle: Twenty New Hymns by Fred Kaan and Doreen Potter. Carol Stream, Ill.: Agape, 1975.

Joyful Noises: Hymns for Humans by Burrell Gluskin. Downers Grove, Ill.: CCS Publishing House, 1975.

Songs of Praise, Volume I. Ann Arbor: Word of God, 1975.

Worship II: A Hymnal for Roman Catholic Parishes. Chicago: G.I.A. Publications, 1975.

Early American Hymns. Minneapolis: A.M.S.I., 1976.

Hymnal Supplement II. N.p.: Church Pension Fund, 1976.

Hymns for the Family of God. Nashville: Paragon Associates, 1976.

Westminster Praise. Edited by Erik Routley. Chapel Hill, N.C.: Hinshaw Music, 1976.

Ecumenical Praise. Carol Stream, Ill.: Agape, 1977.

Hymns of the Syrian Orthodox Church of Antioch. Lodi, Calif.: Archdiocese of the Syrian Orthodox Church, 1977.

New Hymns I. Minneapolis: A.M.S.I., 1977.

The New National Baptist Hymnal. Nashville: National Baptist Publishing Board, 1977.

Lutheran Book of Worship. Minneapolis: Augsburg Publishing House, 1978.

Songs of the Spirit. Philadelphia: Friends General Conference, 1978.

Songs for the Feast, by Willard F. Jabusch. Chicago: World Library Publications, 1978.

Welsh and English Hymns and Anthems of the Welsh National Gymanfu Ganu Association, Inc. Warren: Cox Lithographing, 1979.

The Calvin Hampton Hymnary: Twenty New Hymntunes with Various Texts. Chicago: G.I.A., 1980.

Songs of Thanks and Praise. Edited by Russell Schulz-Widmar. Chapel Hill, N.C.: Hinshaw Music, 1980.

Lift Every Voice and Sing: A Collection of Afro-American Spirituals and Other Songs. New York: Church Hymnal Corporation, 1981.

The Hymns and Ballads of Fred Pratt Green. Carol Stream, Ill.: Hope Publishing, 1982.

Lutheran Worship. St. Louis: Concordia Publishing House, 1982.

The Hymnal 1982 according to the Use of the Episcopal Church. New York: Church Hymnal Corporation, 1985.

Faith Looking Forward: The Hymns and Songs of Brian Wren. Carol Stream, Ill.: Hope Publishing, 1983.

AMEC Bicentennial Hymnal. Nashville: African Methodist Episcopal Church, 1984.

Exalt Him. Kansas City: Lillenas, 1984.

Glory and Praise. Phoenix: North American Liturgy Resources, 1984.

Hymnal Supplement. Carol Stream, Ill.: Agape, 1984.

Lift Every Heart: Collected Hymns 1961-1983 and Some Early Poems by Timothy Dudley-Smith. Carol Stream, Ill.: Hope Publishing, 1984.

The Hymn Texts of Fred Kaan. Carol Stream, Ill.: Hope Publishing, 1985.

Hymns: The Church of Jesus Christ of Latter Day Saints. Salt Lake City: Church of Jesus Christ of Latter Day Saints, 1985.

Rejoice in the Lord: A Hymn Companion to the Scriptures. Edited by Erik Routley. Grand Rapids: William B. Eerdmans, 1985.

The Seventh-day Adventist Hymnal. Washington: Review & Herald Publishing Association, 1985.

The Hymnal for Worship and Celebration. Waco: Word Music, 1986.

New Hymns for the Lectionary: To Glorify the Maker's Name. Music by Carol Doran, words by Thomas H. Troeger. New York: Oxford University Press, 1986.

Worship, 3d edition: *A Hymnal and Service Book for Roman Catholics.* Chicago: G.I.A. Publications, 1986.

Songs of the People. Minneapolis: Augsburg Publishing House, 1986.

The Hymnal of the Christian Methodist Episcopal Church. Memphis: CME Publishing House, 1987.

Lead Me, Guide Me. Chicago: G.I.A. Publications, 1987.

Now the Joyful Celebration: Hymns, Carols, and Songs by Jaroslav Vaida. St. Louis: Morning Star Music Publishers, 1987.

Psalter Hymnal, including the Psalms, Bible Songs, Hymns, Ecumenical Creeds, Doctrinal Standards, and Liturgical Forms of the Christian Reformed Church in America. Grand Rapids: CRC Publications, 1987.

A Singing Faith, by Jane Parker Huber. Philadelphia: Westminster Press, 1987.

A Singing Heart, by Margaret Clarkson. Carol Stream, Ill.: Hope Publishing, 1987.

Spirit Touching Spirit. Burnsville, Minn.: Prince of Peace Publishing, 1987.

Gather. Chicago: G.I.A. Publications, 1988.

Songs of Rejoicing: Hymns for Worship, Meditation and Praise. Edited by John Worst and David P. Schap. New Brunswick: Selah Publishing, 1989.

The United Methodist Hymnal. Nashville: United Methodist Publishing House, 1989.

The Collegeville Hymnal. Edited by Edward J. McKenna. Collegeville, Minn.: Liturgical Press, 1990.

The Presbyterian Hymnal: Hymns, Psalms, and Spiritual Songs. Louisville: Westminster/John Knox Press, 1990.

Trinity Hymnal. Atlanta: Great Commission Publications, 1990.

The Worshiping Church: A Hymnal. Carol Stream, Ill.: Hope Publishing, 1990.

A Year of Grace: The Collected Hymns of Carl P. Daw, Jr. — Hymns for the Church Year. Carol Stream, Ill.: Hope Publishing, 1990.

The Baptist Hymnal. Nashville: Convention Press, 1991.

Women and the American Religious Pilgrimage: Vida Scudder, Dorothy Day, and Pauli Murray

L. DeAne Lagerquist

> Memory is the thread of personal identity, history of public identity. Men who have achieved any civic existence at all must, to sustain it, have some kind of history, though it may be history that is partly mythological or simply untrue.
>
> RICHARD HOFSTADTER

In *Pilgrims in Their Own Land,* Martin E. Marty provides us with a pattern of corporate public identity woven from the threads of personal identity. The pattern he reveals in both public and personal American religious life is pilgrimage. The motif of the large scale and that of the small are variations of one another. His narrative is vivid with the lives of people in pursuit of their own sacred goals. Late in the book, Marty suggests that "a view of an individual pilgrim may serve better than talk about pilgrimage."[1]

Pilgrimage may seem an obvious motif to sustain the history of American religion. There is, after all, the powerful public mythology of the Pilgrims. And to the extent that this American nation constructs its identity on biblical typology, Hebrew pilgrimage through the wilderness and Christian pilgrimage toward an otherworldly home are available as shared plots. But neither the civic mythology of the Pilgrims nor

1. Marty, *Pilgrims in Their Own Land: Five Hundred Years of Religion in America* (Boston: Little, Brown, 1984), p. 432.

biblical sojourning is the source for the pattern of pilgrimage Marty weaves. He takes his title and theme from Jacques Maritain's observation in mid-century that Americans are like "pilgrims in their own land." By this Maritain meant that Americans are not settled but perpetually on the move, prodded by a dream. This American way of being, this constant movement, Maritain suggests, can engender a spiritual awareness of the "impermanence of earthly things."[2] A pilgrimage usually takes one through foreign or unfamiliar land, not familiar territory. But Maritain's remark, become Marty's title, highlights the peculiarity that even in their own long-sought and hard-won land, Americans continue to be unsettled, on the move, in pursuit of something else.

Although Marty recognizes that "women were major contributors to the story of American religion all along" and gives them sympathetic, respectful attention, they do not have a central place among the pilgrims in this volume.[3] Most women appear in passing, mentioned because of a relationship to a noted male figure; if a woman is noted for her own achievement, it is usually without much elaboration. A half dozen women receive fuller consideration: Isabella of Spain, Anne Hutchison, the Grimké sisters, Ellen G. White, and Mary Baker Eddy — two founders of religions, two social reformers, a religious "rebel," and the patron of Columbus and Spanish religious reform. Each pursued a goal that might be construed as sacred, whether establishing a new religion, striving for a more perfect society, or advocating a purer church. Further, each departed from what was expected of a woman and thus achieved a release from social norms and expectations that typically characterize pilgrimage.[4] Similar observations could be made about women such as Ann Lee and Elizabeth Cady Stanton, who are treated more briefly.

Surely women of the past may be well understood as pilgrims in the sense that Marty uses the term. His application of it to these women points the way, leaving the trail open for others to explore. Beyond the mere appropriateness of the name for female as well as male American religious figures, the situation of myriad women in the United States today can be enriched by remembrance of the lives of women who have preceded them. Women require a history no less than men do; Richard Hofstadter's remark quoted at the head of this essay

2. Maritain, cited by Marty in *Pilgrims in Their Own Land,* p. 31.

3. See Marty, *Pilgrims in Their Own Land,* p. 249.

4. See Edith Turner, "Pilgrimage: An Overview," in *The Encyclopedia of Religion,* vol. 11, ed. Mircea Eliade (New York: Macmillan, 1987), p. 327.

applies to women as well as to men. For women determined to live within the Christian churches that gave birth to their faith, Marty's motif of pilgrimage in one's own land offers much sustenance. It acknowledges their rootedness in and loyalty to tradition and heritage while expecting exploration and modification.

The image of a pilgrim — never fully at home, ever vigilant, eternally hopeful — fits well many Christian women whose experience of their church is both life-giving and a perpetual struggle with forces determined to undo them because they are women. This motif lends order and thus meaning to their individual lives. But the pattern alone is not enough. It must be filled with and given credibility by the details of real lives if it is to be of value to contemporary women, just as Marty's work is rendered valuable to his readers by the richness of the individual lives that make up his narrative. While Marty has most often peopled his history with the powerful, his work is accessible to the ordinary reader, and he acknowledges the value of their lives and stories. He has encouraged my own investigations, which more frequently look to the less well known, to women who are sometimes unnamed but without whom the church would not have endured.

In this essay I focus on three women more famous than many I have studied, but perhaps not all generally familiar, in order to show how the details of their individual lives animate the motif of pilgrimage in one's own land and how together they can give direction to women whose pilgrimages continue today. Vida Scudder, Dorothy Day, and Pauli Murray — a college professor, a social activist, and a lawyer and priest — were all loyal but unconventional members of traditional churches. They exercised leadership but usually without the benefit of official status. The three lives together span over a century from the Civil War into the mid-1980s, years of much change for American women. That each woman conceived of her life in terms of movement, either as a journey or a pilgrimage, suggests that they might approve of this effort to understand their lives and careers in terms of pilgrimage in one's own land.

Vida Scudder

Vida Dutton Scudder reflected on her life in a volume entitled *On Journey,* published in 1937, when she was more than seventy years old. The volume's title suggests that she saw movement in her life, perhaps a sort of impermanence. The title is not only metaphorical — she did travel widely — but her physical journeys did not constitute the whole of Scudder's life pilgrimage. Perhaps the more significant pilgrimages took place in the context of her struggle to deal with the privilege that came from her family connections, her education, and her profession; in her efforts to establish dialogue between Christians and socialists; and in her provisional loyalty to the Christian church. In her autobiography she describes herself as being in "the position of a migrating bird, poised for an instant on a tree. The bird is sure of its direction, but presently it must resume its flight."[5] Although she does not refer to these pursuits as pilgrimages, they did involve her in journeys toward sacred goals.

In retrospect, although Scudder's life was full of overlapping and sometimes competing interests, it nonetheless appears harmonious. However, her clarity of direction and purpose emerged gradually. Her first memory, being shushed after Lincoln was shot, foreshadowed her adult involvement in public matters; it also prefigured the anxiety of her youth — that she lived life secondhand, not directly but from a distance. During her childhood years in Europe with mother and aunt, she developed both "devotion to beauty and awed intuition of the human past."[6] What she did not develop were contacts with people. Describing herself after a second European trip in her teens, Scudder wrote, "[I] was not wholly a happy young creature. [I] was unable to find reality anywhere . . . for I always felt as if in a dream, with the substantial world just round the corner."[7] This sense of living secondhand continued through her education at Boston Latin School and Smith College, from which she graduated in 1884.

Young Vida did not know early what her vocation would be. Her life was punctuated by "awakenings" followed by increased insight and conviction. After graduation from Smith, she accompanied her mother, her friend Clara French, and Clara's mother on a trip to Oxford. Describing the year she spent there, Vida used words such as "awakening," "quickened imagination," and "turning point." She "woke up to the realities of modern civilization."[8]

She received only a small inheritance, and it became clear that she would have to seek employment. Two years after the Oxford sojourn, she took a position teaching English at Wellesley College, her

5. Scudder, *On Journey* (New York: E. P. Dutton, 1937), p. 334.
6. Scudder, *On Journey,* p. 30.
7. Scudder, *On Journey,* p. 49.
8. Scudder, *On Journey,* p. 78.

vocation as a teacher suddenly heard and answered. However, this was not the whole of her calling, and the classroom was not the only goal of her pilgrimage.

Her family connections, education, and employment gave Professor Scudder a secure place in Boston life. Of the three women we are considering here, Scudder had the strongest claim to insider status in American society, yet she was never easy there. The "plethora of privilege" she became aware of in England continued to weigh heavy on her after her return to the States. With a group of other young college women she organized the College Settlement Association to carry out work much like, but independent of, that begun by Jane Addams and Ellen Star Gates in Chicago. Never a full-time resident, she spent regular evenings and weekends, as well as several vacations, away from her Back Bay home at Dennison House in Boston's South End. Here, among Irish and Italian immigrants, the daughter of old New England families found life lived directly. Through these contacts she became involved in the emerging labor movement. She delivered a speech in Lawrence, Massachusetts, during the 1912 strike that led some supporters of the college to call for her resignation. A compromise was struck whereby she temporarily suspended her popular course examining the social ideals of English literature. The conflict between academic obligations and Scudder's developing radicalism also surfaced when she denounced a gift for faculty pensions from Andrew Carnegie as tainted money.

Conflicts between social reform activities and academic responsibilities and the compromises they demanded, as well as obligations to her mother and the strain of a daily commute to Wellesley, brought on a dramatic collapse in 1901, followed by a period of bed rest and two years of relative calm. Scudder had for over a decade been a member of the Society of the Companions of the Holy Cross, Episcopal women pledged to intercessory prayer for social change, but in the next years she followed a renewed resolve to learn to pray. And, while in Europe, she found two guides for her continued exploration of Christianity: Francis of Assisi and Catherine of Siena.

In 1912 Scudder and her mother built a house and moved to Wellesley. The relocation brought withdrawal from some Boston activities, particularly Dennison House, where new leadership had proved less congenial to Scudder's socialist convictions. Despite the title she gave to the section of her autobiography treating these years — "Ebbing Tides" — Scudder continued to be very active. Even before the College Settlement Association was organized, Scudder had participated in numerous groups devoted to labor and radical social causes, several of which, such as the Society of Christian Socialists, combined religious and social concerns. She continued her efforts in these areas, as when she helped organize the Church League for Industrial Democracy in 1919. She continued to teach until 1927, often holding seminars in her attic study. The Franciscans remained a major interest, especially after her retirement. Scudder died in 1954 at the age of ninety-three.

Throughout her long life, Scudder struggled with a sense that she was separated from life, living it secondhand. In her autobiography she described her existence as movement "in a garden enclosed, if not a hothouse, an enclosure of gracious manners, regular meals, comfort, security, good taste. I liked the balmy air." Perhaps this seems an odd image for the life of a pilgrim from whom we expect movement and unsettledness. But she went on to say, "Yet sometimes it suffocated me. I wanted to escape, where winds buffeted, blowing free. The spirit of adventure . . . filled [me] with a biting curiosity about the way the Other Half lived, and a strange hunger for fellowship with them."[9] Precisely this intense discomfort with the privileges enclosing and protecting her in her own native habitat fitted Scudder for a pilgrim life seeking a resolution to her uneasiness. Like other women of her generation, Scudder may have found that her college training compounded her sense of being out of place and ill-suited for life in the world into which she was born. Fortunately among her parents' families were missionaries (including her father) whose devotion to a cause was respected and aunts who took unusual paths; one, a homeopathic doctor, shared a house with Vida and her mother. These precedents may have eased her journey into a profession and encouraged her commitment to social reform activity. Even so, her mother was never reconciled to Scudder's radicalism, and Scudder herself was unsure whether an inherited income or an earned income was the more moral source of support.

Introducing her collection of essays *The Church and the Hour: Reflections of a Socialist Churchwoman,* Scudder ventured to include other Christians in her dilemma, "caught on the branches of a great tree, the tree of privilege."[10] What she suggested for these others serves well as a description of her own response: "They do not quite know how to climb down, but they have the axe of the law in their hands, and they can apply themselves to sawing off the branch they sit on. No less than

9. Scudder, *On Journey,* pp. 139-40.

10. Scudder, *The Church and the Hour: Reflections of a Socialist Churchwoman* (New York: E. P. Dutton, 1917), p. 35.

this, probably is demanded of them by their religion, and it is consoling to reflect that, though a tumble may hurt, the ground is a good place after all." The socialist churchwoman was unwilling to accept that Christianity need be segregated by class. Indeed, she found such a notion impossible to accept having once learned to pray "Thy Kingdom come on earth."[11] Her uneasiness with privilege was intensified by her faith, which seems to have anticipated the insights of liberation theology in the vocabulary of the Social Gospel. She attempted to resolve her discomfort with privilege not by withdrawing further into it but rather by engaging more actively in efforts to dismantle the basis of her privilege — the first goal of her life pilgrimage.

While her criticism of the world order sprang as much from moral as political grounds, Scudder was willing, even eager, to engage in conversation and cooperation with those who held similar goals even if they were based in other convictions. Such interaction and joint endeavor toward the transformation of society was the second goal of Scudder's pilgrimage. She counseled religiously and politically motivated reformers to listen to one another and was an active participant in several organizations with compatible goals, among them the Church League for Industrial Democracy. The notion that Christians and social reformers might cooperate was perhaps as surprising to the radicals as to some Christians. Scudder urged the critics not to despise the efforts of religious people. Her membership in the Socialist Party provided one avenue for this urging, as did the letters she wrote to the editors of *The Masses* in the 1910s. "It is high time for you to recognize that anti-Church radicals do not absorb radicalism any more than Church-members absorb Christianity," she wrote. "Among these disciples [of a Living Lord] a considerable number find pungent and penetrating treatment of Churchianity and civilization in *The Masses* as welcome as flowers in May. They agree with you not all the time, but much of the time."[12]

Although well aware that the church could not as a body take a single social position, Scudder was convinced that if the church would "speak her own language," significant correspondence would emerge between that distinctly Christian view and "economic theories quite at variance with those on which society now more or less uneasily reposes."[13] Again and again in her essays she sounded the characteristic

11. Scudder, *The Church and the Hour,* p. 34.
12. Scudder, *The Church and the Hour,* pp. 99-100.
13. Scudder, *Church and the Hour,* p. 24.

note of the Social Gospel movement, the call to the kingdom of God.[14] Although she knew that this had not always been the church's position, Scudder believed that praying for the coming of God's reign was incompatible with renouncing the world or withdrawing from it. Making this petition in her prayer was central to Scudder's understanding of her own commitments and action. Her social radicalism was supported by a deep concern for the things of the spirit, a connection dramatically symbolized by the red flag positioned alongside a crucifix in her private place of prayer. In her essay "A Plea for Social Intercession," Scudder suggests that "Intercession is the counterpart in the life within of social work in the life without."[15] And as she meditated on the social meaning of the church year with the aid of her prayer book, she noted that the prayers both tie the spiritual and the social together and unite the pray-er with "the vital continuity of a corporate life down through the ages."[16]

The continuity of corporate life provided a basis for Scudder's attainment of a provisional loyalty to the Christian church, which constitutes a third sort of pilgrimage in her life. Her struggle was less with unbelief (though as a young woman she did struggle with particular doctrines) than with institutional commitment. Her understanding of the nature of belief both prevented a resolution of the difficulty and made progress possible. In marked contrast to the fundamentalists, Scudder responded to the uncertainty of their common age, "the supreme test of faith,"[17] with a sense of adventure. Particularly in this context, her comments from *On Journey* offer an implicit suggestion that faith is a pilgrimage:

> To remain a member of an historic Church is not to achieve finality. A creed is not an imprisoning wall, it is a gate, opening on a limitless country which can be entered in no other way. I am within that country, Laus Deo, but I have only begun to explore it; I am finding it, now glorious in beauty, now arid and forbidding. Again and again the explorer hesitates in a maze of paths pointing in sundry directions. But he can not stop; the religious life never suffers one

14. For a more complete examination of Scudder's role in the Social Gospel movement, see Susan Lindley, " 'Neglected Voices' and *Praxis* in the Social Gospel," *Journal of Religious Ethics,* Spring 1990, pp. 75-84.

15. Scudder, *The Church and the Hour,* p. 123.

16. Scudder, *Social Teachings of the Christian Year* (New York: E. P. Dutton, n.d.), p. 6.

17. Scudder, *Church and the Hour,* p. 72.

> to stand still. I will not say what happens, as he pauses, irresolute; but there are Guides.[18]

Scudder herself stands as a guide for others exploring that country.

Dorothy Day

Dorothy Day is probably the best known of the three women we are looking at. She was born in 1897, after Scudder had already been teaching for a decade. Like Scudder, she wrote an autobiography, *The Long Loneliness,* published when she was fifty-five. The title evokes the pilgrim's enduring sense of isolation and homelessness. The book chronicles Day's life into the first decades of the Catholic Worker movement. In her regular column in the movement newspaper, she explicitly applied the figure of pilgrimage to herself and her readers: "We should always be thinking of ourselves as pilgrims anyway."[19] In the column, entitled "On Pilgrimage," Day wrote about life in the St. Joseph hospitality house and reflected upon religious life in general.

Also like Scudder, Day undertook a fair number of physical journeys throughout the United States, Mexico, and, late in her life, Europe. Her father was a journalist whose work took the family from New York to California when she was a child. Although the family's stay in the San Francisco area was brief, Dorothy recalled the 1906 earthquake. Most of her childhood was spent in Chicago, where her father's improving career allowed a move to the Lincoln Park area. Here the growing girl encountered both the beauty of Anglican worship and the spectacle of poverty — the latter after reading Upton Sinclair prompted her to take her infant brother on walks through the areas west of their neighborhood. A Hearst scholarship funded two years at the University of Illinois spent largely in independent reading and conversation.

In 1915 Day followed her family back to New York, determined to work as a journalist. Her father was firmly opposed to women in his own field, so she was not allowed to live at home. Through her newspaper work, Day became acquainted with individuals who moved in radical and bohemian circles. Seemingly on a whim, she and a friend

18. Scudder, *On Journey,* pp. 232-33.

19. Day, quoted by William D. Miller in *Dorothy Day: A Biography* (San Francisco: Harper & Row, 1982), p. 379.

went to Washington to demonstrate for woman's suffrage and spent time in jail on a hunger strike. She was also involved in antiwar activities and took nurses' training. Day herself characterized these as years of searching, recording that she traveled a bit, living in both Chicago and New Orleans. Scholars have filled in more details from this period, activities that Day believed would detract from the spiritual aim of her autobiography. None of them requires significant revision of Day's self-assessment, however. Her interest in the poor continued as did her determination to write, but Day's life lacked a central focus.

The middle section of her autobiography, entitled "Natural Happiness," begins, "The man I loved, with whom I entered a common-law marriage, was an anarchist, an Englishman by descent, and a biologist."[20] It ends, "And when I returned to New York, I found Peter Maurin — Peter the French peasant, whose spirit and ideas will dominate the rest of this book as they will dominate the rest of my life."[21] In the period of time that is bracketed by these two observations, Day's life took several turns along the path that led to her mature vision. She used income from the movie rights to a novel she had written to buy a little beach house on Staten Island. There she shared a gentle life with anarchist Forster Batterham. Awaiting the birth of their child, Day became increasingly attracted to Roman Catholicism, apparently out of a desire to give the child what she herself lacked. In retrospect, her determination was firm: "I knew that I was going to have my child baptized, cost what it may. I knew that I was not going to have her floundering through many years as I had done, doubting and hesitating, undisciplined and amoral. I felt it was the greatest thing I could do for my child."[22] Further, "I felt that 'belonging' to a Church would bring that order to her life which I felt my own had lacked."[23] Tamar was baptized, and the cost did prove to be high. Batterham was opposed on principle to both religion and marriage. When Day was baptized in 1927, her intimate relationship with him ended. Her companions in faith were primarily saints she read about and the priests to whom she confessed in the next years spent in Los Angeles and Mexico and then back in New York.

Meeting Peter Maurin in 1932 brought Day into living contact

20. Dorothy Day, *The Long Loneliness: The Autobiography of Dorothy Day* (San Francisco: Harper & Row, Publishers, 1952), p. 113.

21. Day, *The Long Loneliness,* p. 166.

22. Day, *The Long Loneliness,* p. 136.

23. Day, *The Long Loneliness,* p. 141.

with a Catholicism hospitable to her early commitment to the poor and gave her an audience for her journalism. In the chapters of her autobiography recounting the first two decades of the Catholic Worker movement that Day and Maurin founded, the woman seems to merge into the movement and its activities — publishing the paper and establishing and maintaining the houses of hospitality, the retreats, the farms. To many people Dorothy Day *was* the movement until her death at eighty-three in 1980. Through those years she was consistently obedient to Catholic authorities, disciplined in worship, and indefatigably active on behalf of the poor and in promoting peace.

If Vida Scudder's pilgrimage was a struggle with life lived secondhand, Dorothy Day's was a struggle with loneliness. Although her family had deep roots in the United States, they were not among the elite, so Day did not carry the same burden of privilege that weighted Scudder. However, she did find herself always a bit of a misfit and dissatisfied. As a social radical, even her early unformed spiritual strivings marked her as odd; as a Catholic, she was oddly concerned with the social implications of faith. Even on the beach with Batterham, she was longing for something else, something more, something beyond the loveliness of their shared life. Throughout her autobiography this theme shapes her pilgrimage, although any positive statement of the object of her personal longing is far more elusive than Scudder's desire to cut off the branch of privilege. Two objects present themselves: the need for a resolution to the conflict of spirit and flesh and the need for a teacher.

The conflict of spirit and flesh developed early in Day's life. She introduces it when describing her teenage years in Chicago. It continued to surface during the years with Batterham especially, but long after that as well. Day maintained that women are more material than men, more inclined to think of home and children, more unfulfilled without a mate. As a consequence, she thought, women tend to "complicate the issue by an emphasis on the personal . . . and [to go] against their own best interests."[24] Despite the happiness of overflowing love she experienced with Batterham, Day took the difficult path of leaving behind that life for the one it opened to her. "Forster had made the physical world come alive for me and had awakened in my heart a flood of gratitude," she recalled. "The final object of this love and gratitude was God. No human creature could receive or contain so vast a flood of love and joy as I often felt after the birth of my child."[25] Nonetheless, neither conversion nor

24. Day, *The Long Loneliness,* p. 60.
25. Day, *The Long Loneliness,* p. 139.

her work in the Catholic Worker movement resolved the conflict of spirit and flesh or provided the synthesis reconciling the "body and soul, this world and the next" that Day longed for. The retreats of the forties and fifties did go some distance toward resolving the tension in a perfectionist fashion, however.

Day frequently noted her lack of a teacher during her years of searching. Despite her natural striving for spiritual adventure and her attraction to almost any form of religion that passed into view, she found no one to direct her in her searching until the time of her pregnancy. Then she allowed herself to be instructed, even consenting to Sister Aloysia's demand for memorization. In the years immediately following her conversion, the saints — victorious rather than living — were her teachers. Finally, Peter Maurin took responsibility for her education, directing Day's reading and lecturing her on history. The lives of the saints, the social teachings of the Catholic Church, and the work of great novelists became for Day the guides that Scudder had promised would be made available to all those who explore the limitless country inside the gates of a creed. If these guides did not overcome her profound loneliness, they at least suggested its purpose.

Day's loneliness was also ameliorated by the group of fellow pilgrims she found — or drew together — in the Catholic Worker movement. Their companionship gave immediacy and flesh to the mystical body of Christ. And because this community included the saints of the past as well as the workers of the present, it spanned time as well as space. Of course Day was well aware of the deficiencies and failings of her companions, as those within the movement were aware of hers. So too she knew of the scandal of the church not living up to its ideals. But as a personalist she asked what *she* could do, continuing in obedience to call the church to be its best. As Vatican II brought changes to liturgical practice and the turmoil of the sixties called for more innovations, Day preferred the older ways. Despite the experiences of her own youth, she had little patience for young people's rebellion and unwillingness to be guided. Her loyalty to the church appears to have been less anguished than Scudder's, although her work continually prodded the institution to attend more actively to the least among them.

As Day cast about for a way beyond her loneliness and lack of direction, her early concern for the poor remained firm. In her teens she felt that her life "was to be linked with theirs, their interests were to be my interests."[26] This calling directed her life pilgrimage through its

26. Day, *The Long Loneliness,* p. 38.

various stages. Her preconversion involvement in the developing labor movement and the birth of the Catholic Worker movement in the midst of the Great Depression shaped Day's keen interest in the lives of working people and engendered sympathy for their needs. Personally she was supportive of union efforts, and Catholic Workers participated in strikes. The last time she was arrested, in 1973, Day was marching with Cesar Chavez and the United Farm Workers in California.

Nevertheless, in her vocation for the poor, Day focused more on direct aid than on agitation for social reform. In response to the question, "How close are you to the worker?" Day described the life she and other Catholic Workers lived: "Going around and seeing the sights is not enough. To help the organizers, to give what you have for relief, to pledge yourself to voluntary poverty for life so that you can share with your brothers is not enough. One must live with them, share with them their sufferings too. Give up one's privacy, and mental and spiritual comforts as well as physical. . . . We have lived with the unemployed, the sick, the unemployables." She continued, melding radical and Christian language: "Going to the people is the purest and best act in Christian tradition and revolutionary tradition and it is the beginning of world brotherhood."[27] She wanted to give the people not only food but also a sense of human dignity and meaning unavailable through government programs and more organized charity.

This was grueling work that exhausted many. Some left because they were tired, others because they could not abide the conditions, and still others to pursue different paths toward a new society. Day herself was worn down by conditions at the St. Joseph hospitality house, by internal divisions, by frequent travel to lecture and visit Workers, and by the demands of Tamar and her growing family. She had some comfort from her sister Della, with whom she maintained a close relationship, however, and, beginning in the 1940s, a series of public and private retreats that she organized served to refresh her for the work. "It is not only for others that I must have these retreats," she wrote. "It is because I too am hungry and thirsty for the bread of the strong. I too must nourish myself to do the work I have undertaken; I too must drink at these good springs so that I may not be an empty cistern and unable to help others."[28] Although portrayals of Day often emphasize her selflessness, she was not unaware of the importance of attending to her own needs if she was to continue. Her faithfulness in

27. Day, *The Long Loneliness,* pp. 214-16.
28. Day, *The Long Loneliness,* p. 263.

worship may be taken as a sign of obedience to the disciplines of the church; without denying that, it may also be an evidence that Day took care to nourish herself.

Increasingly she became convinced that the means by which one makes a journey is significant as well as the destination. She considered writing a biography of St. Therese of Lisieux, whose life taught her the truth of "the little way" of constancy and faithfulness in the small things as the means to overcome daunting evils. During the 1950s she observed, "I see around me sin, suffering, and unutterable destruction. There is misery, materialism, degradation, ugliness on every side. All I see some days is sin. The problem is gigantic. Throughout the world there is homelessness, famine, fear, and war and the threat of war. We live in a time of gigantic evil. It is hopeless to think of combating it by any other means than that of sanctity. To think of overcoming such evil by material means, by alleviations, by changes in the social order only — all this is utterly hopeless."[29] If she did not end poverty or bring world peace, she did broaden the vision of her church so that ecclesial concern for the poor and for peace no longer seems odd.

Pauli Murray

Like Vida Scudder, Pauli Murray was a lifelong member of the Anglican Church; unlike Scudder, but like Day, she was not a child of material or social privilege. Although she refused to consider herself an outsider, both her sex and her race raised barriers throughout her life. Dismantling both types of barriers for the benefit of others was a major goal of her life pilgrimage. Murray entitled her autobiography *Song in a Weary Throat: An American Pilgrimage.* In it she chronicled a life that paralleled several major social movements of her time and recorded her involvement in the reforms of the New Deal, in the early stirring of the civil rights movement, and in the beginnings of the women's movement. Thus her life illustrates well Marty's vision of the large-scale national pilgrimage as a reflection of the small-scale personal pilgrimage and vice versa.

From childhood Murray was well aware that her birth in 1910 coincided with the founding of the Urban League and came only a year after the founding of the National Association for the Advancement of Colored People. (That year Scudder was nearing fifty and Day was

29. Day, quoted by Miller in *Dorothy Day,* p. 431.

entering adolescence.) Although orphaned at a young age, Murray gained an abiding sense of her mother's family and their heritage as she grew up in the care of her aunt Pauline Dame in the Fitzgerald home. Photographs of four generations of ancestors surrounded her on the parlor walls, and their stories were told. As an adult she recorded stories of both her Fitzgerald grandparents in *Proud Shoes: The Story of an American Family.* In this household she learned pride in self, family, and race and received an abiding faith — pride and faith that sustained her in later years.

Coming from a family of teachers, Murray was determined to secure a quality education for herself. To overcome the deficiencies of her "colored school" degree, she took an additional year of high school in New York City before entering Hunter College. She graduated in the midst of the Depression and took WPA employment before applying to the University of North Carolina for graduate work. When her application was denied on the basis of her race, the NAACP declined to try the case, which was weakened because her legal residence was no longer North Carolina. Nonetheless, Murray herself regarded her efforts as "part of a tradition of continuous struggle, lasting nearly twenty years, to open the doors of the state university to Negroes, struggle marked by modest beginnings and several bitter defeats before the victorious breakthrough."[30] Nor was this to be her only contribution to the larger cause of civil rights.

In 1940 Murray and a companion were jailed in Virginia for violating Jim Crow laws on an interstate bus. Their careful documentation of the incident that led to their arrest and their exemplary conduct in jail did not gain the verdict they hoped for, but the experience prefigured Murray's entry into the legal realm and her activities while a student at Howard Law School during World War II. With other students who found Jim Crow laws especially offensive in light of the "wartime appeal for sacrifice on behalf of freedom," she was part of two well-orchestrated sit-ins conducted to desegregate restaurants in Washington, D.C.[31] As in the case of her application to the University of North Carolina, Murray and her colleagues were a bit ahead of the general movement in their combination of Gandhi's nonviolent re-

30. Murray, *Pauli Murray: The Autobiography of a Black Activist, Feminist, Lawyer, Priest, and Poet* (Knoxville: University of Tennessee Press, 1987), p. 128. This is a reprint of the volume originally entitled *Song in a Weary Throat: An American Pilgrimage.*

31. Murray, *Pauli Murray,* p. 201.

sistance and "American techniques of showmanship." She graduated from Howard experienced in direct confrontation and well versed in the less dramatic techniques of civil rights law.

Her high standing at Howard won Murray a graduate scholarship that she hoped to use at Harvard Law School. Although at the time Harvard did not admit women, Murray was characteristically determined to "raise the issue in such a way that its law school would be unable to avoid it."[32] Her experience in racial struggle had taught her the value of following "whatever administrative procedure was available," and without much hope of success she proceeded. While she could not budge Harvard, the encounter with the school and the response of Howard colleagues left the young lawyer profoundly aware that she was a minority within a minority — an "unabashed feminist" as well as an advocate of civil rights. She took her scholarship money to the University of California at Berkeley.

She devoted the next decades to advancement of her race and her sex through legal channels and education. To those not aware that she was motivated by these goals, her activities might seem like aimless wandering. But if Murray's life, like Scudder's and Day's, is properly understood as a pilgrimage, then even wandering would have been purposeful: it was movement in pursuit of a dream even when the dream appeared to be a long way from realization. The title for Murray's autobiography is part of a line from her poem "Dark Testament"; the whole line reads, "Hope is a song in a weary throat." No doubt in these years Murray was often weary, living as she did on the edge of financial ruin. However, reading her description of her work in private law practice, writing *Proud Shoes,* caring for her aged aunts, running for office, compiling *States' Laws on Race and Color,* studying at Yale, and teaching at the Ghana School of Law, Benedict College, and Brandeis University, one hears a song of hope rather than a litany of weariness. Each activity allowed Murray to chip away at the barriers that sex and race placed in the paths of other people like her and helped her move toward the goal of her pilgrimage.

By the 1960s the nation was alive with intensified civil rights agitation. Murray took part in the 1963 March on Washington despite her disappointment in its male leaders' inattention to women. She spent a year working with rural Southern students at Benedict College. Then in the late 1960s she went to Brandeis to help found and teach in an Afro-American Studies program. Here she found herself in the midst

32. Murray, *Pauli Murray,* p. 242.

of an increasingly radical movement the members of which promoted strategies for advancing their race that were at odds with her own. The conflict was clear in a classroom dispute over terminology. Murray held that *Negro* was a term of dignity, worthy of use, but neither her experience, her record, nor her reasoning were convincing to the young black men in her class. She came to see that her own search for identity had been more private than those of her students. She anchored herself "in the immediate American past, which had produced [her] mixed racial origins with all their Ishmaelite implications — a stance that made both blacks and whites uncomfortable."[33] Her students may have thought she had sold out by adapting to the mainstream. She viewed her position not as "blind imitation of dominant values but a choice of those verities, handed down through centuries of human experience, that enriched the quality of life. Chief among these was the sacredness of the individual, who in Biblical tradition, is created in the image of God, and from that vision followed [her] obligation to work with others to transform the planet Earth into a place where each individual would have an opportunity to fulfill his or her highest creative potential."[34] Unlike her students and the militant leaders they followed, Murray continued to hope for and work toward a society in which people of all races would cooperate for the good of all. This ultimate goal of her life pilgrimage made her a fellow traveler with both Day and Scudder, though the specific paths of their journeys diverged.

Beginning in the early 1960s, Murray's pilgrimage brought her into the growing women's movement, and the domain of her pilgrimage expanded to include the Episcopal Church. In 1961 John F. Kennedy appointed Murray's old friend Eleanor Roosevelt as the chair of the President's Commission on the Status of Women. Murray served on a committee and wrote an important report exploring the value of litigation under the Fifth and Fourteenth amendments. In retrospect the Commission's work seems quite moderate, but its significance cannot be measured only through its reports. Doing the work forged an informal network of women that mobilized to support the inclusion of a prohibition of discrimination on the basis of sex in Title VII of the 1964 Civil Rights Act. Again, Murray's legal training and experience with racial civil rights issues gave her the knowledge and skills needed to play a quiet but decisive role. That she herself was subject to restrictions imposed by race and sex made her an especially effective advocate.

33. Murray, *Pauli Murray,* p. 391.
34. Murray, *Pauli Murray,* p. 396.

This same network gave birth to the National Organization for Women in 1966.

From her childhood, the church played a role in Murray's life. She described Saint Titus Episcopal, a black mission in Durham, as an extension of her family. One of her aunts married its rector. However, her adult feelings toward the church were ambivalent: "I could neither stay away entirely nor enter wholeheartedly into Christian community."[35] Thus she continued to participate in worship but remained indifferent to other aspects of parish life and the larger organization. In the mid-1960s small changes began to take place at St. Mark's, her New York parish: her friend Renee Barlow was elected to the vestry, and occasionally a woman read the lessons. To Murray's eyes, these steps only served to make the usual male dominance of worship leadership more evident. Finally one Sunday Murray filled with rage and walked out of the eucharist service. "I wandered about the streets full of blasphemous thought," she recalled, "feeling alienated from God. The intensity of this assault at the deepest level of my devotional life produced a crisis of faith. . . . If the present church customs were justified, then I did not belong in the church and it became a stumbling block to faith."[36] Two years later the World Council of Churches Uppsala Assembly helped convince Murray to accord her church the sort of provisional loyalty that Scudder had given it decades before. In subsequent years she became active in efforts to expand laywomen's participation and to secure women's ordination.

Still Murray was not ready to consider the possibility that her life's pilgrimage might lead to a third path — pastoral ministry in addition to law and education. She separated life into distinct zones of sacred and secular, viewing herself as too worldly for ministry, lay or ordained. This changed through her increased involvement in the church and the death of Renee Barlow. The friendship between Murray and Barlow grew out of their shared faith. When Renee died, Pauli was called upon to minister to her in the role of the clergy, as she had also done when her Aunt Pauline died. (This involved reading Scripture and praying; while these are not uniquely clerical tasks, Pauli preceived them as such, and did them in part because no priest was present.) Although she resisted, Murray recognized these occasions as signs that God was calling her to a new task. In 1973, prior to church approval of women's ordination, she was accepted as a postulant and enrolled in

35. Murray, *Pauli Murray,* p. 369.
36. Murray, *Pauli Murray,* p. 370.

General Theological Seminary. After study and field work at St. Philip's Chapel (a parish she visited as a child when its rector was her aunt's husband), Murray was ready for ordination. When, at age 67, she was one of the first women regularly ordained in the American Episcopal Church, Murray was once again on the crest of a wave of change, as she had been in the civil rights movement and the secular women's movement. A few weeks later she celebrated the eucharist at the Chapel of the Holy Cross in Chapel Hill in which her grandmother had been baptized as a slave and sent to sit in the gallery by her white father's sister. This scene closes Murray's autobiography. "All the strands of my life had come together. Descendant of slave and slave owner, I had already been called poet, lawyer, teacher, and friend. Now I was empowered to minister the sacrament of One in whom there is no north or south, no black or white, no male or female — only the spirit of love and reconciliation drawing us all toward the goal of human wholeness."[37] In these words Murray expressed the goal of the pilgrimage that had taken her down several paths. Here for a moment the dream and its realization merged. She continued on this path until her death in 1985.

Guides

These three American churchwomen lived in the land of American Christianity, but each pilgrim was also prodded by a dream of what the church, the nation, even human society could be. They did not rest content with the world that was given to them or within the boundaries it assumed for them; rather, they pressed on toward what might be. Although none of them achieved the goal of her pilgrimage, each one glimpsed it and by her life moved herself and others toward it. Together Murray, Day, and Scudder may serve as guides for other women who find themselves uneasy travelers through the same land.

Facing the barriers to leadership and participation that femaleness comprised during their lifetimes, these women refused to be excluded from the church. To the contrary, they held themselves responsible for the mending required to make their church what it should be but was not. They shared a sense of continuity with the church through the ages at the same time that they cultivated contemporary community through friendships and groups such as the Society of the

37. Murray, *Pauli Murray,* p. 435.

Companions of the Holy Cross and the Catholic Worker. Scudder confessed, "I am no longer accuser, but penitent; am I not a member of the Mystical Body? Is it not composed of those like me?"[38] Murray was also supported by her family's heritage of racial pride and her awareness of the long history of civil rights struggles.

In addition to having cultivated community and friendship with like-minded people and having claimed membership in the church across time, these women shared two other characteristics that suggest sustaining strategies for contemporary women. Related to their refusal to be excluded was their indefatigable persistence in pursuit of their goals. They may have hoped for the kingdom of God to come quickly, for the reconciliation symbolized in the eucharist to spread rapidly, but all three were practical in undertaking their journeys. They proceeded by putting one foot in front of the other. This was Day's "little way." This was how Murray made her way, exhausting every procedure available. Each woman held the church responsible to her notion of its best ideal, even while recognizing its shortcomings.

However, this idealism did not prevent any of them from forging alliances with people some others might have regarded as suspect, as outsiders. Scudder articulated her willingness in her letters to *The Masses.* Though Day's view were less wide-ranging, she made them clear by her participation in various labor and peace efforts. As Suzanne R. Hiatt has remarked, "The theme of [Murray's] life was the pursuit of justice for all; and she meant *all* — white, black, native American, poor, female, male — all God's human creatures."[39] She refused to allow the many facets of her own identity to be divided and worked resolutely for both racial and sexual civil rights in several arenas.

Memory of these women's activities and personal identities becomes part of the history that can sustain other women (and men) on similar journeys, as Hofstadter's assertion about the role of history for personal identity suggests. The telling of their lives also seems to echo Monica Wittig's oft-quoted admonition: "You say you have lost all recollection of it, remember . . . you say there are no words to describe it, you say it does not exist. But remember. Make an effort to remember. Or, failing that, invent."[40] While Wittig wrote of a mythic world of

38. Scudder, *On Journey,* p. 370.

39. Hiatt, "Pauli Murray: May Her Song Be Heard at Last," *Journal of Feminist Studies in Religion* 4 (Fall 1988): 72.

40. Wittig, *Les Guerilleres,* trans. David LeVay (New York: Avon Books, 1971), p. 89.

laughing women who were not slaves, these three women give witness that they remembered the church as ideal and labored to invent it as reality. They offer a view of the church as open and of faith as an adventure. The memory of their example urges other women to cling to the conviction that they too are responsible members of the church, to refuse to be silenced, and to draw upon the resources its saints and spiritual disciplines offer them for their pilgrimage.

RELIGIOUS FUNDAMENTALISM

The Fundamentalism of the Enclave: Catholic and Protestant Oppositional Movements in the United States

R. Scott Appleby

FUNDAMENTALISM WITHIN Protestant Christianity has been characterized by a strong tendency toward institutional and theological separatism interrupted by occasional episodes of intradenominational collaboration and coalition-building for religious and political purposes. Twice in this century Protestant fundamentalists have emerged from periods of relative quiescence in order to wage public campaigns designed to influence what Martin E. Marty has often called "the *the* culture." Judging by the inflated rhetoric of the fundamentalists themselves regarding their goals and intentions vis-à-vis American society, one might conclude that these efforts have met with mixed results at best. But fundamentalist influence on the culture of American evangelicalism, and thus on the general religious life of the nation, is indisputable. Perhaps the most compelling evidence of this influence is found in the very endurance of Protestant Christian fundamentalism across generations — the staying power of this subculture within a subculture. Fundamentalists have been able to retreat to their own enclaves sustained by a formidable institutional network, there to be nourished and renewed in the struggle for a Christian America.[1]

In contrast, Roman Catholic "fundamentalists" have yet to sus-

1. For examples of fundamentalist enclaves nurtured by educational networks, see Susan D. Rose, *Keeping Them Out of the Hands of Satan: Evangelical Schooling in America* (New York: Routledge, 1988); and Alan Peshkin, *God's Choice: The Total World of a Fundamentalist Christian School* (Chicago: University of Chicago Press, 1986).

tain an effective or prolonged countermodernist campaign or build far-reaching institutional networks. In the twenty-eight years following the close of the Second Vatican Council there have been signs of the effort to do so in the establishment of publishing houses, institutes, seminaries, colleges, and "wildcat parishes" that serve as the major channels for Catholic traditionalist activity. But far more of these efforts have failed than have succeeded, and even the fate of the "movement" itself as a distinct Catholic subgroup was cast into doubt by the death of rebel archbishop Marcel Lefebvre in February 1991.[2]

Why has American Protestantism been able to nurture fiercely conservative independent churches and sustain separatist communities while American Catholic oppositional movements have either died on the vine or failed to thrive? Theologians attribute this to the reforming spirit of Protestantism and to its expansive ecclesiology: the proliferation of independent churches and splinter groups is only to be expected when anti-institutionalism is a defining religious impulse. Historians point to the irony of world-renouncing Protestants adapting to the world with far greater flexibility than Catholics. In order to explain the greater frequency and vigor of antimodernist separatist movements within Protestantism, they emphasize the longer history of religious modernization within the mainline churches. Meanwhile, the Catholic Church effectively fought off modernization within its ranks until the mid-twentieth century. In other words, liberal Christians have been irritating conservative Christians for a longer time and in far greater numbers in Protestant denominations than in the Catholic Church.[3]

Marty has drawn the relevant implications of these historical and theological statements in suggesting that the Catholic variant of religious fundamentalism labors under burdens that hinder it from becoming a viable American religious subculture — "viable" in terms of its ability to influence nonfundamentalist Catholics in significant ways. Catholics who flee the Church and its modern adaptations are immediately on terra incognita. When they attempt to abandon what they believed to be the true and perfect society, Marty points out, they

2. See William D. Dinges, "Roman Catholic Traditionalism," in *Fundamentalisms Observed,* ed. Martin E. Marty and R. Scott Appleby (Chicago: University of Chicago Press, 1991).

3. See, for example, the account of Protestant battles in Martin E. Marty, *Modern American Religion: The Irony of It All, 1893-1919* (Chicago: University of Chicago Press, 1986), pp. 208-37.

have no place to go.[4] Roman Catholics find their communal identity in an unbroken tradition embodied and preserved in the papal and episcopal magisterium. Alienation from the Church is thus a profoundly serious and disorienting step that requires the reconstruction of Catholic self-understanding for those who would be "fundamentalists."

What Marty's observation may teach us about the American Catholic community in particular, and American religion in general, is the subject of this essay. Marty has also demonstrated the guiding method of inquiry for such an essay with his extensive work in comparative religious fundamentalisms. "Fundamentalism," as defined for comparative purposes, is a useful conceptual lens with which to examine a variety of religious movements sharing a sustained opposition to modernizing and secularizing influences within a religious tradition and in the surrounding culture. Comparative study demonstrates, for example, the prominence of apocalyptic imagery and eschatology in fundamentalist worldviews. One finds confirmation of this generalization in the prominent role that apocalypticism plays in the religious imagination of Catholic fundamentalists. The fundamentalist reconstruction of Catholic religious identity seems to require an eschatological vision of a remnant church victorious over its many enemies. Such a vision reinforces and gives meaning to the present-day sense of siege and justifies the naming of apostates.

But how can we account for the relative obscurity of these Catholic movements of opposition, the secrecy in which their activities are shrouded, and their failure to organize or mobilize a statistically significant minority of aggrieved Catholics? Why has American Protestant fundamentalism been more prominent and influential in American culture than any analogous movement arising within Catholicism? Are the limitations to both Catholic and Protestant movements inherent in their respective religious imaginations?

With these questions in mind, I have studied the reactions of evangelical and fundamentalist Protestants and conservative Catholics to cultural and religious developments in the 1960s.[5] By most reckon-

4. Marty has made this point in his teaching and in communications with me. See also Marty, *An Invitation to American Catholic History* (Chicago: Thomas More Press, 1986).

5. Although I am including the two distinct groups of conservatives and traditionalists in one general category of "Oppositional Catholics" — that is, Catholics who oppose the modernization of Catholicism and particularly the liberal implementation of the decrees of the Second Vatican Council — I have attempted in this essay to indicate matters on which the groups are dissimilar. Apocalyptic

ings "the sixties" was a critical period in the development of American religion. Striking and surprising transformations (or attempted transformations) of American society coincided with a quantum leap forward in the efficacy of communications technology that led to the immediate dissemination, exaggeration, and distortion of these actual and attempted transformations.[6] In the signs of the times many conservative Christians found an ominous portent: secular humanism, a virulent form of cultural modernism, was being codified and institutionalized as the reigning ethos of the once-Christian nation.[7] Opposition movements and oppositional mentalities formed in reaction to the perceived conspiracy of liberalizing agents within the respective religious traditions and secularizing forces in the larger mainstream culture. To the conservative religious mind, the religious liberals were either unwitting dupes or unacknowledged allies of the New Left.[8]

The cumulative impact of the sixties, as perceived and interpreted by conservative Christians, not only inspired the public reemergence of fundamentalism as a self-conscious opposition movement of American Protestantism but also provided the cultural requirements for initial manifestations of a fundamentalist mentality within American Catholicism. Protestant fundamentalists achieved a victory of sorts in their efforts to restrain the erosive forces of secularism within their churches, but traditionalist Catholics, would-be restorers of a long-lost medieval Catholic cultural hegemony, created little more than a ripple on the ecclesial waters.

Considering conservative Roman Catholics and evangelical Protestants as one — in their perceptions of the sixties at least — is a justifiable relaxation of religious historical categories for comparative purposes. Because the communications/entertainment industry and the public schools and universities had played and were playing a major role in the process by which the *the* culture was secularized, feisty and discerning conservative Christians, who were able to launch a

---

thought, for example, is more broadly characteristic of traditionalist than of conservative thought, as is open opposition to the current pope.

6. See the essays in *Progress and Its Discontents,* ed. Gabriel A. Almond, Marvin Chodorow, and Roy Harvey Pearce (Berkeley and Los Angeles: University of California Press, 1982).

7. See George M. Marsden, "Unity and Diversity in the Evangelical Resurgence," in *Altered Landscapes: Christianity in America, 1935-1985,* ed. David W. Lotz (Grand Rapids: William B. Eerdmans, 1989), pp. 61-76.

8. See William O'Neill, *Coming Unglued: An Informal History of the Sixties* (New York: Basic Books, 1979), p. 45.

counterattack almost immediately, counted it a blessing that they had fortified their own alternative institutions of socialization for the better part of the twentieth century. In 1884 Catholic bishops had mandated the establishment of a Catholic school in every parish, a wildly ambitious goal that was approached but never fully realized in the twentieth century, while fundamentalist Protestants had been building a vast network of separatist schools, radio stations, and publication houses since "going underground" in the 1920s.[9]

Yet Protestant conservatives were strikingly more successful than their Catholic counterparts in the effort to sustain a fundamentalistic subculture in the United States after the 1960s. Protestants had forsaken, or been forsaken by, sheltering traditional institutions decades prior to Pope John XXIII's call for Catholic *aggiornamento;* they had learned to move within the confines of modernity, to imitate its successes, even to contribute as Christians to its achievements. In 1962 Catholics were just beginning to shake off the cobwebs of a 400-year-old fortress mentality designed to keep out the elements of modernity identified and condemned categorically by Pope Pius IX in the 1864 *Syllabus of Errors,* including democracy, science, and "progress" unfettered by revealed moral norms. American Catholics were thus relatively inexperienced in the game of religious-modernization-to-combat-modernity. Put simply, conservative Protestants were modern Christians in ways that Catholics were not, and as such were much better qualified to become successful fundamentalists.

This mention of fundamentalism as a modern (and largely twentieth-century) phenomenon raised terminological and definitional questions. There has been much discussion of the term *fundamentalism* of late and whether it can appropriately be applied even to certain segments of conservative evangelicalism in the United States, much less to ultraconservative or traditionalist segments of American Catholicism (and still less to Hindus, Sikhs, Jews, and Muslims elsewhere). This is not the place to rehearse the particulars of that discussion. Suffice it to say that for a comparative paper that tries to make sense of larger religious trends in the sixties and beyond, the term *fundamentalism* is a construct indicating directions and emphases within conservative reli-

9. On Protestant activities, see Joel A. Carpenter, "Fundamentalist Institutions and the Rise of Evangelical Protestantism, 1929-1942," *Church History* 49 (March 1980): 62-75. On Catholic activities, see James Hennesey, *American Catholics: A History of the Roman Catholic Community in the United States* (New York: Oxford University Press, 1981), p. 182.

gion. I use the term here much the way Robert Wuthnow uses it to describe one of two poles to which post–World War II American religious groups gravitate.[10] The Fundamentalism Project, an interdisciplinary cross-cultural study directed by Martin Marty, offers the following historical-comparative definition of the term.

> Religious fundamentalism has appeared as a tendency, a habit of mind, found within denominations and embodied by certain representative individuals and movements. This tendency manifests itself as a strategy or set of strategies by which beleaguered believers attempt to preserve their distinctive identity as a religious people or group. Feeling this identity to be at risk in the contemporary era, they fortify it by a selective retrieval of doctrines, beliefs, and practices from a sacred past. These retrieved "fundamentals" are refined, modified, and sanctioned in a spirit of shrewd pragmatism: they are to serve as a bulwark against the encroachment of outsiders who threaten to draw the believers into a syncretistic, areligious, or irreligious cultural milieu. Moreover, these fundamentals are accompanied in the new religious portfolio by unprecedented claims and doctrinal innovations. Drawing on the strength of these innovations and the new supporting doctrines, the retrieved and updated fundamentals are meant to regain the same charismatic intensity today by which they originally forged communal identity from the formative revelatory religious experiences long ago.
>
> By selecting elements of tradition and modernity alike, fundamentalists seek to remake the world in the service of a dual commitment to the unfolding eschatological drama (by returning all things to submission to the divine) and to self-preservation (by neutralizing the threatening "other"). Such an endeavor often requires charismatic and authoritarian leadership, depends on a disciplined inner core of adherents, and promotes a rigorous sociomoral code for all followers. Boundaries are set, the enemy identified, converts sought, and institutions created and sustained in pursuit of a comprehensive reconstruction of ecclesial and/or political society.

In this sense, contemporary fundamentalism is at once both derivative and vitally original. In their effort to reclaim the efficacy of religious life, fundamentalists have more in common than not with other Christian revivalists of the past two thousand years. But despite the fact that nostalgia for a golden era, a sacred past, a bygone time of origins is a hallmark of fundamentalist rhetoric, Christian fundamentalism in-

10. Wuthnow, *The Struggle for America's Soul: Evangelicals, Liberals, and Secularism* (Grand Rapids: William B. Eerdmans, 1989).

tends neither a simple return to such an era nor an artificial imposition of archaic practices and life-styles. Fundamentalism is, on the contrary, a child of the modern age, a hybrid of certain late nineteenth-century religious sensibilities and twentieth-century scientific culture.

By defining fundamentalism as a tendency or habit of mind, I am able to generalize not only about thousands of independent or affiliated fundamentalist churches (each of which is unique, tied as it is to the personality of a pastor), which form only a portion of the larger Protestant evangelical community, but also about the spectrum of Christian churches, including the Roman Catholic Church.[11]

In order to be considered fundamentalist to any extent, a community must exhibit, among other traits, a certain degree of self-consciousness in proclaiming and living the faith. Faith held literally in an age of myth and metaphor is held *over against;* it must be chosen consciously.[12] And the very act of choosing faith does something important to the traditional form of religious practice; among other things, it lends the faith a self-conscious, contra-acculturative, and perhaps even militant cast.

The American Catholic community of the decades prior to Vatican II exhibited certain features of a fundamentalist mentality. Even as the immigrant flock was absorbed by and assimilated into a larger pluralist culture in the twentieth century, the community sustained a separatist, defiant subculture that required an infallible authority, a guarantee of "inerrancy" in interpreting Scripture and tradition, and a perch above the vicissitudes of history from which to preserve the transcendent character of revelation against the erosions of historical criticism, radical skepticism, and relativism. American Catholicism at times adopted a strident and condemning tone toward outsiders, refusing to dialogue with those who did not accept, and sometimes openly scorned, its most cherished doctrines and practices. And, as the cheerfully triumphalist standard-bearers of the neo-Thomist revival proclaimed, the Church yearned to transform American culture from within.[13]

Prior to the Second Vatican Council, however, Catholics were selectively "fundamentalist," "separatist," and "oppositional." They

11. Martin E. Marty and R. Scott Appleby, "Conclusion: An Interim Report on a Hypothetical Family," in *Fundamentalisms Observed,* p. 835.

12. Nancy T. Ammerman makes this point in "North American Protestant Fundamentalism," in *Fundamentalisms Observed,* p. 14.

13. See William Halsey, *The Survival of American Innocence: American Catholicism in an Age of Disillusionment* (Notre Dame, Ind.: University of Notre Dame, 1985).

opposed the Protestant worldview that seemed to inform the textbooks and teaching of the public school system, and so they separated their children from that system by building their own alternative system (or by instructing the children in Catholic "fundamentals" in CCD classes). Lay Catholics were free to marry other Catholics of any ethnic background, but they were not to marry "outsiders," non-Catholics who might lure them from the practice of the faith. Catholic politicians traveled in packs, as did Catholic businessmen. In short, American Catholics living in the aftermath of the *Syllabus of Errors* looked with suspicion and distrust on the dominant American Protestant ethos and challenged it selectively even as they made inroads into mainstream political culture, a process culminating in the election of John F. Kennedy as president of the United States. Thus, before the 1960s Catholic attitudes toward the external culture were informed by a fundamentalist orientation, but the institutional church itself was not the primary concern of oppositional or separatist forces. The enemy was outside the fortress, driven there by papal vigilance. Catholics felt fully secure in their identity as Catholics only within the boundaries of the institutional Church — boundaries drawn with great care by canon law, magisterial pronouncement, and parochial custom.

That sense of security diminished for Catholic conservatives almost immediately following the Second Vatican Council. Oppositional sensibilities formed in reaction to implementations of the conciliar decrees that seemed to undermine the faith itself. Catholic conservatives came to define themselves over against the liberal interpretation of the Council. They were unable to appeal "above" the authority of a general council to the authority of the pope, because the succession of popes from John XXIII to John Paul II affirmed the Council at every opportunity, without the slightest hesitation. So those who rejected the Council's legitimacy were in open defiance of the pope as well. Catholic conservatives have thus remained in full communion with the hierarchy but strive to be faithful to the "authentic traditions" of the Church and to an "authentic reading" of Vatican II. Their dissent from liberal Catholicism on religious matters often takes place within the local church structures, whereas their dissent from liberalism and secular humanism on sociopolitical matters may be expressed through a variety of extraecclesial organizations. "Most conservative Catholics took their beliefs for granted until, sometime after Vatican II, they realized that many of those beliefs were being called into question," the conservative Catholic historian James Hitchcock has written. "Issues like the ban on artificial means of contraception, or the exclusively male celibate priesthood, loom much larger than they might otherwise for the simple reason that they have been important rallying points for Catholic liberals. Conservative Catholics have been deliberately and even stubbornly countercultural in making a firm stand at precisely those points where Catholic teaching is most strongly attacked."[14]

Small groups of conservatives, many of them looking for leadership to the French archbishop Marcel Lefebvre, either rejected the Council openly, arguing that its decrees were not authentic and binding, or maintained an ambiguous attitude toward the decrees. These so-called traditionalists held that the Council Fathers were "modernists" and repeated the warnings of Pius X, the pope who had condemned modernism as "the synthesis of all heresies" in 1907. Modernism threatened to destroy the Church from within, Pius had written, by imposing a secular scientific worldview on the faithful, by subjecting the sources of revelation to the methods of historical and literary criticism, and by reinterpreting supernatural truths according to modern needs and sensibilities. In the aftermath of Vatican II, the traditionalists feared that modernism was infecting the very heart of the Church itself. In response they mounted an antimodernist movement in which opposition to the enemy within took precedence over opposition to the enemy outside the Church. The battle was for hegemony — that is, for the control of ideology, resources, and education that had been wrested away from the true Church by the misguided liberals and modernists holding key positions of authority in the postconciliar Church. The immediate problem for these Catholic counterhegemonists was finding a place to go now that the *the* church, like the *the* culture, had been sidetracked into secularism. The fundamentalist arsenal that militant Catholic conservatives ransacked was also missing a crucial weapon — a proven knack for manipulating modern instrumentalities and attitudes.[15]

14. Hitchcock, "Conservative Catholic Activism," in *Fundamentalisms Observed,* p. 113.

15. This dalliance with modernity is a complex but important trait of fundamentalism. Even as they oppose many of the cultural consequences of modernization (such as "atheistic materialism," "evolutionism," and "secular humanism"), fundamentalists have proven themselves adept at manipulating the technological products of modernity, from the small-arms weaponry used by Jewish and Islamic fundamentalists in the Middle East to the effective use of mass media of communication by Protestant televangelists. In contrast, Catholic oppositional groups seem not to be shrewdly selective adaptors of the modern. Even Fulton Sheen's popular television hour was not decidedly countercultural and in any event was popular at a time when Catholicism had not yet experienced its own internal revolution.

The Sixties as Secular-Hegemonic: The Errant Academy and Clergy

"The critical decade" of the sixties is dated variously and often refers to a period longer than ten years. For the purposes of historical analysis, the "decade" could, for example, begin in 1962, the year in which the Second Vatican Council opened; and historian Robert Booth Fowler, among others, has made a convincing argument that the culmination of the process occurred as late as 1976, dubbed "the year of the evangelical" by the secular press.[16] Taking a slightly different approach, Leonard Sweet has suggested that there were two "sixties." The first, which lasted roughly from 1960 to 1967, was a time of great expectations, optimism, and newness — as in the New Frontier, the New Morality, the new humanity. Even the death-of-God movement "did not represent one of Christianity's more funereal moods; it constituted one of the decade's most high-spirited youth demonstrations (the average age of its four theologians in 1960 was 34.5) against selfishness, hatred, injustice, and entrenched authority."[17] In contrast to this intoxicating beginning, the second "sixties," which lasted from 1967 to 1971, was, like a morning-after hangover, characterized by disorientation and disintegration. The rebellious questioning of authority and irreverence toward tradition gave way to a crisis of identity as mainline Protestant churches experienced what Benton Johnson has called "a second great depression."[18] Evangelicals stepped briskly into the clearing left by the departed and demoralized liberals.

Sweet's dividing line also makes sense in the case of American Catholics, who had a newly elected Catholic president of the United States, a universally beloved pope, and a thrilling ecumenical council to be near-euphoric about in the "first sixties" but then suffered their own hangover in the "second sixties." The changed relations between clergy and laity took their toll in pastoral confusion, conciliar decrees were implemented amateurishly, and the Novus Ordo Mass led willy-nilly to undisciplined and unauthorized liturgical experimentation. As in the case of Protestantism, the ensuing crisis of identity inflated the

16. See Fowler, *A New Engagement: Evangelical Political Thought, 1966-1976* (Grand Rapids: William B. Eerdmans, 1982).

17. Sweet, "The 1960s: The Crises of Liberal Christianity and the Public Emergence of Evangelicalism," in *Evangelicalism and Modern America,* ed. George Marsden (Grand Rapids: William B. Eerdmans, 1984), p. 30.

18. Johnson, quoted by Sweet in "The 1960s," p. 31.

stock of those church members who had stubbornly held fast to the tried-and-true traditions and worldview. They felt at least partially vindicated when the old Roman authoritarianism returned with Pope Paul VI's vigorous restatement of mandatory clerical celibacy and the ban on artificial birth control.

While the "two sixties" thesis correctly identifies a shift in mood and tactics for both Catholics and Protestants, it may also give short shrift to the multitextured character of the entire period by overlooking the pain and ambiguities experienced even by the liberals in the first phase as well as the consolidation of reforms in the otherwise fragmented second phase. From the perspective of conservative Christians, to the extent that any such generalization holds, "the sixties" was a bittersweet experience, a sophomoric experiment that produced, at best, mixed results. By the end of 1963, the decade had this feel about it. While the symbolic significance of John F. Kennedy's election to the presidency has been repeatedly noted by historians of American Catholicism, less attention has been paid to the symbolic significance of his assassination. Coupled with the setbacks suffered by the status quo ante curial faction at the Vatican Council, the death of Kennedy betokened a season of frustrated hopes for those who would come to be called traditionalist Catholics. Moreover, 1963 was the first year of the new dispensation outlawing prayer in American public schools, a development that annoyed conservative Protestants almost as much as the increasingly secular content of public school textbooks did.[19] The frustrations of both groups seemed to merge and culminate in 1973, the year in which the U.S. Supreme Court handed down the landmark ruling on abortion. Looking back on the period from 1963 to 1973, Erling Jorstad recited this litany of fundamentalist grievances:

> First, a constitutional amendment was proposed that could have been interpreted so as to prevent women from fulfilling their biblical role as submissive wives, serving primarily in the household. Second, the family was further attacked as social agencies and legislatures sought to define the limits of physical punishment permitted in a father's attempts to discipline his children. Third, the IRS began to take on the task of investigating the finances of religious agencies and determining what "counted" as true religion (at least for tax purposes). Fourth, civil rights arguments began to be extended to those (especially

19. See Ronald B. Flowers, *Religion in Strange Times: The 1960s and 1970s* (Macon, Ga.: Mercer University Press, 1984), pp. 140-60.

> homosexuals) whose lives were deemed grossly immoral by fundamentalists. Fifth, not only could children not pray in school, they were also being taught "values clarification" and other "humanist" ideas that undermined the unwavering beliefs and traditions their parents held dear. Sixth, even Christian schools could not do their work without government agencies imposing certification restrictions that seemed to strip them of their theological power.
>
> And finally, *Roe v. Wade.* All the forces seeking to destroy traditional families and moral society seemed to converge in a court ruling that abortion was a matter of private choice.[20]

Angry conservatives, Catholic and Protestant alike, became angrier as the secularizing agents who orchestrated such moves seemed to proceed with impunity, obviously assuming that the future was theirs. Certainly no prominent non-evangelical commentators on religion in the 1960s considered as a serious possibility the resurgence of a conservative, much less a fundamentalist, trend in American Christianity. The Zeitgeist fostered the expectation of unyielding "progress" toward a liberal, liberating, and ecumenical consensus. Fundamentalists went largely unnoticed in the literature, and conservative churchmen were pictured as an endangered species.[21]

There was one mid-sixties development, however, that did trouble sympathetic observers of religion and that, in hindsight, was not unrelated to the subsequent growth of conservative churches. This was the widening gulf between an activist clergy and a stay-at-home laity whose primary interest seemed to be in preserving a traditional sacred space that, for a few hours a week, would continue to provide a center of spiritual renewal and a safe haven from the world outside. The people in the pews perceived the world outside as increasingly "other" — as venal, corrupt, libertarian, amoral, and cut adrift from its presumed Judeo-Christian biblical moorings. In the popular mind, liberalization and the New Morality seemed to go hand in hand with the surging bureaucratization and elitism in the denomination as in the federal government.[22] This trend flew in the face of a widely held

20. Jorstad, "The Political Rebirth of American Evangelicals," in *The New Christian Right,* ed. Robert C. Liebman and Robert Wuthnow (Hawthorne, N.Y.: Aldine, 1983).

21. See the discussion of this oversight in *Religion and America: Spirituality in a Secular Age,* ed. Mary Douglas and Stephen Tipton (Boston: Beacon Press, 1982), esp. pp. 3-78.

22. See Wuthnow, *The Struggle for America's Soul,* p. 14.

conviction among the rank and file membership of the churches that religious organizations were to be above all else "responsible for treasuring and enhancing, embodying and transmitting the ideals and qualities that earlier generations have found good . . . [and] concerned more with conserving the tried and true than with exploring or experimenting with the new."[23]

This popular consensus about the role of religion and the churches was directly at odds with a consensus forming among academic and religious elites. Reflecting on the disenchantment with leaders, Sweet contends that the ranks of evangelical churches swelled in part because "modernist [mainline Protestant] churches made a cult of the cultivated and distanced themselves as never before from their social environment and the religiosity of middle class Americans."[24]

Indeed, the historian who relies exclusively on the "mainstream" literature on religion produced in the period will grossly underestimate the size and ultimate importance of the evangelical groundswell in the United States. Outside the evangelical camp, strikingly little attention was given to this form of popular religion. One of the most respected secular observers of religion was the accomplished sociologist Milton Yinger. Yinger had immersed himself in his subject and had done pioneering work in black religion, among other topics. He studiously avoided the shallow cliches of many secular intellectuals, such as the facile identification of religious fundamentalism with the political right wing, and he frankly acknowledged that sociology can provide only one of several possible valid perspectives on religion. Yet despite his strenuous objectivity, Yinger completely overlooked the evangelical revival. He did refer to evangelicals and fundamentalists, unlike some sociologists who ignored them altogether, but, as Robert Booth Fowler points out, it was usually to denounce them as the unfortunate remnants of a rapidly receding past.[25] Yinger did, however, notice the important fact that evangelicals and the more secular intellectuals had at that time strikingly different class and educational backgrounds.

Yinger's scientific approach was exceptional. Among secular intellectuals in general the study of civil religion and "exotic" religions was in vogue at a time of widespread disillusionment with American

23. Dean M. Kelley, *Why Conservative Churches Are Growing: A Study in Sociology of Religion* (Macon: Mercer University Press, 1986), p. 147.

24. Sweet, "The Modernization of Protestant Religion in America," in *Altered Landscapes*, p. 31.

25. Fowler, *A New Engagement*, pp. 15-17.

imperialism. Academics joined left-wing radicals in holding "the national religion" responsible for many of America's excesses, and they introduced and celebrated Eastern religions and, later, feminist theologies as necessary correctives to Western, patriarchal, and WASP orientations.

From an evangelical perspective, the emphasis on civil religion and on exotic sects such as the International Society of Krishna Consciousness, the Meher Baba movement, Synanon, Zen Buddhism, the Divine Light Mission, and many others was an indication that the liberal professors, and the secular media that popularized the fads they endorsed, "no longer took Christianity seriously as a system of truth."[26] When Robert Bellah, the dean of the civil religionists, declared that what religious life and "renewal" he could find in America "has come outside the Protestant tradition," evangelicals knew that judgment to be wrong. And when Harvey Cox, whom evangelical intellectuals perceived as "the most celebrated popular religious thinker in America" during the period, trumpeted *The Secular City* even as he was *Turning East,* he seemed to evangelicals to be extolling what they considered transitory in American religion while ignoring the much more serious and enduring growth of the evangelicals. In the 1960s Cox announced a "New Breed" in the church in America — the social activist — but, predictably, social activism within evangelicalism failed to attract his attention. Other authors of the New Left era routinely stated what they considered obvious — namely, that the "irrelevance of traditional Christian teachings has been acknowledged" among religious Americans, though "practice probably outlasts faith."[27] Even William G. McLoughlin concluded that evangelicals and fundamentalists had reached their peak in 1964.[28] Indeed, the "New Religious Consciousness" included every intellectually respectable movement — Dewey's "religion," Whitehead's process theology, death-of-God theology, black theology, cults, and even the religion of Alpha Waves — but not evangelicalism.

Many non-evangelical Protestants were also suspicious of the liberal academy. A significant number of ministers in mainline churches

26. Fowler, *A New Engagement,* p. 18.

27. Bryan Wilson, "Religion and the Churches in Contemporary America," in *Religion in America,* ed. William McLoughlin and Robert N. Bellah (Boston: Houghton-Mifflin, 1968), pp. 74-75. Also see S. S. Acquaviva, *The Decline of the Sacred in Industrial Society* (Oxford: Basil Blackwell, 1979).

28. McLoughlin, "Is There a Third Force in Christendom?" in *Religion in America,* p. 42.

became social activists and in so doing made common cause with liberal academics protesting racial segregation, WASP cultural imperialism, and the Vietnam War. Traditional theology gave way to a new gospel of social justice that was not always warmly received by middle-class congregations. What seemed threatened in this development was the once-reliable touchstone of Christian theodicy.

Rank-and-file American Catholics were also perplexed by the sudden liberalization of priests and nuns who now became "the professional religious." The fact that priests and religious were, ironically, often more secularized than their lay counterparts reflected the very intensity with which religious elites confronted the changed ecclesiastical circumstances of the Vatican II era; the crisis of religious identity was for them directly personal and professional and weighed more heavily on them than on most laypeople. As a result of the Council, far more priests and religious began studying for advanced degrees than was formerly the case. There was a great increase in the number of priests, religious, and laypeople formally certified as experts in religious education, liturgy, and other aspects of church life. Diocesan bureaucracies grew as new offices of worship, social justice, urban ministry, and personnel were created and the new professionals were placed in charge of them. Priests and religious were encouraged to attend conferences and seminars designed to acquaint them with the new theology, and the most gifted priests were taken from the parish setting and placed in bureaucratic leadership positions. The professionalization and specialization of ministries in the Catholic Church that occurred in the wake of the Council reinforced in those priests and sisters the momentum away from a vertical faith and generated a corresponding interest in public issues.[29] Meanwhile, due in part to their detachment from the institution of the Church on a daily basis and their relative lack of exposure to the teaching of the conciliar theologians, many laypeople adhered to traditional beliefs more closely than did the clergy and women religious. Conservative activists were convinced that a moderate liberalism became the conventional wisdom in most clerical circles in the 1960s. They regarded the professionalization of the clergy with considerable suspicion.[30]

29. See R. Scott Appleby, "Present to the People of God: The Transformation of the American Catholic Parish Priesthood," in Jay P. Dolan et al., *Transforming Parish Ministry: The Changing Roles of Catholic Clergy, Laity, and Women Religious* (New York: Crossroad, 1989), pp. 54-78.

30. See Hitchcock, "Conservative Catholic Activism," p. 115.

Fundamentalist Responses to the Secularized Academy and Clergy

The litany of conservative woes must be interrupted in order to consider the respective responses of our two nascent post-sixties fundamentalist cultures.

The Protestant fundamentalist subculture was readily mobilized for effective action in response to the perception of secular hegemony in American religious and political culture. An impressive network of private institutions was already in place, and large sectors of the evangelical community in which the fundamentalist impulse or tendency originated were nurtured by a protective institutional cocoon. At the same time, when these evangelicals did enter the public order, they moved more freely in the larger mainstream culture than did Catholics, for that culture had been shaped by a Protestant rather than a Catholic ethos. Fundamentalist Protestants were thus more experienced in dealing directly with "the enemy" and had in fact perfected the art of selective mimesis.[31] Their shrewd imitation of the secular culture that they opposed was most evident in their use of electronic media and modern marketing techniques, but it was also apparent in a popular theology preached from the pulpits that interpreted American individualism and material culture in benign terms. Protestant fundamentalists took as their starting point the assumptions of the mainstream culture, which they implicitly acknowledged without explicitly accepting: the starting point was also a point of departure.[32]

Mark Silk has recently commented, for example, on the way in which one strand of the counterhegemonic fundamentalist movement successfully and shrewdly cloaked itself in the exotic garb of the New Religious Consciousness even as it offered what it marketed as an orthodox Christian interpretation of the signs of the times:

> In its radical turning towards new forms of belief and religious practice, the counterculture was symptomatic of a larger rejection of American spirituality before Vietnam. Indeed, the era's most striking assault on the "general consensus" governing postwar religion came from a source diametrically opposed to the New Reli-

31. On selective mimesis, see Rene Girard, *Violence and the Sacred* (Baltimore: The Johns Hopkins University Press, 1972).

32. On Protestant fundamentalist use of the media, see Jeffrey K. Hadden and Anson Shupe, *Televangelism: Power and Politics on God's Frontier* (New York: Henry Holt, 1988).

gious Consciousness. At the same time that Castañeda was leading the way into the Brave New World of psychedelic anthropology, another figure on the UCLA campus was busy adapting his calling to the Age of Aquarius. He was a staff member of the local Campus Crusade for Christ named Hal Lindsey, and in 1970 he worked his lectures and sermons up into a small volume called *The Late Great Planet Earth.* Though scarcely noticed even by the evangelical press, it became the best selling book of the decade with scores of printings ultimately flooding the United States with some 16 million copies.[33]

The conservative American Catholic response to the perceived secularism in clergy and academy betrayed no such intimacy with the Age of Aquarius, with the propagandization and mass marketing of a cause, or even with the rudiments of effective protest action in a religiously voluntarist nation. Disgruntled Catholic conservatives and traditionalists, then as now, were notably ineffective as counterhegemonists. They staged poorly attended rallies, met clandestinely in homes or in the so-called wildcat parishes, shrouded themselves rather desperately in secrecy and apocalypticism, muttering about the vengeance of the Blessed Virgin, and took heart when a muckraking American priest went on the lecture circuit or, later, when an aging French rebel archbishop consecrated a few of his own. Although they, too, were troubled by the social disintegration and moral dissolution of American society telegraphed by the drug culture, pornography, and *Roe v. Wade,* Catholic conservatives and traditionalists expended most of their contra-acculturative energies writing nasty letters to Rome tattling about the various misdeeds of the liberal American clergy and episcopacy and pleading for a "strict constructionist" reading of the documents of Vatican II. Their central concern was that the Roman Catholic Mass be celebrated in the Tridentine rite, in Latin rather than in the English.

In summarizing lay Catholic discontent in the late sixties and seventies, Hitchcock revealed its parochial focus:

> The perception was widely shared that most dramatic changes following upon the Second Vatican Council — the Mass celebrated in the vernacular, the abandonment of many traditional religious practices such as Friday abstinence from meat, the reformulating of traditional doctrines, ecumenical relations with other religions, a

33. Silk, *Spiritual Politics: Religion in America since World War II* (New York: Simon & Schuster, 1989), pp. 156-57.

> more flexible approach to moral questions, deeper involvement in social and political issues — could not have taken place without eventual clerical encouragement and support. A capsule summation of conservative complaints in the United States would read somewhat as follows: "Our worship is no longer a truly sacred action, and liturgical rules are widely ignored. Our children are not being taught authentic Catholic doctrine in the schools. Everywhere people are given dubious or distorted ideas about what the Second Vatican Council really taught. Most of those responsible for such abuses are priests and religious. When confronted, they adamantly refuse to change. Complaints to the bishop either go unheeded or are summarily rejected. In some cases the bishop himself is actively sympathetic to dissenting clergy."[34]

It was not that the Catholic conservatives' objection to the sixties was less strenuous than that of the Protestants or that the traditionalists lacked a will to power in the world, ultimately, as well as within the Church. But for Catholics the Church is the divine means to salvation, and they are bound to it in ways that evangelicals are not bound to their institutions. Because the One True Church, destined ultimately to rule this world, had lost its medieval theocratic bearings, traditionalist Catholics were committed first to the restoration of Catholicism rather than to the Catholicization of America. Thus the nostalgic aspects of traditionalist discourse did not, as in the evangelical-fundamentalist case, hearken back to the sacred origins of this nation or to a pinnacle of purity and hegemony in the mid-nineteenth century but rather to a more distant, pre-American, pre-Enlightenment past. The heroes of the traditionalists were those churchmen who had valiantly resisted the modern debunking of that sacred past (e.g., "Pope St. Pius X," who had secured his place in the traditionalist pantheon by embodying antimodernism).

In the post-Enlightenment era, therefore, the Catholic who continued to prefer the medieval theocratic or neo-Scholastic tradition became a traditional*ist*. That is, she was forced to fight for tradition (as she understood it) and thus became militant, defining herself over against the agents of modernization within the Catholic hierarchy and priesthood. Cloaked in the garb of the Blue Army or the Legion of Christ, or shrouded in the secrecy of Opus Dei, she strove to keep alive the traditional Catholic witness to the supernatural.

34. Hitchcock, "Conservative Catholic Activism," pp. 114-15.

Separatism after the Sixties

In this context the name *traditionalist* indicates a type of fundamentalism that is inveterately separatist. Thus it serves well the task of contrasting the conservative Catholic and Protestant reactions to the perception of encroaching secularism in the 1960s and 1970s.

Protestant fundamentalists could never have influenced American society and politics to the extent that they did in the seventies and eighties had they continued to insist on the strict separatism and exclusive focus on soul-winning that defined their mission before the critical decade. Instead, they were able to direct their considerable institutional resources outward. Furthermore, the separatist impulse that had provided those institutions with their *raison d'être* did not abate in the 1960s; it was expressed in the extraordinary proliferation of Christian day schools and academies, a new generation of evangelical publishing houses and enterprises, and a dramatic growth in the media empire.[35] The new generation of alternative institutions were separatist in ethos but activist in orientation. The schools, for example, continued to foster a "total Christian environment" while providing students with the vocational and technical training needed for success in a hostile and un-Christian job market. But they were also now actively arming others for direct confrontation with the secular-hegemonic culture.[36] Thus the protean Falwellians could claim continuity with the historic fundamentalist subculture even as their penchant for coalition-building and power politics necessitated a move toward an expansive New Evangelicalism.[37]

The successful Protestant shaping of the foundation myths of the nation precluded the possibility that angry evangelicals and fundamentalists might confine their counterhegemonic reaction to the sixties to ecclesial issues alone. When Falwell and, subsequently, Reagan evoked Winthrop's Puritan city shining on a hill as the icon of a morally renewed America, it was a calculated and shrewd political move. Both

35. See Marsden, "Unity and Diversity in the Evangelical Resurgence," pp. 61-76.

36. See Rose, *Keeping Them Out of the Hands of Satan;* and Peshkin, *God's Choice.*

37. See Joel A. Carpenter, "From Fundamentalism to the New Evangelical Coalition," in *Evangelicalism and Modern America,* pp. 3-16. For the strict separatists who published *The Sword of the Lord,* Falwell's appropriation of the term "New Evangelical" in the 1980s confirmed their suspicions that he was not a true fundamentalist; see *The Sword of the Lord* 55 (1989): 1.

men knew that the mere historical fact that the founding documents of the nation had explicitly prohibited sectarian hegemony would be lost in the affirmations of a "Judeo-Christian nation." The active participation of the religious right in local and national politics was a return; the promise to "get America back on track" was an act of *repossession.*

A quite different tack was taken by the Catholic fundamentalists. Catholics could not as readily cite either historical or ideological precedent for a formative role in the mainstream political culture of the United States — no matter how vigorously they had tried to do so at times.[38] Indeed, Catholics had frequently been cast as the consummate outsiders, a fate seemingly confirmed by Al Smith's defeat in the 1928 presidential election. Their one presidential success story ran but a thousand days; and Kennedy had campaigned for the office at a calculated distance from the historic faith tradition to which he belonged.

Neither could Catholics compete with Protestants as interpreters of the national-religious myth: colonial Maryland was not the repository of American memory that Pilgrim Massachusetts was, and it was not until 1881 that an American Catholic leader, Baltimore archbishop James Gibbons, encouraged his co-religionists to celebrate the national Thanksgiving holiday enthusiastically. Fourteen years later, a papal encyclical expressed gratitude that, "unopposed by the Constitution and government," American Catholics were "free to live and act without hindrance," but it warned nonetheless that American-style separation of church and state was not to be considered a model for authentic Catholic societies, which should "enjoy the favor of the laws and the patronage of public authority."[39] A century later Pope John Paul II was sharply critical of the freethinking style of American Catholics. Those Catholics who would reform American society could not take for granted the premises and bedrock values by which it was governed.

Concern about jeopardizing their hard-won social and economic status in American society may also have made Catholics in the 1960s and 1970s reluctant to express discontent in protest movements reach-

38. Among other examples of proponents of the claim that American Catholicism fully embodies the best values in the American political-philosophical tradition, see the account of the political rhetoric of the social action priest John A. Ryan in Joseph M. McShane, *"Sufficiently Radical": Catholicism, Progressivism, and the Bishop's Program of 1919* (Washington: Catholic University Press, 1986); and the account of the political rhetoric of Archbishop John Ireland in Marvin R. O'Connell, *John Ireland and the American Catholic Church* (St. Paul: Minnesota Historical Society Press, 1988).

39. Quoted by Hennesey in *American Catholics,* p. 200.

ing beyond the narrowly ecclesial. By 1965 the G.I. Bill and postwar prosperity had begun to convey American Catholics up the immigrant escalator; by the 1980s Irish-American Catholics had attained a socioeconomic rank only slightly below that of American Jews. But their enhanced status and security did not lead to a more vital traditionalist movement.

Countercultural American Catholics did not mount a successful public campaign on their own after the 1960s. A public expression of discontent with American society was conveyed not through traditionalist channels but, ironically, through ecumenical alliances with fundamentalist Protestants in the Moral Majority or, later, in the Francis Schaeffer–inspired antiabortion movement Operation Rescue.[40]

Catholic Oppositional Movements: A Fundamentalism of the Enclave

The study of comparative fundamentalisms suggests that Catholic traditionalists in the United States belong to a cross-cultural category of "fundamentalisms of the enclave." Equipped with the insights offered by cultural theory (a hermeneutic device developed by the anthropologist Mary Douglas),[41] comparative historian Emmanuel

40. On Operation Rescue, see Garry Wills, "Evangels of Abortion," *New York Review of Books,* 15 June 1989.

41. See Mary Douglas, *Cultural Bias* (London: Royal Anthropology Society, 1978); *Essays in the Sociology of Perception,* ed. Mary Douglas (London: Routledge & Kegan Paul, 1982); Mary Douglas and Aaron Wildavsky, *Risk and Culture* (Berkeley and Los Angeles: University of California Press, 1982); Mary Douglas, *How Institutions Think* (Syracuse: Syracuse University Press, 1986); and Aaron Wildavsky and R. Ellis, *Cultural Theory* (Boulder: Westview, 1990). Briefly put, cultural theory proposes that in any social context, shared cultural ideas (about time and space, human and physical nature, ethics, etc.) will be structured in such a way that individuals within it can negotiate their way through the constraints they experience in daily life to make sense of the world they live in. Social contexts are determined by two sorts of constraints (or claims): group constraints and grid constraints. Group constraints involve constraints of incorporation — the extent to which people are restricted in their social relations by their commitment to a human group. Grid constraints involves constraints of categorization — restricting how (rather than with whom) people interact by virtue of their category (gender, color, age, formal rank, etc.). By combining the group / grid dimensions, Douglas developed a typology designed to facilitate comparative analysis. This typology consists of three major (and two minor) social contexts. Each carries with it, as posited above, its own "cultural package," which, together with its prescribed mode of behavior (and

Sivan of Hebrew University, Jerusalem, has drawn a compelling cross-cultural portrait of the religious enclave. Sivan's study draws on examples from Islam, Judaism, Protestant fundamentalism, and Catholic traditionalism.[42]

Fears in traditional religious communities of losing large numbers of members seem to be the essential impulse (at least at the leadership level) for the creation and maintenance of fundamentalist movements of this type. Norman Birnbaum was describing pre–World War II Eastern European Jewry when he reported their fear that "the number of defectors is on the rise, while the distinction maintained in the past between apostates and those faithful to the Covenant has gotten blurred,"[43] but the formula is echoed in the words of the pioneers and latter-day proponents of Islamic, Protestant, and Catholic fundamentalism as well. The fear of erosion of a traditional community inspires the circling of the wagons. Sivan writes,

> The enclave is usually the response to a community's problem about its boundary. Its future seems to be at the mercy of members likely to slip away. For some reason, usually the appeal of the neighboring central community, it cannot stop its members from deserting. Devoid of coercive powers over the members, it cannot punish them; lacking sufficient resources, it cannot reward them. The only control to be deployed in order to shore up the boundary is moral persuasion. The interpretation of this type of community is thence in opposition to outside society.[44]

In briefly illustrating the ways in which Catholic traditionalists and some conservative activist groups approximate a fundamentalism of the enclave, I shall consider (1) a self-appointed traditionalist group — Lefebvre's Pope St. Pius X Society; (2) a personal prelature that nonetheless remains a secretive society of ultraconservative lay Catholics and priests — Opus Dei; and (3) a conservative activist group that,

---

organization), makes it into a way of life. The three major types are *hierarchy* (which is more or less assured of its outer group boundary and invests most of its energy in controlling its various and separate compartments and keeping them in smooth interaction), a *market* context (individually negotiated social networks with little interference of group or grid), and *enclave*.

42. Sivan, "The Enclave," in *Accounting for Fundamentalisms: The Dynamic Character of Movements*, ed. Martin E. Marty and R. Scott Appleby (Chicago: University of Chicago Press, forthcoming).

43. Birnbaum, quoted by Sivan in "The Enclave."

44. Sivan, "The Enclave."

unlike the other two groups, originated in the United States — Catholics United for the Faith. These groups take different positions on the meaning and significance of Vatican II and differ in their responses to the Council. But they share the important family resemblance of self-conscious and organized opposition to the postconciliar Church. Indeed, each of these groups is motivated by a fear of losing members of the traditional society that was the preconciliar Church.

These groups also share a sense of dispossession. They have lost a prominence in the religious community that is rightly due to them, and this loss of prominence is tied directly to the sagging prestige of orthodoxy. The enemy — postconciliar liberal or "modernist" Catholics who control appointments in major universities, who run the seminaries, who participate in mainstream public discourse — are considered usurpers. Catholics United for the Faith (CUF) is a lay apostolate the members of which describe themselves as "ordinary Catholics" who are dissatisfied with the tepidity of postconciliar Catholic moral teaching, with the "woeful" state of the liturgy, and especially with the Catholic schools — the substance of the curriculum, the educational content and method, and the philosophies and theologies said to be informing them. CUF members are also concerned about the perceived neglect of traditional devotional practices, such as group recitation of the rosary, days of recollection, and novenas. They know that they are a minority within the postconciliar Church but feel strongly that they are its most faithful witnesses to "authentic Roman Catholicism."[45]

As a minority with limited popular support, traditionalists and conservative activists rely on a powerful and often shrill moral clarion call to awaken passive Catholics from their dogmatic slumbers. But these groups must also seek alternate sources of influence, including the backing of wealthy individuals (e.g., business tycoons with personal fortunes from pizza or beer franchises). This pattern is indicative of the enclave mentality. "An enclave's outer boundary is leaky, due above all to the material and social temptations of the central community; that is, the community which enjoys prestige and cultural hegemony, has access to governmental sanctions as well as to resources (whether the state's or wealthy individuals')," Sivan writes. "Virtually all the beleaguered enclave can offer is moral rewards . . . and charity contributions by ultra-orthodox benefactors."

45. The minority status of the Catholic conservatives and traditionalists is documented by Andrew Greeley in "Who Are the Catholic 'Conservatives'?" *America,* 21 September 1991, pp. 158-62.

But how does one come to wield moral authority? Cultural theory posits that the enclave must stress the voluntary character of the membership and the fact that members are specially chosen (in religious enclaves, elected to salvation by God):

> The value of each member is highlighted and the enclave must put in relief the oppressive and morally defiled outside society as opposed to the community of virtuous insiders. A sort of "wall of virtue" is thereby constructed, separating the saved, free, equal (before God or before history) and morally superior enclave from the hitherto-tempting central community. Who but the depraved would like to cross such a boundary and join the defectors and the evil outsiders? The most obvious bricks of the wall of virtue are the short-hand terms used within fundamentalist communities to convey the identity of the real, the true-blue, full-fledged Christians, Muslims or Jews. The tradition is presented as shrunken and under siege, nay even persecuted. The faithful are depicted as the Believing Remnant, the Last Outpost, Covenant Keepers, in fundamentalist writings in the United States. All the rest are cut from an inferior cloth; they are lesser affiliates of the same tradition if not worse, outright rejects — apostates and disbelievers.[46]

One need not look far to find analogues among the American Catholic oppositional movements. The oldest traditionalist journal in the United States is *The Remnant,* published by Walter Matt in St. Paul, Minnesota. The name of the journal aptly conveys the traditionalist self-understanding: they believe themselves to be the enclave within which the remaining true believers find mutual encouragement and support. In the decade following the Council, *The Remnant* came to play an important role in linking the nascent traditionalist movement in the United States with its European counterpart. Although unaffiliated with any traditionalist organization, Matt's paper developed a reputation as the unofficial voice of Archbishop Lefebvre in the United States before the latter established his own headquarters and publishing

46. Sivan, "The Enclave." Usage is not limited to nouns; it covers adjectives as well — e.g., a "Christian home (or attitude)," an "Islamic solution" *(hall islami),* "Jewish Jews" *(yidn Yudn, Volljuden).* The adjective is invariably positive, signifying the sole type in full accordance with the tradition. References to the scriptural basis of that tradition crop up in synonyms: "Bible believers" (or, in adjectival form, "biblical standard"), a "Koranic way of life" *(Nahj Kur'ani),* "Torah-true" (in Yinglish, or its Hebrew equivalent, *Ne'emanei ha-Torah, yahadut ha-Torah;* and *Bnei Torah* for yeshiva students and graduates).

sources in this country. The righteous character of the dissident Catholic community is a recurring theme found in the pages of *The Remnant* and is also conveyed in Lefebvre's description of his followers as "Zealots of Elijah" and "the leaven of the dough."[47]

The polluted outside casts a heavy shadow upon the dissidents inside the enclave. A Manichean sensibility, dividing the world into realms of light and darkness, informs fundamentalisms of the enclave, and Catholic traditionalism is again no exception. Given their view that the world is going through a period of exceptional infidelity in which religious doubt and contempt for traditional morality are blatant, traditionalist Catholics find the apocalyptic aspects of traditional devotions intellectually and emotionally satisfying — a characteristic that is also beginning to characterize conservative groups such as the Blue Army, which sees in the twentieth-century apparitions of the Virgin Mary in Fatima, Lourdes, and Medjugorje evidence that God has allowed things to deteriorate radically as a prelude to chastising the world.[48]

Secrecy is especially important in a Manichean world. Because the enemy is ubiquitous and adopts countless disguises, the remnant church must also mask its efforts to restore Catholicism to its previous glory. Because the hierarchy itself includes modernists, Catholic oppositionists must be extremely cautious, even dissembling, in their relationships with Catholic priests and laity outside the enclave. Among Catholic oppositional movements, Opus Dei has most frequently been cited for its secretive ways and its resistance to control by the Catholic hierarchy. The hope of reducing the number of its potential ecclesial "keepers" was likely what motivated Opus leaders to have the society elevated from the status of a secular institute to a personal prelature answerable directly to the pope — a petition Pope John Paul II granted in 1982. The suspicion of priests and bishops "outside the enclave" is evident in the Opus insistence that its members interact only with Opus priests. Wary of "contamination" by outsiders, the leaders inserted a clause in the 1982 constitution that excluded from membership in the society anyone who had even studied in a non-Opus seminary.[49]

At the same time, Opus members are taught to act with overt deference to diocesan bishops and other Catholic religious officials

47. On *The Remnant*, see Dinges, "Roman Catholic Traditionalism," p. 69.

48. See, for example, Mark Miravalle, *Heart of the Message of Medjugorje* (Steubenville, Ohio: Franciscan University Press, 1988); Lucy Rooney and Robert Faricy, *Medjugorje Journal* (Chicago: Franciscan Herald Press, 1988).

49. Michael Walsh, *The Secret World of Opus Dei* (London: Grafton, 1989), p. 94.

outside the enclave. Because Opus is committed to working within the Church in order to save it from itself, its leaders hesitate to hand their opponents in the hierarchy any excuse to disband or penalize them. By the same reasoning, Opus restricts its members from participating *as Opus members* in any form of public activism. In practice this means that Opus members who are involved in the pro-life movement or who write articles in the Catholic or secular press are not to be identified as belonging to the society. The fear of exposure, infiltration, and persecution is perhaps understandable among believers under siege, fighting against a tide of secularism and apostasy. This anxiety also inspires the organization's virulent denials of any affiliation with political parties or "public" causes.[50]

Because of the diffuse presence of traditionalists and conservative activists throughout the United States, the sheltering enclaves of the Catholic oppositionists are institutional rather than strictly geographic. Catholic traditionalist dissent in the United States has found expression in a variety of different forms. Many of the traditionalist "parishes" that formed in the wake of the Council were first located in homes, hotel rooms, and meeting halls until suitable facilities could be found. These parishes are ministered to by individual priests and range in size from a few dozen to several hundred parishioners. Traditionalist dissent has also found an outlet through independent publishing initiatives. In the United States, Hugo Kellner, Fr. Lawrence Brey, William F. Strojie, and Solange Hertz are among the better-known traditionalist apologists who have produced an assortment of anticonciliar literature. Aside from the independent chapels and anticonciliar publishing initiatives, traditionalist aspirations have also found expression in quasi-ecclesial organizations such as the Catholic Traditionalist Movement, Inc. (CTM), the Orthodox Roman Catholic Movement (ORCM), Catholics for Tradition, Roman Catholics of America, Traditional Catholics of America, Union Catholica Trento, the Saint Pius V Association, Liqa Katholisher Traditionalisten (LKT), and Archbishop Lefebvre's Society of Saint Pius X.[51]

50. Walsh, *The Secret World of Opus Dei,* pp. 15, 98, 122. Despite the claims of uninvolvement in political affairs, there is a growing literature on the alliances between Opus Dei priests and right-wing regimes in Spain and in Latin America. On this point, see Walsh, *The Secret World of Opus Dei,* pp. 130-58; and Penny Lernoux, *People of God: The Struggle for World Catholicism* (New York: Viking, 1989) pp. 302-50.

51. Catholic traditionalism itself is an international, segmented, and loosely organized montage that has grown steadily in the last quarter century. Vatican estimates place the number of active traditionalists worldwide at sixty thousand to eighty

Catholics United for the Faith provides another cohesive network for Catholic oppositionists. Founded in 1968 to support the pope following the intense attack on *Humanae Vitae,* the organization is international in scope and has a membership of approximately twenty thousand, with headquarters in New Rochelle, New York. The national center consists of a board of directors, national officers, and staff members — together numbering about twenty-five people. There are about 150 local chapters, where much of the actual work of the organization is carried out. Such chapters form after individual Catholics in a particular town or diocese discover others in their area like themselves who are disturbed over the direction the Church is taking and come together for mutual support. CUF members usually send the bishop a list of grievances about parish liturgies, parochial education, diocesan policies, and the political and sociomoral statements of Catholic leaders. "Self-appointed watchdogs of orthodoxy," they often find themselves dissatisfied with the bishop's response and send material to the Vatican concerning irregularities in the American Church. CUF activists scrutinize sermons very carefully and analyze their theological content. The "canon within the canon" for CUF is *Humanae Vitae.* Assent to the teaching of the encyclical is a unique litmus test of one's orthodoxy and, thus, of belonging to the Church. Paul VI's ban on artificial birth control is an appropriate litmus test precisely because it was widely rejected and because many clergy claimed it was not strictly binding. Those who disobey its moral teaching thereby demonstrate an unwillingness to acknowledge full papal authority and the supernaturalist worldview supporting it.[52] CUF provides its members with intellectual

---

thousand. These figures do not include many sympathetic supporters of the traditionalist cause who remain unaffiliated. Traditionalism is also generally understood to be both larger and more militant in Europe (especially France) than in the United States, where there are some ten to fifteen thousand active participants. An additional clue to the scope of the movement can be adduced in part by the size of Archbishop Lefebvre's priestly fraternity, the largest and most visible traditionalist organization. As of 1986, Lefebvre had ordained some 250 traditionalist priests. His Society of Saint Pius X operated a worldwide (twenty-three countries) network of schools, priories, and religious foundations including 339 churches and 6 seminaries (Switzerland, West Germany, United States, France, Australia, Argentina) with over 250 candidates studying for the priesthood. See Dinges, "Roman Catholic Traditionalism," p. 68.

52. See M. Timothy Iglesias, "CUF and Dissent: A Case Study in Religious Conservatism," *America,* 11 April 1987, p. 305. As the CUF journal *Lay Witness* put the matter in 1980, "Those who begin doubting the church's teaching on contraception generally go on to deny her teachings on a whole host of other subjects such as abortion, the indissolubility of marriage, pre- and extra-marital chastity, and so on."

resources to use in their local fights, including periodic detailed critiques of particular catechisms and other books that the group deems objectionable. It sponsors both national and local conferences at which appropriate speakers address the members. In 1988 the organization cosponsored publication of a series of new catechisms that it hoped would replace many of those previously in use.[53]

Opus Dei ("The Work of God") is a third expression of Catholic opposition to the implementation of the reforms of Vatican II. An international, predominantly lay organization founded in Madrid in 1928, it claims seventy-two thousand members worldwide, with approximately three thousand in the United States.[54] Opus Dei is in a sense innovative; it differs from unions, associations, and lay organizations on the one hand and from traditional religious orders and congregations, tertiary orders, and secular institutes on the other "because of the intimate integration between priests and laity, which changes the status of priest and laity, because of the emphasis on spirituality and personal formation, because of the centralization of spirituality around the laity, because of the will always repeated — and emphatically proclaimed — of being withdrawn from any political or social option, because of the will — also emphatically proclaimed — of being withdrawn from any social class distinction."[55] Clergy and religious live their priestly mis-

53. See Hitchcock, "Conservative Catholic Activism," p. 117.

54. The prelature of Opus Dei develops its apostolates through two sections, one for men and one for women. For ruling the prelature, the prelate has the assistance of two councils (one for each section). The prelate is elected in a general congress summoned for that purpose. The candidate has to be a priest with no less than five years of experience. His position lasts for life and has to be confirmed by the pope. The General Council helps the prelate in ruling the Male Section. The Female Council is ruled by the prelate with the general secretary vicar, the vicar for the Women's Section, and the Central Office, which is similar to the General Council of the Male Section and has analogous functions. All the directors of these organisms are named for a period of eight years. Members are divided into four grades: *numerarii* ("numeraries," celibate priests and laity who constitute the leading group of the movement); *agregati* (celibate priests and laymen engaged in the coordination of external work); *supranumerarii* ("supernumeraries," priests and laity who work in their profession according to the ideals of the movement); and *cooperatores* (the rest of the cooperators, among whom there are also non-Catholics). It is estimated that 2 percent of the members of Opus Dei are priests. There are Regional Councils, subject to the General Council, which is presided over by a general president (the prelate). See Walsh, *The Secret World of Opus Dei,* pp. 96-105.

55. Joseph Comblin, "Movimientos e ideologias en America Latina," in *Fe cristiana y cambio social en America Latina* (Salamanca: Ediciones Sangueme, 1972), quoted by Hitchcock in "Conservative Catholic Activism," p. 119.

sion and consecrated life inside the movement. They constitute a new kind of clergy, neither secular nor regular, because they are integrated into and at the service of the movement. Opus Dei fosters the development of dynamic religious elites as guardians of spiritual values and moral authority. It tends to establish communities near major universities (e.g., Columbia in New York City), and most of its recruits hail from the professional classes — doctors, lawyers, engineers, and businessmen.[56]

Conclusion

These Catholic oppositional movements operate within strictly set institutional and ideological boundaries; in fact, they are sustained and defined *as movements* by their maintenance of these boundaries, and a great deal of their corporate energy goes into these activities rather than into efforts to reach a broader constituency. Thus, for example, Catholic conservatives who do become involved in mass media tend to produce programs directed to a select Catholic audience rather than to a broad "silent majority" of American Christians hungering for spiritual nourishment.[57]

Because modernism has penetrated decisively into even those institutions of the Roman Catholic Church that once safeguarded the sacred deposit of faith, Catholic "fundamentalists" see themselves as an elite remnant preserving the memory of the fundamental truths and works of the tradition. Outside the Church there is no salvation, but the Church itself has become infected. In some traditionalist eschatologies God will preserve the sacred deposit through the agency of Mary, the symbol of the true Church, and her faithful devotees. In some

56. Hitchcock, "Conservative Catholic Activism," p. 119.

57. An example is the Eternal Word Network. A common format on EWN is the talk show, which features guests firm and devout in their Catholic faith. It includes theologians, activists in various organizations, people engaged in charitable work, and people with inspiring personal stories to tell. There is little overt controversy, but from time to time both the guests and Mother Angelica, the host, enlighten viewers as to official Church teaching and warn against corrupting social and religious influences. In 1988, after trying unsuccessfully to develop a national television network of their own, the American bishops voted to affiliate with Mother Angelica's operation, but she terminated the affiliation in 1990 after disputes about programming. See Daniel W. O'Neill, *Mother Angelica: Her Life Story* (New York: Crossroad, 1986).

scenarios, God will exact punishment on those who have turned away from the True Church. This apocalypticism leads to an exclusivist and Manichean sensibility shared in various degrees by Catholic oppositional groups.[58]

These cosmic and eschatological concerns are reflected in the Catholic traditionalist emphasis on spiritual and liturgical reform, an otherworldly or supernaturalist orientation that eclipses any impulse toward the building of concrete programs of social action or religiocultural reform. In contrast to Protestant fundamentalists, these groups have failed to mount a sustained campaign of sociomoral activism on matters of concern to the general public. Part of the reason for this lies in the orientation to a golden age of the past: American Catholic traditionalists take the Counter-Reformation and the pontificates of Pius IX and Pius X as their historical models for the social order.

Successful American Christian fundamentalist movements — those oppositional movements that effectively launched counter-hegemonic drives in American denominations and in the secular political culture — were able to moderate the impulse toward separatism that followed from the collective revulsion engendered in conservative Christians in the wake of the transformations and attempted transformations of the sixties. Ironically, the world-affirming, sacramentally oriented Roman Catholic Church bequeathed to its most ardent members and would-be "fundamentalists" a corporate identity built largely upon the principled renunciation of the modern world. Meanwhile, the heirs of the world-renouncing Reformation had been culturally and theologically reborn many times over in the intervening centuries. Protestant fundamentalism was cradled rather comfortably in the American South when the challenges of the critical decade called them once again to shape the moral agenda of the nation — or, at least, to make the attempt.

Even as the United States experienced the sixties, and evangelicals positioned themselves to shape the reaction, however, the Catholic cosmos was in flux, the center of "divine activism" shifting from heaven to earth. Religious liberty was in; the old theocratic yearnings seemed pointless now to all but a handful of American Catholic intellectuals. Trapped inside the old ecclesiology that told them they had nowhere else to go for salvation, the traditionalists could only flail in frustration in the hope of restoring the soul of the True Church. The shining American city would have to wait.

58. For a skeptical analysis of the phenomenon by a conservative Catholic, see E. Michael Jones, "Medjugorje: The Untold Story," *Fidelity* 8 (Sept. 1988): 18-41.

Fundamentalism Twice Removed: The Emergence and Shape of Progressive Evangelicalism

TIMOTHY P. WEBER

IN 1976 Martin Marty observed that looking at American religion without giving evangelicalism its due "would be comparable to scanning the American physical landscape and missing the Rocky Mountains."[1] Since the seventies, evangelical religion has been hard to miss. In 1976 *Newsweek* magazine proclaimed the "Year of the Evangelicals,"[2] and shortly thereafter *Time* called evangelicalism "A New Empire of Faith."[3] Scholars have produced a steady stream of books and articles on the movement, which makes defining the nature and extent of evangelicalism one of the growth industries in the study of American religion. Nevertheless, there is still much work to be done. What historian Leonard Sweet wrote in 1984 remains true in the nineties: "There are three indisputable facts about the evangelical tradition in America. First, it is important. Second, it is understudied. Third, it is diverse."[4]

In this essay I will focus on Sweet's last point — evangelical diversity. Specifically, I will examine the rise in the sixties and seventies of a distinctly ecumenical and progressive brand of American evangelicalism. I intend to show where the movement came from, outline its main concerns and constituency, and analyze its prospects.

1. Marty, *A Nation of Behavers* (Chicago: University of Chicago Press, 1976), p. 80.

2. Kenneth Woodward, "Born Again!" *Newsweek*, 25 October 1976, pp. 68-78.

3. "Back to that Oldtime Religion," *Time*, 36 December 1977, pp. 52-58.

4. Sweet, "The Evangelical Tradition in America," in *The Evangelical Tradition in America*, ed. Leonard I. Sweet (Macon: Mercer University Press, 1984), p. 1.

Issues of Definition and Classification

As in any academic pursuit, the first scholars to take up a subject get to define terms and set the boundaries of inquiry. Among the first to study evangelicalism in the 1970s were a number of evangelical historians.[5] To a large extent, the work of George Marsden, Mark Noll, Nathan Hatch, Joel Carpenter, Donald Dayton, Grant Wacker, and others have determined how people inside and outside evangelicalism view it. According to Leonard Sweet, by writing their own history, these scholars "are engaging with and criticizing their own tradition — and thereby setting the scholarly agenda for years to come."[6]

Much of that agenda has centered on matters of classification and definition. At first glance, evangelicalism seems too diverse to be defined accurately and too varied to be considered a single movement. For example, what do fundamentalist Baptists, Christian Reformed, Free Methodists, black Pentecostals, Orthodox Presbyterians, Nazarenes, members of the Churches of Christ, charismatic Episcopalians, Mennonites, Missouri Synod Lutherans, Assemblies of God, and conservatives in mainline Protestant denominations have in common?[7]

After years of trying, scholars still have a hard time defining what evangelicalism is and how many kinds there are.[8] Even those who speak about evangelicalism as a whole must begin by identifying its parts. In a 1974 study, for example, Richard Quebedeaux identified five distinct evangelical subgroups;[9] two years later Robert Webber counted fourteen.[10] Cullen Murphy looked under the "vast tent of evangelical faith" and discovered a twelve-ring circus.[11] It is not surprising, then, that Catholic Thomas Stransky calls evangelical Protestantism a "con-

5. Douglas Sweeney, "The Essential Evangelical Dialectic: The Historiography of the Early Neo-Evangelical Movement and the Observer-Participant Dilemma," *Church History* 60 (March 1991): 70-84.

6. Sweet, "Wise as Serpents, Innocent as Doves: The New Evangelical Historiography," *Journal of the American Academy of Religion* 56 (1988): 402.

7. For an ethnographic study of such evangelical diversity, see Randall Balmer, *Mine Eyes Have Seen the Glory: A Journey into the Evangelical Subculture in America* (New York: Oxford University Press, 1989).

8. The most sophisticated attempt at definition and classification to date can be found in *The Variety of American Evangelicalism,* ed. Donald W. Dayton and Robert K. Johnston (Knoxville: University of Tennessee Press, 1991).

9. Quebedeaux, *The Young Evangelicals* (New York: Harper & Row, 1974).

10. Webber, *Common Roots* (Grand Rapids: Zondervan, 1976), pp. 25-35.

11. Murphy, "Protestantism and the Evangelicals," *Wilson Quarterly* 5 (August 1981): 105-16.

fusing conglomeration"[12] and Nazarene Timothy Smith sees it as a kaleidoscope or mosaic.[13]

Donald Dayton believes that such diversity makes it difficult, if not impossible, to speak of evangelicalism as a single entity. In fact, he thinks that the word *evangelical* has outlived its usefulness. He and William Abraham, who are both Wesleyans, claim that the label is "an essentially contested concept," whose core meaning is in dispute, even among those who use it.[14] In their view, the term *evangelical* is not adequate to cover the profound differences between, say, ecstatic Pentecostals and rationalistic Presbyterians or entirely sanctified Nazarenes and community-minded Mennonites. Furthermore, Dayton argues that the term has been commandeered by a single party within American Protestantism, fundamentalists out of the Reformed tradition. Consequently, Dayton has called for a "moratorium on the use of the term, in the hope that we would be forced to more appropriate and useful categories of analysis."[15] Few if any scholars have joined the boycott, though Dayton's arguments have forced others to pay closer attention to the complexities involved in studying evangelicalism.

Despite these difficulties, George Marsden still speaks of an "evangelical denomination" made up of people with common convictions and loyalty to a complicated infrastructure of institutions.[16] Evangelicals are united by the teachers they admire, the schools they attend, the books they read, the religious language they use, the organizations they support, and the beliefs they hold. According to Marsden, "The meaningfulness of evangelicalism as such a 'denomination' is suggested by the fact that today among Protestants the lines between evangelical and nonevangelical often seem more significant than do denominational distinctions."[17]

12. Stransky, "A Look at Evangelical Protestantism," *Theology, News and Notes* 35 (March 1988): 24.

13. Smith, "The Evangelical Kaleidoscope and the Call to Christian Unity," *Christian Scholar's Review* 15 (1988): 125-40.

14. See Dayton, "The Use of Scripture in the Wesleyan Tradition," in *The Use of the Bible in Theology: Evangelical Options,* ed. Robert K. Johnston (Atlanta: John Knox Press, 1985), pp. 121-22; and Abraham, *The Coming Great Revival: Recovering the Full Evangelical Tradition* (San Francisco: Harper & Row, 1984), p. 72.

15. Dayton, "Doubts about the Category 'Evangelical,'" in *The Variety of American Evangelicalism,* p. 251.

16. Marsden, "The Evangelical Denomination," in *Evangelicalism and Modern America,* ed. George Marsden (Grand Rapids: William B. Eerdmans, 1984), pp. vii-xvi.

17. Marsden, "The Evangelical Denomination," p. ix. This was also Marty's observation in *A Nation of Behavers.*

Robert Johnston sees evangelicalism as an extended family of diverse groups and individuals whose "family resemblance" comes from "a dedication to the gospel that is expressed in a personal faith in Christ as Lord, an understanding of the gospel as defined authoritatively by Scripture, and a desire to communicate the gospel both in evangelism and social reform. Evangelicals are those who believe the gospel is to be experienced personally, defined biblically, and communicated passionately."[18]

Even if one grants this family resemblance, it is still necessary to identify evangelical "types" that roughly correspond to the different ways that the term *evangelical* has been used since the sixteenth century.[19] *Classical evangelicals* are loyal to the doctrines of the Protestant Reformation: the absolute authority of Scripture, justification by faith alone, and an Augustinian view of human nature that rejects notions of free will in favor of divine sovereignty. They hold passionately to their historic creeds and downplay the importance of personal religious experience in doing theology. In the American context, strict Lutherans and Calvinists belong in this category — for example, Missouri Synod Lutherans, conservatives in the Evangelical Lutheran Church of America, Christian Reformed, Orthodox Presbyterians, and nineteenth-century Old School Presbyterians.

Pietistic evangelicals also stand in the Reformation tradition but add the experiential emphases of Anabaptism, pietism, Puritanism, and the spiritual awakenings of the eighteenth and nineteenth centuries. They are basically religious pragmatists who would rather conduct revivals, promote "higher life" movements, and reform society than engage in scholastic theological debates. In this category belongs most of the evangelical establishment of the nineteenth-century: Methodists, holiness people, Baptists, Oberlin Perfectionists, New School Presbyterians, and everyone else who felt comfortable under the revivalist's tent, including the Pentecostals of the early twentieth century.

Fundamentalist evangelicals incorporate elements from the other two evangelical traditions but are primarily known for their rejection of liberal, critical, and evolutionary thinking and their strong defense of a few Christian "fundamentals" in opposition to various modern-

18. Johnston, "American Evangelicalism: An Extended Family," in *The Variety of American Evangelicalism,* p. 261.

19. See Donald Dayton, "The Limits of Evangelicalism: The Pentecostal Tradition," in *The Variety of American Evangelicalism,* pp. 47-48; and Max Stackhouse, "Religious Right: New? Right?" *Commonweal* 29 (Jan. 1982): 52-56.

isms. Included in this type are what Marsden has called "card-carrying fundamentalists"[20] who display a militant and separatistic spirit and their more moderate "neo-evangelical" offspring who after World War II tried to reform some of fundamentalism's more disagreeable features.

Needless to say, these are only types, not rigid categories. Pentecostals and holiness people, for example, though basically pietistic, have been greatly influenced by fundamentalist evangelicals; people in the Christian Reformed Church, though "classical" in their commitment to historic creeds, have a strong pietistic streak as well; and fundamentalists, though "pietistic" in their emphasis on "getting saved" and holy living, are also much like classical evangelicals in their concern over precise doctrine.

What holds these evangelical types together? Evangelicalism basically consists of a constellation of common beliefs and behaviors, shared theological convictions, and an ethos. Evangelicals believe that the Scriptures are inspired by God and constitute the ultimate authority for faith and life; that Jesus Christ is the incarnate Son of God whose life was characterized by supernatural power and divine authority; that salvation is based on the grace of God, not human goodness, and comes through personal faith in Christ; and that Christian conversion entails holy living and sharing the gospel with others. In other words, evangelicals combine a commitment to more or less historic Christian orthodoxy (usually interpreted through a traditional Protestant grid) and a particular view of the Christian life as personal conversion and ongoing renewal. Thus, evangelicals believe certain things and behave in certain ways.[21]

Yet, as members of an extended family, evangelicals are free to develop their own distinct traditions, which sometimes produces conflict. Big families include different kinds of people, from kissing cousins to embarrassing distant relatives. Though evangelicals frequently fight, compete, and question each other's parentage, they have on the whole been able to recognize the family resemblance and pull in the same theological and missional directions.[22]

20. Marsden, "Fundamentalism and American Evangelicalism," in *The Variety of American Evangelicalism,* p. 26.

21. In the mid-1970s, Marty observed the close connection between these two elements in evangelicalism and fundamentalism; see *A Nation of Behavers,* pp. 80-105.

22. I have been following my argument in "Premillennialism and the Branches of Evangelicalism," in *The Variety of American Evangelicalism,* pp. 5-21.

It is my contention that it is time to add another evangelical "type" to the list — *progressive evangelicals.* These "progressive" or "open" or "ecumenical" evangelicals, as they have been called,[23] are also committed to basic Christian orthodoxy and the evangelical ethos, but with a well-developed sense of modernity. In contrast to the "pre-critical" perspective of many pietistic evangelicals and the "anti-critical" stance of fundamentalist evangelicals, progressives are "post-critical" in their willingness to use the methods of modern scholarship to analyze and advance the gospel. Progressive evangelicals, in other words, are well aware of their current context — a pluralistic and secular society in which Christianity has become "old news" — and are prepared to respond to their intellectual and social environment in ways that sometimes frighten and alienate other evangelicals. As I see it, progressive evangelicalism currently consists of a union of elements from the post–World War II "new evangelical" attempt to transform fundamentalism, the large traditional segment within mainline Protestantism, and other reform-minded believers within classical and pietistic evangelical branches.

The Emergence of Progressive Evangelicalism

To understand this type of evangelicalism, one must know something about the "neo-evangelical" effort to reform fundamentalism after the Second World War. By the 1940s many fundamentalists realized that their militancy and separatism had marginalized them in American society. In a flurry of self-criticism, a group of younger fundamentalists rejected their movement's isolationism, anti-intellectualism, social conservatism, and general bad manners.[24] They remembered and longed for the time when evangelical religion had power and respect in society. Because the term *fundamentalism* had so many bad connotations, these reformers started using *evangelicalism* instead and launched a well-coordinated strategy to achieve their goals. They envisioned a "new evangelicalism" (Harold John Ockenga's term) that

23. See George Marsden, *Reforming Fundamentalism: Fuller Seminary and the New Evangelicalism* (Grand Rapids: William B. Eerdmans, 1987); Dayton and Johnston, *The Variety of American Evangelicalism;* and Clark Pinnock, "Defining American Fundamentalism: A Response," in *The Fundamentalist Phenomenon,* ed. Norman J. Cohen (Grand Rapids: William B. Eerdmans, 1990), pp. 38-54.

24. For example, see Carl F. H. Henry, *The Uneasy Conscience of Modern Fundamentalism* (Grand Rapids: William B. Eerdmans, 1947).

could again capture the culture for Christ and effectively engage modern thought.[25]

In 1943 they organized the National Association of Evangelicals (NAE), which included moderate and less separatistic fundamentalists as well as holiness and Pentecostal people. In 1947, radio preacher Charles E. Fuller and Harold John Ockenga, the pastor of Boston's prestigious Park Street Church, founded Fuller Theological Seminary in order to promote worldwide evangelism and elevate evangelical scholarship. A few years later, Carl F. H. Henry, one of the foremost new evangelical intellectuals, and other religious and business leaders started *Christianity Today,* which became *the* magazine of the movement. These reformers also established specialized ministries to reach high school and college students: Young Life, Youth for Christ, and Campus Crusade for Christ. A young Southern Baptist evangelist named Billy Graham was the symbol of the evangelical renaissance and quickly became one of the most admired men in America. In short, the new evangelical network offered a full-blown alternative to militant fundamentalism, which condemned "neo-evangelicalism" as a dangerous compromise with apostasy and an obvious departure from orthodoxy.[26]

To many others, however, it looked as if the evangelical establishment of the nineteenth-century was making a comeback. Certainly the NAE included a broad alliance of pietistic and fundamentalist evangelicals. But the people who ran the show — and tried to mold the entire movement to fit their own theological and social concerns — nearly all came from what Dayton calls the "presbyterian paradigm," which embraced the kind of Reformed scholasticism taught at the old Princeton Seminary, where theology was rationalistic (in the Scottish common-sense style), ready to do battle for the faith, and

25. On this point, I have found very helpful George Marsden's *Understanding Fundamentalism and Evangelicalism* (Grand Rapids: William B. Eerdmans, 1991), pp. 62-82. For an insider's view of this strategy, see Harold John Ockenga, "From Fundamentalism, through New Evangelicalism, to Evangelicalism," in *Evangelical Roots: A Tribute to Wilbur Smith,* ed. Kenneth Kantzer (Nashville: Thomas Nelson, 1978), pp. 35-46.

26. For analyses by militant fundamentalists of the new evangelicalism, see Robert P. Lightner, *Neo-Evangelicalism* (Des Plaines, Ill.: Regular Baptist Press, 1965); George W. Dollar, *A History of Fundamentalism in America* (Greenville, S.C.: Bob Jones University Press, 1973); John R. Rice, *I Am a Fundamentalist* (Murfreesboro, Tenn.: Sword of the Lord, 1975); and David O. Beale, *In Pursuit of Purity: American Fundamentalism since 1850* (Greenville, S.C.: Unusual Publications, 1986).

firmly tied to the doctrine of biblical inerrancy.[27] Many of these leaders graduated from the same schools: Wheaton College, Gordon College and Divinity School, Princeton Seminary, and its more conservative offshoot, Westminster. Their perspective dominated the coalition's elite corps. For example, although elements from classical, pietistic, and fundamentalist evangelicalism flowed together in the founders and faculty of Fuller Seminary, the institution wanted to become the new Old Princeton, and so the Wesleyan perspective was nowhere to be seen.[28]

One example of the new evangelical bent toward Reformed orthodoxy can be seen in *The Evangelicals: What They Believe, Who They Are, Where They Are Changing* (1975), which was one of the first attempts to explain the evangelical renaissance.[29] In an essay entitled "The Theological Boundaries of Evangelical Faith," John Gerstner found "real" evangelical theology only in the classical Reformation tradition that he traced through Calvin, Edwards, Hodge, and Warfield (three out of four Princeton men).[30] Gerstner mentions John Wesley only in passing and totally ignores the movement he founded. Likewise, because Charles Finney lapsed from Calvinist orthodoxy, Gerstner concludes that "the greatest of nineteenth-century evangelists became the greatest of nineteenth-century foes of evangelicalism."[31] Gerstner's placing of Finney and the Wesleyan tradition outside authentic evangelicalism shows how limiting the presbyterian paradigm could be. To correct this bias, a later revised edition of *The Evangelicals* included a new chapter on the Arminian contribution to evangelicalism.[32]

Under the surface, the coalition was marked not only by diversity but also much divisiveness. In fact, just as *Time* and *Newsweek* announced the emergence of a new evangelical empire, one of its

27. See Dayton, "The Use of Scripture in the Wesleyan Tradition," pp. 121-36.

28. See Marsden, *Reforming Fundamentalism*.

29. *The Evangelicals: What They Believe, Who They Are, Where They Are Changing*, ed. David F. Wells and John D. Woodbridge (Nashville: Abingdon, 1975). For other examples of this genre, see Bruce L. Shelley, *Evangelicalism in America* (Grand Rapids: William B. Eerdmans, 1967); Donald G. Bloesch, *The Evangelical Renaissance* (Grand Rapids: William B. Eerdmans, 1973); and Bernard L. Ramm, *The Evangelical Heritage* (Waco, Tex.: Word Books, 1973).

30. Gerstner, "The Theological Boundaries of Evangelical Faith," in *The Evangelicals*, pp. 21-37.

31. Gerstner, "The Theological Boundaries of Evangelical Faith," p. 27.

32. Vinson Synan, "Theological Boundaries: The Arminian Tradition," in *The Evangelicals: What They Believe, Who They Are, Where They Are Changing*, rev. ed. (Grand Rapids: Baker Book House, 1977), pp. 38-57.

leaders warned of its imminent collapse.[33] In 1976 Carl F. H. Henry observed that "the evangelical lion is nonetheless slowly succumbing to confusion about its own identity. The cohesion that American evangelicals had shown in the sixties has been fading in the seventies through multiplied internal disagreements and emerging counterforces."[34] Despite early signs of promise, evangelicals had not quickened the national conscience and were now debating among themselves the limits of biblical criticism, the truth of biblical inerrancy, the relationship between evangelism and social concern, and the advisability of political involvement. He noted the growing restlessness of the movement's younger scholars, many of whom were trained at non-evangelical institutions and who now openly criticized the establishment's older leadership. What *Newsweek* saw as the possible wave of the future Henry viewed as a toothless beast past its prime: "It is time that the evangelical movement sees itself for what it is: a lion on the loose that no one today seriously fears."[35] Four years later, Henry was even more discouraged: "By the early 1970s the prospect of a massive evangelical alliance seemed annually more remote, and by mid-decade it was gone."[36]

In retrospect, Henry's concern over the demise of evangelical unity was overdone. As Joel Carpenter has observed, "you can't lose what you never had."[37] Nevertheless, to those used to being in charge, the loss of consensus seemed obvious, especially on the issue of how higher criticism fit into evangelical scholarship. In fact, reforming fundamentalists had never seen eye to eye on this question. New evangelicals believed that, if properly used, the methods of modern scholarship would support the Scriptures, not undercut confidence in them, and they criticized fundamentalists for not taking scholarship seriously.[38] But they never settled on the limits of biblical criticism or whether its findings ever justified abandoning accepted conservative positions.

33. For one of the first analyses of the tensions within post–World War II evangelicalism, see Martin E. Marty, "Tensions within Contemporary Evangelicalism: A Critical Appraisal," in *The Evangelicals*, pp. 170-88.

34. Henry, *Evangelicals in Search of Identity* (Waco, Tex.: Word Books, 1976), p. 22.

35. Henry, *Evangelicals in Search of Identity*, p. 96.

36. Henry, "American Evangelicals in a Turning Time," *Christian Century*, 5 November 1980, p. 1060.

37. Carpenter, quoted by Sweeney in "The Essential Evangelical Dialectic," p. 78.

38. See Mark A. Noll, *Between Faith and Criticism: Evangelicals, Scholarship and the Bible in America* (San Francisco: Harper & Row, 1986), p. 154.

In *Between Faith and Criticism* (1986), Mark Noll showed that evangelical scholars eventually formed two parties around these issues. "Critical anti-critics" used scholarship mainly to protect the Bible against its detractors. In their view, if modern research overthrew conventional views of the Bible, then Scripture's credibility was ruined, along with all certainty in matters of salvation. Thus critical anti-critics worked hard to support traditional notions of authorship, dating, literary transmission, and the Bible's historical and scientific accuracy. For them, belief in biblical inerrancy required traditional interpretations of the text.[39] For example, evangelical scholars must affirm that the great fish really swallowed Jonah and that all the events in the gospels happened exactly the way they were recorded. To do less would be to call into question the truthfulness of the rest of the Bible and cast doubt on the character of God.

"Believing critics," on the other hand, were willing to let go some traditional interpretations if the findings of modern research were convincing, but they denied that they were rejecting the Bible's inspiration and authority when they did so. Thus they were less tied to older views of authorship and much more interested in matters of literary genre and authorial intent. For them, the value of the book of Jonah as divine revelation did not depend on the historicity of the story (God could have inspired the author to write a parable), and the gospels contained edited materials that served the authors' literary (as well as God's revelational) purposes. Thus believing critics more eagerly explored the historical and cultural dimensions of the Bible and the human character of inspiration. Furthermore, they were willing to question whether *inerrant* was the best term to describe the Bible that God had given, though some progressives were still willing to speak of inerrancy if they could define it.[40]

While both groups considered themselves to be bona fide evangelicals, they quickly squared off. Of course, this was not the first time reformers of one generation criticized reformers of the next for going too far. Once begun, reform is hard to stop and often has unintended consequences. As fundamentalist *reformers,* the first new evangelicals wanted change; but as *fundamentalist* reformers, they did not want too much. As Marsden has pointed out, they "still saw themselves fighting for the fundamentalist cause in the fundamentalist-modernist controversies. For most of them it was thus extremely important not to move

39. Noll, *Between Faith and Criticism,* pp. 156-57.

40. See Noll, *Between Faith and Criticism,* pp. 158-60.

too far from fundamentalism — to put a left boundary on the course they set." On the other hand, their more progressive protégés "were one more step removed from the fundamentalist-modernist wars: those contests were for them second hand."[41] Reforming fundamentalists were naive to believe that they could earn graduate degrees at top universities and do advanced theological scholarship without changing some opinions in the process. The road that fundamentalist reformers took was more dangerous than many imagined. Progressives, now twice removed from fundamentalism, simply went beyond the point on the road where reforming fundamentalists were comfortable.

By the mid-1960s, then, the conservative wing needed a way to limit fundamentalist reforms and found it in inerrancy. After all, the doctrine was important to a number of other conservative Christian traditions, it was tied to issues of authority that always surfaced in debates with liberals, and it seemed to be an antidote to the poison of untraditional interpretations.[42]

The inevitable collision between conservatives and progressives finally came at a June 1966 meeting at Wenham, Massachusetts (Gordon College), where about fifty scholars discovered irreconcilable differences in their approaches to the Bible. Though the argument that started at Wenham was ostensibly over the doctrine of inspiration, there were other issues at stake. According to Marsden, the inerrancy debate was also about "what kind of movement the new evangelicalism would be. Would it continue as essentially a refurbished version of fundamentalism, with a conspicuously defensive stance? If so, a stress on inerrancy would serve to guard the movement from innovation. Or would openness and tolerance be the more immediately conspicuous traits of the new evangelicals?"[43]

For ten years these disagreements remained in academic circles, but then Harold Lindsell decided it was time to take them public. In *The Battle for the Bible* (1976), Lindsell claimed that all evangelicals throughout church history had affirmed biblical inerrancy, and those who disavowed it now were not true evangelicals. Especially worrisome to Lindsell were those institutions that had once accepted inerrancy but now rejected it — seminaries such as Fuller, where he had once taught and served as vice president. Once inerrancy was denied, he argued, institutions started down the "slippery slope" to apostasy.

41. Marsden, *Reforming Fundamentalism,* p. 231.
42. Marsden, *Reforming Fundamentalism,* p. 227.
43. Marsden, *Reforming Fundamentalism,* p. 229.

Holding to inerrancy was the way for institutions and individuals to preserve their doctrinal orthodoxy. Thus evangelicals must purge their ranks before it was too late.

Needless to say, Lindsell's book stirred up the evangelical rank and file as well as evangelical historians and theologians, who amassed evidence for and against his thesis. Jack Rogers and Donald McKim argued that inerrancy was the product of Protestant scholasticism, not the historic doctrine of the church; but John Woodbridge countered that it had been the church's teaching from the beginning.[44] Daryl McCarthy claimed that inerrancy was central to a Wesleyan doctrine of Scripture; while Paul Bassett showed that Wesleyans historically stressed the Bible's sufficiency in matters of salvation, not its inerrancy in historical and scientific details.[45] It seemed that everyone could find something in Luther and Calvin to support his or her view.[46] Even though a few inerrantists criticized Lindsell for overstating his case and being too divisive,[47] *The Battle for the Bible* did force evangelicals to choose up sides.

Fuller Seminary championed the progressive party. It denied Lindsell's charge that it was subverting evangelical orthodoxy and argued that old-fashioned piety and the latest scholarship can coexist. Its president, David Allan Hubbard, contended that a high view of Scripture is possible without inerrancy and that evangelical scholars must be free to follow the text of the Bible wherever it leads.[48] At Fuller the choice was not between *inerrancy* and *errancy*. One could affirm the

44. Jack B. Rogers and Donald K. McKim, *The Authority and Interpretation of the Bible: An Historical Approach* (San Francisco: Harper & Row, 1979); John D. Woodbridge, *Biblical Authority: A Critique of the Rogers/McKim Proposal* (Grand Rapids: Zondervan, 1982).

45. Daryl E. McCarthy, "Inerrancy in American Wesleyanism," in *Inerrancy and the Church,* ed. John D. Hannah (Chicago: Moody Press, 1984), pp. 279-321; Paul Bassett, "The Theological Identity of the North American Holiness Movement," in *The Variety of American Evangelicalism,* pp. 72-108.

46. See Mark A. Noll, "The Word of God and the Bible: A View from the Reformation," *Christian Scholar's Review* 8 (1978): 25-31.

47. See Carl F. H. Henry, review of *The Battle for the Bible,* by Harold Lindsell, *New Review of Books and Religion* 1 (Sept. 1976): 7; and Richard Lovelace, "Inerrancy: Some Historical Perspectives," in *Inerrancy and Common Sense,* ed. Roger R. Nicole and J. Ramsey Michaels (Grand Rapids: Baker Book House, 1980), pp. 15-47.

48. See Fuller's self-defense in "The Authority of Scripture at Fuller," *Theology, News and Notes,* Special Edition (1976); *Biblical Authority,* ed. Jack B. Rogers (Waco, Tex.: Word Books, 1977); and David Allan Hubbard, *What We Evangelicals Believe: Expositions of Christian Doctrine Based on "The Statement of Faith" of Fuller Theological Seminary* (Pasadena: Fuller Theological Seminary, 1979).

Bible's infallibility, authority, and trustworthiness without having to explain all its difficulties.

The conservative party insisted that inerrancy was crucial for evangelical theology. In the fall of 1978, about three hundred scholars organized the International Council on Biblical Inerrancy in Chicago. After a few days of deliberation, they issued a carefully nuanced document, the "Chicago Statement on Biblical Inerrancy," which acknowledged numerous difficulties in the biblical text but affirmed that "being wholly and verbally God-given, Scripture is without error or fault in all its teaching, no less in what it states about God's acts in creation, about the events of world history, and about its own literary origins under God, than in its witness to God's saving grace in individual lives." It also warned that denying inerrancy undercuts belief in Scriptural authority and harms both individuals and churches. Carl Henry wondered whether the Council's "achievements are too slim to accomplish its hoped for goal of a new Reformation predicated on biblical inerrancy,"[49] but its members produced a series of scholarly works to defend their position.[50]

In general, the debate was not very edifying, nor even instructive. Both sides admitted various levels of imprecision in the biblical text, but they could not agree on what constituted an error or how far the term *inerrancy* could be qualified before it lost its meaning. In some circles, inerrancy became essentially a shibboleth: it did not matter what one meant by the word as long as one used it. Ironically, conservatives quickly discovered that simply affirming inerrancy was not enough: one could accept the doctrine and still come to unacceptable conclusions. In the early eighties, for example, two prominent evangelical scholars affirmed inerrancy but seemed to question the historicity of some gospel accounts. As a result, Ramsey Michaels lost his job at Gordon-Conwell Theological Seminary, and Robert Gundry was expelled from the Evangelical Theological Society.[51] Consequently, the

49. Henry, "The Chicago Statement on Biblical Inerrancy," *Eternity,* February 1979, pp. 44-46.

50. The International Council on Biblical Inerrancy sponsored the following books: *Inerrancy,* ed. Norman L. Geisler (Grand Rapids: Zondervan, 1979); *Biblical Errancy: Its Philosophical Roots,* ed. Norman L. Geisler (Grand Rapids: Zondervan, 1981); *Challenges to Inerrancy,* ed. Gordon Lewis and Bruce Demarest (Chicago: Moody Press, 1984); *Inerrancy and the Church,* ed. John D. Hannah (Chicago: Moody Press, 1984); and *Hermeneutics, Inerrancy, and the Bible,* ed. Earl Radmacher and Robert Preus (Grand Rapids: Zondervan, 1984).

51. See "The Issue of Biblical Authority Brings a Scholar's Resignation,"

inerrancy party sought to establish hermeneutical guidelines that would guarantee traditional interpretations by limiting the use of biblical criticism.[52] After all, inerrancy seems beside the point if those who accept it cannot agree on what the Bible means.[53]

With so little room for compromise, neither side made many converts from the other.[54] Inerrancy was both a theological issue and a political weapon for institutional control.[55] In well-publicized conflicts, conservatives overwhelmed progressives in the Lutheran Church, Missouri Synod, in the 1970s and the Southern Baptist Convention in the 1980s. So close on most issues, the two camps nevertheless saw themselves as moving in opposite directions. By 1979 Lindsell concluded that "the term *evangelical* has been so debased that it has lost its usefulness." Rather than share it with progressives, he suggested that conservatives start calling themselves *fundamentalists* again.[56] That was the last thing most conservative evangelicals wanted to do, though they clearly shared with fundamentalists many of the same anti-critical concerns.

The Shape of Progressive Evangelicalism

Despite their differences with fundamentalist evangelicals, progressives have not yet created a separate infrastructure of organizations, as reforming fundamentalists once did. There are only two thoroughgoing progressive evangelical seminaries (nondenominational Fuller Seminary in Pasadena and the Evangelical Covenant Church's North Park

---

Christianity Today, 15 July 1983, pp. 35-38; and Leslie R. Keylock, "Evangelical Scholars Remove Gundry for His Views on Matthew," *Christianity Today,* 3 February 1984, pp. 36-38.

52. See *Hermeneutics, Inerrancy, and the Bible: Hermeneutics, Authority, and Canon,* ed. D. A. Carson and John D. Woodbridge (Grand Rapids: Zondervan, 1986); and *Inerrancy and Hermeneutics,* ed. Harvie M. Conn (Grand Rapids: Baker Book House, 1988). The International Council on Biblical Inerrancy published its own statement on hermeneutics in 1982.

53. See Robert K. Johnston, *Evangelicals at an Impasse: Biblical Authority in Perspective* (Atlanta: John Knox Press, 1979).

54. See Michael Bauman, "Why the Noninerrantists Are Not Listening: Six Tactical Errors Evangelicals Commit," *Journal of the Evangelical Theological Society* 19 (Sept. 1986): 317-24.

55. See Richard V. Pierard, "The Politics of Inerrancy," *Reformed Journal* 34 (Jan. 1985): 2-4.

56. Lindsell, *The Bible in the Balance* (Grand Rapids: Zondervan, 1979), pp. 319-20.

Theological Seminary in Chicago), but progressives can be found on the faculties of most other evangelical schools. Parents from both parties send their children to the same evangelical colleges, many of which are now quite progressive. Conservatives and progressives often attend the same local congregations, though progressives can also be found in mainline denominations as well as those affiliated with the NAE. Both can be found reading and writing for the same evangelical publishers (Zondervan, Baker, Eerdmans, Multnomah, Word, InterVarsity, etc.), but progressives also want to work with non-evangelical publishers and university presses.

Though no well-developed progressive infrastructure exists, new alliances are visible. One of the most important is "Christian feminism," which took shape after the publication of Letha Scanzoni and Nancy Hardesty's *All We're Meant to Be* (1974). Responding to strong currents in society, many evangelicals found resources in the Bible and the historic evangelical tradition for a Christian version of "women's liberation" that upheld traditional sexual mores and the importance of the family.[57] Since the mid-seventies, these evangelical "egalitarians" have laid an extensive biblical, theological, and historical foundation for their views, which has caused an intense and often divisive debate within congregations, denominations, and parachurch organizations. Though widespread among progressives, feminist views are still anathema to many other evangelicals and have generated a strong backlash.[58]

Similarly, progressive scholars tend to join different professional societies than their more conservative colleagues. Noll discovered that conservatives are more likely to be members of the Evangelical Theological Society (ETS), which requires scholars from a variety of theological disciplines to affirm that "The Bible alone, and the Bible in its

57. See, for example, Mary J. Evans, *Woman in the Bible* (Downers Grove, Ill.: InterVarsity Press, 1983); *Women, Authority and the Bible,* ed. Alvera Mickelsen (Downers Grove, Ill.: InterVarsity Press, 1986); Mary Stewart Van Leeuwen, *Gender and Grace: Love, Work, and Parenting in a Changing World* (Downers Grove, Ill.: InterVarsity Press, 1990); Janette Hassey, *No Time for Silence: Evangelical Women in Public Ministry around the Turn of the Century* (Grand Rapids: Zondervan, 1986); and Ruth Tucker and Walter Liefeld, *Daughters of the Church: Women and Ministry from New Testament Times to the Present* (Grand Rapids: Zondervan, 1987).

58. For the range of views on this issue, see *Women in Ministry: Four Views,* ed. Bonnidell Clouse and Robert G. Clouse (Downers Grove, Ill.: InterVarsity Press, 1989). Antifeminists organized themselves into the Council on Biblical Manhood and Womanhood in 1987 and issued the "Danvers Statement." See also *Recovering Biblical Manhood and Womanhood: A Response to Evangelical Feminism,* ed. John Piper and Wayne Grudem (Wheaton, Ill.: Crossway Books, 1991).

entirety, is the Word of God written, and is therefore inerrant in the autographs." More progressive Bible scholars gravitate toward the Institute for Biblical Research, where they are free to use far-ranging critical methods and are not required to sign an inerrancy statement.[59] Progressives also tend to join the American Academy of Religion (AAR) and the Society of Biblical Literature (SBL). In recent years ETS and AAR/SBL meetings have been scheduled in tandem, but people who attend one usually do not go to the other.

Progressives are also more likely to interact with liberal Protestants and Catholics than was the older evangelical establishment. During the sixties and seventies, a significant number took part in the World Council of Churches' debate over the nature of mission in the modern world. Though the evangelical emphasis on conversion and proclamation did not win out over the liberal definition of mission as identification with the world's social and political struggles, many evangelicals came to the conclusion that it was important for them to participate in the discussion.[60] Even showing up to talk was a sign that for some evangelicals the values of tolerance and cooperation had replaced the fundamentalist emphasis on militancy and separatism.[61]

In other words, understanding the other person's point of view is just as important for progressives as contending for the faith was for fundamentalists. For example, in the introduction to *Theological Crossfire: An Evangelical/Liberal Dialogue,* which he co-authored with Delwin Brown, a process theologian from the Iliff School of Theology in Denver, Clark Pinnock wrote that they wanted to see if one can "dig a middle channel between liberals and evangelicals. We wonder whether one can be evangelical and liberal at the same time and actually avoid both heresy and idolatry."[62] But by the end of the exercise, it was obvious that no middle ground had been discovered. The differences between the two approaches were profound, but Pinnock was pleased with the process anyway. "The conversation proved to be mutually stimulating," Pinnock concluded. "Both of us were forced to face up to hard questions. . . . We experienced more than one awkward moment. It certainly

59. Noll, *Between Faith and Criticism,* pp. 158-59.

60. See *The Conciliar-Evangelical Debate: The Crucial Documents, 1964-1976,* ed. Donald McGavran (South Pasadena, Calif.: William Carey Library, 1977).

61. Fundamentalists believe that such values invariably lead one astray. See Ed Dobson, *In Search of Unity: An Appeal to Fundamentalists and Evangelicals* (Nashville: Thomas Nelson, 1985), especially pp. 66-72.

62. Pinnock and Brown, *Theological Crossfire: An Evangelical/Liberal Dialogue* (Grand Rapids: Zondervan, 1990), p. 14.

forced me to address some of the challenges of modernity I would have preferred to bypass. . . . It proved to be an occasion of growth for us both."[63] Needless to say, no self-respecting reforming fundamentalist would ever say that, but such civility is common among progressives.

There seems to be little left of the old defensiveness. Theology-as-apologetics, which was so central to fundamentalist evangelicalism, is less common among progressives. When Richard Mouw of Fuller Seminary set out to analyze the various "isms" that challenge modern Christianity, he avoided the older show-where-they-are-wrong-and-then-nail-them-to-the-wall approach. Instead, he recognized that these mistaken and sometimes destructive ways of thinking are "distortions of the truth" that people find attractive because of authentic human "hopes and fears." It is never enough to expose, then refute error. One must also ask why truth-seekers have not found it in historic Christianity. In their sinfulness, Christians sometimes distort the truth too.[64] In Mouw's approach, there in none of the older triumphalism and intellectual cockiness. When asked to reflect on how his own mind has changed, Mouw said he was feeling more humble and hopeful than in the past — and working for a kinder and gentler evangelicalism.[65]

Such openness becomes easier with the realization that evangelical theology itself is diverse. In a recent survey of systematic theology in America, Gabriel Fackre counted six subsets among evangelicals: old, new, justice and peace, charismatic, fundamentalist, and ecumenical.[66] Similarly, Robert Johnston has shown that while evangelicals are united around a core of theological beliefs, they arrive at their conclusions in remarkably different ways. In a book on how evangelicals use the Bible in doing theology, Johnston found that evangelical theologians operated as philosophical rationalists, Barthians, straightforward biblical exegetes, liberationists, and those who take the early church fathers nearly as seriously as they do the Bible.[67]

More evangelical theologians are paying attention to the historical development of their own theology and are learning from social

63. Pinnock and Brown, *Theological Crossfire,* p. 254.

64. Mouw, *Distorted Truth: What Every Christian Needs to Know about the Battle for the Mind* (San Francisco: Harper & Row, 1989).

65. Mouw, "Humility, Hope and the Divine Slowness," in *How My Mind Has Changed,* ed. James M. Wall and David Heim (Grand Rapids: William B. Eerdmans, 1991), pp. 21-31.

66. Fackre, "Reorientation and Retrieval in Systematic Theology," *Christian Century,* 26 June–3 July 1991, p. 653.

67. Johnston, *The Use of the Bible in Theology,* pp. 3-5.

scientists and missiologists that all theologies are "contextual" in that they are shaped to a significant degree by their time and place. Growing interest in "globalization," which takes seriously the multicultural nature of Christianity and seeks to overcome evangelical parochialism, has the potential to change significantly how theological educators teach evangelicalism's future leaders.[68] Naturally, not all evangelical theologians like this approach (it smacks of cultural relativism and a denial of propositional revelation that transcends time and place), but progressive theologians are willing to take such issues on.[69]

Because the theological issues that concern them are not exclusively evangelical,[70] progressives often look for help to traditional elements within the Protestant mainline churches. Many evangelicals find great compatibility with such people as Gabriel Fackre of Andover Newton and Thomas Oden of Drew University, whose theologies are basically conservative and orthodox without being fundamentalist.[71] In fact, "evangelical ecumenicals" and "ecumenical evangelicals" find it easy to get along.

Other evangelicals openly embrace the catholic tradition. Donald Bloesch and Robert Webber (Presbyterian and Episcopalian, respectively) issued the "Chicago Call" in the late seventies, urging fellow evangelicals to consider their commonality with the universal church.[72] Elsewhere

68. The Association of Theological Schools has identified globalization as one of the crucial issues for theological education in the 1990s. For an account of Denver Seminary's efforts at globalization, see Robert Stivers, "Evangelicals in Transition," *Theological Education* 27 (Spring 1991): 33-50.

69. For an example of such contextualized theology, consult the following work by William Dyrness: *Christian Apologetics in a World Community* (Downers Grove, Ill.: InterVarsity Press, 1983); "How Does the Bible Function in the Christian Life?" in *The Use of the Bible in Theology,* pp. 159-74; and *How Does America Hear the Gospel?* (Grand Rapids: William B. Eerdmans, 1989).

70. Johnston also identified the five hottest questions facing evangelical theologians today: What is the role of our present context in the shaping of our theology? What role can tradition play in theological formulation? Are there limits to the critical study of the Bible? Is there a central biblical message or schema that can control our theologizing? and How should the role of the Spirit be understood in theology? (*The Use of the Bible in Theology,* pp. 5-17).

71. For a sense of Fackre's position, see *The Christian Story,* 2 vols. (Grand Rapids: William B. Eerdmans, 1987), and "The Use of the Scripture in My Work in Systematics," in *The Use of the Bible in Theology,* pp. 200-226. For a sense of Oden's position, see *After Modernity . . . What?* and "Back to the Fathers: An Interview by Christopher A. Hall," *Christianity Today,* 4 September 1990, pp. 28-31.

72. See *The Orthodox Evangelicals: Who They Are and What They Are Saying,* ed. Robert E. Webber and Donald Bloesch (Nashville: Thomas Nelson, 1978).

Bloesch has called on evangelicals to explore and affirm their catholicity, and Webber has argued that evangelical theology and worship need to be rooted in the patristic age more than in the nineteenth and twentieth centuries.[73] This interest in "catholic evangelicalism" often includes a preference for sacramentalism and high-church worship, which is a far cry from the low-church, antisacramental, and revivalistic style of most evangelicals in the pietistic and fundamentalist traditions. Progressives who take the catholic tradition seriously usually conclude that fundamentalist evangelicalism, from which so many of them have come, is not nearly as "orthodox" as fundamentalists themselves believe. As Jaroslav Pelikan has recently shown, in their zeal to defend the historic faith against the modernist threat, fundamentalists developed their own ahistorical and eccentric theology.[74] When some progressives call themselves "orthodox," they are referring not only to historic evangelical theology but to historic catholic theology, East and West.[75]

To this point, we have been considering progressive intellectuals and academics, but there are also pragmatic progressives who have much in common with pietistic evangelicals of the last century — ecclesiastical entrepreneurs who put fulfilling Christ's mission above maintaining theological precision. What makes these people "progressive" rather than merely "pietistic" is the modern context and their typically modern response to it. According to the experts,[76] America is now an "unchurched" and "postdenominational" society, which means that though Americans retain an amazingly high interest in spiritual things, most downplay the connection between personal spirituality and institutional religion.[77] In the past twenty years, a number of

73. Bloesch, *The Future of Evangelical Christianity: A Call for Unity amidst Diversity* (Garden City, N.Y.: Doubleday, 1983); Webber, *Common Roots*.

74. Pelikan, "Fundamentalism and/or Orthodoxy? Toward an Understanding of the Fundamentalist Phenomenon," in *The Fundamentalist Phenomenon*, pp. 3-21.

75. Much of this evangelical/Catholic/Orthodox dialogue has taken place at the Institute for Ecumenical and Cultural Research in Collegeville, Minnesota. See also Anthony Ugolnik, *The Illuminating Icon* (Grand Rapids: William B. Eerdmans, 1989), which is one of the first attempts to introduce evangelicals to Eastern Orthodox traditions. Richard Mouw wrote the foreword for the book.

76. Lyle Schaller, *It's a Different World* (Nashville: Abingdon, 1985); Kennon Callahan, *Effective Church Leadership* (San Francisco: Harper & Row, 1990); Tex Sample, *U.S. Lifestyles and Mainline Churches* (Louisville: Westminster/John Knox Press, 1990).

77. See George Gallup, Jr., and Jim Castelli, *The People's Religion: American Faith in the 90's* (New York: Macmillan, 1989); and Robert Bellah et al., *Habits of the*

mainline Protestant denominations have lost up to a quarter of their membership.[78] What are evangelicals prepared to do to penetrate such a culture?

Pragmatic progressives are willing to do just about anything, even adopting a "marketing" approach to religion in which the consumer comes first.[79] In a postdenominational society in which "brand-name" religion means very little, many progressives drop "Baptist" or "Presbyterian" or "Mennonite" from their church's name if it will get the unchurched through the front door. Or they will make their churches "seeker-sensitive" and "user-friendly" by eliminating whatever trappings might put off baby boomers who are ready to give religion another try. Often attracting thousands of members, these "full-service" churches offer something for everyone — groups for youth, young mothers, the recently divorced and never married, empty-nesters and retirees, people with every kind of addiction, and the physically fit who do aerobics to Christian rock and roll.[80]

The well-publicized model for the megachurch is the Willow Creek Community Church in suburban Chicago. In the late 1970s, a former youth worker named Bill Hybels decided to start a new congregation for the unchurched. He went door-to-door and asked people why they did not go to church and what kind of church might interest them; then he organized Willow Creek on the basis of what they said. The results were impressive, if unconventional by evangelical standards. Eventually, thousands of people came, many of whom had little or no previous church affiliation, and enjoyed sermons without hell-fire and brimstone. At Willow Creek people are nurtured and affirmed, not frightened into making a decision for Christ. The evangelical gospel is still there, to be sure, but it is packaged in new ways.

This application of "church-growth" principles has its critics

---

Heart: Individualism and Commitment in American Life (Berkeley and Los Angeles: University of California Press, 1985).

78. Wade Clark Roof and William McKinney, *American Mainline Religion: Its Changing Shape and Future* (New Brunswick, N.J.: Rutgers University Press, 1987).

79. See the following titles by George Barna: *Marketing the Church* (Ventura, Calif.: Regal Books, 1988); *The Frog in the Kettle: What Christians Need to Know about Life in the Year 2000* (Ventura, Calif.: Regal Books, 1990); and *User Friendly Churches: What Christians Need to Know about the Churches People Love to Go To* (Ventura, Calif.: Regal Books, 1991).

80. See "A Time to Seek," *Newsweek*, 17 December 1990, pp. 50-56; "Superchurches and How They Grew," *Time*, 5 August 1991, pp. 62-63; and "Baby-boomers Flock to Full-Service Churches," *USA Today*, 6 August 1991, pp. 1D, 4D.

who claim that in their desire to reach the unchurched, the megachurches are in danger of destroying their distinctiveness as evangelical churches. As Peter Berger and other sociologists of religion have shown, traditional religions survive only as long as their "sacred canopies" — the forms and values that provide the "plausibility structures" that make religious worldviews believable and distinguish insiders from outsiders — stay intact.[81] During the fifties and sixties, fundamentalist evangelicals (including new evangelical reformers) had a clearly defined religious subculture. They knew who they were (and who they were not) by what they did and did not do, by the songs they sang, how they dressed, and what they believed. They had their own religious jargon so that they could distinguish between *real* Christians like themselves and everybody else.[82] But what happens when such distinctiveness is denied and the sacred canopy develops gaping holes? Sociologist James Hunter has observed that evangelicalism is quickly losing its "symbolic boundaries," its distinctive patterns of belief and behavior. Without such characteristics, he warns, it is unlikely that evangelicalism can survive as an identifiable movement.[83] This observation certainly applies to these market-driven churches. A consumer approach to religion does well at meeting people's "felt needs," but it has a much more difficult time creating "communities of memory" or resisting the self-centered individualism that so characterizes American society.[84]

But pragmatists are not overly concerned about such issues. For them the most important thing is that the gospel is being preached and people who might not otherwise listen are tuning in. This is fairly standard for pragmatic evangelicals: in the 1820s Charles Finney scandalized his more traditional contemporaries by using his revivalistic "New Measures," and throughout the nineteenth century evangelicals did what they could to reach immigrants, the newly educated, or other people who had little interest in what they had to offer. Parts of evan-

81. See Berger, *The Sacred Canopy: Elements of a Sociological Theory of Religion* (Garden City, N.Y.: Doubleday, 1967).

82. See Patricia Klein et al., *Growing Up Born Again: A Whimsical Look at the Blessings and Tribulations of Growing Up Born Again* (Old Tappan, N.J.: Power Books, 1987). Sociologist Nancy T. Ammerman presents a study of life within a single fundamentalist congregation in *Bible Believers: Fundamentalists in the Modern World* (New Brunswick, N.J.: Rutgers University Press, 1987).

83. Hunter, *The Evangelicals: The Coming Generation* (Chicago: University of Chicago Press, 1987).

84. See Bellah et al., *Habits of the Heart.*

gelicalism have always been adaptive and even accommodating to the culture.[85]

At present it is not easy to identify the boundaries of progressive evangelicalism. In general, the movement is characterized by its commitment to modern scholarship, its openness to culture, and its willingness to form new alliances. But it is possible to provide a shorthand definition. In the mid-1970s Martin Marty identified an evangelical as anyone who found evangelist Billy Graham or his viewpoints acceptable.[86] Likewise, in the 1990s, one might define a progressive evangelical as anyone who finds the mission and style of Fuller Seminary acceptable. Since declaring its progressive agenda in the early seventies, Fuller has become the largest nondenominational seminary in the world and has created a constituency that extends far beyond its institutional boundaries. Thus it is both an educational institution and the vanguard of a movement. Virtually all of the concerns of progressive evangelicalism have been championed at Fuller, and its changing student body provides a rough outline of the movement's demographics: increasing numbers of women, people of color, mainline Protestants, Pentecostals, and charismatics — as well as those who desire a more open style of evangelicalism than they have experienced before. Fuller's broadly distributed "Mission Beyond the Mission" (1983), which marked out as critical concerns world evangelization, the renewal of the whole church, solid scholarship, the moral health of society, family values, and an involvement in social issues, is the closest thing to a "platform" ever produced by progressive evangelicals.[87]

Conclusion

In the emergence of progressive evangelicalism, do we see history repeating itself? According to George Marsden, "It can be plausibly argued that evangelicalism's rounding off of the sharp edges of the gospel message between 1960 and 1985 paralleled the gentle modifications of the gospel by Protestant liberalism in the later nineteenth century."[88] Are progressive evangelicals merely following the old "modernist impulse" that produced evangelical liberalism in the last century?

85. See Nathan O. Hatch, "Evangelicalism as a Democratic Movement," in *Evangelicalism and Modern America,* pp. 71-82.

86. Marty, *A Nation of Behavers,* p. 83.

87. Marsden, *Reforming Fundamentalism,* pp. 265-67.

88. Marsden, *Understanding Fundamentalism and Evangelicalism,* p. 80.

That is certainly what many fundamentalist evangelicals believe progressives are doing, and sociologists of religion have documented a certain "slippage" along the edges of evangelical belief and behavior in recent years as well. In the early 1980s James Hunter surveyed students and faculty members from sixteen evangelical colleges and seminaries to determine the "coming generation's" beliefs and behaviors.[89] He found that those surveyed were less likely than their evangelical forebears to hold to biblical inerrancy, insist that people who have never heard of Christ will suffer eternally in hell for not accepting his offer of grace, and take the creation accounts in Genesis 1–2 literally. Hunter also discovered that most young evangelicals were nearly indistinguishable from the rest of society in their desire for self-fulfillment rather than self-sacrifice and that among younger evangelicals there was a significant movement away from older hierarchical notions of gender roles toward a decidedly more egalitarian view of the sexes and family life. Behaviorally, he found that the next generation of evangelical leaders were less willing than their elders to observe traditional taboos against drinking alcohol, smoking, dancing, going to movies, and playing cards that had been part of evangelical piety in America since before Victorian times.

Many of these changes can be attributed to the fact that higher education, which is increasingly common among evangelicals, invariably creates a willingness to question old ideas and ways of doing things. But Hunter believes something more significant has occurred: usually without knowing it, evangelicals have engaged in extensive "cognitive bargaining" with the modern world. Since World War II, evangelicals have stopped resisting the dominant culture and started accommodating to it.[90] This tendency is common even among conservatives who believe that they are "holding the line" against modernity.[91] Thus, Hunter's findings provide some support for those who think that evangelicalism has passed this way before.

How serious are these changes? Do they mark the beginning of

89. The surveyed institutions included Wheaton, Gordon, Westmont, Taylor, Messiah, George Fox, Bethel, Seattle-Pacific, and Houghton colleges and Fuller, Gordon-Conwell, Westminster, Asbury, Talbot, Wheaton Graduate School, and Denver seminaries (*Evangelicalism*, p. 9).

90. An early warning was sounded by Richard Quebedeaux in *The Worldly Evangelicals: Has Success Spoiled America's Born Again Christians?* (San Francisco: Harper & Row, 1978).

91. Hunter, *American Evangelicalism: Conservative Religion and the Quandary of Modernity* (New Brunswick, N.J.: Rutgers University Press, 1983).

a wholesale departure from evangelical orthodoxy? Not necessarily, says Hunter: "In substantive terms, the continuity in conservative Protestant theology in America is plainly discernible. . . . Evangelicals have, by and large, been successful at maintaining the cognitive boundaries which encompass theological orthodoxy as they have defined it." Nevertheless, "there is less sharpness, less boldness, and accordingly, a measure of opaqueness in their theological vision that did not exist in previous generations."[92] While he rejects the conclusion that evangelical theology as practiced by the coming generation is becoming more liberal, he does believe that the tradition is "conforming in its own unique way to the cognitive and normative assumptions of modern culture." The pressures of pluralism, codes of civility, and the pervasiveness of critical thought have changed the tone, if not the content, of their theology.[93]

The content of progressive evangelical theology is still well within the parameters of evangelical orthodoxy. Again, Fuller Seminary can be used as case in point. When progressives there dropped inerrancy and premillennialism from the Seminary's "Statement of Faith" in 1972, many conservatives concluded that Fuller had "gone liberal." But the revised Fuller statement remained thoroughly evangelical in its affirmation of the doctrine of the Trinity; of Christ's virgin birth, sinless life, atonement, and bodily resurrection; of justification by faith alone; and of the Bible as divinely inspired and the "only infallible rule of faith and practice."[94] Liberals, as a rule, do not maintain Nicene and Chalcedonian orthodoxy or use the Bible as the final, authoritative source for theology. Such commitments make Fuller substantially different from non-evangelical seminaries, where continuity with historic Christianity is not nearly as important. Likewise, in ecumenical discussions, evangelical progressives still set themselves apart from other ecumenical Christians by their insistence on the authority of Scripture and the need for sinners to "name the Name" of Jesus in order to be saved. So, although progressive evangelicals are criticized by conservatives for being too

92. Hunter, *Evangelicalism,* p. 46.

93. What skews Hunter's study to some degree is his baseline of comparison: one gets the impression that the "previous generations" with which he compares the "coming generation" were essentially fundamentalist evangelicals, who represent only one part of the broad evangelical tradition. Nevertheless, he is correct in showing that many evangelicals today are heading in a more progressive direction.

94. See Marsden, *Reforming Fundamentalism,* p. 268; see also the "Statement of Faith," *Fuller Theological Seminary Catalog, 1988-89,* pp. 9-10.

liberal, they are also criticized by liberals for being too conservative. Progressives are still willing to draw lines theologically.

Boundaries are less clear on behavioral matters. Hunter found that "the moral boundaries separating Christian conduct from worldly conduct have been substantially undermined," especially in the areas of smoking, drinking, dancing, and the like.[95] The least change has occurred in views toward sexual practices, though even here Hunter discovered some growing tolerance. That this is an area of disagreement can be seen in the debate among evangelical feminists over homosexuality. The Evangelical Women's Caucus International was founded in the mid-1970s to promote a feminist perspective in conservative evangelical circles. Over the years, the EWCI avoided passing resolutions at its plenary conferences, but in the 1986 meeting in Fresno, California, a group calling itself "Lesbians and Their Friends" presented a resolution recognizing the "presence of the Lesbian minority" in the organization and asked the Caucus to take "a firm stand in favor of civil rights protection for homosexual persons." At a sparsely attended business meeting, the resolution passed 80 in favor, 16 opposed, and 23 abstaining. Fearing that the resolution identified the EWCI with radical feminism and would cut off effective ministry in most evangelical churches, a number of members withdrew and formed another egalitarian organization, Christians for Biblical Equality, which is progressive theologically but still traditional on the question of homosexuality.[96] Likewise, the Fuller Seminary catalog contains a "Statement on Sexual Standards" that declares "premarital, extramarital and homosexual forms of explicit sexual conduct to be inconsistent with the teaching of Scripture" and threatens disciplinary action against any faculty member, student, or staff person who engages in such conduct.[97]

The biggest danger progressives face is that of being co-opted by the culture they are trying to save, which is pretty much what happened to liberal evangelicals in the last century.[98] To counteract this threat, a number of progressives are engaging in sophisticated cultural analysis, especially in the area of popular culture and the media, in

95. Hunter, *Evangelicalism,* p. 58.

96. See Nancy Hardesty, "Evangelical Women Face Their Homophobia," *Christian Century,* 10-17 September 1986, p. 768; and Beth Spring, "Gay Rights Resolution Divides Membership of Evangelical Women's Caucus," *Christianity Today,* 3 October 1986, pp. 40-41, 43.

97. *Fuller Theological Seminary Catalog, 1988-89,* p. 156.

98. See Martin E. Marty, *Modern American Religion,* vol. 1, *The Irony of It All, 1893-1919* (Chicago: University of Chicago Press, 1986).

order to show Christians how they can understand and resist cultural forces that they cannot easily avoid. This is a much different approach than that of the fundamentalist separatism that avoided worldly practices but often absorbed worldly values (as the recent televangelist scandals demonstrated).[99] Whether this new kind of separatism will succeed remains to be seen, but it is further evidence that progressives realize that cultural openness demands special vigilance.[100]

Will progressive evangelical scholars be able to create and sustain the kind of scholarly orthodoxy to which they aspire? Some observers believe that the theological foundation on which they build may be too thin. Bernard Ramm, one of the early reforming fundamentalists who followed the more progressive trajectory, recently declared that "*there is no genuine, valid working hypothesis for most evangelicals to interact with the humanity of Scripture in general and biblical criticism in particular.*"[101] Mark Noll has asked whether "believing criticism," which tries to combine modern scholarship and an evangelical view of the Bible, is even possible, and if evangelicals presently possess a strong enough intellectual base to support "genuine biblical scholarship."[102] To improve their standing in the academic world, evangelical biblical scholars must be "technically competent, theologically informed, and hermeneutically self-conscious. Such work will never dominate the academic marketplace, at least as higher learning is presently constituted in the West. But it will receive at last some of the recognition that it deserves there, and will do so, moreover, while enhancing its contribution to the church."[103] That is not as much as progressive evangelicals hope for or think they are capable of, but it may be a realistic assessment of present possibilities.

Can the current wave of evangelical progressives succeed where their nineteenth-century counterparts failed? Is it possible to embrace modern scholarship (and modern values) and remain evangelical in the

99. See Quentin J. Schultze, *Televangelism and American Culture: The Business of Popular Religion* (Grand Rapids: Baker Book House, 1991).

100. For examples of progressive evangelical cultural analysis, see *American Evangelicals and the Mass Media,* ed. Quentin J. Schultze (Grand Rapids: Zondervan, 1990); Kenneth A. Myers, *All God's Children and Blue Suede Shoes* (Westchester, Ill.: Crossway Books, 1989); and Quentin J. Schultze et al., *Dancing in the Dark: Youth, Popular Culture, and the Electronic Media* (Grand Rapids: William B. Eerdmans, 1991).

101. Ramm, *Beyond Fundamentalism: The Future of Evangelical Theology* (San Francisco: Harper & Row, 1983), p. 114; italics his.

102. Noll, *Between Faith and Criticism,* pp. 163, 174.

103. Noll, *Between Faith and Criticism,* pp. 184-85.

process?[104] The progressives will have to demonstrate over the long haul that they can let go of biblical inerrancy, or at least downplay its importance, without also abandoning other doctrines considered foundational to an evangelical faith. Likewise, they will have to show that they can "market" the gospel to baby boomers without destroying their own identity. Maybe most important, progressives will have to pay careful attention to the fact that the churches that most successfully adjusted to the spirit of the age at the end of the last century are today in serious decline. To survive into the next generation, progressives must be able to distinguish between adaptation and accommodation. As the Bible cautions, it is possible to gain the whole world and lose one's own soul (Matt. 16:26).

104. For a sociologist's answer, see Robert Wuthnow, *The Restructuring of American Religion: Society and Faith since World War II* (Princeton, N.J.: Princeton University Press, 1989); and Wuthnow, *The Struggle for America's Soul: Evangelicals, Liberals, and Secularism* (Grand Rapids: William B. Eerdmans, 1990).

American Fundamentalists and the Emergence of a Jewish State

YAAKOV ARIEL

IN 1982 Menachem Begin, then Israel's prime minister, presented Jerry Falwell, a leading evangelist and leader of the Moral Majority, with a medal of the Jabotinsky Order, an organization associated with Begin's Likud party. Observers both of American religion and Middle East politics could not avoid noticing the friendship that had developed between the Israeli government and conservative evangelical elements within American Protestantism. The special interest that this segment of American Protestantism had in supporting a national Jewish home in the land of Israel was noticeable from the beginnings of the fundamentalist movement and derived from the eschatological premillennial hope that has been an important component in the worldview and set of beliefs of many American fundamentalists.

The Beginnings

The eschatological hope to which millions of American fundamentalists adhere is called *dispensationalism.* This school of premillennialist expectation was crystallized in Britain in the 1830s by John Darby and the group he led, the Plymouth Brethren.[1] Dispensationalists assert that

1. On dispensationalism, see Clarence B. Bass, *Background to Dispensationalism* (Grand Rapids: William B. Eerdmans, 1960); Arnold D. Ehlert, *A Bibliographic History of Dispensationalism* (Grand Rapids: Baker Book House, 1965); Dave MacPherson, *The Incredible Cover Up: The True Story of the Pre-Trib Rapture* (Plainfield, N.J.: Omega Publications, 1975); and Timothy P. Weber, *Living In the Shadow of the Second Coming* (Grand Rapids: Zondervan, 1983).

history is divided into a number of eras, in each of which God has a different plan for humanity. The present era is the penultimate one, to be followed by the millennium, the reign of Jesus on earth for a thousand years. Dispensationalists believe that God did not leave humanity in the dark, that his plans for the present and future dispensations are recorded in the Bible and can be deduced from the sacred text.

In the dispensationalists' understanding of the course of human history, God has a different plan for three categories of human beings: the Jews, the church, and the rest of humanity. They define the church as the body of the true believers, those who have undergone an inner experience of conversion in which they accepted Jesus as their personal Savior and have taken it upon themselves to live saintly Christian lives. They alone will be saved and spared the turmoils and destruction that will precede the arrival of the Messiah. One of the particular characteristic components of dispensational premillennialism has been the belief in the secret, any-moment rapture of the church. The arrival of Jesus, according to this scheme, will take place in two stages. First Jesus will come for his saints. The true believers will be raptured from earth and meet Jesus in the air. Those believers who died prior to the rapture will rise from the dead and be raptured from earth together with all the other true believers. These saintly persons will remain with Jesus in the air for seven years and thus be spared the turmoils and miseries that will be inflicted on those who remain on earth in those years. For the latter this period will be marked by natural disasters — earthquakes, floods, and famine — as well as wars and murderous dictatorial regimes. By the time Jesus returns, about two thirds of humanity will have perished.[2]

For the Jews, this period will be known as "the time of Jacob's trouble." The Jews will return to their ancient homeland "in unbelief," without accepting Jesus as their Savior, and establish a political commonwealth there. This will not be the millennial Davidic kingdom by any means, but merely a necessary development in the advancement of the messianic timetable. The Jews, living in spiritual blindness, will let themselves be ruled by Antichrist, an impostor posing as the Messiah who will be worshiped as God. Antichrist will inflict a reign of terror in the course of which many true believers will be martyred.

The arrival of Jesus and the true believers will end Antichrist's rule. Jesus will crush this Satanic ruler and his armies and will establish

2. For details of this eschatological hope see, for example, Hal Lindsey's dispensationalist best-seller *The Late Great Planet Earth* (Grand Rapids: Zondervan, 1971).

the millennial kingdom. Those Jews who survive the turmoils and terror of the Great Tribulation will then accept Jesus as their Savior. There will follow a period marked by the righteous rule of Christ on earth in which all nations will live in their lands. The Jews will inhabit David's ancient kingdom, and Jerusalem will serve as the capital of the entire world. They will become Jesus' right-hand people, assisting him in administering the earth. In addition, they will function as evangelists of the millennial kingdom, strengthening the knowledge of God among the nations of the earth.

This new view of prophecy and Israel's role in history gained ground among American evangelicals in the decades following the Civil War. Conservative members of major denominations that were shaped by nineteenth-century revivalism, such as Baptists, Presbyterians, Methodists, Congregationalists, and Disciples of Christ, accepted the new messianic hope. The premillennialist belief in the Second Coming of Christ in its dispensationalist form became a major component of the emerging fundamentalist movement that developed among American evangelical Protestants in those years.

Fundamentalists objected to many of the developments that had taken place within American culture and religion. In particular they reacted negatively to the rise of a new "modernist" trend within American Protestantism and to the willingness of Protestants of evangelical background to accept what they, the fundamentalists, saw as dangerous and destructive teachings such as the higher criticism of the Bible.[3] In reaction to the new trends, these conservative Protestants began to emphasize what they considered to be the major fundamental components of their religious tradition. Central among them were the insistence on the inerrancy and authority of the Bible, the need to undergo a personal experience of conversion in order to be saved, and, in many cases, the expected arrival of the Messiah and his reign on earth for a thousand years. Premillennialism became, to a large degree, the philosophy of history for this group. It reflected their interpretation of the world's situation as well as their understanding of their position as the faithful remnant within an apostate culture. To this day it has served to reassure them that they know the course of history and that whatever social, economic, political, or environmental developments take place, they will certainly survive the turmoils.

Since the end of the nineteenth century, most American evan-

3. See George Marsden, *Fundamentalism and American Culture* (New York: Oxford University Press, 1982).

gelists have adopted the premillennialist hope and promoted it in their sermons. It has become part and parcel of the evangelist's message. Millions of Americans have thus adopted a belief in the centrality of the Jewish people in God's plans for humanity as part of a larger worldview. Evangelists often sell their audience a package of beliefs which includes the conviction that one must undergo a conversion experience in order to be saved, an understanding of the Bible as inerrant and authoritative, a premillennialist critique of civilization and understanding of history, and a messianic hope in the imminent establishment of the kingdom of God on earth. Premillennialist views of the role of the Jewish people in God's plans for humanity are essentially connected with the fundamentalists' claim to read the Bible literally and to deduce God's plans for the present and future dispensations from the Bible.

There had been messianic movements in American history that attracted the loyalties of thousands of supporters even before the rise of dispensationalism. The largest of these movements was probably that headed by William Miller in the 1830s and early 1840s.[4] But there is a striking difference between Miller and his disciples and other similar messianic movements on the one hand and groups associated with the new dispensationalist belief on the other. The Millerites and groups like them were ostracized by mainline Protestants and found themselves outside the American religious canon. With the rise of dispensationalism, however, a messianic belief was favorably received within major Protestant denominations and established a durable influence on the heart and center of American society. Over time the dispensationalist conviction came to be associated almost exclusively with members of a well-defined camp within American conservative evangelical Christianity. Although this group has stood in opposition to major trends in American culture and at times aroused suspicion and rejection in progressive circles, it can by no means be viewed as a marginal religious sect. In the 1970s and 1980s it proved itself to be one of the largest and most influential groups within American culture, with direct influence on major national leaders.

The premillennialist view of the Jewish people and their role in history evoked a new interest in the fate of the Jews and the prospect of their restoration to Palestine. The 1880s and 1890s saw an emergence

4. On William Miller and the messianic movement he led, see Leon Festinger, *When Prophecy Fails* (Minneapolis: University of Minnesota Press, 1956); and *The Disappointed,* ed. Ronald L. Numbers and Jonathan M. Butler (Bloomington, Ind.: Indiana University Press, 1987).

of an aggressive evangelical movement in America to spread the gospel among the Jews, one that gave rise in later years to "messianic Judaism," a movement of Jews who embraced Christianity but wished at the same time to retain their Jewish identity. Another manifestation of the new interest American evangelicals began showing in the Jewish people was a series of initiatives directed toward the national restoration of the Jews in Palestine.

One such outstanding initiative was that of William Blackstone in 1891. A lay Methodist, Blackstone was converted to the dispensationalist belief in the imminent Second Coming of Christ while a successful businessman in Chicago in the 1870s. He decided to dedicate himself to evangelism and to the propagation of the premillennialist belief. His first book, *Jesus Is Coming,* became a premillennialist best-seller; it was translated into forty-two languages and enjoyed a circulation of over a million and a half copies. In this book as in others, Blackstone emphasized the centrality of the Jewish people in the events associated with the End of the Age and the expected kingdom. In 1889 Blackstone visited Palestine, where he was deeply impressed by the developments that the first wave of Zionist immigration had brought about in a country he had considered to be a desolated land. He viewed the agricultural settlements, the new neighborhoods in Jerusalem, and the economic developments connected with it as "signs of the time" indicating that an era was ending and the great events of the end of the age were to occur very soon.[5]

After returning from the Holy Land, Blackstone decided to take a more active line in his approach to Jewish national restoration. In 1891 he organized a petition urging the president of the United States to convene an international conference of the world powers aimed at giving Palestine back to the Jews. More than four hundred eminent Americans signed Blackstone's petition — congressmen, governors, mayors, publishers and editors of leading newspapers, prominent clergymen, and notable businessmen. The petition reflected the warm support that the idea of the Jewish restoration to Palestine could receive among the American public, but it had little effect in causing the American government to take any meaningful action regarding its request.[6]

Blackstone continued for many years in his attempts to persuade the American government to help restore the Jews to their ancient

5. See Blackstone, *Jesus Is Coming,* 3d ed. (Los Angeles: Bible House, 1908), pp. 211-13, 236-41.

6. See Yaakov Ariel, "An American Initiative for a Jewish State: William Blackstone and the Petition of 1891," *Studies in Zionism* 10 (1989): 125-37.

homeland. He devised a theory that has been a cornerstone of the American premillennialist attitude toward Zionism ever since. The premillennialist leader asserted that the United States had a special role and mission in God's plans for humanity, that of a modern Cyrus: to help restore the Jews to Zion. God chose America for that mission on account of its moral superiority over other nations, and America would be judged according to the way it carried out its mission. This theory enabled fundamentalists to combine their messianic belief and understanding of the course of human history with their sense of American patriotism. Although they criticized the course American culture was taking and were far from happy with many of the developments that had taken place in American civilization, they remained loyal citizens of the American commonwealth. In this way they were significantly different from other American religious groups that held intense messianic beliefs, such as the Jehovah's Witnesses, which defined themselves at least in part in terms of opposition to American culture.

One of Blackstone's successes lay in getting major church bodies such as the Presbyterian Church, U.S.A., to endorse his plan for an American initiative that would bring about the establishment of a Jewish state in Palestine. In 1916, Blackstone organized a second petition calling upon the president of the United States to help restore Palestine to the Jews. This time his efforts were coordinated with those of the American Zionist leadership. Leaders of American Zionism such as Louis Brandeis, Steven Wise, and Jacob de Haas saw Blackstone's efforts as beneficial to the Zionist cause and maintained a warm relationship with him, encouraging him to pursue his cause. Blackstone did not keep his premillennialist motivations secret from his Zionist friends. He sent them his published works and expressed his opinions in correspondence with them as well. It might be that this group of Jewish leaders was unaware of the actual scope of Blackstone's involvement with attempts to evangelize the Jews. In any event, they were certainly not bothered by his prediction that great turmoils were awaiting the Jews in the events of the end of the age or his belief that the Jews would accept Jesus as their Messiah when he arrived to crush Antichrist and establish his kingdom. These Zionist leaders did not take the premillennialist doctrine seriously; they dismissed it as an eccentric conviction and focused instead on the support it might provide for Zionist aspirations.[7] Such an attitude

7. See Yaakov Ariel, "William Blackstone and the Petition of 1916: A Neglected Chapter in the History of Christian Zionism in America," *Studies in Contemporary Jewry* 7 (1991): 68-85.

characterized both the Zionist and, later on, the Israeli reaction to the fundamentalist support.

The events of World War I, with its unprecedented killing and destruction, filled American premillennialists with apocalyptic thoughts; they were convinced that the war was part of the events of the end of the age. They interpreted the Balfour Declaration and the British takeover of Palestine as further indications that the ground was being prepared for the arrival of the Lord. Their joy over these developments dominated two "prophetic conferences" that took place in Philadelphia and New York in 1918.[8]

Fundamentalist Attitudes toward Jews, Judaism, and Zionism

Premillennialists have viewed modern Jews as the historical Israel, God's chosen people, the subjects of the biblical prophecies about a restored Davidic kingdom in the land of Israel, and hence they believe that these Jews are destined for a glorious future in the millennial kingdom. There has been a tendency among premillennialists to see themselves as friends of the Jews; they often refer to themselves, in fact, as "Christian Zionists." This group of conservative Protestants has often expressed vocal opposition to the harassment of Jews and expressed sorrow at the unhappy record of the Christian treatment of the Jews throughout history. As far as fundamentalists are concerned, their interest in and affection for the Jews have been best manifested in the realm of missions. Their "witnessing" to the Jews has, from their point of view, been an expression of their goodwill and love for that people.

But these are not the only feelings fundamentalists have had for the Jews. Many of them have expressed frustration and anger concerning the Jews' refusal to accept Jesus as their Savior. Blackstone, the ardent Christian Zionist, expressed the opinion that that tragic mistake had brought upon the Jews "centuries of sorrow." It was because of the Jewish refusal to recognize the messiahship of Jesus, he complained, that the kingdom of God on earth did not materialize when Jesus appeared for

8. See Arno C. Gaebelein, "The Capture of Jerusalem and the Great Future of That City," in *Christ and Glory: Addresses Delivered at the New York Prophetic Conferences, Carnegie Hall, November 25-28, 1918*, ed. Arno C. Gaebelein (New York: Our Hope, 1919); and Albert E. Thompson, "The Capture of Jerusalem," in *Light on Prophecy: A Coordinated, Constructive Teaching, Being the Proceedings and Addresses at the Philadelphia Prophetic Conference, May 28-30, 1918*, ed. William L. Pettingill, J. R. Schafter, and J. D. Adams (New York: Christian Herald Bible House, 1918).

the first time.[9] With all their appreciation for the Jewish role in history, many fundamentalists shared traditional prejudices against the Jews.

One can find in the sermons and writings of many leading evangelists, for example, remarks about Jews that refer to them as shrewd businessmen.[10] The traditional, Orthodox Jewish way, they asserted, was that of "judicial blindness." Observing the Law had become completely futile after Jesus' sacrifice on the cross and could not bring observant Jews salvation. Nevertheless, as long as Jews kept to their old beliefs and ways and waited for the Messiah, they were ready to fulfill their heroic role in the millennial age. Reform or secular Jews, on the other hand, had turned their backs on their historical mission.[11] Fundamentalists maintained the stereotypical view of Jews as disproportionately active in various movements of social and political unrest, which in their eyes aimed to undermine Christian civilization.[12]

It was therefore not very surprising that a sociological survey sponsored by the B'nai B'rith Anti-Defamation League in the early 1960s concluded that members of conservative evangelical churches were more likely to hold prejudices against Jews than members of mainline and liberal churches.[13] A similar survey done in the mid-1980s came out with more positive results,[14] no doubt a result of intensified preaching among evangelicals since 1967 on the positive role of Jews in history and the fact that they have come to know more about Jewish people generally.

Although fundamentalists view the Jews as a category of people in God's plans for humanity with a decisive role to play in the millennial events, they have been engaged in aggressive missionary work among the Jews. Their interest in evangelizing the Jews is connected to their messianic hopes, and is based on the assumption that the majority of the Jewish people will remain unconverted despite their efforts until the arrival of the Lord. They have interpreted the conversion of some Jews

9. Blackstone, *Jesus Is Coming,* p. 84.

10. In one of his sermons, Jerry Falwell exclaimed that "A few of you here today don't like the Jews. And I know why. He can make more money accidentally than you can on purpose" (Falwell, quoted by Flo Conway and Jim Siegelman in *Holy Terror* [Garden City, N.Y.: Doubleday, 1982], p. 168).

11. See Arno C. Gaebelein, *The Conflict of the Ages* (New York: Our Hope, 1933), p. 147.

12. See, e.g., Arno C. Gaebelein, "Aspects of Jewish Power in the United States," *Our Hope* 29 (1922): 103.

13. Charles Y. Glock and Rodney Stark, *Christian Beliefs and Anti-Semitism* (New York: Harper Torchbooks, 1966).

14. L. Ianniello, press release by the Anti-Defamation League, New York, 8 January 1986.

in each generation as a sign that all Jews will eventually recognize their true Messiah. In the premillennialist understanding, converted Jews join the body of the true believers that will be spared the miseries of "the time of Jacob's troubles." Bringing the gospel to individual Jews is therefore an act of charity toward them. In addition, spreading the Christian message in its premillennialist interpretation has been viewed as a mission in and of itself. In the dispensationalist eschatological scheme, 144,000 Jews (12,000 from each tribe) will adopt the Christian belief when the rapture takes place and will serve as evangelists to their brethren.[15] These people will recognize that the dramatic events occurring before their eyes correlate with the Christian prophecies to which they had been exposed. It is considered essential, therefore, to spread the knowledge of Christ among the Jews, even if only a few of them accept him in this age. The amount of manpower and resources that the fundamentalist community has been willing to dedicate to the evangelization of the Jews provided an indication of its interest in, and compassion for, that people. Jews have, of course, seen the matter differently. They see the attempts at proselytization as a threat to their national survival. They have felt the old fears and resentments of a minority religious community resisting attempts to make it dissolve into the faith of the majority.

Despite their enthusiasm for the rise of the Zionist movement and for the settlement of Jews in Palestine, fundamentalists have resented the secular character of that movement. They have complained that the Zionists have been unaware of the true role and significance of their mission. Although Zionism has proved a blessed tool for carrying out God's plans, it has also, in terms of the perceptions and motivation of its participants, been a vainglorious attempt on the part of Jews to solve "the Jewish problem" without accepting Christ. Such a secular attempt is, of course, bound to fail. Jews will attain their physical and national security, say the dispensationalists, only when they are ready to recognize their Savior.[16]

Between the Wars

It was many years before Blackstone's attempts to advance the Zionist cause were actively pursued by his fellow premillennialists. Still,

15. Joseph A. Seiss, "Who Are the 144,000?" *The Glory of Israel* (1903): 10.

16. See William E. Blackstone, *The Heart of the Jewish Problem* (Chicago: Chicago Hebrew Mission, 1905).

American fundamentalists maintained a profound interest in the events that were taking place in the life of the Jewish people, and especially in the development of the Jewish community in Palestine. They interpreted many of the struggles and turmoils that befell the Jewish nation in the period between the two world wars in light of their own eschatological beliefs. Leading fundamentalist journals with strong premillennialist leanings, such as *Our Hope, The King's Business, The Moody Monthly,* and the Pentecostal *Evangel,* regularly published news on developments that took place in the life of the Jewish people, the Zionist movement, and the Jewish community in Palestine. Fundamentalists were encouraged by the wave of Zionist immigration to Palestine in the early years of the British administration of the country, and events such as the opening of the Hebrew University in 1925 and the new seaport in Haifa in 1932 were publicized in their periodicals. Fundamentalists interpreted these developments as signs that the Jews were energetically building a commonwealth in their ancient land and that the great events of the end of the age were to occur very soon.[17] Excited by hopes of the Second Coming, they lashed out at the British for putting restrictions on Jewish immigration and settlement and criticized the Arabs for their hostility toward the Zionist endeavor and for their violence against the Jews. Trying to block the building of a Jewish commonwealth in Palestine was seen as equivalent to putting obstacles in the way of God's plans for the end of the age. Such attempts, they asserted, were futile, and the Arabs would pay dearly for their rebellious attempts.[18]

But despite all their resentment of British policy, American fundamentalists did not press their protest beyond the pages of their own journals. They did not mount any organized effort to combat the British policy regarding Palestine, such as petitioning the British government to open Palestine to large-scale Jewish immigration or appealing to the government of the United States to intervene with the British government to change its policy. One explanation for this reticence may have been the fact that, in general during that period, fundamentalists were not very active politically as a group. After the Scopes trial in 1925, they withdrew, to a large degree, from the public arena. Fundamentalist

17. See, e.g., George T. B. Davis, *Fulfilled Prophecies That Prove the Bible* (Philadelphia: Million Testaments Campaign, 1931); and Keith L. Brooks, *The Jews and the Passion for Palestine in Light of Prophecy* (Los Angeles: Brooks Publications, 1937).

18. James Gray, "Editorial," *Moody Bible Institute Monthly* 31 (1931): 346.

leaders did not see themselves as influential national figures whose voices might be heard by the policymakers in Washington or as people who could advance a political agenda on the national or international levels. And this self-perception did not change until the 1970s.

There were some American Protestant leaders in the 1930s and 1940s who organized to express their pro-Zionist sentiments and to help advance the cause of the Jewish national home in Palestine. In 1932, for example, the Pro-Palestine Federation was founded, and in 1942 the Christian Council on Palestine. Remarkably, it was mainline and liberal Protestants who led these Protestant pro-Zionist organizations. Although liberal Protestantism in general could not be described as supportive in those years of the idea of a Jewish state,[19] thousands of Protestant clergymen did join these organizations, including some prominent liberal Protestant leaders and such outstanding progressive thinkers as Reinhold Niebuhr and Paul Tillich. These organizations voiced their opinion and were active throughout the international debates that accompanied the establishment of the state of Israel in 1948. But there was no pro-Zionist fundamentalist organization of similar character created during that period.

The passivity that characterized the fundamentalist attitude toward major developments in the life of the Jewish people is exemplified by their reaction to the fate of the Jews under the Nazis. The fundamentalist journal *Our Hope* was among the first to alert its readers to the devastating scope of the destruction of European Jewry.[20] Arno C. Gaebelein, the journal's editor, expressed his horror at the German regime's treatment of the Jews. He viewed the Nazis' position vis-à-vis Jews as a rebellion against God and predicted the downfall of their regime. Gaebelein, like some other American premillennialists, took particular offense at Nazi attempts to change basic Christian concepts, as in the "Aryanization" of Jesus.[21] For fundamentalists like Gaebelein who saw themselves as biblical literalists, the Nazis' innovations in the realm of Christianity as well as their secular "pagan" ideology in general were indications of the anti-Christian and diabolical nature of their regime. But for all their anger at the Nazis and their sympathy for the persecuted Jews, they did not organize to fight the Nazi policy. Their

19. See Herzl Fishman, *American Protestantism and a Jewish State* (Detroit: Wayne State University Press, 1973).

20. See David Rausch, "*Our Hope:* An American Fundamentalist Journal and the Holocaust, 1937-1945," *Fides et Historia* 12 (1980): 89-103.

21. See, e.g., *Our Hope* 44 (1938): 686.

sympathetic reaction to the plight of the Jews manifested itself mostly on the pages of their journals. One exception was an organization, some of whose active members were conservative Protestants, that was established to help with the absorption of Jewish refugees from Europe in America.

The fundamentalist interest in the Jewish people and their actual involvement in the life of that nation found its expression in that period mostly in the realm of missions. The missionary activity among the Jews continued in the period from the 1920s to the 1940s with great vigor. The evangelical agencies were the main expression during that period of the particular interest fundamentalists took in the Jews and their willingness to invest their hopes, energy, and financial resources in trying to convert them.

A few American premillennialists visited Palestine during the period from the 1920s to the 1940s and thus had an opportunity to watch closely the developments among the Jewish community there. They sent home enthusiastic reports of the scenes they saw. The immigration of tens of thousands of Jews to the country; the building of new neighborhoods, towns, and villages; the cultivation of hundreds of thousands of acres of land; the establishment of cultural and educational enterprises; and the rejuvenation of the Hebrew language — all these things filled fundamentalists with excitement.[22] These, they believed, were "signs of the time," indications that the current era was ending and the arrival of the Messiah was imminent.

Fundamentalists criticized the secular character of the Zionist movement. They were disappointed that the Jews were unaware of the real significance of their national restoration in Palestine. But their immediate reaction to the Zionist endeavor was enthusiastic and warm. Some of their reports on the developments in Palestine are reminiscent of those of American Jewish supporters of the Zionist cause of that period, such as articles in the publications of the Hadassah women's organization.

The years between the two world wars saw a rise in overt anti-Semitism in America, and fundamentalists varied in their reactions to the phenomenon. There were leading figures in the fundamentalist camp who voiced opposition to anti-Semitism and denounced harassment of Jews. They denied, for example, the truthfulness of both traditional blood libels and of the accusation that the Jews were conspiring

22. See George T. B. Davis, *Rebuilding Palestine according to Prophecy* (Philadelphia: Million Testaments Campaign, 1935).

to take over the entire world, as suggested in the *Protocols of the Elders of Zion*. There were others who were more open to anti-Jewish sentiments. Although no openly anti-Semitic movement arose within the ranks of core premillennial fundamentalists, there were nonetheless a few fundamentalist activists who openly adopted a socially and politically exclusivist white Protestant "nativist" stand during the 1920s and 1930s. Some of these persons, such as Gerald L. K. Smith, labored on the margins of fundamentalism.[23] Others, such as Gerald Winrod, founder and head of the Defenders of the Christian Faith, received more widespread recognition in fundamentalist circles.[24] Charles Fuller, one of the leading evangelists in America from the 1920s to the 1940s who adhered to the premillennialist hope, participated in the activities of Winrod's organization.[25]

Many central leaders in the fundamentalist-premillennialist camp had mixed and complicated reactions to anti-Semitism. Such fundamentalist activists and scholars as Arno C. Gaebelein, William B. Riley, and James Gray reaffirmed in their writings the centrality of the Jewish people in God's plans for humanity and the glorified future that awaited that people in the messianic age. Gaebelein, for one, raised his voice against harassment of Jews around the world and militated against such old-time accusations as the blood libel. At the same time, these men accepted the *Protocols of the Elders of Zion* as authentic.[26] They saw secular, "modern" Jews as fallen people who had let themselves be deluded by all types of distorted teachings and ideologies. As these Jews abandoned traditional, Orthodox Judaism, which at least had kept them prepared for their heroic tasks in history, and did not in turn accept Christianity, they were left with no moral guidelines. They had let themselves become instruments of Satan. Moreover, Gaebelein and others in the fundamentalist camp associated secular Jews with various social and political movements that aimed to undermine Christian civilization.

23. On Smith and his activity, see Glen Jeansonne, *Gerald L. K. Smith: Minister of Hate* (New Haven: Yale University Press, 1988).

24. See Ralph L. Roy, *Apostles of Discord* (Boston: Beacon Press, 1953).

25. See George L. Marsden, *Reforming Fundamentalism: Fuller Seminary and the New Evangelicalism* (Grand Rapids: William B. Eerdmans, 1987), p. 39.

26. See Arno C. Gaebelein, "Jewish Leadership in Russia," *Our Hope* 27 (1921): 734-35; James M. Gray, "The Jewish Protocols," *Moody Bible Institute Monthly* 22 (1921): 589; and William B. Riley, *Wanted — A World Leader!* (Self-published, n.d.), pp. 41-51, 71-72.

The Birth of the Jewish State

The fundamentalist response to the establishment of the state of Israel in 1948 was one of passive support. Fundamentalist journals had published sympathetic articles about the Zionist struggle for a Jewish state, and some American statesmen with conservative evangelical leanings had supported the Zionist cause in the political and diplomatic struggles that preceded the birth of Israel,[27] but no particular pro-Zionist evangelical lobby developed, and fundamentalists as a group did not raise their voice in favor of the Zionist political cause. In the late 1940s conservative evangelicalism was beginning to recover its prestige in the American public arena. One example of this was the successful career of Billy Graham, who got his start in those years. But this segment of American Protestantism was not yet actively organized on the national level around its particular causes.

After the birth of Israel, American premillennialists observed the young Jewish state with great interest in an attempt to interpret its significance for the advancement of God's plans and purpose in the ages. While they were not enthusiastic about the secular character of Israeli government and society, some of the things they saw filled them with enthusiasm and enhanced their messianic hopes.[28] The mass emigration of Jews to Israel in the 1950s from Asian, African, and East European countries was one cause for encouragement. This was undoubtedly a significant development, one that had been prophesied in the Bible, and a clear indication that the present era was terminating and the events of the end of the age were beginning to occur.

Contrary to the perceived view, fundamentalists did take notice and show concern over the fate of hundreds of thousands of Palestinian Arabs who lost their homes in 1948 and became refugees in Arab lands. Although American premillennialists criticized the Arab hostility against Israel and supported the Israeli state in its struggles with its Arab neighbors, they also stressed the belief that the land of Israel could maintain an Arab population alongside its Jewish population and that

27. See Dwight Wilson, *Armageddon Now! The Premillenarian Response to Russia and Israel since 1917* (Grand Rapids: Baker Book House, 1977).

28. See Louis T. Talbot and William W. Orr, *The New Nation of Israel and the Word of God* (Los Angeles: Bible Institute of Los Angeles, 1948); M. R. DeHaan, *The Jew and Palestine in Prophecy* (Grand Rapids: Zondervan, 1950); William L. Hull, *The Fall and Rise of Israel* (Grand Rapids: Zondervan, 1954); Arthur Kac, *The Rebirth of the State of Israel: Is It of God or of Men?* (Chicago: Moody Press, 1958); and George T. B. Davis, *God's Guiding Hand* (Philadelphia: Million Testaments Campaign, 1962).

Israel had an obligation to respect human rights and treat the Arabs with fairness. One such fundamentalist was John Walvoord, president of the Dallas Theological Seminary, an ardent premillennialist supporter of Israel.[29] A few conservative evangelical churches, such as the Southern Baptists, the Christian and Missionary Alliance, the Assemblies of God, and the Plymouth Brethren, have worked among Palestinian Arabs for years. In striving to reconcile premillennialist teachings with the hopes and fears of Arab congregants and potential converts, they strongly emphasized that the ingathering of the Jews in the land of Israel and the eventual reestablishment of the Davidic kingdom would not necessitate the banishment of Arabs from that land. Ironically, premillennialists accepted, in some ways, Martin Buber's ideal of "a land for two people."

The fledgling Israeli government was not aware of the special attitudes of the conservative evangelical elements within American Christianity toward the new state. Israeli officials could not tell the difference between its mainline supporters and its conservative evangelical supporters. They did not grasp the roots and motivations of "Christian Zionists."[30] They were certainly unaware of the details of the dispensationalist eschatological hopes and had never heard of such terms as "the Great Tribulation" and "the time of Jacob's trouble." David Ben-Gurion, Israel's first prime minister, believed that Christian supporters viewed the establishment of the state of Israel as the ultimate fulfillment of biblical prophecies, the reestablishment of the Davidic kingdom, rather than simply a step toward the realization of the millennial kingdom. When he gave expression to his views when addressing an international Pentecostal conference in Israel in 1961,[31] the Israeli officials that sat at the opening session were puzzled by the coolness of the Pentecostal reaction to the prime minister's speech. They certainly were not aware that messianic hopes encouraged not only support for Zionism and for Israel but also aggressive missionary activity among the Jews. When Oral Roberts visited Israel in 1959, Ben-Gurion

29. See Walvoord, *Israel In Prophecy* (Grand Rapids: Zondervan, 1962), p. 19.

30. A striking example of this failure to understand can be found in Michael Pragai's book *Faith and Fulfillment* (London: Valentine Mitchell, 1985). The author, who served as the head of the department for liaison with the Christian churches and organizations in the Israeli Foreign Office for many years, demonstrates a complete lack of knowledge of the nature of the fundamentalist support of Zionism and of the differences between fundamentalist and mainline/liberal churches.

31. Yona Malachy, *American Fundamentalism and Israel* (Jerusalem: Institute of Contemporary Jewry, 1978), 106-11.

granted him an audience.[32] The Israeli leader demonstrated a knowledge of the nature of Roberts's activity as an evangelist, but it could well be that he was unaware of Roberts's missionary work among the Jews. At any rate, secular Israeli leaders were not particularly bothered by the Christian missionary activities. Their view of such activities was often cynical — they were not to be taken seriously and were, in any event, doomed to futility.[33] Any conversions to Christianity that did take place were attributed to socio-economic motivations, and it was assumed that spiritual persuasion had little to do with it.

The Israeli government tried to build good relations with Christian groups and considered it essential to assure them that the government would not interfere with their work. The evangelical missions continued their operations in Israel without interruption. Evangelical missionaries were more than mere proselytizers of Jews; they often publicized Israel and its problems in evangelical circles, writing books, sending articles to journals back home, broadcasting on evangelical radio stations, or giving lecture tours.[34] The Orthodox parties and other activists protested against the missionaries' work in Israel, and some Orthodox Jews occasionally attempted to harass missions, but the government refused to change its policy, and the police were given the task of preventing interference with missionary work.[35]

The Six-Day War and Beyond

The Six-Day War had a dramatic effect on American fundamentalist attitudes toward Israel. In fact, it probably had a stronger effect on the historical perceptions of American fundamentalists than did the birth of Israel in 1948. Since the French Revolution and the Napoleonic wars in the late eighteenth and early nineteenth centuries, there has probably not been a political-military event that has provided so much fuel for the engine of prophecy as the short dramatic war between Israel and its neighbors in June 1967, a war that led to the Jews taking over the historical sites of Jerusalem. The dramatic and unexpected Israeli

32. For Roberts's perspective on the visit, see "The Spell of Israel over Me," *Abundant Life,* July 1959; and David E. Harrell, *Oral Roberts: An American Life* (Bloomington, Ind.: Indiana University Press, 1985), p. 137.

33. See, e.g., David Eichhorn, *Evangelizing the American Jew* (New York: Jonathan David, 1978).

34. See, e.g., Robert L. Lindsey, *Israel in Christendom* (Tel Aviv: Dugit, 1961).

35. Per Österlye, *The Church in Israel* (Lund: Gleerup, 1970).

victory, and the territorial gains it brought with it, strengthened the premillennialists' conviction that Israel was created for an important mission in history and was to play an important role in the process that would precede the arrival of the Messiah.[36]

After the war it became clear to those waiting for the Second Coming that Israel now held the territory on which to rebuild the Temple and reinstate the priestly sacrificial rituals.[37] Many premillennialists expected the imminent building of the Temple as part of the events of the end of the age. One such person who decided to give God a hand was Dennis Rohan, a young Australian who had joined the Church of God and become an ardent premillennialist. After spending some time as a volunteer in an Israeli kibbutz, Rohan visited Jerusalem in July 1969 and there, convinced that God had designated him for that task, planned and executed the burning of the El-Aksa Mosque on the Temple Mount, in an attempt to secure the necessary ground for the building of the Temple. The mosque was damaged, Arabs rioted, Rohan was arrested, put to trial, found insane, and sent to Australia to spend the rest of his life in an asylum.[38] Many premillennialists learned their lesson; an open promotion of the idea that the Jews should begin building the Temple would provoke Arab hostility, embarrass the state of Israel, and hurt the fundamentalist image. Although many American fundamentalists were happy to discover that Jewish groups such as Ateret Cohanim were preparing themselves for the operation of the rebuilt Temple's ritual works and sacrifices, most of them refrained from openly working for the construction of that holy site. But not all. A few organizations and groups in the 1970s and 1980s openly advocated the building of the holy Jewish shrine. A few conservative evangelical individuals and institutions have kept close contact, for example, with the Jerusalem-based Temple Mount Foundation. Chuck Smith, a noted minister and evangelist whose Calvary Chapel in Costa Mesa, California, is one of the largest and most dynamic evangelical churches in America, invited Stanley Goldfoot, the founder and head of the Temple Mount Foundation, to come to California and lecture in his church. He also secured financial support for exploration of the exact site of the Temple.

36. See, e.g., L. Nelson Bell, "Unfolding Destiny," *Christianity Today* 9 (1967): 1044-45.

37. Raymond L. Cox, "Time for the Temple?" *Eternity* 19 (January 1968), 17-18; Malcolm Couch, "When Will the Jews Rebuild the Temple?" *Moody Monthly* 74 (December 1973): 34-35, 86.

38. Jerusalem District Court Archive, Criminal File 69/173, pp. 503, 1206.

One of the noted explorers of the Temple Mount has been Lambert Dolphin, a Californian physicist and leader of the "Science and Archeology Team." Using sophisticated technological devices and methods, they concluded that the Temple's real location had been between the two major Moslem shrines, El-Aksa and the Dome of the Rock, and that it could be rebuilt without destroying them, thus providing a "peaceful solution" to the problem of how to build the Temple at a site that is holy to the Moslems.[39]

Arab hostility toward Israel and a perception that the Moslems were standing in the way of the rebuilding of the Temple certainly did not add to a more positive fundamentalist attitude toward Islam. Fundamentalists have not taken the liberal road of interfaith dialogue, and they have often regarded Islam as a a superstitious apostate faith.[40] As the trend toward liberalization in the Soviet Union and Eastern Europe progressed from 1987 to 1990, providing new freedoms for the churches, some fundamentalists began to question whether Russia was in fact the northern evil empire of which the prophecies spoke. In 1990 and 1991 some fundamentalists began to suggest that perhaps Saddam Hussein and Iraq were meant to fulfill that function.[41]

During the 1970s and 1980s Arab and pro-Arab antagonists of Israel have taken notice of, and tried to counter, the fundamentalist support of Israel. Among other things, they have warned against what they consider to be the potential dangers of the fundamentalist attitude. Some of them asserted that American fundamentalists could be expected to endorse any request of Israel for military and economic support and that in case of a conflict between America and Israel, they would stand by Israel.[42]

In the 1970s and 1980s, fundamentalists were counted among Israel's most ardent supporters in the American public arena and often

39. See Yisrayl Hawkins, *A Peaceful Solution to Building the Next Temple in Yerusalem* (Abilene: House of Yahweh, 1989).

40. Such attitudes toward Islam are evident in the sermons and writings of J. Willem van der Hoeven, founder-head of the International Christian Embassy, among others. See, e.g., Van der Hoeven's sermon "Jerusalem: The Christian Embassy, 1990," audiotape, 22 August 1990. See also Peter A. Michas, *What Is Islam?* (Poway, Calif.: Christian Mid-East Conference, n.d.).

41. See John Elson, "Apocalypse Now?" *Time,* 11 February 1991, p. 64.

42. See, e.g., Davey M. Beegle, *Prophecy and Prediction* (Ann Arbor: Pryor Pettengill, 1978); *All in the Name of the Bible,* ed. Hassan Haddad and Donald Wagner (Chicago: PHRC, 1985); and Grace Halsell, *Prophecy and Politics: Militant Evangelicals on Road to Nuclear War* (Westport, Conn.: Lawrence Hill, 1986).

voiced their approval of American political and economic support for Israel.[43] They have also involved themselves in such Jewish issues as the demand to facilitate Jewish immigration from Russia.

The period following the Six-Day War was marked by massive American support for Israel in terms of money, arms, and diplomatic backing. Many fundamentalists saw support for Israel as going hand in hand with American interests. Their pro-Israeli stand was, from their point of view, an expression of love and concern for the Jews and an appreciation of the importance of the state of Israel in the advancement of the ages. It was, at the same time, a fulfillment of one of America's major goals in history and an advancement of America's immediate interests. But their support for Israel is not unconditional. When they see a conflict between such support and American self-interest, they are more reluctant to endorse Israeli requests. For example, when the American government decided to sell sophisticated AWACS intelligence planes to Saudi Arabia in 1981, the Israeli lobby in Washington attempted to block the deal. Stalwart evangelical supporters of Israel accepted the position of the American government that the sale would not undermine Israel's security and that it was essential for maintaining good relationships with Saudi Arabia.

The years following the 1967 Middle East war saw a dramatic rise in the fundamentalists' position in America. Growing in numbers and self-confidence, they have become more visible and aggressive. In the stormy 1960s, many Americans viewed fundamentalist churches as anachronistic, marginal, and irrelevant to the general cultural trends. In 1976, when Jimmy Carter was elected president, they discovered in surprise not only that evangelicalism was alive and well but that as a matter of fact it had grown in numbers and influence. Carter, however, was a disappointment to fundamentalists. He was not a premillennialist and did not promote specific evangelical issues, and although he took an interest in the Middle East and brought Egypt and Israel together to sign a peace treaty, the role he filled was that of an American statesman rather than that of an evangelical Christian. The messianic hope of paving the way for the Davidic kingdom was not his concern.

Was Ronald Reagan influenced in his Middle East policy by the premillennialist understanding of the course of history? Reagan made

43. See, e.g., Peter L. Williams and Peter L. Benson, *Religion on Capitol Hill: Myth and Realities* (New York: Oxford University Press, 1986); Allen D. Hertzke, *Representing God in Washington* (Knoxville: University of Tennessee Press, 1988); and Mark Silk, *Spiritual Politics* (New York: Torchstone, 1989).

a few remarks that caused people to speculate about whether he held to the fundamentalist messianic convictions.[44] (These remarks might have been written for Reagan by advisers in an attempt to appease fundamentalist supporters.) Reagan's policy toward Israel could be summarized on the whole as extremely friendly and supportive, but while the president's remarks could have been understood to imply a dispensationalist understanding of Israel's role in history and of America's duty to assist that state, Reagan never made a remark about Israel with explicitly premillennialist overtones.

In the 1970s and 1980s, dozens of pro-Israeli fundamentalist organizations emerged in the United States. Besides mustering political support for Israel among American evangelicals, they also organized lectures, distributed materials on Israel and its historical role, and organized tours to the Holy Land. One such organization was the Friends of Israel Gospel Ministry, of Bellmaur, New Jersey, a group headed by Elwood McQuaid, who has written a good deal on Jewish topics in the evangelical world.[45] Another example was the Washington-based American Christian Trust. Some of the fundamentalist organizations that muster support for Israel are also engaged in proselytizing Jews. The years following the Six-Day War also saw an increase in the actual presence and activity of fundamentalists in Israel. Fundamentalist tours to that country increased, as did the numbers of field-study seminars and volunteers coming to kibbutzim such as Project Kibbutz, organized by Oral Roberts University. Even institutions of higher education were established in Israel by American evangelicals, one of these being the Holy-Land Institute set up by Douglas Young, president of Trinity Evangelical Divinity School in Deerfield, Illinois, which had a premillennialist, pro-Zionist orientation.

In 1981, when, following the Israeli Knesset's Jerusalem Law, many states closed their consulates in Jerusalem, a group of European and American fundamentalists established the "Christian Embassy" there. This institution, composed of charismatic premillennialists, became the largest of "Christian Zionist" establishments. In addition to offering lectures and distributing material about Israel and its role in history, the "embassy" organizes groups of visitors to the Holy Land and collects money for various Israeli enterprises such as the absorption of Russian immigrants.

44. See Martin Gardner, "Giving God a Hand," *New York Review of Books,* 13 August 1987, p. 22.

45. See, e.g., McQuaid, *It Is No Dream* (Bellmaur, N.J.: Friends of Israel Gospel Ministry, 1978).

In the late 1970s, as the evangelical influence on American political life became more and more apparent, the Israeli government began to take notice of this segment of American society and took measures to establish contact with it.[46] Among other things, Menachem Begin appointed Harry Horowitz as a special liaison for American evangelicals. Israeli officials spoke at fundamentalist conferences, and evangelists met with Israeli leaders as part of their touring schedules in Israel. After the Israeli bombing of the Iraqi atomic plant in 1981, Begin called Jerry Falwell and asked him to back Israel on the issue. He was scheduled to speak at Criswell's First Baptist Church in Dallas but had to cancel his speech because of the death of his wife. But despite all these efforts to establish contacts, the Israeli leadership has often remained ignorant of the real motivation and nature of the fundamentalist friendship. When on one occasion Begin exclaimed that "the Christians in America supported Israel," it was obvious that he did not realize that premillennialist evangelicals were only one segment of American Christianity.

One example of the Israeli ignorance of the nature and scope of the evangelical interest and involvement with Israel can be found in its reaction to attempts by Christian fundamentalists to evangelize Jews in that country. One of the Begin government's earliest acts of legislation was intended to restrict such missionary activity by outlawing the "buying" of converts through economic incentives. The successful legislative initiative reflected the long-standing resentment that Orthodox and other Jews felt toward these evangelistic incursions, but in the end it proved to be ineffective legislation because it was based on the Jewish myth that Christians buy Jews' souls. When the issue was being debated prior to the enactment of the legislation in 1978, many evangelicals were worried that the law might bring their activity to an end. They were relieved when they saw the wording of the law that the Knesset eventually came up with, since it clearly did not place restrictions on the sort of work they did. But the fact remains that the Begin coalition had tried to halt the evangelization of Jews in Israel without realizing that this activity was carried out by the same elements in Christianity with whom it was trying to establish a friendly relationship.

The intensive involvement and interest of fundamentalists in events in the life of the Jewish people, and especially in the developments that led to the establishment of the Jewish state and in the

46. "Israel Looks on U.S. Evangelical Christians as Potent Allies," *Washington Post*, 23 March 1981, p. A11.

ongoing history of that state, has continued for more than one hundred years. Events in the life of the Jews and their state have consistently given this conservative segment of American Protestantism "signs" that the ground is being prepared for the arrival of the Messiah, that the present era is coming to an end and the eschatological drama is at hand. Whereas at the end of the nineteenth century the signs were the emergence of Zionism and new Jewish settlements in Palestine, in the 1980s and early 1990s it was the Israeli war in Lebanon, in which Israel enlarged its territory to include more of David's ancient kingdom, and later on the large immigration from the Soviet Union, which meant that the ingathering of Israel was being completed. When the Gulf War broke out in the beginning of 1991 and Iraq directed a number of missile attacks at Israel, many premillennialists saw these acts of violence as connected in some way to events of the apocalypse.

The understanding of current events in light of prophecy is in the eyes of the beholders. Dispensationalism is convincing for a certain segment of American Protestants who see themselves as "Bible believers." Many fundamentalists have adopted eschatological beliefs emphasizing the role of the Jews at the end of the age as part of an overall worldview. Events in the life of the Jewish people have served these fundamentalists as a source of reassurance, validating not only their messianic conviction and their view of the course of history but also their critique of society and culture. It might be argued that they have derived from the Zionist movement and the state of Israel much more than they have given that state. The self-perception of the Zionists has not been much influenced by the interest that fundamentalists have taken in them; indeed, for the most part, Jews have not taken notice of the fundamentalists at all. The latter, on the other hand, would have had to rewrite almost their entire literature, theological and popular, if they had not seen in the history of Zionism so many signs to point to as proofs that they had read the Scriptures correctly and that history is proceeding according to plan.

A Select Bibliography of Works by Martin E. Marty

In reviewing Martin E. Marty's career as an author, the words *prolific* and *eclectic* spring immediately to mind, but even these are inadequate to describe the 3,000-plus titles, including books, chapters in books, introductions, prefaces, columns, scholarly and journalistic articles, encyclopedia entries, lectures, a weekly column in *The Christian Century (M.E.M.O)*, and a fortnightly newsletter *(Context)*, which draw on a variety of disciplines and focus on subjects ranging from American religious history to French philosophy to Zsa Zsa Gabor.

Thus our first principle of selection was to limit the bibliography to works in the fields covered in the present volume: American religious history, public religion, and religious fundamentalisms. While this omits major areas of Marty's research, such as his extensive writings on health, faith, and medical ethics, on Christian pastoral life and theology, and on the Lutheran tradition, it nonetheless includes over 1,000 titles. The second principle of selection, therefore, was to limit the bibliography to representative works in these three areas — books, the more important journal articles and chapters, and the occasional review essay. This leaves us with approximately 300 titles. This bibliography was compiled by Patricia A. Mitchell and R. Scott Appleby.

A. Religious History

Books

The Noise of Conflict, 1919-1941. Vol. 2 of *Modern American Religion.* Chicago: University of Chicago Press, 1991.

Religion and Republic: The American Circumstance. 1987. Reprint. Boston: Beacon Press, 1989.

An Invitation to American Catholic History. Chicago: Thomas More Association, 1986.

The Irony of It All, 1893-1919. Vol. 1 of *Modern American Religion.* Chicago: University of Chicago Press, 1986.

Pilgrims in Their Own Land. Boston: Little, Brown, 1984.

Where the Spirit Leads: American Denominations Today. Edited. Atlanta: John Knox, 1980.

Faith of Our Fathers. Vol. 4 of *Religion, Awakening, and Revolution.* Wilmington, N.C.: Consortium, 1977.

The Pro and Con Book of Religious America: A Bicentennial Argument. Waco, Tex.: Word Books, 1975.

Protestantism in the United States: Righteous Empire. 2nd ed. New York: Macmillan, 1986.

What Do We Believe? The Stance of Religion in America. With Stuart E. Rosenberg and Andrew M. Greeley. New York: Meredith Press, 1968.

The Religious Press in America. With John G. Deedy and David W. Silverman. San Francisco: Holt, Rinehart & Winston, 1963.

Second Chance for American Protestants. New York: Harper & Row, 1963.

The Infidel: Freethought and American Religion. Cleveland: Meridian Books, 1961.

The New Shape of American Religion. New York: Harper & Row, 1959.

A Short History of Christianity. New York: Meridian Books, 1959; Reprint. Philadelphia: Fortress Press, 1980. Revised edition, 1987.

Articles and Chapters

"Forum: Sources of Personal Identity: Religion, Ethnicity, and the American Cultural Situation." In *Religion and American Culture* 2 (Winter 1992): 8-18.

"Religion in America." Reprint of United States Information Agency edition, 1989. In *Making America: The Society and Culture of the United States,* edited by Luther S. Luedke. Chapel Hill, N.C.: University of North Carolina, 1992.

"The Binding Tie of Cohesive Sentiment: Complementing the Constitution." In *Threescore Years and Ten: Essays in Honor of Rabbi Seymour Cohen,* edited by Abraham Karp, Louis Jacobs, and Chaim Zalman Dimitrovsky. Hoboken: KTAV, 1991.

"Civic Virtue: The Framers' Worries — And Our Own Post Script to the Bill of Rights." *Religious Education* 86 (Fall 1991): 492-504.

"Protestantism and the American Way of Life/America and the Protestant Way of Life." *Chicago Studies* 30 (August 1991): 161-76.

"New Visibility for the Invisible Institution." Review of *The Black Church in the African-American Experience,* by C. Eric Lincoln and Lawrence H. Mamiya. *Georgia Historical Quarterly* 75 (Summer 1991): 385-400.

"A Scripted Nation" (the Bartlett Lecture at Yale). *Mayflower Quarterly,* August 1991, pp. 264-67. Reprinted from *Reflections,* Winter 1990.

"On Medial Moraine: Religious Dimensions of American Constitutionalism" (the 1988 Overton A. Currie Lecture in Law and Religion). In *Symposium: Religious Dimensions of American Constitutionalism,* a special issue of *Emory Law Journal* 39 (Winter 1990): 1-8.

"Reflections on the Protestant Experience." In *The Catholic Church and American Culture,* edited by Cassian Yuhaus. Mahwah, N.J.: Paulist Press, 1990.

"The Twentieth Century Protestants and Others." In *Religion and American Politics: From the Colonial Period to the 1980s,* edited by Mark A. Noll. New York: Oxford University Press, 1990.

"The Bible and American Cultural Values." *New Theology Review* 2 (February 1989): 6-15.

"Christliches Waehlerverhalten in den USA." *Evangelische Kommentare* 22 (January 1989): 11-12.

"Living with Establishment and Disestablishment in Nineteenth-Century Anglo-America." In *Readings on Church and State,* edited by James E. Wood, Jr. Waco, Tex.: Baylor University, 1989.

"Reflection on the Life of Joseph Sittler." *Currents in Theology and Mission* 16 (February 1989): 27-28.

"Religion in America, 1935-1985." In *Altered Landscapes: Christianity in America, 1935-1985,* edited by David W. Lotz. Grand Rapids: William B. Eerdmans, 1989.

"The Sacred and Secular in American History." In *Transforming Faith: The Sacred and Secular in Modern American History,* edited by M. L. Bradbury and James B. Gilbert. New York: Greenwood Press, 1989.

"The Tribulations of the Center: Transformations of Mainline American Religion." In *Center Ideas and Institution,* edited by Lian Greenfield and Michel Martin. Chicago: University of Chicago Press, 1989.

"The Clergy." In *The Professions in American History,* edited by Nathan O. Hatch. Notre Dame, Ind.: University of Notre Dame Press, 1988.

"In the Combat Zone over American Values: The Vision of One America versus the Vision of Many Americas" (the Roy H. Witherspoon Lecture, 1988). Published by University of North Carolina, Charlotte, 1990.

"Presidents and Religion." In *Science, Religion and the Humanities,* edited by Kenneth W. Thompson. Washington: University Press of America, 1988.

"Uncle Sam versus John Q. Public." *American Heritage,* July-August 1988, p. 58.

"The Virginia Statute Two Hundred Years Later." In *The Virginia Statute for Religious Freedom,* edited by Merrill D. Peterson and Robert C. Vaughn. New York: Cambridge University Press, 1988.

"American Tribalism." *Liberty,* September/October 1987, pp. 18-19.

"The Bible in American Culture." *Perspectives* 2 (June 1987): 406.

"First Amendment." *American Heritage,* May-June 1987, p. 71.

"Freedom of Religion and the First Amendment." In *The Bill of Rights: A Lively Heritage,* edited by Jon Kukla. Richmond: Virginia State Library and Archives, 1987.

"The Impact of Technology on American Religion." In *Technology, the Economy, and Society: The American Experience,* edited by Joel Colton and Stuart Bruchey. New York: Columbia University Press, 1987.

"Irony (Fig.) and (Lit.) in Modern American Religion." In *Trajectories in the Study of Religion,* edited by Ray L. Hart. Atlanta: Scholars Press, 1987. Reprinted from *Journal of the American Academy of Religion* 53 (June 1985).

"War's Dilemmas: The *Century* 1938-1945," and "Peace and Pluralism: The *Century* 1946-1952." In *A Century of the Century,* by Linda Marie Delloff et al. Grand Rapids: William B. Eerdmans, 1987.

"Anne Hutchinson on Trial." In *A Sense of History: The Best Writing of American Heritage,* ed. Byron Dobell. Boston: Houghton Mifflin, 1986. Reprint of "Anne Hutchinson on Trial," *American Heritage,* December 1984, p. 27.

"Church and State." Excerpt from "Invitation to American Catholic History," *Overview* 20 (August 1986): 6-9.

"God's Country: The Argument over Who Owns America." *The Critic,* Fall 1986, pp. 72-81.

"Presidents and Religion." In *The Virginia Papers on the Presidency,* vol. 21, edited by Kenneth W. Thompson. Washington: University Press of America, 1986.

"Transpositions: American Religion in the 1980s." *The Annals of the*

American Academy of Political and Social Science 480 (July 1985): 11-23.

"Religion in America since Mid-Century." In *Religion and America,* edited by Mary Douglas and Steven M. Tipton. Boston: Beacon Press, 1984.

"The American Experience of Salvation." *Chicago Studies,* April 1983, pp. 69-82.

"The Electronic Church." In *Eerdmans' Handbook to Christianity in America,* edited by Mark A. Noll. Grand Rapids: William B. Eerdmans, 1983.

"Freedom of Religion and the First Amendment." *Virginia Cavalcade,* Spring 1983, pp. 158-71.

"Power and Powerlessness in American Religion Today." *Religion* 21 (October 1983): 1-5.

"Religious Trends in America." In *Dialogue* (Washington, D.C.: USIA, 1983), pp. 41-46. Reprinted from *Daedalus.*

"America's Iconic Book." In *Humanizing America's Iconic Book,* edited by Gene M. Tucker and Douglas A. Knight. Chico, Calif.: Scholars Press, 1982.

"The Catholic Ghetto and All Other Ghettos" (ACHA Presidential Address). *The Catholic Historical Review* 17 (April 1982): 185-205.

"Religion in America since Mid-Century." *Daedalus* (Winter 1982): 149-64.

"Religious Power in America: A Contemporary Map." *Criterion* 21 (Winter 1982): 27-31.

"The Many Faces of Religion in America." *TOPIC,* no. 127 (1980): pp. 45-52.

"North America: The Empirical Understanding of Religion and Theology." In *What Is Religion? An Inquiry for Christian Theology,* edited by Mircea Eliade and David Tracy. New York: Seabury Press, 1980.

"Of Darters and Schools and Clergymen: The Religion Clauses Worse Confounded." In *The Supreme Court Review 1978,* edited by Philip C. Kurland and Gerhard Casper. Chicago: The University of Chicago Press, 1979.

"Religion in Amerika." *Evangelische Kommentare* 12 (April 1979): 200-202.

"The Changing Role of Religion in American Society." In *The National Purpose Reconsidered,* edited by Dona Baron. New York: Columbia University Press, 1978.

"Here Am I: Send Me, Send Me! The Missionary Movement, Then and Now." *American Heritage* 29 (February/March 1978): 70ff.

"The Protestant Experience and Perspective." In *American Religious Values and the Future of America,* edited by Rodger Van Allen. Philadelphia: Fortress Press, 1978.

"The American Tradition and the American Tomorrow." In *Tomorrow's American,* edited by Samuel Sandmel. New York: Oxford University Press, 1977.

"Ethnicity: The Skeleton of Religion in America." In *Denominationalism,* edited by Russell E. Richey. New York: Harper & Row, 1977. Reprint of article in *Church History,* March 1972.

"God's Almost Chosen People." *American Heritage* 28 (August 1977): 4-7.

"The Land and the City in American Religious Conflict" (the 1976 H. Paul Douglass Lecture). *Review of Religious Research* 18 (Spring 1977): 211-32.

"A Map of Religious America." *Journal of Current Social Issues,* Spring 1977, pp. 4-9.

"In 2076, It Still Will Be True That We Are a Religious People." *U.S. News and World Report,* 5 July 1976.

"Isaac Backus." In *Heritage of '76,* edited by Jay Dolan. Notre Dame, Ind.: University of Notre Dame, 1976.

"Living with Establishment in Nineteenth-Century Anglo-America." *Journal of Church and State* 18 (1976): 61-78.

"The Lost Worlds of Reinhold Niebuhr." *American Scholar,* Autumn 1976, pp. 566-72.

"The Love Affair of America's Religious World with the Printed Word." *Religious Media Today,* April 1976, pp. 11-14.

"The Light at the End of the Burrow: A Mid-Decade Report on American Religion." *Currents in Theology and Mission* 2 (August 1975): 192-204.

"Pentecostalism in the Context of American Piety and Practice." In *Aspects of Pentecostal-Charismatic Origins,* edited by Vinson Synan. Plainfield, N.J.: Logos, 1975.

"The Revival and the Revolution." In *Religion American Style,* edited by Patrick H. McNamara. New York: Harper & Row, 1975.

"The Revolution of Religion: Isaac Backus, Man of Action." *Elkhart Truth,* 11 July 1975, p. 6.

"The Altar and the Throne: Civil Religion in America." In *Britannica Book of the Year.* Chicago: Encyclopedia Britannica, 1974.

"Religious Behavior: Its Social Dimension in American History." *Social Research* 41 (Summer 1974): 241-64.

"Two Kinds of Two of Civil Religion." In *American Civil Religion*, edited by Russell E. Richey and Donald G. Jones. New York: Harper & Row, 1974.

"Church History." In *Contemporary Christian Trends*, edited by William M. Pinson and Clyde E. Fant, Jr. Waco, Tex.: Word Books, 1972.

"Freedom and Faith: Spiritual Attitudes of a New World." In *American Civilization*, edited by Daniel J. Boorstin. New York: Thames & Hudson, 1972.

"Locating Consent and Dissent in American Religion." *Philosophic Exchange* 1 (Summer 1972): 139.

"Conflict and Consensus in Contemporary American Religion." In *Contemporary Civilization No. 5*, by James F. Findlay. Glenview, Ill.: Scott, Foresman, 1971.

"The North American Situation 1969." In *The Religious Situation, 1969*, edited by Donald M. Cutler. Boston: Beacon Press, 1969.

"Part One." In *What Do We Believe? The Stance of Religion in America*, by Martin E. Marty, Stuart E. Rosenberg, and Andrew M. Greeley. New York: Meredith Press, 1968.

"The Spirit's Holy Errand: The Search for a Spiritual Style in Secular America." In *Religion in America*, edited by William G. McLoughlin and Robert N. Bellah. Boston: Houghton Mifflin, 1968. Reprint of article in *Daedalus*, Winter 1967, pp. 99-115.

"Mary Baker Eddy: Science and Health, 1875." In *An American Primer*, edited by Daniel J. Boorstin. Chicago: University of Chicago, 1966.

"The Protestant Press: Limitations and Possibilities." In *The Religious Press in America*, by Martin E. Marty, John G. Deedy, and David W. Silverman. New York: Holt, Rinehart & Winston, 1963.

"The Protestant Reinterpretation of American Life." In *The Outbursts That Await Us*, by Arthur Hertzberg, Martin E. Marty, and Joseph Moody. New York: Macmillan, 1963.

"Sects and Cults." In *Religion in American Society*, edited by Thorsten Sellin. Philadelphia: Academy of Political and Social Science, 1960. Reprinted in *Annals of the American Academy of Political and Social Science* 332 (November 1960): 125-34; *Not Many Wise*, edited by Thorsten Sellin. Boston: Pilgrim Press, 1962; and *Sociology and Religion: A Book of Readings*, edited by Norman Birnbaum and Gertrud Lenzer. Englewood Cliffs, N.J.: Prentice-Hall, 1968, 1969.

"Interreligious Tensions in America's Third Century" (Seamans Lecture). Special publication of National Conference of Christians and Jews.

B. Public Religion

Books

Pushing the Faith: Proselytism and Civility in a Pluralistic World. Edited with Frederick E. Greenspahn. New York: Crossroad, 1988.

Handbook of Christian Theologians. Edited with Dean G. Peerman. Nashville: Abingdon Press, 1980. Reissue of 1965 World Meridian book. Enlarged edition, 1984.

The Public Church: Mainline — Evangelical — Catholic. New York: Crossroad, 1980.

The Fire We Can Light: The Role of Religion in a Suddenly Different World. Garden City, N.Y.: Doubleday, 1973.

Protestantism. New York: Holt, Rinehart & Winston, 1972.

The Modern Schism: Three Paths to the Secular. New York: Harper & Row, 1969.

Varieties of Unbelief. New York: Holt, Rinehart & Winston, 1964.

Articles and Chapters

"The Religious Dimension of Humanism." *Forum for Honors* 20 (Winter-Spring 1990): 3-10.

"The Academic Study of Religion." *Humanities* 10 (January-February 1989): 26-29.

"Committing the Study of Religion in Public" (presidential address). *Journal of the American Academy of Religion* 57 (Spring 1989): 1-22.

"Committedly Civil — Civilly Committed." In *Quest* 45 (October 1988). Reprinted from *As Others See Us.*

"Mere Pluralism, Utter Pluralism and Civic Pluralism." In *Ethics in American Public Life.* Providence: Brown University, 1988.

"Proselytism in a Pluralistic World." In *Pushing the Faith: Proselytism and Civility in a Pluralistic World,* edited by Martin E. Marty and Frederick E. Greenspahn. New York: Crossroad, 1988.

"Public Religion." *National Forum* 48 (Winter 1988): 8-9.

"History, Education and Policy: A Review." *Religious Education* 82 (Summer 1987): 498-505.

"Religion and the Public Realm." With Harvey Cox. *Humanities Discourse* 1 (July 1987): 4-7.

"Academic Religion Today." *Theology Today* 43 (July 1986): 244-48.

"The Protestant Principle: Between Theocracy and Propheticism." In *Cities of Gods: Faith, Politics and Individualism in Judaism, Christianity and Islam,* edited by Nigel Biggar, James S. Scott, and William Schweiker. New York: Greenwood Press, 1986.

"Religion and Public Life." In *Religion and Public Life: The Role of Religious Bodies in Shaping Public Policy,* edited by Joseph A. Bracken. Cincinnati: Xavier University Press, 1986.

"Hell Disappeared, No One Noticed: A Civic Argument." *Harvard Theological Review* 78 (1985): 381-98.

"What Is Modern about the Modern Study of Religion?" (the University Lecture in Religion at Arizona State University). Department of Religious Studies, Tempe, Arizona, 1985.

"The Conflict of Humanisms." With Colin Williams. In *The Humanist Tradition: Past, Present and Future.* Aspen, Colo.: Aspen Institute, 1984.

"The Role of the Religious Leader in the Development of Public Policy" (response to Cardinal Bernardin). *DePaul Law Review* 34 (Fall 1984): 10-14. Reprinted in *Journal of Law and Religion* 2 (1984): 379-82.

"Twelve Lessons of the Church/State Debate." *Across the Board,* December 1984, pp. 46-51.

Review of *Government Intervention in Religious Affairs,* by Dean Kelley, and *Freedom of Religion,* by Henry B. Clark. *Journal of Law and Religion* 1 (1983): 427-34.

"Christian Humanism among the Humanisms." *Humanities Report* 4 (February 1982): 15-17.

"Science and Theology: On Drawing Proper Lines of Conflict." *Scholar and Educator,* Fall 1982, pp. 3-10.

"Religion and Society." *Revue Francaise d'Etudes Americaines,* October 1981, pp. 157-73.

"Religion and the Humanities: An Assessment." In *Religion and the Humanities.* Research Triangle Park, N.C.: National Humanities Center, 1981.

"This We Can Believe: A Pluralistic Vision." *Religious Education* 75 (January-February 1980): 37-50.

"In Every Way Religious." *Social Research,* Autumn 1979, pp. 580-99.

"On Black, White, Gray, and the Rainbow." In *The Denigration of Capitalism: Six Points of View,* edited by Michael Novak. Washington: American Enterprise Institute, 1979.

"Primacy of the Bible." In *Protestantism,* edited by Hugh T. Kerr. Hauppauge, N.Y.: Barron's, 1979.

"Science versus Religion: An Old Squabble Simmers Down." *Saturday Review,* 10 December 1977, pp. 29-35.

"Churches Behaving Civilly." *Fides et Historia* 7 (Spring 1975): 2-10.

"Civil Religion and the Churches Behaving Civilly." *Theology Today* 32 (July 1975): 175-82.

"Reinhold Niebuhr: Public Theology and the American Experience." In *The Legacy of Reinhold Niebuhr,* edited by Nathan A. Scott, Jr. Chicago: University of Chicago Press, 1975.

"Reinhold Niebuhr: Public Theology and the American Experience." *Journal of Religion* 54 (October 1974): 332-59.

"The Social Meanings of Religion." In *The Occult Establishment.* Chicago: Rand McNally, 1974.

"Christianity and Urban Revolution." In *Christianity: A Revolutionary Catalyst,* edited by Paul K. K. Tong. Glassboro, N.J.: Glassboro State College Press, 1973.

"The Persistence of the Mystical." In *The Persistence of Religion,* edited by Andrew Greeley and Gregory Baum. New York: Herder & Herder, 1973.

"Theology during a Cultural Revolution." In *New Theology No. 8,* by Martin E. Marty and Dean G. Peerman. New York: Macmillan, 1971.

"Religion in a Secularized World" (the Ware Lecture). Twentieth Congress, International Association for Religious Freedom, July 12-20, 1969.

"Secularization in the American Public Order." In *Religion and the Public Order No. 5,* edited by Donald A. Giannella. Ithaca, N.Y.: Cornell University Press, 1969.

"Theology and Revolution." In *New Theology No. 6,* edited by Martin E. Marty and Dean G. Peerman. New York: Macmillan, 1969.

"After the Secular Theology." *Perspective* 9 (Summer 1968): 119.

"Beyond the Secular: Chastened Religion." In *New Theology No. 4,* edited by Martin E. Marty and Dean G. Peerman. New York: Macmillan, 1967.

"Does Secular Theology Have a Future?" In *The Great Ideas Today,* edited by Robert M. Hutchins and Mortimer J. Adler. Chicago: Encyclopedia Britannica, 1967.

"Religion in General and Protestantism in Particular." In *Operation Theology,* edited by Andrew J. Buehner. St. Louis: Lutheran Academy for Scholarship, 1967.

"Whenever God Dies: Protestant Roots of the Problem of God." In *Speaking of God,* edited by Denis Dirscherl. Milwaukee: Bruce Publishing, 1967.

"The Bible and Tradition" (Thomas More-Rosary Symposium Lecture). *The Critic* 24 (August-September 1965): 28.

"The Function of Religion in Society." In *A Time for Decision,* by Paul C. Johnson et al. Lincoln, Neb.: University of Nebraska Press, 1965.

"History of Christianity." *Criterion* 4-6 (1965-67): 41-42.

"Alternative Approaches in Church-State Relations." In *Church and State under God,* edited by Albert G. Huegli. St. Louis: Concordia, 1964.

"The Church and Its Polity." In *Theology in the Life of the Church,* edited by Robert W. Bertram. Philadelphia: Fortress Press, 1963.

"Protestantism-in-Pluralism." *Commonweal,* 12 July 1963, pp. 416-18.

"The Age after Christendom." *Dialog* 1 (Autumn 1962): 14.

C. Comparative Fundamentalisms

Books

Fundamentalisms and Society: Reclaiming the Sciences, the Family, and Education. Edited with R. Scott Appleby. Chicago: University of Chicago Press, 1993.

Fundamentalisms and the State: Remaking Polities, Economies, and Militance. Edited with R. Scott Appleby. Chicago: University of Chicago Press, 1993.

Fundamentalisms Observed. Edited with R. Scott Appleby. Chicago: University of Chicago Press, 1991.

Religious Crises in Modern America. Waco, Tex.: Baylor University Press, 1981.

Articles and Chapters

"Fundamentals of Fundamentalism." In *Fundamentalism in Comparative Perspective,* edited by Lawrence Kaplan. Amherst: University of Massachusetts, 1992.

"The Fundamentalism Project: A User's Guide," and "Conclusion: An Interim Report on a Hypothetical Family." In *Fundamentalisms Observed,* edited by Martin E. Marty and R. Scott Appleby. Chicago: University of Chicago Press, 1991.

"Fundamentalisme in Vogelvlucht." In *Naar de Letter: Beschouwingen oveer Fundamentalisme,* edited by Pieter Boele van Hensbroek, Sjaak Koenis, and Pauline Westerman. Utrecht: Cip-Gegevens Konninklijke Bibliothek, 1991.

"Fundamentalisms Observed: A Hypothetical Family." With R. Scott Appleby. *Bulletin of the American Academy of Arts and Sciences* 45 (November 1991).

"The Fundamentalism Project at Midpoint." *Criterion* 29 (Winter 1990): 19-23.

"A Field Guide to Fundamentalism." In *1989 Britannica Book of the Year.* Chicago: Encyclopedia Britannica, 1989.

"Christian Soldiers: American Fundamentalism in (British)." *The Tablet,* 23 April 1988, pp. 460-61.

"Fundamentalism as a Social Phenomenon." *Bulletin of the American Academy of Arts and Sciences* 42 (November 1988): 15-29.

"Reassessing the New Christian Right." *Chicago Catholic,* 22 July 1988. Reprint of *Context,* 15 July 1988, p. 9.

"Fundamentalism as a Social Phenomenon." In *Piety and Politics: Evangelicals and Fundamentalists Confront the World,* edited by Richard John Neuhaus and Michael Cromartie. Washington: Ethics and Public Policy Center, 1987.

"A Historian's Letter to a Fundamentalist Neighbor." *Miami Herald,* 29 March 1987, p. 4.

"Morality, Ethics, and the New Christian Right." In *Border Regions of Faith: An Anthology of Religion and Social Change,* edited by Kenneth Aman. Maryknoll, N.Y.: Orbis Books, 1987.

"Modern Fundamentalism." *America,* September 1986, pp. 133-35.

"Fundamentalism." *Fundamentalist Journal,* December 1984, pp. 14-15.

"Fundamentalism as a Social Phenomenon." In *Evangelicalism and Modern America,* edited by George Marsden. Grand Rapids: William B. Eerdmans, 1984.

"Fundamentalism as a Social Phenomenon." *Review and Expositor* 79 (Winter 1982): 19-30.

"Now and Then: Precursors of the Moral Majority." *American Heritage* 33 (February/March 1882): 98-99.

"A Christian View of the Moral Majority." *Social Issues Resource Series* 2 (April 1981): 5-13.

"Ethics and the New Christian Right." *Hastings Center Report* 11 (August 1981): 14-21.

"Torn Apart on New Christian Right." *The Lutheran,* 18 March 1981, pp. 8-10.

"Twelve Points to Reconsider." *Face to Face* 8 (Winter 1981): 16-18. Reprint from *Context*.

"Fundamentalism Reborn." *Saturday Review,* May 1980, pp. 37-38, 42.

"In Search of the Moral Majority." *Miami Herald,* 21 December 1980, pp. 1, 4.

"An Evaluation of the 'Born-Again' Movement." *Catalyst* 10 (Winter 1978): 3.

"The Explosion in Evangelical Television." *Laity Exchange* (London), December 1978.

"The Shape of Religious Thought and Assumptions." In *Evangelicals Face the Future,* edited by Donald E. Hoke. South Pasadena, Calif.: William Carey Library, 1978.

"Evangelism in the U.S. — What Has It Been? What Will It Be?" *New World Outlook,* January 1975, pp. 8ff.

"Tensions within Contemporary Evangelicalism: A Critical Appraisal." In *The Evangelicals,* edited by David F. Wells and John D. Woodbridge. Nashville: Abingdon, 1975. Reprinted in *Contemporary American Theologies II: A Book of Readings,* edited by Deane William Ferm. New York: Seabury Press, 1982.

"What's Ahead for Evangelism?" In *Mission Trends No. 2,* edited by Gerald H. Anderson and Thomas F. Stransky. New York: Paulist Press, 1975.

"The Younger Generations: Cultic Conservatism on the Right." *Current,* May 1961, p. 18. Reprint from "When Conservatism Becomes Cultic." *Christian Century,* 22 March 1961.

D. Contemporary Religious Issues

Books

The Word: People Participating in Preaching. Philadelphia: Fortress Press, 1984.

A Cry of Absence: Reflections on the Winter of the Heart. Boston: Little, Brown, 1983.

Faith and Ferment: An Interdisciplinary Study of Christian Beliefs and Practices. With Joan Chittester. Minneapolis: Augsburg, 1983.

Health and Medicine in the Lutheran Tradition. New York: Crossroad, 1983.

The Place of Trust: Martin Luther. Edited and introduced. San Francisco: Harper & Row, 1983.

By Way of Response. Nashville: Abingdon, 1980.

The Lord's Supper. Philadelphia: Fortress Press, 1980.
What a Modern Catholic Believes as Seen by a Non-Catholic. Chicago: Thomas More Association, 1974.
You Are Promise. Niles, Ill.: Argus, 1973.
These Theses Were Not Posted. Boston: Beacon Press, 1968.
Youth Considers "Do It Yourself" Religion. New York: Thomas Nelson, 1965.
Church Unity and Church Mission. Grand Rapids: William B. Eerdmans, 1964.
New Theology, Nos. 1-10. With Dean G. Peerman. New York: Macmillan, 1964-73.
Religion and Social Conflict. With Robert Lee. New York: Oxford University Press, 1964.
What's Ahead for the Churches. With Kyle Haselden. Kansas City: Sheed & Ward, 1964.
Baptism. Philadelphia: Fortress Press, 1962.
The Hidden Discipline. St. Louis: Concordia, 1962. Revised edition, 1974.
The Improper Opinion: Mass Media and the Christian Faith. Louisville: Westminster Press, 1961.

Articles and Chapters

"How to Draw Guidance from a Heritage: A Protestant Approach to Moral Choices." In *A Time to be Born and a Time to Die: The Ethics of Choice,* edited by Barry S. Kogan. New York: Aldine de Gruyter, 1991.
"Never the Same Again: Post Vatican II Catholic-Protestant Interactions" (Furfey Lecture). *Sociological Analysis* 52 (Spring 1991): 13-26.
"The Machine and the Spirit: Imagining a Humane Technological Future." In *Ethics of Change: Humanistic Values vs. Technological Imperatives,* edited by Jay Booth. Atlantic Center for the Arts, 1988.
"The Meaning of Life." In *The Meaning of Life: According to Our Century's Greatest Writers and Thinkers,* edited by Hugh S. Moorhead. Chicago: Chicago Review, 1988.
"The Many Faces of Technology, the Many Voices of Tradition." In *Traditional Moral Values in the Age of Technology,* edited by Andrew Cecil. Dallas: University of Texas, 1987.
"A Sort of Republican Banquet." In *Religion and American Public Life,* edited by Robin W. Lovin. New York: Paulist Press, 1986. Reprinted from *Journal of Religion* 59 (October 1979): 383-405.

"Tübinger Modelle für Theologie." In *Das Neue Paradigma von Theologie,* edited by Hans Küng and David Tracy. Gütersloh: Gerd Mohn, 1986.

"A Man of Grand Contradictions." *Christianity Today,* 21 October 1983, pp. 8-9.

"Mysticism and the Religious Quest for Freedom." In *God and Human Freedom: A Festschrift in Honor of Howard Thurman,* edited by Henry James Young. Richmond, Ind.: Friends United Press, 1983.

Introduction to *The Varieties of Religious Experience,* by William James. Baltimore: Penguin, 1982.

"Protestant and Jewish Relations." In *Tomorrow's Church: What's Ahead for American Catholics,* edited by Edward C. Herr. Chicago: Thomas More Press, 1982.

"Prophecy, Criticism and the Electronic Media." *Media Development* 28 (1981): 30-34.

"The Reporting of Religious Events by the Media: A Framework for Inquiry." In *The Religion Beat: The Reporting of Religion in the Media.* Rockefeller Foundation, August 1981.

"Franz Bibfeldt, Who?" *The Limen,* 10 April 1980, pp. 1-2.

"Migration: The Moral Framework." In *Human Migration: Patterns and Policies,* edited by William H. McNeill and Ruth S. Adams. Bloomington, Ind.: Indiana University Press, 1978.

"Time Now to Think of Turning Baptist." Review of *Turning East,* by Harvey Cox. *Christianity and Crisis,* 17 October 1977, pp. 236-39.

"Experiment in Environment: Foreign Perceptions of Religious America." *Journal of Religion* 56 (July 1976): 291-315.

"Religion: U.S.A." In *United States: People-Questions.* New York: Friendship Press, 1975.

"Knowledge Elites and Counter-Elites." *Daedalus,* Fall 1974, pp. 104-9.

"Introduction: Bios and Theology." In *New Theology No. 10,* edited by Martin E. Marty and Dean G. Peerman. New York: Macmillan, 1973.

"Introduction: Peoplehood and Particularism." In *New Theology No. 9,* edited by Martin E. Marty and Dean G. Peerman. New York: Macmillan, 1972.

"The Occult Establishment." *Social Research* 37 (Summer 1970): 212.

"The Recovery of Transcendence." In *New Theology No. 7,* edited by Martin E. Marty and Dean G. Peerman. New York: Macmillan, 1970.

"The Future of Christianity — An Historian's View." *Holy Cross Quarterly* 2 (Winter 1969): 17.

"Protestantism: 1975." In *The Future of the Christian Churches in the 1970s.* Monograph prepared for the U.S. Army Chaplain Board, Fort George G. Meade, Maryland, November 1969.

"Christian Hope and Human Futures." In *New Theology No. 5,* edited by Martin E. Marty and Dean G. Peerman. New York: Macmillan, 1968.

"The Religious Situation: Introduction." In *The Religious Situation 1968,* edited by Donald M. Cutler. Boston: Beacon Press, 1968.

"A Future Direction for Catholic Theology." *The Critic* 25 (April-May 1967): 33.

"Luther on Ethics: Man Free and Slave." In *Accents in Luther's Theology,* edited by Heinz O. Kadai. St. Louis: Concordia, 1967.

"Introduction: The Turn from Mere Anarchy." In *New Theology No. 3,* edited by Martin E. Marty and Dean G. Peerman. New York: Macmillan, 1966.

"Introduction." In *New Theology No. 2,* edited by Martin E. Marty and Dean G. Peerman. New York: Macmillan, 1965.

"The Forms and the Future." In *What's Ahead for the Churches,* by Kyle Haselden and Martin E. Marty. Kansas City: Sheed & Ward, 1964.

"Introducing New Theology." In *New Theology No. 1,* edited by Martin E. Marty and Dean G. Peerman. New York: Macmillan, 1964.

"The Nature and Consequences of Social Conflict for Religious Groups." In *Religion and Social Conflict,* by Robert Lee and Martin E. Marty. New York: Oxford University Press, 1964.

"No Ground Beneath Us." In *No Ground Beneath Us: A Revolutionary Reader.* National Methodist Student Movement, 1964.

"Problems and Possibilities in Bonhoeffer's Thought." In *The Place of Bonhoeffer.* New York: Association Press, 1962.

"The Liberal Arts and the Christian Faith: The Approach from Below." In *Discourse,* Autumn 1961, p. 235.

"New Directions in Biblical Thought: Introduction." In *New Directions in Biblical Thought.* New York: Association Press, 1960.

E. Historiography

Books

A Nation of Behavers. 1976. Reprint. Chicago: University of Chicago Press, 1980.

The Search for a Usable Future. New York: Harper & Row, 1969.

Articles and Chapters

"Two Integrities: An Address to the Crisis in Mormon Historiography." In *Faithful History: Essays on Writing Mormon History,* edited by George D. Smith. Salt Lake City: Signature, 1992. Revision of previously published essay in *Journal of Mormon History* 10 (1983): 3-19.

"The Social Context of the Modern Paradigm in Theology: A Church Historian's View." Translation of German work. In *Paradigm Change in Theology,* edited by Hans Küng and David Tracy. New York: Crossroad, 1989.

"We Might Know What to Do and How to Do It: On the Usefulness of the Religious Past" (the Westminster Tanner-McMurrin Lectures on the History and Philosophy of Religion). Salt Lake City: Westminster College, 1989.

"Creative Imagination in Writing Religious History." In *The Incarnate Imagination: Essays in Theology, the Arts and Social Sciences,* edited by Ingrid H. Shafer. Bowling Green, Ohio: Bowling Green University Press, 1988.

"On the Philosophy of Comparative Religion." *Criterion* 27 (Winter 1988): 12-13.

"The Historian as Teacher." In *The Lively Experiment Continued,* edited by Jerald C. Brauer. Atlanta: Mercer University Press, 1987.

"The American Religious History Canon." *Social Research* 53 (Autumn 1986): 513-28.

" 'Storycide' and the Meaning of History." In *Bitburg in Moral and Political Perspective,* edited by Geoffrey Hartman. Bloomington, Ind.: Indiana University Press, 1986. Reprint from *Los Angeles Times.*

"A Curious People — A Usable Past." *Concordia Historical Institute Quarterly* 58 (Fall 1985): 98-102.

"The Difference in Being a Christian and the Difference It Makes — for History." In *History and Historical Understanding,* edited by C. T. McIntire and Ronald A. Wells. Grand Rapids: William B. Eerdmans, 1984.

"Paradigma im Übergang von der Moderne zur Postmoderne." In *Theologie — Wohin?* edited by Hans Küng and David Tracy. Gütersloh: Gerd Mohn, 1984.

"The Idea of Progress in Twentieth-Century Theology." In *Progress and Its Discontents,* edited by Gabriel A. Almond, Marvin Chodorow, and Roy Harvey Pearce. Berkeley and Los Angeles: University of California Press, 1982.

"On Comparing and Connecting Histories." In *In the Great Tradition,* edited by Joseph D. Ban and Paul R. Dekar. Valley Forge, Pa.: Judson Press, 1982.

"A Christian Interpretation of History." In *Conspectus of History,* Vol. 1, no. 5, edited by Dwight W. Hoover and John T. A. Koumoulides. Cambridge University Press for Ball State University, 1980.

"In Defense of History and Humanity." *Chronicle of Higher Education,* 20 May 1974, p. 24.

"The Historical Focus." *Journal for the Scientific Study of Religion* 13 (March 1974): 86.

"Religious Development in Historical, Sociological, and Cultural Context." In *Research on Religious Development: A Comprehensive Handbook,* edited by Merton P. Strommen. New York: Hawthorn Books, 1971.

"The Spirit's Holy Errand: The Search for a Spiritual Style in Secular America." *Daedalus,* Winter 1967, p. 99.

"A Dialogue of Histories." In *American Catholics: A Protestant-Jewish View,* edited by Philip Scharper. Kansas City: Sheed & Ward, 1959.

The Authors

Catherine L. Albanese is Professor of Religious Studies at the University of California, Santa Barbara. She received her Ph.D. from the Divinity School at the University of Chicago in 1972.

R. Scott Appleby is the Associate Director of The Fundamentalism Project of the American Academy of Arts and Sciences and a Research Associate at the University of Chicago. He received his Ph.D. from the Divinity School at the University of Chicago in 1985.

Yaakov Ariel is a lecturer at the Institute of Contemporary Jewry, the Hebrew University of Jerusalem. He received his Ph.D. from the Divinity School at the University of Chicago in 1986.

J. E. Robert Choquette is Professor of the History of Christianity and of Religion in Canada in the Department of Religious Studies at the University of Ottawa, Canada. He received his Ph.D. from the Divinity School at the University of Chicago in 1972.

Jay P. Dolan is Professor of History at the University of Notre Dame, where he is also the Director of the Cushwa Center for the Study of American Catholicism. He received his Ph.D. from the Divinity School at the University of Chicago in 1970.

L. DeAne Lagerquist is Assistant Professor of Religion at St. Olaf College, Northfield, Minnesota. She received her Ph.D. from the Divinity School at the University of Chicago in 1986.

Sally M. Promey is Assistant Professor in the Department of Art History and Archaeology at the University of Maryland at College Park. She received her Ph.D. in History of Culture from the University of Chicago in 1988.

WILLIAM L. SACHS is Assistant Rector at St. Stephen's Episcopal Church in Richmond, Virginia. He received his Ph.D. from the Divinity School at the University of Chicago in 1981.

MARK G. TOULOUSE is Associate Dean and Associate Professor of History of Christianity at Brite Divinity School, Texas Christian University, in Fort Worth, Texas. He received his Ph.D. from the Divinity School at the University of Chicago in 1984.

TIMOTHY P. WEBER is the David T. Porter Professor of Church History at the Southern Baptist Theological Seminary in Louisville, Kentucky. He received his Ph.D. from the Divinity School at the University of Chicago in 1976.

PAUL WESTERMEYER is Professor of Church Music at Luther Northwestern Theological Seminary in St. Paul, Minnesota. He received his Ph.D. from the Divinity School at the University of Chicago in 1978.

JAMES P. WIND is Program Director, Religion Division, Lilly Endowment, Inc. He received his Ph.D. from the Divinity School at the University of Chicago in 1983.